THE NEW PUBLIC MANAGEMENT IN ACTION

THE NEW PUBLIC MANAGEMENT IN ACTION

EWAN FERLIE, LYNN ASHBURNER,
LOUISE FITZGERALD, AND
ANDREW PETTIGREW

Oxford University Press
Oxford · 1996

Oxford University Press, Walton Street, Oxford OX2 6DP

Oxford New York
Athens Auckland Bangkok Bombay
Calcutta Cape Town Dar es Salaam Delhi
Florence Hong Kong Istanbul Karachi
Kuala Lumpur Madras Madrid Melbourne
Mexico City Nairobi Paris Singapore
Taipei Tokyo Toronto
and associated companies in
Berlin Ibadan

Oxford is a trade mark of Oxford University Press

Published in the United States
by Oxford University Press Inc., New York

British Library Cataloguing in Publication Data
Data available

Library of Congress Cataloging in Publication Data
The new public management in action/Ewan Ferlie . . . [et al.].
   Includes bibliographical references.
   1. Civil service—Great Britain.   2. Administrative agencies—Great
Britain—Management.   3. National Health Service (Great Britain)
4. Great Britain—Politics and government—1979–   5. Local
government—Great Britain.   I. Ferlie, Ewan, 1956–
JN421.N49   1996   96–2135
350'.000941—dc20

ISBN 0–19–828902–2
ISBN 0–19–828903–0 (Pbk)

Typeset by J&L Composition Ltd, Filey, North Yorkshire
Printed in Great Britain
on acid-free paper by
Bookcraft (Bath) Ltd., Midsomer Norton, Avon.

ACKNOWLEDGEMENTS

THIS book would not have been completed without the help of many people to whom we are most grateful.

The original research was funded by the then National Health Service Training Directorate, with the support of the National Association of Health Authorities and Trusts. We are grateful for the advice received, particularly from the two chairs of the Project Steering Committee, Sir Robin Buchanan and Mrs Angela Sealey. Dr Charlotte Williamson also gave helpful advice as a Steering Committee member.

We acknowledge with many thanks the contribution to data collection and early analysis of Liz Cairncross who worked as Senior Research Fellow on the Project between 1990 and 1992.

We are grateful for all the cooperation we received in the participating sites in our study. Since anonymity was promised as a condition of access, it is not possible to name individuals publicly. Nevertheless, we are thankful that they took so much time and effort to cooperate with a research project which must have seemed low priority given the magnitude of the immediate managerial pressures on them.

We were also encouraged and stimulated by our dialogue with external academic colleagues, notably Professor Sandra Dawson, Professor David Hunter, Professor John Stewart, Dr Sue Dopson, and Dr Lorna McKee.

May we also thank MBA course designers at the University of Warwick and elsewhere who have given us the early opportunity to try out this material in the classroom. We believe that there is a great hunger for recently derived research-based evidence amongst the growing number of MBA students taking public sector management modules.

As always, we are thankful for the dedicated contribution of the secretarial staff in the Centre both to the research project and to the completion of the subsequent manuscript. We would like to thank both Gill Drakeley (for her patient retyping of endless redrafts) and Ann Jackson, the Centre Secretary.

While we give thanks for such advice and help, the authors are responsible for the accuracy of the data and soundness of the analysis.

E. F., L. A., L. F., and A. P.

CONTENTS

LIST OF TABLES

ABBREVIATIONS

AGM	Annual General Meeting
AMA	Association of Metropolitan Authorities
BBC	British Broadcasting Corporation
BCCI	Bank of Credit and Commerce International
BERA	British Educational Research Association
BMA	British Medical Association
CBI	Confederation of British Industry
CEPP	Centre for the Evaluation of Public Policy and Practice
CSO	Central Statistical Office
ESRC	Economic and Social Research Council
FMI	Financial Management Initiative
FMIP	Financial Management Improvement Programme
GDP	Gross Domestic Product
GP	General Practitioner
HEFC	Higher Education Funding Council
HMO	Health Maintenance Organization
HMSO	Her Majesty's Stationery Office
IVF	In Vitro Fertilization
JP	Justice of the Peace
MBA	Master of Business Administration
MIT	Massachusetts Institute of Technology
NFER	National Foundation for Educational Research
NHS	National Health Service
NPM	New Public Management
OECD	Organization of Economic Cooperation and Development
PAC	Public Accounts Committee (House of Commons)
R and D	Research and Development
RCN	Royal College of Nursing

CHARACTERIZING THE 'NEW PUBLIC MANAGEMENT'

1.1. Introduction

In the 1980s the organization and management of the UK public services came under sustained top-down pressure for change. As a result the well-established organizational paradigms of the public corporation and of the large-scale, standardized, and professionalized Welfare State agency were challenged, as new organizational forms, roles, and cultures emerged. With the benefit of hindsight, it became apparent that these old-style public sector organizations had also possessed the virtues of their vices, with an emphasis on due process, equity of treatment, probity, and accountability.

As similar restructurings proceeded in a large number of different public service settings, so it became clear that a broadly based organizational phenomenon was emerging, now often labelled as the rise of the 'new public management'. While there are a number of studies of particular settings available (see Metcalfe and Richards (1990) for a discussion of change in the higher Civil Service; Pettigrew, Ferlie, and McKee (1992) for change in health care), the new public management has until very recently remained under-analysed as a more general phenomenon. Critical accounts are emerging from scholars trained in the public administration or political science traditions (Pollitt 1990; Hood 1991; Dunleavy and Hood 1994). Organization theorists, by contrast, were in general slow to recognize the significance of the new public management movement (but see Hoggett 1991).

This lack of interest relates to the academic division of labour. The study of public sector organizations has often been left to scholars of public administration while Business School academics usually have privileged the study of private firms. This is surprising given the central role that not-for-profit organizations such as hospitals, universities, and voluntary associations have historically played in the development of organization theory (e.g. the use of universities as a site for the development of the theory of 'loosely coupled organizations': see Cohen and March 1974).

However, we argue that public sector settings remain important sites for organizational analysis especially as there is currently a dearth both of theory and of evidence. We substantiate this assertion in Section 1.2. We then set out the theoretical and substantive context of changes in public sector organization and management in overview form. In Section 1.3, we highlight the role of changing managerial ideologies or bodies of thought in influencing managerial practice. Following this, we outline four competing models of the new public management which have emerged. We then briefly place the new public management in international context in Section 1.4. Section 1.5 outlines some key themes which will be explored throughout the later chapters of the book.

1.2. Key Recent Changes in UK Public Services

No Withering Away

Why should scholars be interested in the study of the public sector? Surely, one might argue, it has withered away to insignificance under the sustained assault of the radical right regimes of the 1980s, now renewed in the USA with the recent shift of Congressional control to radical Republicans.

The picture is more complex than this perspective might suggest (Ferlie 1992). The public sector (here defined widely so as to include transfer payments) continues to exert major significance as an item of expenditure in many OECD countries, growing slightly across the OECD group of seven leading economies during the 1980s. The USA represents the lowest spender, while Sweden can be seen as a high spending outlier. While the UK is in the

Table 1.1. General government total outlays as a percentage of nominal GDP

	1978	1985	1990	1994[a]
USA	30.0	33.2	33.3	33.6
Japan	30.0	31.6	31.7	35.3
Germany	47.3	47.0	45.1	48.9
France	44.6	52.1	49.8	55.3
Italy	42.4	50.9	53.2	56.0
UK	41.4	44.0	39.9	43.2
Canada	38.7	45.3	46.0	48.2
SUBTOTAL	35.0	38.4	38.0	40.2
Australia	32.7	36.5	34.8	37.5
Spain	29.0	41.1	42.0	46.3
Sweden	58.6	63.3	59.1	67.4

Notes: The data are calculated as all current outlays, plus net capital outlays. Current disbursements are made up of current consumption transfer payments, subsidies and interest payments.
[a] The figures for 1994 are estimates.

Source: OECD (1994: annex table 27).

middle of the range, expenditure levels crept up if anything during the 1980s. OECD (1993: 32) comments:

following some success at restraining governmental expenditure during the second half of the 1980s, control appears to have weakened again in the 1990s for most OECD countries: even after allowing for cycle related factors, the share of spending of GDP has increased, on average, by 2.5 percentage points since 1989.

This is because the public sector continues to finance and deliver core goods and services that are of major significance to society as a whole: health, education, R and D, criminal justice, social security. Rising expenditure in the first three sectors is often seen as a hallmark of an advanced post-industrial society; while the growth of expenditure in the last two sectors (e.g. expansion of the prison population) is a reminder of the discontents of such modernity.

UK manpower data suggest a contraction in public sector employment in the 1980s. However, such job losses were heavily concentrated in the national-ized industries, now largely privatized. Public sector employment in health and social care, education, and criminal justice services remains buoyant. The UK public sector may have lost its economic role, but has retained a strong social role.

Public Sector Organizations: Some Changes of the 1980s

A wide raft of different, but interrelated, initiatives and change processes have been apparent in the UK public services of the 1980s (Ashburner *et al.* 1994). These initiatives include not only structural changes, but also attempts to change both process and roles. Some of these initiatives have been facilitated and accelerated by a convergence of technological innovation and cost-drivers: the development of day case surgery in health care would offer a prime example.

The post-1979 UK experience is dominated by a series of 'reform' initiatives apparent across a number of different settings, driven from the top and sustained over a long time period. In terms of the change process, the pattern is distinctively different from the pre-1979 period, which was characterized more by a bottom-up mode of service development. There are a number of key changes apparent, some of which can be seen as contradictory, but they include the following very broad features:

1. There has been a large-scale privatization programme in the sphere of economic activity, with the sale of many nationalized industries to workers and shareholders. The UK public sector has indeed virtually ceased to exist in the sphere of direct economic activity.

2. Those social policy functions which have remained in the public sector have been subjected to processes both of managerialization and of market-ization. There are increasing attempts to create 'quasi-markets' within the

Table 1.2. UK public sector and private employment by major categories (at mid-year) (000s)

A

Year	Central government				Local authorities						
	HM Forces	NHS	Other	Subtotal	Education[a]	Health and Social Services	Construction	Police and civilians	Other	Local authority community programme	Subtotal
1979	314	1,152	921	2,387	1,539	344	156	176	782	—	2,997
1980	323	1,174	896	2,393	1,501	346	152	181	776	—	2,956
1981	334	1,207	878	2,419	1,454	350	143	186	766	—	2,899
1982	324	1,227	849	2,400	1,434	352	132	186	761	—	2,865
1983	322	1,227	835	2,384	1,434	360	130	187	768	27	2,906
1984	326	1,223	810	2,359	1,430	368	126	187	773	58	2,942
1985	326	1,223	811	2,360	1,429	376	125	187	774	67	2,958
1986	322	1,215	800	2,337	1,452	387	125	188	770	88	3,010
1987	319	1,212	781	2,312	1,486	398	128	191	763	96	3,062
1988	316	1,228	778	2,322	1,504	405	125	194	764	89	3,081
1989	308	1,226	781	2,315	1,444	411	119	195	771	—	2,940
1990	303	1,229	781	2,313	1,431	417	114	199	808	—	2,969
1991	297	1,092	788	2,177	1,416	414	106	202	810	—	2,948

Notes: Components may not add up to totals due to separate rounding.

[a] Excludes polytechnics from Apr. 1989, when they were transferred to the private sector.

Source: CSO (1993: table 48).

B

Year	Public Sector General government	Public corporate				Total	Local authorities Total	self-employed	Work related government training programme[a]	Total workforce in employment
		Nationalized industries including Post Office	NHS Trusts	Other	Subtotal					
1979	5,384	1,849	—	216	2,065	7,449	17,944	1,906	—	25,393
1980	5,349	1,816	—	222	2,038	7,387	17,940	2,013	—	25,327
1981	5,318	1,657	—	210	1,867	7,185	17,160	2,119	—	24,345
1982	5,265	1,554	—	202	1,756	7,021	16,886	2,169	—	23,907
1983	5,290	1,465	—	198	1,662	6,952	16,656	2,219	16	23,624
1984	5,301	1,416	—	195	1,610	6,911	17,149	2,496	175	24,235
1985	5,318	1,137	—	125	1,261	6,579	17,784	2,614	176	24,539
1986	5,347	1,065	—	134	1,199	6,546	17,796	2,633	226	24,568
1987	5,374	870	—	126	996	6,370	18,402	2,869	311	25,083
1988	5,403	798	—	126	924	6,327	19,244	2,998	343	25,914
1989	5,255	727	—	117	844	6,099	20,123	3,253	462	26,684
1990	5,282	682	—	115	797	6,079	20,378	3,298	424	26,924
1991	5,125	516	124	108	747	5,872	19,916	3,298	381	26,028

Note: Components may not add to totals due to separate rounding

[a] Participants in the YTS who receive work experience, participants in the new JTS and some trainees on similar Northern Ireland schemes. Those with contracts of employment are included in the appropriate employment category.

Source: CSO (1993: table 48).

public sector (Ferlie 1992 and 1994) whereby previously line-managed organizations disaggregate into purchasing and providing wings, with relations between them governed by contract rather than hierarchy. Within central government, for example, an increasing number of devolved and quasi-autonomous agencies have been created (the so-called 'Next Steps' agencies). The financing of such quasi-markets remains public, but an increasing number of independent providers may compete for contracts. Other public functions (e.g. civil service roles) are currently subject to market-testing. Such quasi-markets are seen by their proponents as one way of empowering users (e.g. giving parents more choice of schools). New forms of regulation are apparent, compensating for the retreat of direct line management.

3. We see an increased emphasis on 'doing more with less', on securing value for money, on the use of comparative performance indicators and the development of enhanced cost, information, and audit systems. Relative performance is assessed more openly and subject to tight central monitoring.

4. There has finally been a move from maintenance management to the 'management of change'. There is a desire for more visible, active, and individualistic forms of leadership in the public services as seen, for example, in the emergence of high profile chief executive officers. There is a rhetoric of 'culture change management', although supporting evidence remains thin on the ground. The human resource management function has tried to use such developments to negotiate a more strategic role but also acted as a key deregulator of the workplace. The organizational development tradition has continued to offer an alternative and more humanistic management style, most recently regrouping behind the banner of 'organizational learning' movement.

The Changing Political Economy of the Public Sector

Such a wide range of changes should not be seen as socially neutral, but reflect the rise of some constituencies and fall of others. In effect, as the balance of power shifted during the 1980s so a new political economy of the public sector emerged.

First, there has been a clear decline in the power of the public sector unions, partly caused by the changes in the legal framework and also contracting-out (Ascher 1987). Alongside this, there has been a shift from traditional forms of collective pay-bargaining to more contract- and performance-based forms of reward and appraisal (Farnham 1993). Moves to decentralized pay-bargaining in the NHS represent a further stage in this process. Within the Next Steps agencies as well (Corby 1994), there is evidence of significant moves away from the traditional Whitley system.

Secondly, there is now evidence of some erosion of the autonomy of professionals within the public sector (traditionally a highly professionalized sector) (McKinlay and Stoeckle 1988). Teachers have been subjected to imposed pay settlements and had curriculum development responsibilities reduced. Much more extensive forms of monitoring are apparent in higher education, both in respect of research and teaching. Even doctors can be seen as losing ground to the new cadre of general managers in health care. However, the evidence is still slight and it is too early to conclude that this will lead remorselessly to a process of de-professionalization (Elston 1991) as professionals may learn new skills and regroup. We will develop this argument in Chapter 7. Some doctors, for instance, are now moving into quasi-managerial roles as clinical directors. This argument that professional adaptation is taking place—albeit confined to certain subgroups—offers a very different perspective to those analyses influenced by critical theory (Laughlin *et al.* 1992) which argue that professionals are retaining autonomy in their core tasks and that managerialization and marketization are confined to the periphery of the organization. As a result, 'transformatory change' remains an unlikely outcome in these accounts.

Thirdly, public sector managers can be seen as a gaining group (Pollitt 1990; Pettigrew *et al.* 1992; Farnham and Horton 1993). They have indeed been the instrument through which many of the changes have been forced (e.g. headmasters in schools), empowered by the doctrine that 'management must manage'. Lower down the hierarchy, there has been a proliferation of operational management posts in business management, finance, audit, and information functions. Table 1.3 illustrates the growth of posts classified as managerial in the NHS. While some of this growth may be due to reclassification, this trend data still points to very significant expansion of managerial posts. While senior managers in the public sector are now much better paid, they also enjoy less job security and face tougher appraisal tests.

Fourthly, we see the rise of a non-elected élite (Stewart 1993), or appointee state, directing these new-style public services in their role as non-executive directors. Elected and staff representatives have been removed from the boards of many public sector organizations and replaced by appointees. Traditionally, these boards had been seen as no more than rubber stamps but with the influx of senior and skilled personnel, often drawn from the private sector, the picture has changed. Power moved to the apex of new public management organizations in the 1980s and this group has exerted a powerful role in imprinting these newly created organizations. It may be that an 'inner circle' (Useem 1984), as argued by élite theory, will emerge of individuals who hold multiple board positions within the new-style public sector just as, so critics argue, already exists in the corporate sector.

Finally, and most ambiguously of all, whatever happened to the user? Sometimes the new public management movement has been seen as aggravating a 'democratic deficit' (Bogdanor 1994), removing traditional channels of local accountability. Supporters argue that the new public management develops new forms of market-based accountability, giving consumers greater choice between producers (Waldegrave, cited in Weir and Hall 1994). Such

Table 1.3. Health and personal social services workforce: summary

	Unit	1982	1988	1989	1990	1991	1992
Health service staff and practitioners, and local authority social services staff		1,079,511	1,078,106	1,084,714	1,086,678	1,087,933	1,080,504
Health service staff and practitioners		876,167	842,137	845,960	846,336	850,653	845,264
Directly employed staff:							
Medical and dental staff	Wte	41,502	44,794	46,256	47,392	48,567	49,589
Nursing and midwifery staff	Wte	397,081	403,883	405,281	402,066	396,136	382,019
General and senior managers[a]	Wte	—	1,235	4,609	9,676	13,338	16,692
Administrative and clerical	Wte	108,803	114,716	116,842	120,040	127,367	135,009
Professional and technical staff	Wte	67,239	79,775	81,168	83,987	86,876	89,819
Ambulance staff	Wte	18,324	18,761	18,862	18,131	18,192	17,725
Works professional and maintenance staff	Wte	27,129	22,654	21,183	19,921	18,349	17,915
Ancillary	Wte	170,525	107,619	102,360	95,689	85,893	78,995
Other	Wte	—	—	—	—	6,095	7,304
SUBTOTAL	Wte	830,603	793,437	796,561	796,902	800,812	795,067
Family Health Service Authority Practitioners	No.	45,564	48,700	49,399	49,434	49,841	50,197
Local authority social services	Wte	203,344	235,969	238,754	240,342	237,280	235,240

wte = whole time equivalent

[a] A new management class was introduced in phases from 1984 following the Griffiths Report (1983). There was one general manager in each health authority and hospital and community health services unit. Senior managers were introduced in 1987 with up to seven senior posts at board level in each health authority; from 1989 senior management posts extended below board level and to family health service authorities and HCHS units. Most of these posts replaced those formerly counted within the administrative and clerical and other staff groups

Source: Department of Health (1994).

experiments are, however, yet to make a sustained impact and the jury is still out on whether the new public management will in the end empower users (Ferlie *et al.* 1994). Many suspect that the failure to produce a robust model of public accountability represents the Achilles' heel of the new public management.

1.3. The NPM as Rising Bodies of Managerial Thought

The 1980s certainly witnessed the importation of a number of management techniques new to the public sector, but behind these surface manifestations of change lies the rise of new sets of key managerial ideas and beliefs. Both the rise of diagnostic-related group forms of classification (Kimberly *et al.* 1993) and of total quality management initiatives and ideas (CEPP 1994) have for instance been seen as 'presenting' phenomena, behind which lie more general processes of new sets of managerial ideas being transported into the public sector.

The emergence of the broad new public management movement can hence be seen as an example of a more general process whereby bodies of managerial thought rise and fall (Child 1969; Barley and Kunda 1992). Such bodies of thought contain both descriptive and normative (perhaps ideological) elements. They may be linked to social constituencies, either management practitioners or management intellectuals.

There may be strong fads and fashions in management thought, fanned by fashion-setters, such as professional associations, the specialized media, or management consultants (Abrahamson 1991). The corporate management fad in 1970s local government would be a good example of this time-limited phenomenon. Ideas are diffused through management best sellers, where the volume of sales may exceed the quality of the analysis (Rhodes 1994). However, such managerial fads follow each other with bewildering speed, and are unlikely to make a major impact on receiving organizations.

The new public management has been seen by critics as a market-based ideology invading public sector organizations previously infused with counter-cultural values (Laughlin 1991). But it has also been seen by others (Ashburner *et al.* 1994) as a management hybrid with a continuing emphasis on core public service values, albeit expressed in a new way. However, many would agree that the new public management should now be seen as a major break point in public sector management (Dunleavy and Hood 1994) of much greater significance than the usual fad or fashion.

'Ideology' represents a vast and complex field within social science, and we can do little more here than touch on some of the key debates (see Boudon 1989; Hartley (1983) for an organizational behavioural view of the term). Pollitt sees (1990: 10–11) the new public management movement as an ideological thought system, characterized by the importation of ideas generated in private sector settings within public sector organizations.

For Hood (1991), the new public management movement has been shaped by the emergence of bodies of theory such as 'new institutional economics' (Downs 1967; Niskanen 1971; O. E. Williamson 1975 and 1985). This body of work includes such areas as bureau maximization theory; transaction costs theory; principal–agent theory, and quasi-market theory. It provided a set of sophisticated ideas which enjoyed rising influence throughout the 1980s.

Such theory has sharp implications for the restructuring of public agencies. Public choice theory (Niskanen 1971) predicts that government agencies over-supply collective goods because of budget maximization behaviour in the absence of effective market forces (but for a critique see Dunleavy 1991). The requisite response is to cut back on 'wasteful' government by splitting up collusive systems and provider cartels, introducing external regulation, downsizing and contracting-out, and providing stronger incentives for performance.

The New Public Management and Alternative Idea Systems

Some key trends observable in the organization and management of the public services in the 1980s have already been briefly described. But what does this disparate, and at times contradictory, set of traits mean? Indeed, sometimes the new public management seems like an empty canvass: you can paint on it whatever you like. There is no clear or agreed definition of what the new public management actually is and not only is there controversy about what is, or what is in the process of becoming, but also what ought to be.

At least four new public management models can be discerned and while each of them represents a move away from traditional public administration models, they also contain important differences and distinctive features. A contest for interpretation is apparent between proponents of these four models, and the degree of influence they achieve in the field may wax or wane over time.

In essence, these four models represent our initial attempt to build a typology of new public management ideal types. Typology-building is a key analytic technique within social science (Weber 1946; Miles and Snow 1978; Mintzberg 1979 and 1983; Porter 1980 and 1985) but typology construction requires careful thought (Doty and Glick 1994) if the categories derived are to be meaningful, exhaustive, and mutually exclusive. We will return to the adequacy of our initial typology in Chapter 9.

NPM Model 1: The Efficiency Drive　NPM Model 1 can be seen as the earliest model to emerge, dominant throughout the early and mid-1980s, but now coming under increasing challenge. It represented an attempt to make the public sector more business-like, led by crude notions of efficiency. Government advisers drawn from the private sector (Griffiths Report 1983) and advisory bodies (such as the Audit Commission) played an important role in diffusing these ideas within the public sector. To its critics, it reflected an inappropriate and imported model of private sector management which took no account of the distinctive properties of public sector organizations (see Pollitt's critique of so-called neo-Taylorian approaches within the new public management; see also Hood 1991, J. Stewart and Walsh 1992).

Core themes include:

- an increased attention to financial control; a strong concern with value-for-money and efficiency gains; getting more from less; a strengthening of the finance function; a growth of more elaborate cost and information systems;
- a stronger general managerial spine; management by hierarchy; a 'command and control' mode of working; clear target-setting and monitoring of performance; a shift of power to senior management;
- an extension of audit, both financial and professional; an insistence on more transparent methods for the review of performance; more standard setting and bench-marking; greater use of protocols as a means of assessing professional performance;
- increased stress on provider responsiveness to consumers; a greater role for non-public sector providers; more market-mindedness and a customer orientation; market-like experiments at the margins (e.g. income generation) but as yet no moves to fully fledged quasi-markets;
- deregulation of the labour-market and increasing the pace of work; erosion of nationally agreed pay and conditions and collective agreements; a move to highly paid and individually agreed rewards packages at a senior level, combined with more short-term contracts; much higher turnover at senior management level within the public sector;
- a reduction in the self regulating power of the professions; a shift in power from professionals to management; a drawing in of some professionals into the management process; more transparent forms of professional self-regulation, with a stronger lay presence;
- some empowerment of less bureaucratic and more entrepreneurial management, but still with tight retrospective accountability requirements upwards;
- new forms of corporate governance (Ferlie *et al.* 1995); marginalization of elected representatives and trade-unionists; moves to a board of directors model; a shift of power to the strategic apex of the organization;

The driver for NPM Model 1 is often seen as the new Thatcherite political economy. The public sector was here diagnosed as bloated, wasteful, over-bureaucratic, and underperforming. It was seen as part of the problem and not as part of the solution, with the result that recurrent institutional reforms were led from the top of the political system in a way which would not have been conceivable in the 1970s.

But it would be simplistic to see all the new public management-style changes currently observable as an epiphenomenon of Thatcherism. Some of the new organizational forms and styles (e.g. core–periphery split; management through influence) now increasingly apparent are not readily compatible with the concern to keep direct management control characteristic of NPM Model 1 and an explanation must be sought elsewhere.

NPM Model 2: Downsizing and Decentralization   NPM Model 2 can currently be seen as of increasing significance, undermining and contradicting some of the earlier changes brought about as a result of the diffusion of NPM Model 1 ideas. It springs from the argument that the historic shift towards large, vertically integrated, organizations apparent in the 1900-75 period appears to have gone into reverse. This has resulted in some very general organizational developments including: organizational unbundling and downsizing; a search for greater organizational flexibility; a move from a high degree of standardization; increased decentralization of strategic and budgetary responsibility; increased contracting-out; and a split between a small strategic core and a large operational periphery.

These trends are seen as common to both private and public sectors, at least within the Western European and North American cultures which represent a similar broad cultural context. When compared, say, to Mediterranean family-based or Far Eastern clan-based patterns of organization (Clegg 1990), for instance, the old style, large-scale, rationalized, and hierarchical bureaucracy (whether in the private or the public sector) appears to be particularly strong as an organizational form in early–mid-twentieth century Western European or North American societies.

Historically, both public bureaux delivering mass services and large-scale corporations delivering standard products and in control of their markets can be seen as representing a 'Fordist' mode of production which reached its apogee in the post-Second World War period (Hoggett 1991). In organizational terms (Clegg 1990: 178), Fordist enterprises can also be seen as highly bureaucratized, with a hierarchy of offices, rules, and regulations and an impersonal, formal climate of relations. Indeed, critics of corporate life pointed to the bureaucratic pathologies observable there (Whyte 1956) as much as in the public sector.

From the late 1970s onwards, accelerating shifts towards 'post-Fordist' models of organization have been apparent in both the private and the public sectors. These new organizational forms are characterized by a shift for flexibility and the unbundling of vertically integrated forms of organization (Hoggett 1991). Large organizations are typically downsizing, contracting functions out, and splitting up internally into more autonomous business units (Kanter 1989). The point is that very similar trends are evident in the private and the public sectors alike. In essence, the old question, why do firms replace markets?, has been stood on its head: why do markets replace firms? (O. E. Williamson 1991).

This model was less overtly dominant than Model 1 during the 1980s but can now be seen as of rising importance. It represents the expression within the public sector of the trends discussed above. Within NPM Model 2, key indicators include:

- an extension of the early stress on market-mindedness to more elaborate and developed quasi-markets; a (still ambiguous) shift from planning to quasi-markets as the mechanism for allocating resources within the public sector;
- a move from management by hierarchy to management by contract; the emergence of looser forms of contract management; the creation of more loosely coupled (critics would argue fragmented) public sector organizations at local level;
- a split between a small strategic core and a large operational periphery; market-testing and contracting-out of non-strategic functions;
- delayering and downsizing; a drastic reduction in the payrolls of public sector organizations; moves to flatter organizational structures; staff reductions now at the higher tiers as well as lower down the organization;
- a split between public funding and independent sector provision; the emergence of separate purchaser and provider organizations; the formation of purchasing organizations as a new organizational form;
- moves from the 'command and control' form of management associated with NPM Model 1 to new management styles, such as management by influence; an increased role for network forms of organization; stress on strategic alliances between organizations as a new form of coordination;
- an attempt to move away from standardized forms of service to a service system characterized by more flexibility and variety.

NPM Model 3: In Search of Excellence   NPM Model 3 is most obviously associated with the 'excellence' stream of the 1980s, influential through best-selling texts (Deal and Kennedy 1981; Peters and Waterman 1982). In part it represents the application to the public services of the human relations school of management theory (Meek 1988) with its strong emphasis on the importance of organizational culture. It rejects the highly rationalistic approach of NPM Model 1 and instead highlights the role of values, culture, rites, and symbols in shaping how people actually behave at work. There is a strong interest in how organizations manage change and innovation.

In turn, NPM Model 3 can be subdivided into bottom–up and top–down approaches. The bottom–up approach has been historically better developed, emphasizing long-standing themes of organizational development and learning. The 'learning organization' movement of the late 1980s represents the latest relabelling of this tradition (Senge 1990; Pedler *et al.* 1991; Jones and Hendry 1992; Jones 1994). Studies which reveal the role of highly committed, bottom–up, product champions in stimulating innovation in public sector settings also reflect this approach (Bennett and Ferlie 1994*a*). In these approaches, processes are seen as important as well as organizational out-comes, distinguishing them from more narrowly task-focused models.

These accounts do not necessarily accord top management a privileged role in the change process. Strong collective cultures can act as organizational glue within high commitment organizations more effectively than line management hierarchies. Deviants, heretics, and rockers of boats (Pettigrew 1985) can play a critical role in triggering off processes of strategic change. Leadership can come from small teams or networks as well as charismatic senior managers (Petti-grew, *et al.* 1992). People or groups may learn within organizations (Jones 1994) even if the organization does not learn at a corporate level. Normatively, this stream tends to be linked with the more humanistic management models which have shaped the organizational development tradition with an emphasis on self-development and participation.

However, Dunphy and Stace (1988) recognize the limited validity of the bottom–up organizational development perspective in explaining the increased number of coercive and 'transformatory' reorganizations of the 1980s. This top–down variant of the NPM Model 3 emphasizes what it sees as the plastic and changeable nature of corporate culture (see Meek (1988) for a critique), leading to explicit attempts to manage processes of cultural change. There is an emphasis on charismatic rather than transactional forms of leadership, often in turn associated with attempts to secure corporate turnrounds. Such leader-ship is often seen as personal rather than team-based, coming from a senior manager who inspires the organization with a new vision.

NPM Model 3 can be characterized by the following indicators:

- in the bottom–up form: emphasis on organizational development and learning; recognition of organizational culture as a form of glue; top–down backing for bottom–up product champions; radical decentralization with performance judged by results;
- in the top–down form: explicit attempts to secure culture change; projection of a top–down vision; managed culture change programmes; stress on charismatic forms of top–down leadership; identification of charismatic private-sector role models for the new-style public sector; more intensive corporate training programmes; the growth of corporate logos, mission statements, and uniforms; an explicit communications strategy; a more assertive and strategic human resource management function.

NPM Model 4: Public Service Orientation   NPM Model 4 is presently the least well developed and is still to reveal its full potential. It represents a fusion of private and public sector management ideas, re-energizing public sector managers by outlining a distinct public service mission (Osborne and Gaebler 1992), but one compatible with received notions of high quality management derived from transferable good practice in the private sector. It thus confers legitimacy on a new-style public sector which claims to have broken with the pathological aspects of the past, but which retains a sense of distinctive identity and purpose. Critics argue that these accounts contain a number of internal contradictions (du Gay 1993).

The Public Service Orientation model (J. Stewart and Clarke 1987; J. Stewart and Ransom 1988; Ranson and Stewart 1994) is an example of this genre, taking ideas from the private sector but applying them in a distinctively public sector context. This new public management variant attracts supporters from the left of centre (see Hodge 1991; Hodge and Thompson 1994) and includes a strong focus on securing the accountability of services to local users and citizens (not so much to customers) which is not apparent in other variants.

NPM Model 4 can be characterized by the following key indicators:

- a major concern with service quality (e.g. the use of quality initiatives; the rise of total quality management); a value-driven approach but based on a mission to achieve excellence in the public services;
- reflection of user (rather than customer) concerns and values in the management process; reliance on user voice rather than customer exit as the characteristic source of feedback; a concept of citizenship;
- a desire to shift power back from appointed to elected local bodies; scepticism as to the role of markets in public services;
- stress on the development of societal learning over and above the delivery of routine services (e.g. community development work, assessment of social need);
- a continuing set of distinctive public service tasks and values; management of the distinctive politics of collective provision; a stress on securing participation and accountability as legitimate concerns of management in the public sector.

Alongside a proclamation of difference, however, lie attempts to adapt ideas generated in private sector contexts (e.g. total quality management, organizational learning) to public sector organizations. The criteria for deciding which ideas can diffuse across, and which should not, are rarely made explicit and may be largely normative in nature.

1.4. The New Public Management in International Perspective

For Hood (1991), the new public management is emphatically not a parochial British development but a striking international trend in public administration observable from the mid-1970s onwards. Dunleavy and Hood (1994) point to the durable and wide-ranging nature of the new public management agenda, implying that it has more staying power than the usual managerial fad (we will consider later in the book why this should be the case). Hood (1991) sees the rise of the new public management as associated with increased attempts to curb the rise of government and a shift towards privatization. Gray and Jenkins (1995) point to the international diffusion of the new public management model, aided by growing popular and intellectual disenchantment with the role of government and with high levels of taxation.

Yet Osborne and Gaebler's view (1992) that there is universal convergence on an agreed new public management model is simplistic and overdeterminist. They may indeed be guilty of a crude Anglo-Saxon ethnocentrism. As Dunleavy and Hood (1994) argue, politicians and citizens still have the power to choose between a range of alternative future patterns of organization of the public services. The brief review of the diffusion of the new public management movement possible here suggests that while it is of international rather than parochial UK significance, it has had highly variable international impact and that different variants have emerged in different countries, depending on local history, culture, and political and managerial leadership.

Anglo-Saxon Contexts

One argument is that new public management style ideas have had more impact in Anglo-Saxon political cultures than in Continental Western European contexts (Marsh 1994). While the rise of the new public management has been evident within the Anglo-Saxon grouping of countries, it cannot be seen solely as a function of the New Right but appears to be a broader development apparent in a range of political contexts.

New Zealand can be seen as an extreme case and as a rapid mover, yet here new public management-style ideas were embraced by a Labour government. Between 1984 and 1990 dramatic changes were brought in to the organization and management of the public sector (Boston 1987). The stated aims behind the restructuring have been to increase the efficiency of the public sector and to improve the accountability of public services to the Executive and to Parliament, although much concern has also been expressed about the social costs.

Boston (1987) has identified three main streams of activity. First, the Government has commercialized many of the functions performed by public organizations. Second, wherever possible, the commercial and non-commercial activities of departments have been separated and the trading activities transferred to public corporations. The final area concerns human resource management policy with moves away from national systems of pay-bargaining to a more decentralized and enterprise-based system. A new accountability regime for chief executive officers has been introduced (Boston 1992) with increased emphasis on fixed term contracts, performance-based pay, and performance reviews.

Wistrich (1992) has drawn attention to the intellectually coherent approach to the new public management evident in the New Zealand case, as evinced in key documents such as the 1987 Treasury Report *Government Management: Brief to the Incoming Government.* Explicit theories such as public choice theory and the principal–agent model are used to justify public sector reorganization. She sees the Treasury as acting in the role of think-tank for the movement, supplying intellectual rigour and coherence.

The Australian case is again complicated by a division of responsibility between a federal government and states, sometimes controlled by different political parties. A reform movement has been evident in the Australian public sector since the early 1980s, and many of the themes—more markets, sharper incentives, importation of private sector techniques—can be seen as new public management-orthodox (Marsh 1994).

Zifcak's (1994) elegant comparative analysis of the fate of the UK Financial Management Improvement Initiative and Canberra's Financial Management Improvement Programme argues that the Australian programme had greater long-term impact than the UK reform programme. Superficially, it might appear that both governments were responding in the same way to similar economic and intellectual contexts, but on a closer examination substantial differences in the change process can be discerned.

Originally the Australian Labour Government led by Hawke placed greater stress on a democratic and equity-based agenda, although this was abandoned as economic conditions worsened in the mid-1980s. It came into office with a detailed and comprehensive plan for reform. Its reform style could, however, be seen as more consensual and less top–down than in the UK, with the development of a strong coalition between political and bureaucratic leaders which was strong enough to embed the reforms within the machinery of government.

An analysis of the American case (Pollitt 1990) suggests a more neo-Taylorian (NPM Model 1) approach, with a scientistic, generalist, and mea-surement-based approach to management dominant. However, the pressure for public sector reform predated the election of Reagan, with the 1978 Civil Service Reform Act being enacted during the Carter administration. This provided for the introduction of performance appraisal and merit pay systems within the Civil Service, along with new demotion and dismissal procedures. With the election of Reagan, the more developmental aspects of the Carter programme were curtailed.

However, the new administration's initial hope of a drastic scaling-back of the scope of government proved difficult to implement. Instead, the Presiden-tial Private Sector Survey on Cost Control (or Grace Commission) (1982–4) was asked to report on ways of securing better value in the civil service using private sector 'best practice' as a template. Its main diagnoses of the reasons for public sector failure can be specified as follows:

- Congressional 'interference' with the day-to-day management of Federal agencies;
- lack of continuity of personnel, especially at the higher levels;

- lack of incentives to seek greater efficiency and economy;
- inadequate system-wide accounting and management information systems;
- lack of strong central management of finance and accounting.

Nevertheless, Pollitt (1990: 93) assesses the impact of American new public management initiatives as rather weaker than those in the UK. This is first of all due to the extreme pluralism characteristic of the American political system, with a Republican president having to negotiate with a Democrat-controlled congress (at that stage) and well-organized special interest groups to get his proposals through. These difficulties continued to bedevil Clinton's plans for health care reform in the early 1990s. Political power in the UK in the 1980s, by contrast, was far more concentrated at cabinet or even prime ministerial level. Secondly, there was a relatively weak presidential commitment to securing institutional reform with the result that the persistent, top-level, political clout so apparent in the UK case was not evident in the American case. Thirdly, the mechanism used to achieve change—the Grace Commission—was itself flawed. It failed to ally itself with reformist elements which were in any case emerging within the Federal Civil Service and took an excessively didactic and politically naïve stance, alienating potential supporters in the Congress.

Osborne and Gaebler (1992) can be seen as the American public sector top seller of the early 1990s, supplying ideas and recipes to the new Clinton administration. Written in consultancy rather than academic mode, the quality of the theoretical analysis can certainly be questioned (Rhodes 1994). On the other hand, it has had major policy and management impact. It is therefore better analysed as a phenomenon than as a text: what is it selling and why are so many public service managers buying?

Osborne and Gaebler in effect move the American debate from NPM Model 1 to a fusion of NPM Models 2 and 3. The State is recast in the role of enabler rather than provider. They argue that government is moving away from those standardized, mass production, models of service delivery which arose in the 1900-40 period towards a new form of entrepreneurial government which is more concerned to use public resources in new ways to maximize productivity and effectiveness. This echoes many of the arguments for greater organizational flexibility, adaptability, and customer orientation to be found in the private sector 'excellence' literature.

For practising public service managers, this model represents a means of regaining social and political legitimacy. The public sector is no longer criticized for failing to live up to private sector best practice. Instead, some of the distinctive conditions, and special challenges, of managing in the public domain are recognized. However, public sector managers are enjoined to cast off their old role as administrators and to become more entrepreneurial, results-focused, and market-based, all traits seen as characteristic of the high status private sector business community.

In a critical review, du Gay (1993) notes that Osborne and Gaebler's analysis blurs conventional distinctions between public and private sector modes of behaviour. Rather than representing a simple colonization of the public by the private, their model can be seen as a hybrid form whereby government takes on a more entrepreneurial character (this concept of hybrid organizational forms will be developed in later chapters). But the bureaucratic character undergoing displacement retains virtues as well as vices, such as its emphasis on equity, due process, and probity. This raises the question of accountability, especially of the hived-off operational functions, managed by the small strategic core on a contractual basis.

European Contexts

Central and Eastern Europe offers a separate and distinctive context where public sector reform programmes are currently aimed at a drastic scaling-down of the Marxist-Leninist State (Hendrych 1993; Balazs 1993). While the public sector is in retreat, the issues and processes involved are very different from the Anglo-Saxon experience.

Western Europe offers some intriguing comparisons. France's health care reforms (we here draw on Bach 1994) have focused on cost containment and improving management. Both Conservative and Socialist Governments in the 1980s adopted evolutionary policies of cost containment, but with only partial success. Despite its centralist reputation, the French health care system can be seen as complex and fragmented, with the central state, local government, the semi-autonomous sickness funds, the medical profession, and the trade unions all playing important roles. Most finance is provided through the sickness funds which are organized along corporatist lines, with a strong trade union presence and indeed leadership role.

Further reforms were enacted in 1991, providing hospitals with more autonomy in setting their investment budgets and over-staffing. A cadre of hospital managers is beginning to emerge, equipped with better information systems and more actively scrutinizing medical behaviour. However, there was also a recognition in the 1991 reforms of the need to improve hospital social relations (Bach 1994: 601-2) in the light of recent industrial disputes. A board was created in each hospital, enabling nursing staff to join the medical profession in having specific senior level representation. The 1991 reforms also placed new obligations on managers to involve medical staff in decision-making and required the establishment of more consultative committees. These developments can of course be seen as very different from contemporary UK changes which are much more managerialist in character.

Despite its large public sector, Sweden can be seen as a relatively cautious mover in public service reform throughout the 1980s. There is some evidence that traditional democratic values have continued to inform Swedish public sector reorganizations to a much greater extent than has been apparent in the

UK. Thus Fudge and Gustafsson's (1989) analysis of the Swedish case highlights recent moves to decentralization, securing greater productivity, ensuring value, greater choice, and service to the public, all of which resemble some of the UK new public management themes already discussed. However, important differences remain. Sweden is seen as retaining (Fudge and Gustaffsson 1993: 33) a social responsibility model, which is different from market-led models with their stress on efficiency. The Swedish model continues to emphasize humanistic concerns and there is thus a greater stress on such themes as participation.

This brief international review suggests that first of all there is no simple convergence on one new public management model, but rather that a range of options is available. Secondly, it suggests that the UK (along with New Zealand) may be fruitfully seen as a 'fast mover', at least in terms of proclaimed intent, when compared internationally.

This raises the further question of what connection can be established empirically between proclaimed change at system-wide level and actual change at the level of the organization, small group, or indeed individual role. Zifcak's (1994) analysis raised the possibility that the top–down and power-led approach characteristic of the UK case might well be associated with a higher probability of implementation failure. We will need to return to these important organizational-change questions in later chapters.

1.5. Some Underlying Themes and Questions

A number of academic and policy debates will be explored throughout the book and returned to in Chapter 9. Here we briefly rehearse four overarching themes which can be seen as threads which will connect the subsequent chapters.

Sectoral Differences and Similarities

Do the developments now apparent within the public sector essentially mirror trends within private sector organizations or does the public sector display an idiosyncratic pattern of evolution? This raises the question of whether the two sectors should be seen as more similar than different, or as more different than similar. We can furthermore ask: how do the four ideal types of the new public management already reviewed respond to this question?

While NPM Models 1–3 stress intersectoral similarity (albeit in very different ways), NPM Model 4 emphasizes difference. Of course, a long-standing debate is apparent within management studies between those who argue that management roles and skills are generic across organizational settings (the general management model) and contextualists who feel that they are specific either to an individual managerial job (R. Stewart 1975) or indeed to a sector (J. Stewart and Walsh 1992).

The view that core managerial roles and skills were indeed transferable from the private to the public sector (and the flow was generally seen as unidirectional) gathered strength in the 1980s. It was strongly associated with NPM Model 1. For influential policy advisers of the 1980s, such as Griffiths (Griffith Report 1983), the differences between private and public sector settings had been much exaggerated: both could benefit from an active and assertive general management function.

Public administrative theory, however, argues that roles and skills are not readily transferable from the private to the public sector, because the nature of the tasks undertaken is fundamentally different (Pollitt 1990; Hood 1991). In the public sector, there are a series of distinctive conditions (such as a greater role for collective choice, citizenship, notions of need and justice) which are not apparent in the private sector (Ranson and Stewart 1994). Sometimes the public services are seen as comprising a distinct form of work organization. For example, Ackroyd, Hughes, and Soothill (1990) argue that public services have sufficient in common to be seen as a relatively homogenous grouping.

Motivationally, public officials are often seen within these accounts as driven by a strong sense of vocation, reinforced by the presence of strong self-regulating professions with their own ethical codes of practice. This public administrative culture can be seen as a strong guarantor of probity, now threatened by the rise of entrepreneurial management.

No one model of management is in any case readily identifiable within the private sector. Some management writers stress the fragmented, negotiative, and intuitive aspects of much managerial activity there (Kotter 1982; Mintzberg 1973; Pettigrew 1987). An important corollary is that patterns of work and key managerial skills may indeed significantly depend on organizational context even within the private sector (Hales 1986). Thus Whitley (1989) notes that the construction of a general management science is as far away as ever.

So are the proponents of NPM Model 4 correct when they point to some important differences (as well as similarities) between managing in the public and in the private sectors? As we present our evidence, are intersectoral differences more apparent than similarities? The extent to which the public services still present a distinct work context will be re-examined in the concluding discussion, in the light of the data outlined.

Studying Organizational Change

The organizational change theme is another thread which runs across the book but which is explored in particular in Chapters 2, 3, 4, and 7. A distinctive and additive contribution that organization theory can make to the study of public sector management is the analysis of the rise and implementation of new public management style reorganizations as an organizational change process.

A number of analytic distinctions can be usefully drawn (Ashburner *et al.* 1994). For example, the change process may be characterized as top–down, bottom–up, or middle–out (i.e. emanating from middle management), or as a mixture of these modes. Much of the organizational development tradition saw change taking place incrementally, on the basis of consensus, collaboration, and participation (Quinn 1980): the change process had to be 'owned' by the employees. The view was sometimes taken that top–down and power-led change strategies might produce temporary tactical compliance, but would not result in enduring cultural change. Dunphy and Stace (1988) argue that this organizational development tradition, lacking a contextual or environmental element, had difficulty explaining the rise of 'coercive' reorganizations apparent in the 1980s, often introduced at the dictate of newly imposed chief executives.

At this point, the focus began to switch from incremental (or first order) change to transformatory (second order) change (Levy 1986). As the 1980s wore on, the established view that attempts at large-scale change had only superficial effects came under increasing scrutiny as writers explored the possibility of radical or strategic change. Lundberg (1984), for instance, wrote of strategies for engineering major organizational transitions.

There is currently increased interest in examining the circumstances in which such transformatory change may occur. At the same time, empirical assessment criteria for judging whether this form of change has occurred remain undeveloped, reflecting the loose and rather breathless tone of much of the writing in this area.

The earlier work on organizational change from the organizational development tradition also stressed techniques for planned transition management, often at the level of an organizational unit. As the ideas from this tradition mixed with the socio-technical-based analysis emanating from the work associated with the Tavistock Institute (Emery and Trist 1965) so the concepts took on a more holistic form and whilst still incremental in approach, there was greater recognition of the interdependencies within organizations. Even relatively small-scale changes were seen to create unintended consequences and waves of change.

Organizational change can be analysed at a series of levels, including the system-wide level at the highest level of aggregation. For example, Zifcak (1994) compares and contrasts the highly top–down character of the UK case with the more consensual process observable in the Australian case.

This literature suggests a number of key questions for analysis. Should the UK change process be seen as essentially top–down and power-led? If so, to what extent has this approach resulted in transformatory change? What is the balance between planned and unplanned change? How significant are the unplanned consequences of complex organizational action (Merton 1936)? We will argue that unanticipated consequences have been apparent, and in particular that unheralded and hybrid organizational forms are emerging.

Changing Roles and Relationships

Change may occur at group and individual level as well as at the higher level of the entire system. At these lower levels of analysis, change to established patterns of roles and relationships within small élite groups at the highest tiers of local public services are of particular interest. These themes are explored in depth in Chapters 4, 6, and 7, with particular reference to the post-1990 health authorities and trusts. The relative fate of three élite occupational or social groupings are of particular interest in our analysis of new public management style organizations.

A process of managerialization has already been noted at system-wide level. But what does this imply for the role of senior public sector managers within individual units? Has there been a process of role expansion occurring at local level? If so, what are the limits to such role expansion as managerial roles begin to collide with other roles? What is the relationship between the individual manager and the wider managerial grouping or cadre?

Public sector organizations are often highly professionalized (e.g. hospitals, universities) in nature. This raises the question of the changing role and autonomy of professional groups as they are faced with the processes of increased managerialization and marketization seen as characteristic of new public management-style reforms. Often a general process of deprofessionalization is heralded; for example, Keat and Abercrombie (1991) argue that especially for skilled and professional workers, markets underline the autonomy of previously established work practices, constituting them as individualized and compliant competitors rather than as members of a collective craft or profession. However, Whittington *et al.*'s (1994) study of the response of hospital clinicians and scientists in R and D laboratories to increased market pressures paints a more nuanced picture. For top management, the shift to a market-driven regime may entail some risk to control. Control loss might occur not only as professionals manipulate market opportunities and rhetoric for themselves, but also lead to a loss of strategic control over a fragmenting organization. Certainly clinicians with strong external reputations may find themselves empowered by the development of quasi-markets in health care.

Our own analysis in Chapter 7 will develop this more nuanced approach, identifying the potential for professional gains as well as losses and focusing on the development of interesting new hybrid roles as some professionals move into the arena of management.

The third key grouping within the new public management is that of appointed non-executives. The critical sociological tradition has argued that advanced capitalist societies are dominated by a small but tightly integrated power élite (Wright Mills 1956) who controlled key positions within society and whose interests conflicted with the vast majority of the population.

While class theorists accept that there may be divisions within the power élite, these are seen as relatively slight and as overridden by integrating mechanisms which create a tendency towards class-wide unity (Mizruchi 1992). Useem (1984) argues that there exists among leaders of largest firms an inner circle whose multiple board membership enables them to view the world in terms of the long-term interests of business as a whole. Pluralists (Dahl 1961), by contrast, argue that a range of different sub-élites typically negotiate, or even compete, and that the presence of integrating mechanisms or a dominant inner circle should not be assumed.

So we need to distinguish between local and national élites, and as far as appointments to local public sector boards are concerned, members of local élites (except perhaps at chair level) will predominate. We need to investigate whether such members are drawn from a range of backgrounds, or are very narrowly recruited. Members drawn from élite positions in public service, not-for-profit organizations, or academic life may display different value systems from those with a business background. We also need to investigate how powerful non-executives really are, both within the organization and within the wider world. Class theory assumes that non-executives are indeed powerful, as ambassadors of wider class interests. However, this power-based explanation of why it is that individuals seek board status has been questioned by Zajac (1993) who has put forward alternative explanations based on prestige, friendship, or pleasure in the process. Élite theory may then operate with a very crude theory of motivation.

The boards of public service organizations are also of interest because they can often be seen as mixed and multi-role groups which contain representatives of all the three occupational groupings already alluded to. Interrelationships within such mixed groups are sometimes seen in terms of a negotiated order (Hodgson *et al.* 1965; R. Stewart 1991). Although small in size, the boards of public service organizations contain a complex series of distinctive roles and interrelationships (e.g. the relationship between the chair and the chief executive officer, between the chair and the non-executive directors, between the executive directors and the non-executive directors). Chapter 6 will seek to capture some of the decision-making processes observable at board level.

The Strategic Apex of Public Service Organizations

Our empirical data and analysis are concentrated at the level of the strategic apex of local new public management-style organizations, notably the post-1990 restructured health authorities. Critics of this approach could argue that this is to focus at too high a level, and that behaviour at the operational level may be unaffected by developments at this tier. We would, however, argue that this strategic tier has commonly gained power as a result of recent reorganizations and that it now possesses an increasing active and reshaping role. An examination of the strategic behaviour of the board is then urgently needed. Chapters 5 and 6 in particular seek to address this theme.

The first question is whether there is indeed evidence of strategic leadership behaviour at this level. After all, the pre-1990 health authorities were widely criticized for acting as passive rubber stamps (P. Day and Klein 1987; Best and Ham 1989), where the initiative lay with the executive. The adoption of a private sector 'boards of directors' model was advocated on the grounds that it would attract senior and skilled personnel who could play a more strategic role. However, much of the private sector literature also painted a picture of the marginal role of non-executives, except perhaps under conditions of crisis (Mace 1971; Lorsch and MacIver 1989; Pettigrew 1992).

More recent work has helped specify the conditions in which private sector non-executives may achieve a greater level of influence (Pettigrew and McNulty 1995). These include: external stature and prestige, drawing on the external legitimacy of groups such as shareholders and regulators; knowledge of the host sector or business; the quality and extent of personal networks in and outside the board; residual power to reward and sanction; the threat of resignation; and derived power from a good quality relationship with the chair or chief executive officer. The empirical question of whether the non-executive directors on the post-1990 NHS boards can be said to have undergone a transition to a more active influencing and strategic role is then a key one.

There is a second question of how we characterize the nature of the strategic process observed on these boards in the light of the wider strategy literature (FitzGerald *et al.*, forthcoming). Much of the literature on strategic management has an outward facing perspective, and is strongly influenced by rational planning and marketing concepts. However, concepts and models of strategy formulation range from rational planning approaches, through evolutionary and emergent approaches, to the dustbin view of strategy (Whittington (1993) provides a useful typology of concepts and approaches). Clearly, whichever view of strategy one adopts, there are implications for managerial action. The critique by Whittington illustrates the limitations to our knowledge about strategy. Much of the attention hitherto has centred on the content of strategy and the pressure is growing to integrate the study of process, both formulation and implementation, with the study of content (Porter 1991; Rumelt, Schendel, and Teece 1991). There have been few empirical studies of strategy formulation to illuminate what actually happens in an organization and therefore to ask the questions of whether or not, for example, the classical mode is used and whether it is seen as effective.

One study by Grinyer and Norburn (1974) indicates that classical approach to strategy overemphasizes clear choices and underemphasizes the role of informal communications in forming strategy. The empirical data cited in this book have the virtue of drawing on a longitudinal study of boards and strategy formulation, which includes not only real time data, but direct observation of decision-making processes.

Another limitation to the framework of our current thinking on strategy is that the frame of reference is based mainly on organizations in the for-profit sector. There is little recognition that organizations in the new-style public or voluntary sectors may also need to develop strategies to survive against or alongside increasingly competitive counterparts (Wilson and Butler 1990; Shortell *et al.* 1990).

So how do the public sector boards studied make strategy? Are funnelling processes evident so that only a restricted amount of information flows to the board? To what extent is strategy intended or is it emergent in nature? What form does strategic leadership take? The question also arises of how strategy is formed within developing quasi-markets where the system level is under pressure to fragment and the initiative passes to more autonomous local organizations, bound more by contract than by hierarchy (although the extent of this shift in mode of control is still ambiguous). These issues will be addressed in Chapters 3 and 6.

Any discussion of behaviour at local board level also needs to address the question of the accountability of new public management-style organizations. Typically, the creation of new public management-style boards has been marked by a shift in composition from elected and staff representatives to appointed members and sometimes senior managers. Traditional, albeit indirect, channels of downwards accountability to local electors have been eroded. Instead, senses of upwards and managerially driven accountability may be strengthening as tighter line management hierarchies were constructed in key public services during the 1980s.

Recent reorganizations of the public services have been seen by critics as impoverishing traditional concepts of public accountability (Weir and Hall 1994) and as leading to the rise of a 'new magistracy' (J. Stewart 1992) out of democratic control. The spectre is raised of the 'appointee State', with imposed and politically pliable appointees running local public services. There is also some recent evidence which suggests serious failures of probity in public service organizations. While supporters of recent reorganizations have in turn developed new models of accountability, such as market-led account-ability or the developing role of purchasing organizations as tribunes of the people, many are unpersuaded. The accountability debate has escalated in importance and can now be seen as central to the whole future of the new public management. This theme is acknowledged and developed in Chapter 8.

1.6. Approach and Methods

The research team has demonstrated a long standing interest in the study of organizational change processes, both in the private sector (Pettigrew 1985;

Pettigrew and Whipp 1991) and in health care settings (Pettigrew *et al.* 1992; Bennett and Ferlie 1994). The methodology employed has typically been qualitative, based on longitudinal and comparative case study work and informed by organization theory. In one sense, the analysis offered here builds on this well-established approach and tradition.

However, this latest analysis also contains some novel developments. The field of analysis and discussion has moved from health care to the public sector as a whole, although our primary data are reported from health care settings. There is, however, more comparative material cited from other public sector settings, such as education services. The approach is rather more discursive and less directly data-driven than hitherto, and fewer case studies are reported in depth in order to achieve this broader coverage.

Of course, there is still a strong empirical component to our analysis. Data are reported from a number of concurrent health care studies in which the team has been involved (for instance, material from a study of clinical directorates is cited in Chapter 7). We regard the NHS as a good vantage point from which to observe the rise of new public management-style ideas, as it can be seen as an early and rapid mover in this field (for example, adopting general management in 1985; beginning a transition to a quasi-market model in 1991).

The primary study cited is our study of the post-1990 boards of the new health authorities and trusts. Full details of the research design and methodology of this study are contained in the Appendix.

Here it is sufficient to make two important methodological points. First, in this study conventional in-depth case study work was complemented by two national postal surveys administered across the whole population of NHS boards in England. There has then been a broadening of methodology. Secondly, our qualitative methodology has been developed through a move to more emphasis on observational work. We were able to attend board meetings (both public and private components of their agendas) in the eleven sites tracked over a considerable time period. We regard this as a major methodological achievement as very few researchers studying board-room behaviour have so far managed to get inside the boardroom (Pettigrew 1992).

1.7. Plan of the Book

Following this initial overview chapter, the next two chapters will analyse some of the major changes apparent within UK public services initially in a broad and discursive way, although some primary data will be presented from the NHS.

Chapter 2 picks up the organizational change theme already surfaced, focusing on the question of public sector restructuring at a system-wide level. Conventionally, public sector reform programmes have been seen as likely to achieve only very limited impact. The literature on the problems of public sector restructuring is reviewed. Yet the 1980s were also characterized by increasing talk of transformatory change. Is there evidence of transformatory change taking place in UK public service settings? What indeed are the criteria which might enable us to judge the presence of such change? Six criteria are proposed, two at a system-wide level (examined in this chapter) and four at below system-wide level (examined in Chapter 4). The initial assessment against the NHS evidence outlined suggests, at the very least, that the system is moving from inertia to change.

Chapter 3 examines the introduction of quasi-markets within public service settings. This can be seen as an attempt to mimic certain features of private sector organizations and thus relates to the different–similar debate. The experience so far of quasi-markets across different settings within the public sector is reviewed. A novel theory of quasi-markets—stressing their relational character—is presented. Case study evidence is then briefly adduced from two contrasting NHS localities.

Chapter 4 develops the analysis of organizational change commenced in Chapter 2, this time moving down to the unit, group, and individual levels. The theoretic focus also shifts further from the public sector restructuring literature to a focus on organizational change, and in particular the notion of transformatory change. Primary data are presented from the NHS, and compared with secondary material relating to the education sector. We conclude that there is now evidence of significant change occurring, at least in health care.

Chapters 5 and 6 focus in more depth on changes to the strategic apex of public sector organizations. Within the public services, there has been a growth of a private sector 'boards of directors' model, with appointed local boards being asked to take on a more active strategic role. Supporters argue that these changes have facilitated the engagement of skilled and senior personnel with public service management, while critics point to the unrepresentative and unaccountable nature of this leadership cadre. All agree that this is an important area for empirical enquiry, yet systematic empirical data are scarce. Taking the post-1990 NHS health authorities and trusts as a key example, we present our data on board composition and process.

The public services have traditionally been seen as highly professionalized settings. Chapter 7 examines the changing role of professionals within the new public management. Some have argued that the increased power of managers and markets has disadvantaged professionals. We question this and provide a more nuanced interpretation, pointing to the possibility of professional gains as well as losses.

A key difference between private and public sector settings is that the latter can be characterized by a stronger sense of accountability. Chapter 8 addresses the question of public accountability within the new public management, which some have seen as its Achilles' heel. Should new public management-style organizations still be seen as essentially public in nature? What do we mean by the word 'accountability'? Are there alternative models of accountability on offer? We conclude that this represents a major area of concern, and that there is an urgent need to develop more robust models of accountability.

Chapter 9 will seek to draw the results from this empirical suite of chapters together and to offer a more synthetic interpretation, together with suggestions for future lines of enquiry.

PUBLIC SECTOR RESTRUCTURING

2.1. Introduction

This chapter sets the emergence of the new public management in the wider context of public sector restructuring in Britain and other developed countries. Common factors such as the impact of national and world recession and the growth of government have increasingly led to attempts to control public expenditure or to restructure public sectors with the aim that they become more effective and responsive. The emergence of the New Right in Britain has led to the search for answers being focused on an ideological perspective which advocates the primacy of markets for the production and distribution of goods and services. Concomitant with this are the values of individualism and freedom from government which have resulted in the drive for privatization. The impact of this ideology in Britain and elsewhere and its consequences for public sector restructuring need to be analysed.

The two chief characteristics of public sector restructuring and administrative reform on both sides of the Atlantic, prior to 1980, have been the top–down nature of the change process and its limited impact. The lack of impact can be defined both in relation to the extent of the change within the organization and its ability to be sustained over time. The similarities of the experiences across a number of political regimes has led to a level of scepticism as to whether any form of public sector reform is likely to achieve the consequences desired by the instigating government. Given the continuing emphasis on public sector reform it becomes essential that any analysis seeks to understand what might be different in the political context of the latest series of reforms so that this can contribute to the development of a conceptual framework within which the style, nature, and impact of recent restructuring processes can be assessed.

The Political Context

The increasing political influence of the New Right within many countries during the 1980s followed the monetarist reaction against Keynesian economics in the 1970s, associated with economists such as Milton Friedman. In terms of the public sector, there was a more systematic challenging of collectivism in attempts to redefine the role of the State (Massey 1993). In Britain the breakdown of the post-war settlement has given the New Right the opening it needed to challenge the social democratic principles and values which had dominated British politics since 1945 (Farnham and Horton 1993).

In Britain, by the 1970s the political consensus which had been shared by all shades of governments, defining the nature of the political system and forming the framework within which policy decisions had been made, was increasingly being called into question. The slowing down of economic growth world-wide had helped to undermine this edifice, with the least economically efficient countries such as Britain being hardest hit. The Welfare State was seen as responsible for the high level of taxation needed to sustain it and the subsequent levels of inflation. The New Right's perception of the Welfare State was that it was under- and poorly-managed, acted as an unaccountable monopoly, was professionally dominated, and lacking in client involvement. The philosophy of the New Right was that the introduction of markets and the process of privatization would bring both the efficient allocation of resources and choice to consumers and producers.

The 1979 Conservative Government introduced a series of public sector reform initiatives which represented a reaction against this perception of public sector immobility and even ungovernability. Much of the industrial public sector was privatized as part of the process of scaling down the scope of the public sector and transferring responsibilities back to the private sector. Where privatization was not possible the aim was to make the public sector 'more business-like' and the means chosen was the transfer of existing concepts, models, and personnel from the private to the public sector. There was an increased emphasis on financial control, such as securing efficiency, effectiveness, and value for money. Administrators became managers. Where markets did not exist, quasi-markets were introduced. As with other aspects of the new public management, it is not clear that the transfer of models from the private sector to the public was well thought through. In this new enterprise culture (Keat and Abercrombie 1991) markets are preferred to politics as a means of allocating resources and distributing welfare. In the UK this represented a unifying theme in policy-making and is exemplified in the sustained nature and wide scope of public sector reform.

Restructuring via privatization occurred in the utilities and in the industrial public sector, before attention turned to the Welfare State. Here the New Right's central tenet of the supremacy of markets had to be introduced in a way that was more politically acceptable and in a way that reflected the inherently different needs of sectors such as health, education, the criminal justice system, and social services. The reforms experienced within the NHS were typical of the general policy trend within government, yet with key differences which reflect the need for different approaches between the various parts of the public sector. The health sector represents an exemplar of many of the main features of this part of the restructuring process with the growing influence of managerialism, the introduction of quasi-markets, purchaser–provider splits, and management by contract.

The juxtaposition of, on the one hand, the increasing pressure for greater public sector efficiency and, on the other, the rise of the New Right has meant that these two agendas have become inextricably linked. The issue of the nature of the problem facing the public sector and the need for reform must analytically be disentangled from the means whereby they are to be achieved. It is important to note that this feature of public sector reform in the 1980s was not universal. In Sweden, for example, the process of restructuring progressed alongside a continued adherence to democratic principles and a retention of consensus management (Czarniawska-Joerges 1989). Also, the New Right philosophy has not gone unchallenged. An alternative view put forward by Keman (1993) for example, argues that there is no direct evidence that the 'burden' of tax acted as a disincentive for growth and that without a Welfare State there would be increased wage demands and greater inflation. He argues that a large public sector is not a disincentive for growth as the production and provision of public goods and services did not jeopardize the working and viability of the market economy, citing the enormous cross-national differences in economic performance unrelated to the size of each country's Welfare State.

The Restructuring Theme

In examining how aspects of the present government's reform agenda compare and contrast with the past and how this is contributing to the emergence of the new public management, this chapter will first consider theoretical developments as they relate to the theme of restructuring. These will be assessed to ascertain what conceptual frameworks might develop our understanding of recent and current processes in the UK. The chapter next examines the process of public sector restructuring by considering the context of the changes as they emerged historically in the UK, across the wider public sector and with some international comparisons. Developments in the health sector are compared and contrasted with those in other parts of the public sector in terms of the predominant factors and the timing of the government initiatives. The sectoral comparators will thus vary depending upon which feature of restructuring is being addressed. The data from our study of the post-1990 NHS will be used to develop the conceptual framework and to suggest why the number, scope, and size of the changes experienced throughout the 1980s in the UK public sector lead to the need for a fundamental reassessment of the theory of public sector restructuring processes.

The main themes addressed by this chapter are first, to understand the changes which are occurring within the public sector and secondly, to begin to assess whether these mark a significant shift from past experience and whether they can be seen as beginning a process of organizational transformation. In this assessment it is important that the criteria upon which any judgements are made are seen as relating to identifiable organizational factors rather than the more specific and often political objectives set by the government. As shown later in this chapter, some public sector reforms may be introduced for the political expediency of indicating a desire for improvement or reductions in public expenditure, rather than with any great expectation of achievement. We need to understand the extent to which, when measured against stated objectives, reforms can be judged to have succeeded or failed. There also needs to be an analysis of the effects of the reforms on public sector organizations at all levels, in order to understand the significance of the changes, whether they are those intended or not.

In analysing the extent of the changes experienced by the public sector we have distinguished between different levels of change. Moving beyond the simple dichotomy usually drawn between incremental and fundamental change, we discriminate between processes of large-scale organizational change and organizational transformation. In an attempt to develop a more effective theoretical basis upon which to classify different types of organizational change, we have identified six key factors. These, we suggest, can act as indicators of the extent and depth of change and they will be used as the basis of our analysis of the NHS empirical data. The six indicators have been devised in order to enable an assessment of the change process at several levels, from the national, to the sector, to the individual organization and the units within.

1. The extent of multiple, interrelated change across the system as a whole;
2. The creation of new organizational forms at a sector level;
3. The development of multi-layered changes which impact below the whole system at unit level;
4. The creation of changes in the services provided and their mode of delivery;
5. The reconfiguration of power relations;
6. The creation of a new culture, ideology, and organizational meaning.

This chapter with its emphasis on the macro-issues relating to public sector restructuring will focus mainly on the first two criteria. Chapter 4, which introduces the discussion of the nature of transformational change and examines the process of multi-layered change inside the organization, will focus its analysis on the remaining four factors.

2.2. Theoretical Developments

There is a need for a theoretical understanding of restructuring processes that offers a conceptual framework for explaining the perceived limited impact of earlier public sector restructuring. One such attempt focuses on the notion, as outlined by March and Olsen (1983), of reforms as administrative rhetoric (While we use the term 'reform' we are aware of its value-laden connotations. We do not assume that the organizational outcomes of reform processes are necessarily benign, but are aware that the term may also be a device through which self-proclaimed reformers sell their products.) As they have shown from their study of post-war restructuring programmes in the USA, most plans for major reorganization failed to survive normal political trading, although they did stress that these were not set up deliberately to be sacrificial lambs. These attempts at restructuring can be seen as being legitimacy-led rather than efficiency-led, as governments introduced policies which appeared politically attractive and to which organizations had to be seen to conform. A second factor was the short-run political attention afforded each reform effort by national politicians. As less central actors moved to the forefront, not only were the initial issues and impetus which began the reforms diluted, but further dissipation occurred as otherwise unoccupied participants and unresolved issues became part of the reform process. This ambiguity of reorganizations could end up by producing a negative political impact attracting more political opposition than support.

In accepting the apparent failure of each attempt by the US government at administrative reform prior to the 1980s, March and Olsen (1983) examine why it is that with the frustration and disillusionment caused, such exercises continue to be repeated. They see this as being based on an unwillingness to accept political impotence, in a continuing belief that persistence would pay off and as a way of keeping issues alive. For a government to continue an adherence to increasing bureaucratic efficiency, and use reform programmes as a tactic for creating an illusion of progress where none existed, was seen as politically attractive. As March and Olsen note, after several different reform attempts some changes could be discerned. From this, they conclude that bureaucratic reform appears to need long-run commitment, patience, and perseverance. They also note that the initiators of reform seldom attempted to ascertain what really happened as a consequence of their efforts.

Proposals for reform, and their subsequent implementation, can thus be viewed as an ongoing feature of most governments. Using another concept, that of the 'reform cycle' (Brunsson 1989), we can see that while reforms are superficially presented as a dramatic change in agency life, reforming can also be seen as a standard and repetitive process. As Brunsson observed, reforms are easy to start but difficult to finish. Reforms may be oversold or raise undue expectations and lead in turn to the perception of fresh problems for which ever-newer reforms were needed, so that reforming became a steady state. Reforms can also often come in cycles, and this is connected both to strong fashions in the stock of managerial knowledge and to the fact that many agencies are forgetting rather than learning organizations.

Post-1980 research has highlighted two factors which have been identified as having the potential to change the patterns of the past. These are the concepts of 'radical shock' and of 'persistent political will' (March and Olsen 1989). Their discussion of agencies as political institutions examines a strategy of intentional transformation through the process of radical shock, usually via an attempt to impose a significantly different ideology.

Where historical processes are inefficient, it is possible to imagine moving the political system from one (relatively) stable equilibrium to another one that is quite different. This is the sense in which political institutions are essential elements of political change. They are instruments for the branching of history. The Thatcher government's attempts to reform the British civil service may turn out to be an example of such a process (March and Olsen 1989: 64).

In the UK, similar reforms have been evident in the Civil Service, local government, education, and the health service, and are all based on the application of the philosophies of the New Right, which did mark a sea change with the past. The concept of radical shock itself needs to be more fully articulated before it can be established whether it would be sufficient in itself to produce fundamental change. Brunsson (1982) argues that radical changes need to be preceded by and initiated through ideological shifts. Thus if allegiance to the old ideology persists then the context for change is poor. An important conclusion of March and Olsen is that it is easier to produce change through shock than it is to control what new combination of institutions and practices will evolve from the shock. They have also noted that they did not study what effects reforms actually had and this may have led in part to an underestimation of the longer term effects of reform programmes.

Does the concept of persistent political will involve merely the eventual outcome of continuous efforts at reform, each one different from the last, even when the effects are apparently very limited in the short term or seen merely as superficial? Or, on the other hand, is it better understood as a different approach to reform by governments, where a single set of policies continue to be pushed over a long time period? In relation to the present analysis, it is the latter interpretation that will be developed.

The issue of outcomes is an important one; as we have seen, the concept of radical shock can result in unpredictable outcomes. This raises the question of whether such changes should necessarily have been unpredictable. One feature of administrative reform is the policy-led nature of its defined objectives, such as reducing costs or size, and this leads to its success or failure being defined in these terms. Even if little impact is made upon such areas the impact of change in organizational terms might be more significant. It is thus more important in assessing the outcome of reform efforts to focus on the actual changes that resulted. Czarniawska-Joerges (1989) suggests that the impact of earlier and current reforms should be analysed in relation to their effects at the time, especially on changing power relations, rather than in relation to the longer term structural impact. She adds that March and Olsen's failure to find evidence of the impact of public sector reform lies in their adherence to the conventional expectations such as efficiencies, responsiveness, and control. Czarniawska-Joerges's approach may produce a theoretical framework which allows some value to be attached to all reform efforts even when the primary objectives of those initiating the reforms have not necessarily been realized. Where it is useful is in focusing on the process of reform and on how those involved in the implementation process at different levels in the organization try to discover what can be gained from the process by redirecting some aspects of the reform into specific directions which may not be the same as the original objectives. The potential for change can be broader still. Alvesson and Berg (1992) consider that to present a powerfully coercive, though partly false, external image of the changes can have the effect of indirectly influencing human behaviour internally, so the reform effort might not be as totally ineffective as at first assumed. Similarly, Broadbent *et al.* (1991) describe the constitutive nature of the NHS reforms with its potential for changing behaviour. They also observe that this does not mean that behaviour will necessarily change in the way desired, and indeed are sceptical of the long-term impact of reforms on core professional practice.

Unlike March and Olsen who saw the 'symbolic' nature of reforms as a sign of failure, Czarniawska-Joerges identifies the key effect of reform in terms of its 'symbolic accomplishment' which she believes might be as important as more concrete change, if power realignment can be achieved and if reform can appear to change things for the better and thus renew public trust and confidence. Thus the potential importance of symbolic changes, such as changes in terminology and language, which might be dismissed as superficial, needs to be recognized and the effects on culture, ideology, and organizational meaning need to be assessed as well as more substantive aspects of the change process. It is therefore important to recognize that some important symbolic change may result from apparently unsuccessful restructuring processes.

This line of argument raises the issue of whether the change which might be achieved is in fact closely related to the original objectives of the reforms, or is a partly unanticipated consequence of the lengthy, complex, multidirectional, and multilayered process of change itself, whereby in interpretation, selection, and application, the original broad policy intentions can be adapted or modified. This concept of multilayered change would therefore emphasize, among other important variables, the need to understand power reconfigurations within organizations as a consequence of a top–down reform effort, and to explore whether organizational players are empowered enough to be able to avoid the frustration and chaos that leads to the reassertion of previous forms and processes. We expand on the concept of multilayered change and examine further what constitutes fundamental or transformatory change in Chapter 4.

The two chief characteristics of typical administrative reform efforts identified earlier were their top–down nature and their limited impact over time and in extent. In the 1980s a new concept of radical shock, where the scale of the change was expanded, and the concept of persistent political will, where it was the repetitive application of a single set of policy objectives, emerged as significant. In reassessing why attempts at public sector restructuring might no longer be limited in their impact, we note the critical importance of the above two factors. Post-1980 processes of reform may move through the various layers of the organization, reconfigure power relations within the organization, and accord increased attention to the role of symbolic change. It is the cumulative effect of the combination of all of these factors, as encapsulated in our six criteria of transformatory change, which is significant rather than the effects of any one.

2.3. Public Sector Context

International and Cross-sectoral Comparisons

Public sector restructuring and the development of new forms of public sector management are common across many countries as described in Chapter 1. As Eliassen and Kooiman (1993) show, there are several dimensions to the differences in reform patterns which exist across countries and time. The political importance of ideas of efficiency and the use of private management techniques rooted in New Right philosophies, are more predominant in some countries, such as Britain, than in others. Nevertheless, Eliassen and Kooiman found in nearly all countries, major privatization programmes and the introduction of market-led ideas into the public sector. However, they also noted that over time there has been a gradual decline in the use of private sector management mechanisms in public management reforms.

Evidence from the USA prior to the 1980s has shown how attempts at reform within the public sector appeared to be doomed to fail. Initial far-reaching proposals were typically diluted in the course of political trading within a pluralist system and political attention could not be sustained over a long enough time-span. Improbable promises of economies were made in an effort to secure political advantage and the restructuring process was seen much more as rhetorical or symbolic than as a genuine attempt to improve the machinery of government. How does the American experience compare with that of Britain?

Evidence from Britain also shows a well-developed scepticism about the effects of administrative reforms (Fry 1981). A later assessment of the continuing Civil Service reforms led Fry (1984: 334) to conclude that 'The civil service has little choice about wearing the currently fashionable clothes but much the same bodies remain underneath.' Metcalfe and Richards (1990) show the record of administrative reform in Britain to have been poor, with its political appeal being much greater than its administrative impact, as in America. This they see as the consequence of electoral propaganda when politicians promise more than they deliver and political tactics when politicians claim their policies will keep costs down. Once the magnitude of the task becomes apparent then enthusiasm for it evaporates. More fundamentally, Metcalfe and Richards see failure as being based in both conceptual and practical difficulties since the solutions chosen had their origin in the private sector. Whilst acknowledging that some private sector practices can be useful for the public sector, they are critical of reforms which fit the private sector solutions available rather than developing new solutions to fit the specific problems being faced by the public sector.

Studies of attempts at public sector reform post-1980 have begun to suggest that a different process is under way. High priority was given to securing institutional change and the 1980s saw British administrations continuing to prioritize their policies related to public sector reform. Processes of piloting and assessment were not part of the remit. Fry (1984) describes the Government's reforms of the Civil Service as being vigorous and persistent. Metcalfe and Richards (1990) offer an account of the management of change in Whitehall in the 1980s when the pace of change was described as seeming to accelerate, if anything, as the decade wore on. They conclude that the changes instigated in the culture of Whitehall would be difficult, if not impossible, to reverse. Similarly, Benington and Stoker (1989) describe the Thatcher Government's changes and interventions into local government as having occurred with increasing frequency and intensity throughout the 1980s.

In central government, as in health, early reforms were built upon in stages but a major escalation was apparent in 1988 when the Ibbs Report, *Improving Management in Government: The Next Steps*, was published (Efficiency Unit 1988). The report focused on the problem of the lack of management skills amongst senior civil servants who saw their main role as policy support to ministers; there was weak financial control only on the input side, and great difficulty in changing the rules which were centrally prescribed. The creation of agencies was a compromise between remaining part of the government bureaucracy and complete privatization. The agencies, as O'Toole and Jordan (1995) observe, were set up as a means of separating the delivery of services from the policy work. Although envisaged as working within business style regimes, complete privatization remained an ideal. Hogwood's (1993) study of reform within central government also saw the Next Steps agencies as part of the attempt to introduce managerialism and private management logic into the public sector. The main issue not specified by the report was the extent to which the new agencies would be part of the Civil Service or independent of it. Here the main problem identified was that of accountability. This was seen to have suffered in the moves towards increasing autonomy. The proposal that emerged was that as far as possible agency chief executives should be responsible to either the PAC or the House of Commons. Gray and Jenkins (1995) have observed the tension between the conflicting goals of policy and administration where the chief executives are accountable to ministers and the requirement that they operate within a policy framework has meant that there is a limit to how innovative and independent they can be. They suggest that the reason for the apparent success to date is that the Next Steps initiative has avoided areas of strategy and side-stepped problematic issues.

Metcalfe and Richards (1990: 230) use the phrase 'centralize in order to decentralize' to summarize the dilemma of the government in seeking to decentralize and relinquish control but retain a leading role in strategy formulation. They note the absence of reform within the core departments themselves. By July 1990 there were thirty-three agencies employing over 80,000 staff and they considered this to be 'the limits of imitation of business management by government' (1990: 235) because many management problems in government fall outside the scope of the agency idea, because of issues such as accountability, and because of the impact of the political context on management. They see a need for the development of new concepts suited more directly to the needs of the public sector.

By 1993 there were ninety-two agencies which, as O'Toole and Jordan (1995) note, along with the thirty-one executive units of Customs and Excise and the thirty-three units of Inland Revenue, employed more than 60 per cent of the Civil Service. They comment that although this was very fast development which was presented as a success it was far from unproblematic. They question the assumptions upon which the reforms were founded, of government waste and the unquestioning acceptance that decentralization was the answer. They are similar to Metcalfe and Richards in that they believe that reform should be based upon 'rigorous identification of weakness and a coherent and considered plan to remedy those defects' (O'Toole and Jordan 1995: 190). Unlike most other writers on the public sector they recognize the importance of understanding the process of organizational change, the need to establish support for the goals of the change, and the risk of unintended consequences. Whilst they acknowledge that Next Steps has led to change, they question whether it has led to improvement. One key difference between the Next Steps initiative and the health service reforms was that the latter embraced the whole of the health system and not just the provider units. This may mean that Next Steps has reached the stage where the scope for further change is limited unless there are major policy changes which directly affect the central core of departments as well. Gray and Jenkins (1995) believe that the fundamental conflict between the political model of the public sector and the market-driven consumer model, has resulted in merely a symbolic commitment to empowerment.

Nevertheless, Next Steps agencies have been created even in politically sensitive areas. A good example is the Benefits Agency (established as an executive agency of the Department of Social Security), with a workforce of

73,000 and annual payments of £66b (Benefits Agency 1994). Its annual report certainly demonstrates a concern with the first three of the models identified in Chapter 1, such as:

- business planning, performance management, and value for money;
- a rolling programme of market-testing;
- service level agreements (quasi-contracts) with other public agencies; a business plan agreed with ministers;
- more active personnel policies; the management of cultural change; investment in people.

In other parts of the UK public sector, parallel reforms are also under way. Glennerster (1991) considers the reform process as it relates to schools and higher education which he sees as containing some of the elements of an internal market for education. For higher education where there was already an element of competition between institutions the concept can be considered applicable. For schools, however, he sees the outcome as resulting in selection bias rather than competition on efficiency grounds. The outcome overall he sees as leading to mediocrity rather than the reverse.

Goodsir (1993) analyses changes in the police service which resulted from a series of Audit Commission reports between 1988 and 1991 as another example of the Government's wider public sector reforms which were begun in the early 1980s. Similarities with other reform attempts lay in the desire to create a stronger management structure, to reduce the autonomy of the professional senior police officer, and to introduce structural changes to pay and conditions of service. The publication of the Sheehy Report in 1993, which outlined how the above objectives were to be achieved, was met with considerable resistance within the force by those likely to be responsible for its implementation.

There are similar reform processes ongoing in many other countries such as Australia and New Zealand. Zifcak (1994) compared the Australian Government's reform attempts during the 1980s with those in Whitehall. The Canberra initiative was called the Financial Management Improvement Programme, and it spanned the same time period as the British Financial Management Initiative and its successor, the Next Steps. In both countries the aim was to introduce a more managerially oriented administration. He notes the similarities of the contexts for reform despite the different political complexions of the two governments. In Australia, reform was primarily led by economic necessity without the defining context of New Right philosophies. Both sets of reforms aimed at improving public sector effectiveness, but the key difference was the Hawke Government's rejection of the private sector analogy and the emphasis placed upon ensuring the new system was more equitable and democratic. A convergence between the two programmes occurred later as the economic situation in Australia worsened and the democratic and equity agendas were eclipsed. In both countries, it was the vigour with which reform was pursued that Zifcak identifies as comparable and significant. In his analysis of the content and strategy of the two sets of reforms, he identified the key differences which related to the success of the innovation and concluded that the Canberra administration with its greater flexibility, cohesion, and openness was more conducive to managerial innovation.

While the Swedish experience of public sector reform appeared similar to that of Australia at the outset, it was as concerned with protecting traditional public sector values as it was with effectiveness and efficiency. Czarniawska-Joerge's study (1989) of the Swedish submunicipal committee reforms concluded that the significance of the reform effort lay in its ability to facilitate shifts in power within organizations which created organizational learning and helped to give the organization renewed legitimacy, resocialized organizational members, and introduced variety into the routines of organizational life. The ideology behind the Swedish reforms studied was for 'democracy via decentralization' in contrast to a more typical objective of efficiency and effectiveness through decentralization apparent in other political cultures.

Willcocks and Harrow (1992) found that the most striking difference between the UK and other European countries was the broader basis of debate in Europe where it was less likely to be restricted to the efficiency arena and considerations of cost, and more likely to include a review and debate on strategic and policy level issues. The Swedish approach showed how adherence to democratic principles was not incompatible with the reform process. In Britain, with its focus on efficiency via private sector management models, markets, and decentralization, this raises the question of the extent to which adherence to the philosophies of the New Right restricts the range of reforms and the means by which they are to be realized.

The experience of earlier reform processes which might have led to the prediction that the commitment to institutional reform would soon run out of steam has not been fulfilled. However, the criteria upon which the impact of such reforms and the means chosen for their implementation are to be judged must be based on an empirical assessment of their organizational impact as well as their rhetorically stated political objectives.

Restructuring in Health Services

The focus will now turn to one of the major services in the public sector in order to develop an in-depth analysis of the impact of reform. The choice of the health service is predicated upon its size and importance in the economy of the country, the wide range of reforms which are currently being experienced which typify those being introduced elsewhere in the public sector, and its greater level of development when compared with other sectors.

Tables 2.1 and 2.2 illustrate first of all the growing importance of health care

Table 2.1. Share of total expenditure on health in total domestic expenditure (%)

	1960	1970	1980	1990	1991
Australia	4.8	5.6	7.1	8.3	8.6
France	4.3	5.9	7.5	8.8	9.1
Germany	4.9	6.0	8.4	8.8	9.1
Japan	3.0	4.6	6.5	6.7	6.8
Spain	1.6	3.6	5.4	6.4	6.5
Sweden	4.7	7.1	9.2	8.6	8.8
UK	3.9	4.6	5.9	6.0	6.6
USA	5.3	7.4	9.2	12.2	13.3
OECD total	3.9	5.1	6.8	7.5	7.8

Source: OECD (1993).

Table 2.2. Total and public expenditure on health (1991) (in millions of national curency units)

	Total expenditure on health	Public expenditure on health	%
Australia	33,178	22,491	67
France	612,700	453,012	74
Germany	222,000	159,400	72
Japan	30,000,000	21,600,000	72
Spain	3,650,000	3,000,000	82
Sweden	123,600	96,450	78
UK	38,000	31,670	83
USA	751,771	329,960	44

Source: OECD (1993).

in resource terms across many countries and secondly the extent to which such expenditure is still publicly financed, notably in Britain.

In the restructuring process itself, there are also strong parallels between the NHS and the rest of the public sector. At an international level as well, Maynard (1991) has observed that although the structure of health care services varies enormously from country to country, the responses of policy-makers to the difficulties being experienced exhibit similar characteristics. As with many commentators who focus exclusively on the health service, Maynard sees the recent NHS reforms as a response to specific health service problems rather than in any wider public sector context. The problems he highlights are poor data, incentives not related to input–outcome relationships, the extent of variation in the costs between different parts of the service, and the level of ignorance about many costs. These are legitimate concerns but they draw attention away from the more politically or ideologically motivated objectives of the policy changes. A purely NHS perspective might explain the introduction of processes designed to increase efficiency and effectiveness but not those related to governance and accountability issues; nor to the means chosen to achieve the economies. To understand the process of restructuring in the British health service of the 1990s, it is necessary both to understand the wider process ongoing in the public sector and the fate of earlier reforms within the NHS.

Politically driven institutional reforms have been a feature of the NHS since the early 1970s. Attempts at that time to introduce managerial ideas from the corporate private sector centred on structural reform with the reduction in the number of management layers and the creation of consensus management teams. The impact of these reforms was seen as superficial and the subsequent concerns about poor performance resulted in the Royal Commission on the NHS in 1976. The outcome was the Merrison Report in 1979 (Cmnd 7615, 1979) which advised caution and incremental change, and gave little hint of what was to follow. A change of government in 1979 meant that its recommendations were put aside.

The Griffiths Inquiry (Griffiths Report 1983), by contrast, was short and not drawn from a general consensus of the views of the key players within the health sector. The views of its author predominated and included as a central recommendation the proposal for setting up a system of general management aimed at processual as well as structural change. This created the necessary foundation upon which the later reforms following the 1989 White Paper *Working for Patients* (Cmnd 555, 1989), later the 1990 NHS and Community Care Act, were to build. The centrally appointed cadre of general managers were the means to the introduction of such managerial levers as accountability reviews and value-for-money initiatives. These managerializing initiatives were seen by Pettigrew *et al.* (1992) as significant in the speeding-up of the rate and pace of change. What was less clear were the ends to which these changes were working, even when the sustained nature of the reform process in the NHS became apparent. The more cautious approach of the 1980s became the more direct challenge of the 1990s.

Two broad schools of thought have emerged about the impact of health care restructuring. The exponents of one, like Kimberly (1989) in the USA and Davies (1987) in the UK detected, even in the 1980s, a faster pace of change within health care management than might hitherto have been expected. The exponents of the other (Pollitt *et al.* 1991; Harrison *et al.* 1992) judged the changes up to the early 1990s, including those following the 1990 NHS and Community Care Act, to have had limited impact. Pollitt *et al.* were sceptical about the level of real change apparent since they believed that fundamental role renegotiation was not taking place. Laughlin (1991) similarly believed that the language of the market might be absorbed but in such a way as to make little or no impact on the dominant culture and core working arrangements of the organization.

The present study with its longitudinal and in-depth assessment of the changes apparent in the first three years of the NHS reforms affords us an opportunity to examine the reality of the changes occurring and to begin to assess whether recent public sector reforms in general might result in funda-mental, rather than limited and incremental, change.

2.4. Evidence of System-Wide Change

The 1990 NHS and Community Care Act put into operation the latest stage in the NHS reform process, representing an ambitious attempt to move the health service from an essentially planned and line-managed organization to one where resources are allocated to a greater, although still ambiguous, extent through an internal market. The introduction of the concept of 'competition' was to be achieved by the separation of the management of the purchasing function from that of the providers of services. One controversial aspect of the reforms was thus the creation of NHS trust status for providers in the acute, mental health, ambulance, and community sectors. Whilst still being part of the health service, units which took on trust status were to be given some enhanced managerial autonomy and new freedoms. Competition was also to be furthered by allowing GPs to purchase health care direct from providers rather than having it purchased on their behalf by health authorities.

The dominance of this model and ideology has also entailed the introduc-tion of a separate function of purchasing which, in turn, has led to the creation of new organizational forms, new roles, and new ways of working with inter-unit relationships increasingly based on contracts rather than hierarchy.

This section examines the empirical data from our study as they relate to the first two of our six indicators of change outlined in Section 2.1, i.e. the extent of multiple, interrelated change across the system as a whole and the creation of new organizational forms at a sectoral level. Given that the focus of the study was on the creation and operation of the new authorities and boards, this allowed for both a macro-view of the health service as a whole and a micro-view of decision-making processes at this level. The new purchasing authorities and trust boards are important implementors and also shapers of government policy and health care services. Change at this level, in combination with the direct effects of the wide range of other reforms, is likely to have a significant influence over changes at all other levels. The analysis of this data will enable us to examine the nature of the changes that have occurred in relation to their congruence with the reforms' objectives. Are the outcomes of a strategy based on radical shock and persistent political will both unpredictable and difficult to control? Secondly, we will begin to examine the evidence for suggesting that these reforms break with the patterns of the past and are not limited by time or extent. This theme is developed further in Chapter 4.

A number of different but related initiatives were introduced by the 1990 Act, which included not only structural changes but attempted to change both processes and roles. These cannot be seen in isolation but need to be considered alongside the ongoing processes which have resulted from earlier change initiatives. Many of the issues outlined in this section are examined in later chapters in much greater depth, but are important here as part of the total picture. Amongst these are the changes which relate to governance and accountability at board level and issues relating to the role of professionals. In this section first we emphasize the importance of understanding the subsequent interrelationships of different aspects of the reforms, and second we consider three of the major changes evident across the system as a whole: the expanding role of general management, the increasing importance of financial and costing data, and the move from management by hierarchy to management by contract.

Multiple and Interrelated Change

It is not our intention to produce a full analysis of the cumulative effects of all the concurrent changes facing the NHS at this early stage in the development of the book's argument, but to draw attention to the increasingly complex analyses that are necessary when individual change processes begin to interact with others, as different policies work their way through the system.

A prime example of a specific reform, the effects of which can now only be understood when seen in conjunction with other changes, is that of the introduction of GP fundholding. Whilst this could be seen either as further decentralization of the purchasing process or as an increase in managerial control at the level of the general practice, its real purpose was the least well defined of all the reforms. In purchasing terms, it militated against the development at district level of planning for health care in relation to the assessment of needs on a community-wide basis, since purchasing decisions would increasingly be made in relation to individual need at practice level. It made adherence to the traditional values of the NHS for equity problematic as the generous funds made available to fundholders have left the districts comparatively worse off. This has been seen as resulting in the emergence of a two-tier system, since fundholders are in a position to buy relatively more health care for their patients in those areas covered by fundholding budgets, than the district can for the patients of non-fundholders.

Organizationally, fundholding has had a significant impact upon trusts by increasing the complexity and cost of the contracting process as the number of purchasers or customers increases, with the need to deal with potentially large number of different sets of requirements and quality standards. Managerially, not only have trusts had to consider their contractual obligations with the districts, but also with each GP fundholder. Unlike a commercial business, it would pose ethical problems for NHS trusts to create different products for different customers.

Another significant impact of this reform has been on the balance of power within the medical profession. Hospital consultants who now have to ensure the viability of their directorates by attracting the custom of GP fundholders are responding to the needs of GPs in a way that was never previously necessary. GP fundholders have welcomed the greater attention paid to their needs by the providers of health care, and in their capacity of acting on behalf of the patient, the ultimate customer, this is the aspect of the reforms which has the greatest potential to increase consumer choice. Non-fundholders, on the other hand, can find their and their patients' choice restricted to those hospitals where the health authority holds block contracts.

Each of these processes needs to be managed alongside the more direct impact of the reforms being experienced by trusts and purchasers in relation to organizational and role changes, all of which serve to increase the number of interacting variables.

System-Wide Change

Whereas the option to go for trust status or GP fundholding was left to the individual hospitals or practices to decide, the principle of the purchaser and provider split was a system-wide change. The changes to the governance structure were also universally applied. Thus system-wide changes were of both structural and processual kinds. The expanding role of general management was also a central objective of the 1990 Act, but a less easily defined one. The change of structure and composition of the old health authority bodies and the development of trust boards with the inclusion on them of senior management was critical to this process as the new boards were nurtured in the expected development of a more central strategic role in the management of the service. This board level development will be analysed in more depth in Chapters 5 and 6. A change of language was also significant here as general managers of units became chief executives, and senior officers became executive directors. The relative autonomy of the trusts brought greater management responsibilities for reaching the externally set financial objectives and deciding upon the internal organizational strategy for the fulfilment of contracts and future developments.

The management of districts underwent a change of role rather than an increase in the level of managerial responsibility as in family health services authorities. For too long seen as the poor relation, the family health services authorities attained 'equality' with their district cousins in the 1990 Act, as both then reported direct to the Region. The key reason for the Department of Health rejecting the option to merge district and family health services authorities, at that time, was the need to give the family health services authorities time to establish managerial and organizational credibility and thus the strength to be equal partners with the districts. One reason for this was the major focus within health policy to transfer resources from the acute to the primary sector. Historically, the secondary sector has been the main user of resources and if these resources were to be successfully redirected to the primary sector, traditional power bases within the secondary sector needed to be challenged.

Our case study data showed that significant changes were made within the family health services authorities studied as they moved from their purely administrative role to one of developing a strategic overview and managing resources in the primary sector (Ashburner 1993c). In one authority, the previous very formal management structure had been replaced with a more open style, based on teamworking with clearer lines of accountability introduced. The management task for family health service authorities was particularly difficult to achieve given that the main consumers of these resources were GPs who were independent contractors and did not come under the direct management control of the family health services authorities.

Whereas the inclusion of managers on the authorities and trusts for the first time, with the reduction in the number of representatives from within the health care professions, can be seen as a very strong increase in managerialism, there have also been efforts within the acute sector to introduce a greater managerial role for some clinicians at directorate and unit level. With growing numbers of units going for trust status, the clinical directorate system was increasingly being taken up within acute units where each directorate was given budgetary control of their work. On the purchasing authority, the enhanced role of health needs assessment has also served to draw clinicians in the public health role more into management and the setting of contracts for purchasing (Ashburner 1994a).

System-wide change also became necessary in the information and support systems to management. Attempts to upgrade cost and information systems continued, but with a greater sense of urgency as it became increasingly important to provide activity and cost data to support the contracting process. In a quasi-market there is a need for services to be costed in a far more detailed way than is necessary for a command hierarchy. The Resource Management Initiative was piloted in the early 1980s in six sites, but again was taken up much more rapidly in other sites after the 1990 Act. It is both an integral part of the overall change process and a means of increasing the effects of the changes underway from other sources.

At the time of the study, cost and information systems were still being developed but the priority afforded to the finance function at board and management meetings was indicative of a fundamental change in the management strategies that were dominating the operating decisions. Finance appeared as an item at every board and authority meeting studied, and was often the single item taking the longest time on the agenda. The average time spent on finance in a three-hour meeting was 21 minutes for regional, 10 minutes for district, 14 minutes for family health services authorities, but 50 minutes for trusts (Ashburner *et al.* 1993a).

Typical of the changing management processes was the move away from management by hierarchy to management by contract. This represents a structural fragmentation and a major change of control strategy with important consequences for organizational and inter-organizational behaviour. Packwood (1991) sees this as a process of two transformations, from an organization based on a division of labour to one based on knowledge, and from top–down management to decentralized control. In each locality, the relationship between the district and its main acute unit increasingly centred on the setting, monitoring, and financing of the contract. In one study site, the relationship between the two parties became less open and more negotiative with the subsequent reduction in the traditional and informal information sources (Ferlie 1994).

Each speciality has had to define the nature of the service they are providing and the purchasers have brought in quality standards that become integral to the contract. As the amount and quality of the data collected improves there has been increasing emphasis on factual data, such as activity returns and the development of other forms of league tables than simple waiting list statistics.

The changing management role, the development of cost and information systems, and the strengthening of management capacity and influence all combine to result in changes which go beyond the mere structural to those in roles and processes. There was no corner of the NHS that had not been affected in some way by the above changes.

New and Amended Organizational Forms

The creation of new organizational forms may represent a significant breakpoint in organizational life (Romanelli 1991), accelerating the pace both of 'unlearning' past behaviour and learning new behaviour. It may also increase the potential for transformatory change as long-standing rules, conventions, and relationships are broken up and new ones negotiated. Harrison *et al.* (1992), for example, speculate that one possible outcome for the NHS is a move away from a vertically integrated bureaucracy characteristic of the postwar Welfare State (which can be seen as imitative of the Fordist corporation) to a 'post-Fordist' model where organization is fragmented into a larger number of operational units which are then loosely coordinated by a central organization. As shown in the last section, the centre no longer retains control through hierarchy but through a mixture of subcontracting, franchising, and partnership arrangements. This again parallels developments in parts of the private sector (Kanter 1989).

The 1990 NHS Act led to the creation of a number of new organizational forms consistent with this model. The introduction of separate purchaser and provider roles has some parallels with the development of executive agencies in Whitehall under the Next Steps initiative. The move from traditional district health authorities towards new-style purchasing organizations represents more than a simple restructuring, since they no longer have direct managerial responsibility for the provider units in their area, or the need to retain all the typical head office-type functions. Whereas within local authorities, purchasing is one departmental function, within the health service they are unique stand-alone organizations. This new organizational form has emerged gradually with a transient stage between the first and last of the provider units taking trust status.

Purchasing organizations are consequently much smaller in size than the old DHAs, retaining a higher percentage of more senior staff, but with a different mix of functions and skills. Districts have shed a range of typical head office functions such as estates, personnel, training, and health promotion and have much reduced capacities in areas such as finance. As the emphasis has moved from the operational to the strategic, this has resulted in the need for authorities to become more outward facing, especially to the local community, than in the past. The creation of local markets is in theory based upon the health needs assessment process which should form the mainstay of the purchasing process. Purchasers are also responsible for the setting of quality standards, future planning of services, and ensuring contractual performance. Unlike purchasing within local authorities or Next Steps agencies, which are parts of existing organizations given enhanced autonomy, this form of organization within health care represents a totally new creation with new roles and functions.

The pace of development of the three purchasing organizations studied was initially slow but is now accelerating (Ferlie *et al.* 1994) as the organizations consolidate past developments. Of particular interest is the emergence of health needs assessment within the locality, which should develop as a central tenet of the contracting process and the consequent need to develop alliances with external constituencies. In one district studied, the district health authority defined its new role as follows:

The district health authority's role is to assess and identify the health needs of the residents, to promote public health and to secure appropriate services and treatment to meet the identified needs. The Authority is also seen as having an advocacy role in relation to the needs of the population working in close co-operation with other agencies, and is pledged to 'speak out' where necessary.

As the functions based at district level contracted from those typical of a head office function to those pertaining only to purchasing, many small districts saw the necessity of merger with neighbouring districts, or the development of closer working relationships with family health services authorities, or the formation of purchasing consortia. In the districts and family health associations studied, no two developed in the same way. In one case study district, there were no moves to merge either with other districts or the family health services authority and each continued to develop its new role as an autonomous organization. This was because both were amongst the largest authorities in the country and thus there was no pressure of either size or viability. Relationships between the district and family health services authority were traditionally poor and neither side was prepared to initiate closer working. In another equally large district, very early moves were made to combine the operations of the district with the family health services authority despite the then lack of sanctioning of such a move by the Department of Health. There had been a history of good relations and the process of integration began with joint executive appointments. The chief executive of the family health services authority was made deputy chief executive of the district with the remit to ensure that the interests of the primary sector were given due prominence. In the absence of legislation, the two authority boards had to remain separate. In another study district, several districts and family health services authorities joined together to create a purchasing consortium, whilst still retaining their own organization structures. The main consideration here was the perceived need for the family health services authorities to retain their individual identity to continue to develop primary services, which in inner-city locations were less well developed than in other parts of the country.

As the process of formation continues, with growing numbers of directly managed units becoming trusts in each subsequent wave, it might be argued that these 'new' or amended forms are merely transitional stages. This process is indicative of the fragmentation that is occurring as part of the decentralization process, as the new organizational forms continue to take shape.

Although the political spotlight was on the formation of the trusts, these cannot be conceptualized as being a new organizational form as the functions and processes within the organization remain basically the same as before. There are now additional functions with the devolution of estate and personnel services, for example, and new functions of contracting, marketing, and, in some, posts such as risk management or public relations. As noted earlier, the key factor here is the new non-hierarchical management process external to the organization and its relationship with other organizations within the NHS. What is also new is the number, type, and extent of a trust's interrelationships with other units and organizations.

Despite the promise of new freedoms for trusts, these have mainly emerged in the human resource area, but most trusts have taken a very cautious approach so far to the implementation of new pay scales and employment contracts. There has been less freedom on the finance side. The NHS executive, via the outposts set up to monitor trust performance, maintains a very tight control of financial aspects. The most dramatic change is less in their level of external autonomy than in the increased management control internally. Less tangible is the positive effect of employees being able to identify with the unit they work for without having an often distant organization controlling even day-to-day operational issues.

What might emerge as amended organizational configurations are possible mergers between trusts as market pressures force them to seek different markets or reduce local competition in a bid for survival. If a large city hospital were to seek to merge with its neighbouring smaller general hospitals, this might be favourable for securing economies of scale or the rationalization of services but for the district hospitals merged it would mean relinquishing their new-found management control. With the growing pressure for specialist services to be focused at major centres, and the trend away from acute to primary care, smaller district hospitals are looking to merge vertically with, for example, community units. Mergers between London hospitals are already occurring but those between hospitals outside London are not, at this stage, being encouraged. In this scenario a merger thus becomes the politically acceptable way of closing hospitals. Mergers by themselves will not constitute a new organizational form unless they also involve a fundamental repositioning in terms of the service provided. Vertical integration of acute units with community units are presently not being sanctioned but there are signs that health care provision will become increasingly rationalized on a geographical basis. This is not just in response to market mechanisms but to changing methods of health care delivery, the commitment to seamless care, and changing perceptions of where health care should be delivered, with, for example, significant increases in day surgery and moves from hospital to home care. The formation of trusts can therefore be seen as the first stage in a process whereby such new organizational forms could emerge.

A totally new organizational form is emerging in primary care as GP fundholders begin to form multifunds or consortia. The pressure for this is coming both from within and from without. The GPs themselves see the value in strengthening their purchasing power in relation to local providers, and the district purchaser recognizes that as fundholding increases, there is a need for them to consider issues of locality planning of health care provision. Fundholding looks set to increase as previously small exempt practices can now join multifunds, as a growing number of districts now have only fundholding GPs, and as the range of services that GPs can purchase continues to be increased.

In the early stages the amalgamation of several GP practices into one fundholding centre meant that the combined resources enabled a wider range of services to be provided, employing more medically related staff and, for example, augmenting the capacity for minor surgical procedures. As the range of services that GPs can buy increases, it becomes more important that purchasing decisions are based upon similar criteria to those which govern district purchasing: that is, a consideration of health-needs assessment and retaining the viability of local providers and not just as a response to the needs of individual patients or to the lowest price.

The outcome of this is that new organizations are being created in primary care with more management capacity. Practice managers are a fast growing arm of health service management. If the pilot schemes for GPs to hold their total budget becomes the norm then these new organizational forms must of necessity grow in size and complexity. The emergence of the new purchasing organizations at district level has here been described as being in a continuing state of flux and these developments within the organization of primary care merely confirm that this will continue for some time to come with maybe the viability of district-based purchasing also ultimately coming into question.

At the outset of our study the health service regions were large employers with a major role in shaping health services. Within four years they have ceased to exist. First came the outposts, fewer in number, to oversee the embryonic trusts, and then regions were forced to reduce dramatically in size. Functions were further devolved or put out to tender. The newly created executive outposts are down in number from what was fourteen regions to eight and are no longer the top tier of the operational health service, but an extension of the executive (management executive, as was) in the regions. The conclusion drawn for the previous section holds true here; there was no corner of the NHS—even the traditionally powerful and insulated regional tier—that had not been affected in some way by the above changes.

2.5. Conclusion: Moving to System-Wide Change?

This chapter has argued that despite a history of ineffective public sector restructuring, the reform processes launched in the 1980s are having a considerable impact upon one major public sector organization in Britain, the NHS, at least at the systemic level considered so far. Evidence relating to more micro-level change will be presented in Chapter 4. The trends in other parts of the public sector may be slower or the reforms more focused, but the potential of the process for transformational rather than incremental change should not be underestimated. This immediately raises two questions. First, we must distinguish between the intended and unintended consequences of reform efforts. Are the changes which are occurring commensurate with the original objectives which shaped the policy and thus would government deem them effective? Secondly, what has been described above is predominantly structural change which gives little indication of the extent to which behaviour and value systems are being changed. Is it possible that fundamental culture change may be occurring in the NHS and that a new competitive, entrepreneurial ethos could emerge?

The other theoretical question that needs to be explored is how this experience fits in with existing concepts in the reform literature. At this stage in our analysis of the changes which have occurred as a consequence of public sector reform we would seek to refine March and Olsen's (1989) concepts of radical shock and persistent political will. The key mechanism for administering the necessary radical shock to an organization, we suggest, lies in the number and scope of the reforms introduced at any one point in time. The likelihood that these might lead to consequences that are not easy to predict or control is increased by the decision not to pilot any of the reforms before introduction.

The importance of political effort lies as much in consistency as in persistence. In this the important factor is the staged or complementary nature of the series of reforms that are introduced. This goes beyond March and Olsen's (1989) concept where it is the repetitive process of possibly unrelated reforms that they see as ultimately having an effect. The persistence of reforms which build on earlier ones with a common objective means that not only is there reinforcement but also a longer time-span within which the changes can move through the organization and become established. The extent to which the process of reform itself can lead to modifications and adaption of the formally stated objectives as a consequence of the power configurations within the organization being reformed will be explored in greater depth in later chapters.

The staged approach and comprehensive nature of the reform process in the health sector has resulted in it both being in the forefront of government reform but also as an example of politically imposed restraint. With regard to the latter, any suggestion of privatization of provider units as has happened with the purchaser–provider split within local and central government levels was rejected and proposed changes to the funding base to increase the level of private insurance were quickly abandoned. With regard to the creation of a market in health care and of new boards to run both the purchaser and provider organizations, the NHS reforms remained true to the general drift of governmentally sponsored reforms. While both of these aspects of the reforms are discussed in more detail in later chapters, it is notable that similar Home Office-sponsored attempts to introduce a board structure within the police service had to be modified due to strong internal resistance.

Whilst reforms elsewhere in the public sector might not have progressed so far, they can still be seen to have been developed in a series of stages and with the objective of being comprehensive in nature. Whilst the agencies that were set up as a result of the Next Steps initiative were not as clearly identifiable as a new organizational form as were the purchasing bodies in the health service, they none the less represented a significant shift of power away from the administrative traditions of the Civil Service towards the more managerially oriented and financially focused private sector organizational model. Another factor that distinguishes them from the reforms in the health service is the focus of the change. Next Steps involved those parts of the Civil Service concerned with the delivery of services rather than addressing changes across the whole system as was the case in the NHS.

As Hogwood (1993) and O'Toole and Jordan (1995) point out, the Next Steps initiative, although a major development in public administration, was still an incremental development in terms of its introduction, following on as it did from other developments concerned with public expenditure and public management. These included initially the Rayner reviews, followed by the Financial Management Initiative (concerned with management across central government and focused on setting clear objectives, the measurement of outputs and performance, clear responsibility within departments for costs, and improved financial information). The Next Steps was literally just that.

The appointment of a project manager who met regularly with the Prime Minister and submitted six-monthly written reports again shows the level of political will that lay behind the reforms.

While common themes are apparent across the public sector, the natural history of managerial change varies by department. For example, as will be suggested in Chapter 3, the criminal justice system was only slowly exposed to new managerialist ideas, but the scope and pace of change escalated in the early 1990s. By contrast, health care services had been exposed to pressure for managerializing change from the 1980s onwards.

In assessing the effectiveness of reform initiatives there is a danger that organizational consequences may be overlooked if only the broader and political objectives of the reform, such as reduced expenditure, are taken as measures. A better understanding of the significance and outcome of reform programmes can be gained from broadening the aspects of change which are evaluated to include internal organizational ones which occur at multiple levels. It was in order to try to assess the extent of the change within an organization that we devised the six criteria outlined at the beginning of this chapter. It is the combination of a number of concurrent reforms, their top–down nature, and the consistency and persistence of approach over time that leads us to suggest that a process of organizational transformation may be the outcome. Data from our study has shown that for the first two criteria there is clear evidence of significant change. Chapter 4 will examine the study data in relation to the other criteria and introduce the debate on the nature of transformatory change.

In trying to assess whether the reforms have been a success in political terms there remains the need to disentangle the means from the ends. Many countries have sought to increase efficiency in the delivery of public services but have differed in their means. Whilst some like Sweden have retained the requirement for democratic control as central, others, like Britain, have focused on the introduction of market mechanisms, which raises the question of how this affects public sector values of equity and accountability. The focus on using concepts and models from the private sector has led the choice of means in Britain to be particularly narrow and based more rigidly on the tenets of the New Right.

There is a need to question not just whether concepts and models designed for a different context can be so directly transferred but also whether a single solution, such as the use of market mechanisms, can be the answer to the problems of public sector expenditure across a range of different economies. Sorensen (1993) for example, after assessing six different reform strategies, questions the inherent assumption that the public sector is more inefficient than the private sector on the basis that governments pursue a more complicated set of societal objectives, resulting in necessarily different criteria for efficiency. His main conclusion is that there is a need for differentiated reforms and it is impossible to present a universal approach to public management reform.

The context of public sector restructuring and the more recent experience of the effects of specific reform programmes suggest that there is a potential for fundamental change. The introduction of New Right ideologies relating to markets and competition and the increasing level of managerialism have structural manifestations but how far this change process has affected organizational behaviour and values needs to be more closely examined for a clearer understanding of the new public management to emerge.

THE CREATION AND EVOLUTION OF
QUASI MARKETS

3.1. Introduction: the New Public Management and Quasi-Markets

As outlined in Chapters 1 and 2, even those functions which escaped privatization and which remained within the British public sector had by the early 1990s been subjected to profound top–down pressures for change. The legislatively driven attempt to create quasi-markets has been increasingly apparent as a major development in public services management from the late 1980s onwards. The introduction of quasi-markets can be seen as a complex system-wide change which is in turn central to the introduction of other changes. In this chapter, we seek to analyse this phenomenon. First, we will describe recent attempts to create quasi-markets in a number of different settings and review the substantive literature which has so far emerged. Secondly, we will attempt to develop a novel theoretical approach to the understanding of these quasi-markets. Thirdly, we will adduce some empirical data from our NHS study. Finally, we will consider the implications of this data for our understanding of quasi-markets and change processes within the new public management.

3.2. The Quasi-Market Phenomenon

The late 1980s witnessed the most intense period of social legislation since the post-1945 social democratic settlement: notably the Education Reform Act 1988, the Housing Act 1988, the Local Government Finance Act 1988, and the NHS and Community Care Act 1990. Furthermore, these legislative changes represent a significant new departure in policy, rather than an incremental continuation of past policies (Glennerster et al., 1991). Taken together, they can be seen as a bold and dramatic attempt to restructure the British Welfare State.

A common feature within this legislation has been the attempt to create quasi-markets, mimicking market-like mechanisms but in which service (in general) continues to be free at the point of use. The official line was that public services were to become more business-like, but not a business. It was believed that the introduction of quasi-markets would have a range of beneficial effects. Key criteria (Le Grand 1994) include quality, efficiency, choice, responsiveness, and equity.

The application of the word 'market' in this context may be no more than a misleading analogy. To what extent is a quasi-market really like a private sector market at all? The centre often retains a battery of regulatory powers which ensures that quasi-markets are still very inward facing. Alongside the rhetoric of quasi-markets, we still see confusing forays back into the world of strategic planning or direct intervention.

Nevertheless, the quasi-market model is now clearly discernible in a number of different settings (see the brief review below) and contains a number of key features. Public funding is no longer to be allocated solely through planning or through formula funding, but instead through such devices as competitive bidding, or an earmarked budget which can be given to users, or to agents acting on their behalf. They then allocate the budget between competing providers (Le Grand 1991). This sharpens the incentives for performance at the level of the individual providing organization.

At the same time, these quasi-markets can be seen as evolving in a different manner and pace across the public services. What might explain this pattern of variation? Challis *et al.* (1994) propose a typology based on variation in market power and market structure. What is crucial is the degree of concentration on both the purchaser and provider sides. Thus the purchasing function may be more concentrated or more diffuse according to the quasi-market under analysis, as may be the providing function. The greater the degree of concentration, the greater the market power.

Challis *et al.* (1994) argue that the balance between contracts and regulatory institutions as control strategies within quasi-markets will reflect the degree of provider and (especially) purchaser concentration. Where both the purchasing and providing function is concentrated (as in health care), the contract will predominate as a means of control. There is here less concern to prevent abuse of monopoly (provider) power and also this is because the transaction costs fall as the number of contracts diminishes (but see Section 3.3 for a critique of transaction costs theory). They make the point that these quasi-markets have been deliberately created and managed. Each quasi-market is therefore set in a historical and institutional context which may have affected its evolution. We now briefly review the career of the quasi-market phenomenon in a number of key public service settings.

Health Care

Health care presents a mixed picture. In some ways, it can be seen as a relatively fast mover towards the quasi-market model, with rapid diffusion of new style structures such as NHS trust status from 1991 onwards (much faster than grant-maintained status in primary and secondary education) and of new forms of purchaser organization. However, the NHS quasi-market remains highly inward facing, even when compared with social care. Few non-statutory providers, for example, have entered the health care quasi-market, nor are there clear arrangements for the market exit of underperforming NHS provider organizations. There is still strong professional self-regulation. There is less personal finance in the health care system than, for example, in higher education (e.g. the growth of student loans and self-financed courses). While there are indeed few external regulatory bodies (Challis *et al.* 1994), the degree of internal regulation is considerable.

No more than a gleam in an economist's eye in the mid-1980s (Enthoven 1985), by 1989 the main principles of the internal market in health care had become national policy (Cm 555, 1989). The subsequent 1990 NHS and Community Care Act paved the legislative way for the introduction of a quasi-market in health care as the NHS progressively separated out into 'purchasers' (district health authorities acting as macro-purchasers); GP fundholders (acting as micro-purchasers) and 'providers' (NHS Trusts, non-statutory providers). Change of status was elective for the trusts and GP fundholders (but not for purchasing authorities), although there were financial incentives for early adoption.

By April 1994 the vast majority of NHS hospitals had adopted trust status. Small-scale at first, there was also a roll-out of the GP fundholder scheme, particularly in the Shires. This scheme increases the number of purchasers and reduces the degree of purchaser concentration, although as yet GP fundholders can purchase only a limited range of services. A period of recurrent reorganization was also triggered off the purchasing side as powerful macro-purchasers emerged.

The old district health authorities first merged to form larger purchasing consortia, and then increasingly sought closer links with parallel family health services authorities responsible for primary care services. This led in some cases to the formation of joint health commissions. Considerable finance and management time was spent on effecting these transitions, perhaps crowding out other priorities (e.g. meeting 'health of the nation' targets).

This quasi-market can be seen as highly internally regulated. The centre retained formidable powers of regulation, rule-setting, and appointment to key posts. The financial regime in which trusts could operate, for instance, was firmly prescribed, as were pricing formulas. Senior executive appointments were carefully vetted.

There was initially a centrally imposed requirement for 'steady state' and the careful management of change. Alongside quasi-markets, there was also a continuing and confusing recourse to strategic planning. In particular, strategy in London was felt much too important to be left to the quasi-market (Tomlinson Report 1992). Nor was there any clear strategy for market entry or exit: failing hospitals were more likely to be merged than closed down. There was no rapid growth of non-statutory providers, although some creeping expansion of private medicine in the NHS trusts delivering acute sector services (such as surgery and medicine) was apparent.

From 1992 onwards, the pressure for steady state was somewhat relaxed. Macro-purchasers were enjoined to create local contestable markets. GP fundholders were able to switch elective services at the margins, where their local general hospital did not respond satisfactorily to their demands. The NHS trusts were regulated not by the old regions but by newly created NHS management executive Outposts which proclaimed an intention to guide 'with a light touch on the tiller' (whether they achieved this objective is another matter). Trusts were encouraged to bring in new private sources of capital financing. Certainly a number of acute trusts in the urban areas can be seen potentially as in a competitive situation, at least at the margins. Overall, however, the quasi-market in health care should still be seen as inward facing and subject to extensive internal regulation.

In our view, the characteristics of the health care quasi-market derive not so much from the balance of power within the quasi-market as other features of market structure (such as financial and knowledge based barriers to market entry) and external contextual factors such as the high political profile of health care, its high degree of professionalization, and the extreme difficulties in assessing product quality which lead to an increased emphasis on soft indicators such as trust, reputation, and relational markets.

Assessments of the Quasi-Market in Health Care Assessments of the effects of the NHS quasi-market often owe more to belief than to evidence. This is after all a highly politicized field where fragments of evidence are seized upon. There are, however, a number of more independent commentators working in the field.

Economists are often primarily interested in assessing the efficiency consequences of the reforms. Thus Maynard (1993) contends that the NHS reforms are producing both advantages (e.g. scrutiny of clinical decision-making) and disadvantages (e.g. escalating management costs), but that the balance between the two is unknown. He argues that no proper evaluation of the reforms has been carried out and that it is thus impossible to determine whether there have been efficiency gains or not.

This is too defeatist a view. While it is true that there has been no global evaluation of the NHS reforms as a totality (such a synoptic evaluation would in any case be difficult to devise and expensive to implement), there are a number of independent research groups which have been actively assessing particular aspects of the reform programme. The NHS quasi-market can hardly be seen as a research-free zone. We ourselves have, for example, explored the related reforms to NHS corporate governance (see later chapters in this book) but other teams have also been active.

A good recent overview has been provided by Robinson and Le Grand (1994). Some of this research has strong implications for policy and management. Glennerster *et al.*'s (1994) assessment of the GP fundholding scheme drew attention to the ability of GP fundholders to effect micro-level improvements through their purchasing decisions. Although they also had long-term worries about possible cream-skimming or exclusion of very expensive patients, they found that this had not yet had major effects. Moreover it might be possible to counteract any such effects by readjusting the capitation funding formula. They did not, however, fully consider possible conflict between the micro-level purchasing intentions of GP fundholders and the more macro-strategic view espoused by health authority purchasers.

What evidence is there that trust hospitals are more 'efficient' than non-trust hospitals? W. Bartlett and Le Grand (1994) compared the pre-reform cost structures of the first and second waves of hospital trusts and a sample of non-trusts. In many areas, trusts had significantly lower costs than non-trusts. However, these differences could not be attributed to the reforms as the data were taken from the pre-reform period. Rather the results suggested that the first and to a lesser extent second-wave trusts were self-selecting high performers who were already among the most efficient providers.

Le Grand distinguishes between research strategies based on direct research (i.e. primary data collection) and indirect research. The latter approach uses economic analysis to specify the conditions which quasi-markets have to meet in economic theory if they are to attain certain goals (e.g. a market structure consisting of many purchasers and many providers). Secondly, it examines whether there is evidence that these conditions are being met in practice. Critics of the indirect approach might argue that the use of such proxy measures leads to overabstracted and schematic forms of analysis which rest on a set of questionable assumptions.

Le Grand concludes that direct research as yet indicates little real change, and even less that can be attributed to the reforms. As yet, the timescale is too short to show evidence of substantial change. However, some direct and indirect research indicates that, at least in some areas, there is potential for efficiency gains over the longer term. There are equity worries, but so far they can be seen as theoretical rather than empirically substantiated issues.

In our view, such a strategy of indirect research is far weaker than one of direct research. There are of course a range of theoretical approaches which may be usefully developed and utilized—indeed this chapter will seek to develop a theoretical model rooted in the 'new economic sociology'. But all such theories require empirical validation or indeed refutation in the light of evidence.

Social Care

The quasi-market in social care was also created by the 1990 NHS and Community Care Act, as social service departments were expected to move from a traditional provider role to an 'enabling role' which mirrored that of the purchasing authorities on the health care side. New-style care managers can be seen as the social care analogues of the GP fundholders, but with fewer devolved powers. There are thus important differences between the pattern of development observable in health and social care settings.

A priori, the pace of development might be expected to have been slower in social care than health care settings. Social care services are organized at a local level (through local authority social services departments), unlike the NHS which has been seen as a national service. There is a tradition of greater local autonomy in the provision of services. Most unusually for a branch of local government, social services departments were given an expanded role in the Act in relation to needs assessment for residential care. However, the social care provisions of the Act were subject to phased implementation between 1991 and 1993, with the new care management system only introduced in April 1993.

In fact, the pace of change may well have been faster in social care than in health care as a much more outward-facing market has been created. The new agenda resulted in a more radical restructuring of the old publicly delivered social care services than in health care. This may be due to factors related to market structure (e.g. fewer barriers to entry and exit) or to contextual factors (e.g. the lower political profile of the social care issue; the less powerful professions; a covert political desire to break up the unionized culture of the old social services departments).

Relatively loose central exhortations about a mixed economy of care were replaced by more focused requirements to establish and to manage a social care market (Knapp *et al.*, 1994). This quasi-market was actively developed and managed from the top. Financial incentives were created for social services departments to use more private provision (Glennerster *et al.*, 1991; 411). As Flynn and Hurley (1993) indicate, in 1992 the Government allocated £6m to develop and promote the supply of private and voluntary sector home care. There is also a requirement under the new care management system to spend 85 per cent of transferred Department of Social Security funds in the private and voluntary sectors. In 1993 the Government brought in new directions to make local authorities involve private providers in the formulation of community care plans.

The 1990s may well be characterized by the rapid expansion of non-statutory provision within social care, even if funding largely remains public. Domiciliary and day care can be seen as areas of future service growth, although there may already be overcapacity in the private residential care market. Contrary to a priori assumptions, a freer and more externally facing market may develop more rapidly in social care than in health care.

Assessments of the Impact of the Quasi-Market in Social Care   How important has been the shift to the enabling authority in social care? Arguing for continuity rather than change, Lawson (1993) contends that, in general terms, the impact at least by the end of 1992 of the community care reforms was muted. The lack of investment funding together with a refusal to ring fence resources, delays in implementation, and uncertainty about the level of funding to be transferred from the DSS have all contributed to this, together with the continued fiscal squeeze on local authorities through charge-capping.

Social services departments did not always possess the high level of analytical capacity and managerial skill needed to progress change of this complexity, and there was a cultural resistance to adopting new forms of management which were seen as grounded in the private sector. The central agenda was not always accepted by key organizations at local level, and was in danger of being reinterpreted out of existence (Wistow *et al.*, 1992) in the localities. In early 1991 only a minority of (usually Conservative-controlled) local authorities were found to have developed plans to build a social care market (Wistow *et al.*, 1994). Where non-statutory forms of provision were emerging, they were often hybrid trust-type organizations spun out of the public sector and with continuing strong informal links. After the tighter needs assessment procedures introduced in 1993, there was if anything excess capacity in the privately provided residential care market and a shake-out was likely.

Yet there are also signs of the first steps towards real organizational change in social care. Hoyes and Means (1993) report early case study work from two Shire counties. In these localities, there was evidence of a growth of the independent sector. Within one social services department, a process of managerialization was also evident as cost centres were being developed, budgets devolved, and experiments in care management being launched. There was a widespread desire to find new ways of involving consumers as partners in service planning and delivery.

While conventional private sector organizations may continue to find it difficult to enter the social care market, Taylor and Hoggett (1994) speculate that the social care market may in time come to be dominated by new statutory–voluntary hybrids and new not-for-profit or even for-profit organizations set up by ex-statutory workers. Large and sophisticated voluntary organizations, with their well-developed network of key contacts, may also be well equipped to enter the social care market.

A contract and quasi-market-based system may also have implications for those voluntary organizations that have traditionally provided care, and which have often in the past been praised for their flexibility and creativity. J. Lewis (1993) argues that the formalization of relations through the contracting process may have a perverse effect on organizational behaviour, leading to a working to the contract, a loss of nerve, and a retreat from more innovative or challenging forms of service provision.

Primary and Secondary Education

In the case of education, both the new-style providing and the purchasing functions can be seen as more dispersed than either in health or social care. Challis *et al.* (1994) comment that this represents a radical change within the education system. Parents can be seen as having a stronger role in the educational reforms, either than patients in the NHS or clients in social care. Collectively, they are able to trigger a change of organizational form (grant-maintained status). They remain represented on the boards of governors. Their wishes are not filtered through proxies, unlike GP fundholders or district health authorities. Their placement decisions may put real pressure on a school to change. While the scope for choice between schools is limited, there are many more schools in a locality than hospitals and hence some potential for essentially local forms of competition (Glatter and Woods 1994).

Traditionally schools have been managed through local education authorities. The 1988 Education Reform Act diminished these authorities' administrative control over schools in three key ways (Levacic 1994):

- Local management of schools: local education authorities are required to delegate responsibilities to school governing bodies e.g. finance; powers over the appointment, disciplining, and dismissal of staff;
- more open enrolment: a school must generally admit pupils up to its standard admission number; parents may appeal against the refusal of a place at a school with no surplus places;
- grant-maintained status: the Education Reform Act outlined a provision for schools choosing—after a ballot of parents—to opt out of local education authority control and move to grant maintained status.

Levavic notes that while these developments were presented as means of reducing bureaucracy and enhancing choice, they were also accompanied by an increase in central government control (e.g. the national curriculum).

Outside local education authority control, grant maintained schools can behave more as independent agents funded by a per capita grant. However, only a small number of schools (particularly primary schools) have so far elected for grant maintained status: certainly the pattern of diffusion is much slower than that of NHS trusts (King 1994, estimates that about 4 per cent of all maintained schools have made moves in that direction). Sometimes schools have gone for grant maintained status for essentially negative reasons such as a difficult relationship with their local education authority, perhaps fearing the closure of surplus places.

Interesting parallels can be drawn between grant maintained schools and

NHS trusts as new organizational forms. Speaking in January 1991, the then Education Secretary, Kenneth Clark, stated:

'the initiative and creative thinking that I wish to see pervading the whole education service is exemplified above all by those schools that go on to achieve grant maintained status . . . The parallel model in the health service is the NHS Trusts . . . They too are independent of a regional or local tier of administration. I have argued that Trust status would eventually become the 'natural organisational model' for all units providing patient care. I see similar possibilities for grant maintained schools, especially for secondary schools' (quoted in Halpin *et al.* 1991: 409)

Assessment of the Effects of the Education Reform Act   The 1988 Education Reform Act contains a series of measures which taken as a whole seek to restructure the power balance and dominant culture of the educational system. The combined effect of grant maintained schools, open enrolment, and local management of schools has been seen as opening up schooling to consumer pressure and a new 'enterprise culture' (Flude and Hammer 1990) as head-teachers, a new group of bursars, and a minority of active governors engage with the new management agenda. Boards of governors are now expected to take on a much more significant role.

Halpin *et al.* (1991) argue that there is scant evidence that grant maintained schools can be seen as an new organizational form. Often grant maintained status is used to preserve the old (e.g. grammar school status) rather than bring in the new. For parents and pupils, they argue, grant maintained status is not perceived as marking a transformation, or even a transition. Where differences since incorporation can be identified, they usually followed on the consolidation of existing strengths. There may rather be changes to the image of the school, such as a tightening-up of the dress code.

How is power shifting within the education system as the effects of the Education Reform Act diffuse throughout the system? Broadbent *et al.* (1992) argue that a small group of senior staff, working with governors, adopt the new market-orientated and managerial value system, while the rest of the staff retain traditional pupil-orientated values.

However, Simkins (1994) notes the potential contradiction in post-Education Reform Act education policy, also apparent in other sectors, between on the one hand market pressures (e.g. increased parental choice of school and requirements for more published information at school level) and on the other hand strong central control over the National Curriculum and associated testing. At the level of the individual school, Simkins sees local management of schools as leading to a centralization of responsibility in the hands of one or two senior members of staff, sometimes, but not always working with one or two active governors.

Levacic's (1994) assessment of locally managed schools suggests that there is evidence that efficiency levels have been increased as a result of the reforms, although locally managed schools may not be cost-effective for small primary schools. The tentative conclusion so far is that evidence for any resulting improvement in educational standards is sparse.

Ball *et al.* (1994) argue that the quasi-market in education is very far from being a free market, but one which is shaped by institutional and social forces. At an institutional level, both central government and the local education authority play important roles. Central government continues to intervene at system-wide level. At local level, one education authority may seek to preserve the existing comprehensive system; another will actively welcome the quasi-market and seek to develop it. Moreover, patterns of parental choice are influenced by local histories, reputations of schools, and social class (working class parents may be more likely to prefer local schools; middle class parents be more likely to travel).

Other Settings

While we have reviewed developments in health care, social care, and school level education is some detail, it is important to remember that similar developments are also observable in a range of other public service settings.

Higher Education Changes in higher education during the 1980s have involved shifts towards greater managerialism as well as quasi-markets. There is also a move from an early emphasis on imposed expenditure reductions (e.g. the 1981 Universities Grants Committee cuts) to a later agenda of efficient expansion of student numbers. There are dramatic oscillations from one policy to another. It remains to be seen whether these policies complement or will ultimately contradict each other. The higher education system is also note-worthy for a high profile failure of an attempt to introduce an auction system for student places.

The Jarratt Report (1985) heralded a move away from old notions of academic collegiality and the emergence of more directive vice chancellors acting more as chief executive officers. Managerialization has gone furthest in the new universities. The 1988 Education Reform Act removed the old polytechnics from local authority control and they became independent corporations, often led by a more assertive senior management. The Act also provided for the creation of a more directive and business-led Universities Funding Council (now Higher Education Funding Council) to replace the old Universities Grants Committee which had traditionally acted as a buffer between the universities and government.

From the early 1980s onwards there has been pressure on universities to increase the proportion of income derived from private and business sources. This implies more engagement with the market, initially for non-core services (such as conferences). The early Universities Funding Council phase (say, 1988–91) perhaps represented the apogee of market consciousness as more

competitive bidding systems for the allocation of teaching funds were introduced.

Within the then polytechnic sector, requirements for competitive tendering
were stringent (Robertson 1993), and seen very much as price-related. However, early University Funding Council attempts to construct a competitive
tendering exercise in the then university sector came to grief. In the 1990
round, the Universities Funding Council declared that 93 per cent of all
student places tendered were offered at its guide prices. The auction system
was then abandoned (Johnes and Cave 1994).

Other financial shifts such as a move from a block grant to tuition fees
based system and the introduction of student loans for maintenance costs
(but not fees), can be seen as increasing the importance of the student
marketplace for courses (Hocking 1991). A few courses, such as MBAs, can
already be seen in terms of self-financing markets. More general 'top-up fees',
whereby undergraduate students might put in co-financing over and above
public funding, have not, however, materialized, despite growing concern
about quality.

The result is a teaching quasi-market still heavily dominated by the funding
councils. Central government manipulation of tuition fee levels is a powerful
instrument for regulating the rate of university growth, and choking it back if
it is seen as excessive.

The BBC   The BBC is currently moving towards an internal market system
based on a 'producer choice' model, with the subcontracting-out of core
programme-making services to independent providers. Starks (1993) offers
an insider's view of this process.

In 1986 a funding crisis arose after the BBC failed to get Government
agreement to its proposed increase in the licence fee. This led to a decision
to subcontract non-core services (e.g. cleaning) externally. This trend was
accentuated after the 1989 pay dispute, which led to a further need to find
resources to fund pay increases.

In 1991 the Government required the BBC to open up a proportion of its
core business (programme-making) to independent producers, building up to
a 25 per cent set quota.

The internal initiative ('producer choice'), led by John Birt who subsequently became director general, represents an acceleration and intensifica-
tion of this process. It identified problems of overcapacity and a high costs
base. Implemented in April 1993, the producer choice model can be summarized as follows (Starks 1993):

- everyone works in full costs, including overheads, accommodation, and
  capital depreciation;
- programme-makers receive the full costs needed to make their programmes,
  including the money to buy production facilities;
- they can buy their production facilities either internally or externally;

- BBC production facilities must price, and charge for, their services and recover their full costs;
- BBC production facilities exist primarily to serve BBC programme making needs, but can sell spare marginal capacity externally.

The Prison Service The criminal justice system can be seen as relatively favoured in the 1980s, and as insulated from NPM-style pressures. However, this situation changed in the early 1990s, as the services caught up with developments already observable in other parts of the public sector.

To an unusual degree, the police and prison services enjoyed big increases in public funding in the early 1980s, albeit associated with big increases in workload. From 1983 onwards, while increasing pressure was being applied by the Home Office to secure more value for money, this initiative could be seen as relatively modest and self-contained in scale.

In the early 1990s, however, the pace and scope of new public management-style change within the criminal justice system suddenly accelerated. More so than in the other services, there was a sense that existing models of organization and management were in crisis, and that there was a need for new ideas. The 1991-4 period was marked by a burst of White Papers and of legislation.

An important factor was the April 1990 riots at Strangeways Prison which resulted in the commissioning of the Woolf Report (Cm 1456, 1991), largely accepted in Cm 1647 (1991). There was a perception that the prison service was in crisis, given increasing numbers, the deterioration of prison buildings, a preoccupation with security issues, and worsening industrial relations (Player and Jenkins 1994). Despite ever-increasing resources, the quality of service provided could be seen as poor.

Perhaps fuelled by this sense of internal crisis, a period of rapid organizational and managerial change within the prison service began which seems to have survived the rapid shifts evident in other aspects of penal policy. The prison service moved into Next Steps agency status in April 1993, headed by an outside appointment as the new chief executive who was charged with providing more visible leadership. The question of where policy responsibility ended and where operational responsibility began is an important one, and some ambiguity was exposed following the controversy about the escape of prisoners from Parkhurst in early 1995.

An important theme is the beginning of a quasi-market in prison services as privately run prisons (such as the Wolds in Humberside) won their first contracts. These contracts were awarded on quality as well as cost grounds, and it was hoped that newly built privately run prisons would be able to offer higher standards (e.g. integral sanitation). Competitive tendering exercises (e.g. for the contract to rebuild Strangeways) can also be seen as exerting pressure even on winning in-house providers to meet cost and quality criteria.

3.3. Characterizing Quasi-Markets—Some Theoretical Issues

There is therefore a considerable substantive literature emerging on the effects of quasi-markets in a number of different public service settings. Because of its applied and evaluative nature, however, the treatment of theory has often not been sophisticated. Where a theoretical base does exist, it is often taken from standard micro-economics. There are of course interesting exceptions, such as Laughlin's (1992) use of social theory which leads him to analyse the introduction of quasi-markets as a form of cultural contest. Nevertheless, the time is ripe to develop and apply new forms of theory, particularly ones which can handle the social and organizational aspects of quasi-markets.

Approaches Rooted in Economics

Micro-Economic Theory   Ferlie (1992) has argued elsewhere that orthodox micro-economic theory influenced, perhaps over-influenced, the early debate about quasi-markets. Sometimes an explicit theory is evident, although on other occasions a 'theory in use' is more apparent. Early authors were often drawn from university health economics research units (e.g. Brazier, Hutton, and Jeavons 1990) or right-wing think-tanks (e.g. Goldsmith and Willetts 1988; Green *et al.*, 1991). Indeed, the model of a quasi-market in health care was first developed by Enthoven (1985) in an elegant attempt to increase value for money, to sharpen incentive structures and to quicken the pace of organizational change. This vividly contrasted with earlier accounts from other economists such as Arrow (1963) who had argued that it would be unwise to introduce market principles into the health care sector because of the consequent dangers posed by high levels of uncertainty, consumer risk aversion, and producer opportunism. In the new world, the American HMO was taken as an exemplar of a new form of purchaser organization that faced strong incentives to ensure provider performance and had the market power to effect change.

The quasi-market may not depend on the existence of a perfectly functioning neo-classical market for its clout. There may be periodic competition for markets, if not day-to-day competition within markets. As long as there is periodic contestability in the market (Baumol 1982), the new quasi-market forces could exert important effects:

If market contestability can be created and sustained, substantial welfare gains may be achieved. The pace of this process is uncertain but its effects may be significant, obliging managers to restructure the supply side in a fashion which reflects current market demand rather than past history. (Maynard 1991)

Presumably, managers in producer units here respond to increased pressures for performance as signalled by the market—either directly by consumers or by their proxies, that is purchasers—and if they did not, then they would pay the penalty.

Behaviour is here seen as determined crudely by a mix of information regarding product price and quality and of a new structure of incentives rather than as shaped by a mixture of strategic choice, government and professional regulation, social norms, or historic interpersonal networks. A major weakness in these highly axiomatic, micro-economic, approaches is that they fail to consider the question of decision-making inside the organization or across the interorganizational network. In comparing and contrasting the two disciplines of economics and strategic management, Rumelt *et al.* (1991: 19) argue,

Economics has been chiefly concerned with the performance of markets in the allocation and coordination of resources. By contrast, strategic management is about coordination and resource allocation *inside the firm*. This distinction is crucial and readily explains why so much of economics is not readily applicable to the study of strategy and why strategy can inform economics as much as economics can inform strategy.

So standard micro-economic theory primarily directs our attention to questions of efficiency, incentives, and of market structure rather than the internal organization of the producing unit or the question of how markets evolve through time. Its static focus does not therefore handle the question of market process (Nelson and Winter 1982). The firm (or more broadly, organization) is too often narrowly seen as a production function, and the prime focus of innovation as technological. The actual strategic behaviour of the organization remains largely unexplored as the neo-classical assumption of hyperrationality sees the organization as making optimal choices from a sharply defined set of possibilities. This schematic approach is unlikely to prove fruitful in any analysis of how quasi-markets really operate.

Transaction Costs Theory An important development in economic theory over the last twenty or so years has been the emergence of the so-called new institutional economics, or transaction costs perspective, closely associated with the work of O. E. Williamson (1975 and 1985; also in Aoki *et al.* 1990; for a critical review see Ferlie 1992). The prime focus is on the efficiency properties of a range of different ways of organizing transactions. The transaction is seen as the prime unit of economic analysis, rather than, say, a traditional focus on the development of technology.

Here is a rich, sophisticated, and influential attempt to link imaginative forms of economic analysis with other disciplines such as contract law and organization theory, even if the question of efficiency continues to hold centre stage. A central question within this literature is whether it is more efficient for transactions to proceed through the market or to be internalized within an organization. Here the decision rule may depend on the nature of the transaction being considered: where transactions are highly specific then the balance of advantage may lie in internalization. Social institutions are here seen as being shaped by efficiency considerations more than as a result of social or political action or the exercise of power.

Within a transaction costs perspective, the old-style public sector can be seen as an extreme case of the large vertically integrated organization. Originally, Williamson's analysis considered why it was that firms replaced markets. However, it is also possible to ask why it is that markets replace firms. At some point bureaucratic failure is likely, particularly in the handling of routine transactions—and these transactions can be more efficiently organized through the market. Williamson outlines a number of criteria which are likely to determine whether or not the market will be a more efficient allocator of resources.

The transaction costs model has proved influential, and has been adopted as a theoretical base by a number of those seeking to understand the nature of quasi-markets (W. Bartlett 1991), including critics of the reforms (Burke and Goddard 1990).

However, the transaction costs perspective has also come under attack from a number of quarters. Organizational sociologists see the approach as over-emphasizing the role of efficiency at the expense of any consideration of social and organizational power (Perrow 1981; Bauer and Cohen 1983), not to mention the question of ideology or of hegemonic forms of culture. Granovetter (1985) also argues that, like many economists, Williamson operates with an undersocialized conception of human action. For instance, it is the existence of social relations, rather than governance structures or forms of contracting, that ensure the interpersonal trust necessary for economic life. The transaction costs approach assumes that the natural state of man is opportunism rather than trust, and finds it difficult to model behaviour on trustworthy institutions, nor, unlike Schumpeterian economics, does it offer a convincing account of how markets evolve and operate.

The New Economic Sociology   Grossly neglected by the discipline of sociology itself, as well as cognate fields in the recent past (despite classic work such as Polanyi 1957), the sociological analysis of markets has been an expanding field throughout the 1980s. Essentially sociological concepts of social relations, of trust, of reputation, and of obligation are seen as central to the understanding of how markets really work.

White's (1981) article led the revival in signalling a need to build a sociological view of markets. His own view was that markets should be seen as self-reproducing social structures established among specific cliques of firms which evolved roles and niches from observation of each other's behaviour. A historically shaped structure of roles emerges among a stable set of producer firms. However, this early emphasis on the reproducibility of markets over time does not fit situations in which new markets are undergoing a process of creation, nor does it consider the roles which may become apparent after the initial period of market establishment as firms may seek to renegotiate their position in the market (Podolny 1992). We now review a number of different strands of literature which could contribute to the development of a more sociologically informed understanding of quasi-markets.

Relational Markets We have considered the relational view of markets elsewhere at greater length (Ferlie, Ashburner, and Fitzgerald 1993). This model of markets developed out of the concerns of marketeers and is associated with the Scandinavian work of the 1980s (Ford 1990). It was felt that the conventional view of an active marketeer, passive consumers, and an atomistic market restricted understanding of what actually happened in markets. The neoclassical model of markets assumes that markets are populated by individuals or small firms, yet economic life is often dominated by a small number of large and complex firms which behave in a different way.

A number of important implications follow from seeing markets in more relational terms. Unlike individual consumers, corporate buyers might often interact with sellers. The relationship between companies might display a complex history of adaptation, commitment, trust, and conflict. Buyer–seller relationships are but one example of sets of relations which may shape a market, as buyer–buyer and seller–seller relations may also be important.

The interaction process is here not seen as solely revolving around product or service exchange, but also includes important processes of social exchange, undertaken so as to reduce uncertainty and to build trust. The result may be a common value system which emphasizes source loyalty. There is then a tendency to 'keep things in the family' so that buyers, once locked into a set of relationships, may be relatively inert in seeking new sources of supply.

A relational market might display the following signs and symptoms. A relatively small number of well-established buyers and sellers could be locked into long-run contracts or repeat buying. Buying decisions would be made on the basis of soft data (e.g. trust) as well as hard information, with the result that reputation is a key intangible asset on which providers trade.

Social Embeddedness An attack on the assumptions of the 'new institutional economics' was apparent in an important paper by Granovetter (1985). Economic transactions needed to be seen as much more socially embedded than in the transaction costs framework. The focal unit of analysis thus shifted from the transaction to the underlying social relationship. For Granovetter, the problem becomes one of tracing the actual, concrete, interactions of individuals and groups and considering how these networks influence trading and the formation of prices within the market (Granovetter and Swedberg 1992). Others may feel that the continued development of a grounded sociological theory is also of relevance.

A further question is whether the extent of the embeddedness of economic behaviour is changing over time. One view might be that economic behaviour was heavily embedded in social relations in pre-market societies, but becomes much more autonomous with modernization. Modernization is sometimes associated with marketization and the reduction of social ties (Polanyi 1957). This view has been questioned by Granovetter and Swedberg (1992) who argue that even in modern markets patterns of social relations still shape trading. In professional services (e.g. medicine) information on reputation transmitted through organizational and occupational networks is critical in establishing market position.

A key issue in the analysis of quasi-markets thus concerns the long-term effects of the introduction of contracting on patterns of organizational and interorganizational behaviour. Will contracting lead to an atomization of social relations? Socio-legal scholars such as MacNeil (1974, 1978, 1983) (see also Hughes and Dingwall 1990, for an application of the socio-legal approach to this substantive field) have distinguished between various types of contracts, commonly classical, neo-classical, and relational forms of contracts.

The development of a 'relational contract' is seen as resulting from the increased duration and complexity of contracts. Particularly with regard to uncertain, complex, and recurrent exchanges, 'spot' contracts are unlikely to offer an adequate means of structuring the transaction, but rather the contract becomes increasingly embedded in a social relation with its own history and norms. Sociological purists might argue that the term 'relational contract' is almost a contradiction in terms, because in relationships social norms of trust and reciprocity replace contracting as a means for restructuring recurring transactions. MacNeil (1983), however, contends that law facilitates the construction of relations because it fosters cooperation through internal and external values of contract behaviour based on countless past contacts.

Professional networks in particular may prove influential in shaping the relational market. Classically the uncertainty facing consumers in health care and their need to trust the provider could result, even in more market-like conditions, in a continuing willingness to hand over responsibility to professionals who speak with great authority in decision-making. The managerial bloc, although increasing in importance and more willing to confront professionals in some areas, can in general be expected to work in alliance with professionals. Most managers continue to be recruited from within the NHS and attempts to break the mould by bringing in managers from the private sector have generally failed.

In addition, proxy consumers (themselves often professionals such as GP fundholders) may often retain more power within quasi-markets than individual consumers. As a result it can be argued that professional, and to a lesser extent managerial, control will continue to prove more powerful than radical consumerism and will continue to shape the operation of market forces.

One might thus expect well established local cliques and networks to continue to dominate decision-making. Within the quasi-market, there will be continuing barriers to market entry and exit; inherited contracting patterns may be rolled forward and there may be little reletting of contracts.

Institutional Embeddedness   Markets may not only be socially embedded, but also institutionally embedded. This shifts us away from the micro-level analysis of social networks and towards the more macro-level of economic (and indeed social and legal) institutions. While in his most recent work Granovetter (1992) retains his network perspective, there is also more of a focus on an institutional level. However, he argues that existing networks of personal and political relations in turn shape economic institutions which act in effect as 'congealed social networks'. Institutions are to be seen as socially constructed by cliques of actors.

This view still has its roots in social network theory and is very different from the work of those theorists who see institutions more as forces in their own right, independent of individuals' motives and actions. In these accounts, notions of organizational fields, legitimating myths, and institutional discourses assume greater prominence. This is a major area of debate between macro- and micro-theorists which can only be touched upon here (but see Powell and Di Maggio 1991; Dingwall and Strong 1985).

While there is no consensus, and indeed sharply different lines of argument apparent, at least some theorists draw attention to the importance of the institutional context. For instance, Meyer and Rowan (1977) see modern formal organizations as operating in highly institutionalized contexts. Organizations are driven to incorporate the practices and procedures defined by prevailing rationalized concepts of legitimate work (e.g. 'public services should be business-like'). Organizations that do so increase their legitimacy, their flows of resources, and hence their survival prospects, independently of the efficacy of acquired practices and procedures.

New organizational forms (Di Maggio and Powell 1983) may arise not because of efficiency considerations but because of strong fads and fashions in organizational design and strong pressure to conform to centrally mandated templates. The State and the professions are seen as particularly important sources for structuring such organizational fields, especially in public sector settings which relate to powerful professions or which are entirely dependent on flows of state finance. This perspective thus draws attention to the role of government, of national associations (e.g. Association of County Councils) and of the professions in structuring public sector quasi-markets.

Our three central propositions derived from this review of theoretical literature are thus as follows:

- that quasi-markets in the public sector can be best seen in relational terms;
- that quasi-markets in the public sector are, and will continue to be, socially embedded;
- that quasi-markets in the public sector are, and will continue to be, institutionally embedded.

3.4. The Creation and Evolution of Quasi-Markets— Some Empirical Evidence from the NHS

We here describe and analyse the creation and evolution of quasi-markets in health care in two contrasting localities. The focus of analysis is the local interorganizational set as it evolves through time. These accounts illustrate the considerable differences which remain between quasi-markets and neo-classical markets. There is little evidence as yet, at least in these localities, of effective price-based competition. Quasi-market creation is not a mechanistic process but one which is heavily influenced by local context and shaped by higher tiers.

South Shire

These two NHS settings are located in South Shire, a district health authority (now a purchasing organization) and its acute unit (which later achieved second-wave trust status). Of particular interest is the way in which each organization evolved even in a relatively short period of time and the shifting relationship between the two organizations.

The District Health Authority, now a Purchasing Authority   This district health authority has been moving towards a new purchasing role since 1989. The public health function has developed, admittedly from a low base. The district health authority is located in a semi-rural area, with a mainly white, middle class, population. The district health authority has been subjected to a series of reorganizations, moving from its old boundaries (1982–autumn 1991), through a transitional planning consortium stage with two neighbouring districts (autumn 1991–spring 1993), and then to full merger (spring 1993) to form a new and large-scale purchasing organization. These shifts are consistent with national trends. However, the relationship with the family health services authority was slow to develop.

The district was regarded as a well-managed authority. It has long been trying to rationalize and redevelop its acute sector facilities onto one main site, and this agenda has now been picked up by the acute trust. There is then only one acute trust in the old district health authority. There was no loss of financial control in the 1980s, and the district achieved considerable efficiency savings. A distinctive approach to general management was evident with an emphasis on teamwork, devolution, and organizational development. There have been a number of strong authority chairs in this locality, continuing after the 1990 reorganization.

Perhaps because of this past track record of success, the note is one of very substantial continuity at senior management level, and many of the officers in the authority went on to achieve very senior posts in the new consortium and authority. The chief executive officer and director of finance, for instance, both went back ten years. There was little evidence of appointments of outsiders to senior posts. Many of the non-executive members were personally known to the chairman and so could be seen as a coherent social grouping. A senior doctor continued to serve as advisor to the new district health authority until he became medical director on the new trust and then withdrew from the authority.

Between 1989 and 1991 the pace of development of the purchasing function seemed modest at district health authority level. The chair and all but one of the non-executive members, for instance, were continuing members, as were all the executive members. Much time was spent on national initiatives (e.g. reducing waiting list times) and some on continuing management responsibilities for directly managed units. However, with the formation of the purchasing consortium, and as the acute unit prepared to go out to trust status in spring 1992, the pace of change began to accelerate.

The district agreed to full merger from April 1993, under a firm steer from the chief executive officer and the regional health authority, and the non-executives in truth seemed to exercise only a minor role in making these key decisions. With the formation of the larger new authority in 1993, although most of the executive directors won the new posts, only one non-executive from the locality continued onto the new authority. The perception was that the authority was now rapidly developing its novel purchasing role, for example, paying much more attention to liaison with GPs than previously.

However, the district health authority's strategic impact had been more noticeable in relation to mental health and learning disability services (where there were concerned non-executive directors to put pressure on) than in local acute services. The District has been progressively withdrawing contracts from London hospitals in an attempt to develop local services.

The Previous Acute Unit, now a NHS Trust

> Trust status is not an end in itself, it is a way of helping us to do what we were going to do anyway.
>
> > (executive director, NHS trust)
>
> we must be the most organisationally developed hospital in the country.
>
> > (hospital saying)

Another case study took place within the acute hospital group which had previously been this district health authority's Acute Unit, but which achieved second-wave trust status in April 1992. The pattern in this area is for large towns about twenty miles apart each to have their general hospitals, so there is little natural competition for general services. This hospital group is also well placed to benefit from the phased movement of services out of London.

The main site is set in spacious grounds and the plan is to move services presently provided in peripheral hospitals onto the main site. It must also be said that this agenda is longstanding and has proved intractable in the past (due to constraints on capital). The potential for greater freedom over capital was seen as a significant benefit of trust status. The case for going trust was not presented in terms of the market, but in terms of autonomy: 'you are the master of your own ship'. Consultant opinion rapidly swung behind the application for trust status following the collapse of the regional capital programme in 1990, endangering long-hoped-for developments on the main site.

While general management had proved influential at District level as early as 1986, there was a view that it 'never really happened' at hospital level, at least until the appointment of a new unit general manager (with a Human Resources background) from outside the locality in 1990. From very early on, he maintained a distant relationship with the district health authority (usually not attending district health authority meetings). There was also a clearout at middle-management level. At the same time, there was much more emphasis on building an organization based on principles of learning and development, rather than competing solely on price. The trust was therefore developing a strong corporate personality which was rather different from many other acute trusts.

All the executive directors appointed to the board were internal appointments. The chief executive officer had previously been the unit general manager and had steered the successful trust application. Both the medical director and the director of nursing, for example, were long serving and highly respected. The first chair of the trust (local businessman and long-serving member of the bench) was new to the NHS and did not have well-developed networks. He did not take easily to strategic thinking, but preferred to concentrate on improving financial reporting to the board.

However, the non-executives represented a mixture of continuity and change. There were two strong appointments from outside the service who were seen as influential in contributing to the significant changes in culture that were apparent at least at the top of the organization:

I think what we as executive directors who are basically health service professionals have done is start thinking of ourselves as a business, and that, probably, would not have come about so quickly if we had non-executive directors who had come from a similar background to ourselves. (chief executive officer, NHS trust)

However, early expectations of increased autonomy were not always fulfilled. While the trust managed to escape the control of the region, it was monitored by the new management executive outpost which took a keen interest in financial control. At the end of its first financial year, the board agreed to curb elective work in order to restore its financial control. In terms of formulating a long term strategy, the non-executive directors—perhaps surprisingly given their calibre—had less impact than in some of the other acute trusts studied.

The Purchaser–Provider Relationship   Initially, there was pressure from higher tiers to restrain the pace of change and to ensure no surprises. In terms of local market structure, the district health authority was overwhelmingly the prime purchaser of the trust's services. Extra-contractual referral income was relatively small. There was no sign of an expanding private sector and no expressed desire by the prime purchaser to switch basic services between general hospitals. In effect, here was a monopoly purchaser relating to a monopoly provider. By 1993, however, the local market was beginning to develop as more GP fundholders came on stream and a greater plurality of purchasers was evident.

The traditional district–unit relationship has been evolving into a purchaser–provider relationship in which the hospital (now NHS trust) can be seen as a full and equal partner. More and more, the key issues centre on the setting, monitoring, and financing of the contract. So far, one-year block contracts have remained the preferred form of contract locally.

The relationship between purchaser and provider can best be described as *negotiative*. For example, the loading of the contract risk between purchaser and provider is a recurrent concern. The relationship is not fixed, but changes its character subtly through time: 1992, for example, was seen as more difficult than 1993.

There are many areas where the interests of both parties coincide (e.g. repatriation of work from London). Networks (e.g. the clinical network) continue to cross the two bodies. While contact between the two groups of non-executives seemed much weaker, it would nevertheless be erroneous to see the relationship between the two parties as conflictual.

However, it cannot be seen as fully cooperative either. The trust very quickly developed its own identity, based on an ideology of autonomy. The historically close links between the district health authority and 'its' hospital were eroded as larger scale purchasing organizations emerged. There was a feeling within the purchasing authority that as a consequence traditional informal flows of information were drying up. Continuing negotiations were evident in relation to contract-setting and the parties went to higher level arbitration for two years running. For example, there were long negotiations between the two chief executive officers in relation to the signing of the 1992/3 contract where the issues included:

- how to fund the higher than expected increase in activity;
- whether an allowance should be made for backlog maintenance;
- the level of detail of any quality specifications in the contract.

Mid-Shire

The District Health Authority   This shire district has been conterminous with the family health services authority and a social service department. Historically, there was a strong feeling that this was the best configuration and served the public well. This view was partly based on having successfully fought against the proposed split of the county into two health authorities during the 1974 reorganization.

The district health authority contains at its centre a large urban conurbation with a substantial ethnic minority population. The city has three large district general hospitals closely situated next to each other, historically linked by a medical school. In the era of planning, they were developed as a whole, exhibiting cross-site links and complementary strengths. This led to the original proposal from the district that all three units should go into trust status together. The Department of Health indicated that this early proposal would be unacceptable. There has been historically a degree of rivalry between these three sites, with the newest hospital (the one in our study) feeling that it was fighting for recognition.

Outside the city, the pattern of provision is one of local hospitals in medium-sized market towns, which tend to attract intense local loyalty.

In terms of the continuity of senior personnel, this locality shows a more mixed pattern than South Shire. The chief executive officer role has remained stable, and the director of public health has had a long career in the locality, but new executive directors have also been imported from other parts of the NHS (e.g. director of contracts; director of nursing). Before 1990, there had been a clearout of managers and indeed the district general manager had been given the task of sorting out the management which was felt by the region to be of patchy quality. A number of people were moved or retired.

With the exception of the chairman, who had only been appointed eighteen months prior to the Act, all the old authority members changed and new appointments were made to the board in September 1990. The only person to lend continuity was one non-executive director who had previously sat on the regional health authority. In early 1992 two of the non-executive directors announced they were resigning or not seeking re-election. In addition, two others were being considered for the role of chairs in the new trusts. Thus the board moved into a second phase as the first generation of non-executive directors moved on. In addition there were changes on the executive side, as the chief executive officer retired and was replaced by an internal successor.

All the city hospitals eventually went into individual trust status in the fourth wave so to allow time to arrange the split of services. This meant that the district health authority was operating with directly managed units during the 1990-3 period. During this time, it was also completing a large capital build programme sanctioned prior to the Act. There was thus a long transitional phase, during which there was a considerable operational management load. However, the district health authority set about developing the infrastructure by setting up new organizational structures and developing the information base for contracting.

There has been an increasingly strong relationship with the family health services authority leading to a merger of the structures, the agreement to move to the same premises, and a gradual increase in joint appointments. By 1992 many of these items had been effected and the district health authority and family health services association now operate jointly with integrated boards.

The newly appointed director of public health, who has managerial as well as professional skills, has had a major influence on the new-style district health association, and after a slow start (building up staff levels) the needs assessment function has developed strongly. There is an expressed concern for equity and for social justice. They have taken a pragmatic approach, using gross data in the first instance to pinpoint areas of need and then deciding on priorities for more detailed investigation. This in turn has led to the setting of specific health targets.

Given the operational workload, little progress was made on the purchasing strategy until 1992. In early 1992 there was pressure from the non-executive directors to establish a clearer forward strategy. This process was again delayed by the loss of experienced non-executive directors from the board, and the process of reforming and learning started all over again. There is now some evidence that the needs assessment work is proving influential, although there is much work still to be done. The district health authority tends not to look at what alternative providers might have to offer.

An Acute Trust in the City   In this trust, there was also an interesting mix of continuity and change. Given that it was a young unit, it did not see itself as having the same weight of history as the two neighbouring hospitals but also as being more innovative.

While there was some tension between the old unit general manager and the district, the unit general manager was well thought of by some colleagues and staff within the hospital. Relationships historically between the hospital and the district had been poor. The other core appointment was the unit director of finance who had been in post some years and was seen as 'a NHS man born and bred'. Other senior figures such as the chief nurse and senior consultants were also stable.

The unit general manager was not offered the post of chief executive officer designate, and quickly left, hence the embryonic trust was without a chief executive officer at a crucial time. A new chief executive officer was eventually appointed. Other internal managers went on to join the new board as executive directors, offering continuity. One of the district health authority members (an accountant and chief executive officer of his own firm) moved to the trust designate as its chair.

Until 1993 this unit was still directly managed and during this period there were a number of behind-the-scenes rows between unit and district (interestingly, rarely discussed openly in board meetings). The management of the units was deliberately arm's length in nature, and more and more functions were devolved.

During the shadow trust period, a considerable amount of work was done to tighten up on the contracting process and, under pressure from the chair, to improve financial reporting. There was also thought given as to how board meetings should be run, how agendas should be formulated, and how information provided. This represents an interesting example of organizational learning, as the chair had reflected on his prior experience on the district health authority.

The trust's strategy was initially driven by the need to keep as many contracts as possible, after the period of steady state, given their fear that they would lose out to the other two acute trusts. They still do not have a fully elaborated strategy, and this has concerned the non-executive directors. However, they are building on their relationships with local GP fundholders, where they believe they have a good reputation for listening. They have also successfully stressed the high-quality nature of their service (e.g. cardiac care). They certainly recognize that they needed to deal more proactively with the market-place and talked frequently about how to improve their marketing.

The Purchaser–Provider Relationship   Prior to the 1990 Act, the three acute units had been deliberately managed across the city as a set of complementary services to the population and sharing a number of common services, but subsequently evolving into three separate trusts, competing for contracts for similar services.

It is true that substantial change has taken place in the type and nature of the relationships between the three trusts. But they cannot be said to be independent of each other or of the purchaser. Indeed the main purchaser continues, in part, to conceive of the three trusts as an entity, whose role was to serve collectively the population as effectively as possible. The district health authority has thus attempted to develop an open and collaborative relationship with local trusts. It argues that this does not make for a collusive relationship, and there is some evidence to support this view. In relationship terms, the district health authority argues that collaboration works, so that it decided to offer incentives in the contracts for specified improvements to the standards of service, as opposed to punishing lower standards. It was also very successful in deploying waiting list monies to achieve lower waiting times, in conjunction with the trusts.

In overall terms, the three acute trusts are not threatened by out of county providers in terms of the placing of district health authority contracts. There is, however, a threat from the rural GP fundholders placing contracts with their local hospitals within the county, to the disadvantage of all the inner city hospitals.

The nature and tone of the relationship between district and hospital have if anything improved since the establishment of the trust (and the new chief executive officer). The relationship is cordial, without being close. It is interesting to note that there is virtually no contact between the trust non-executive directors and district health authority personnel, either executive directors or non-executive directors. The chair maintains his relationships and acts as a channel of communication, and the medical director has his own clinical network, but the other non-executive directors are isolated.

However, there is evidence of some competition and of a market emerging between the three acute city trusts, particularly in the location of certain specialties. One of the other trusts in particular is seen as behaving in a predatory manner. The district health authority has already taken some 'three into two' decisions which have impacted adversely on the trust studied, concentrating contracts on the two bigger and longer established trusts. This produced a long fight and generated the feeling at the trust studied that they had been unfairly treated.

Quasi-Markets in Practice

So far the pace of development of the two local health care markets studied since 1990 has been slow. They remain very much inward-facing and regulated markets. Few alternative providers have moved centre stage, indeed some detect a weakening of the position of private sector health care providers as more business-like management emerges in the NHS Trusts, reducing waiting times for elective work and undercutting the private sector. Persistently failing NHS providers face unclear arrangements for market exit. Competitive forces thus remain relatively marginal, unsurprisingly so when these systems grew up as essentially planned and interdependent organizations. There have as yet been few major changes to services. Contracting is often still based on crude block contracts, rather than more market-sensitive cost and volume contracts.

However, as our initial review indicated, it may be that the quasi-market in health care is developing more slowly than in other services which are less politically sensitive, are less dominated by powerful professions, display fewer sunk costs and service interdependencies, or are characterized by an internal sense of crisis and failure. These contextual features shape the pace of market development just as much as the market structure highlighted by Challis *et al.* (1994) (Ball *et al.*, (1994) make a similar argument in respect of the education service).

However, there are the first signs that the pace of market development within health care is beginning to accelerate, with the relaxation of steady state, the expansion of GP fundholding, and the liberalization of regulations concerning the use of private capital. Eventually cost and information systems may develop further so that more sensitive forms of spot purchasing become possible at least in terms of the information technology. There was some evidence of competition emerging in some of the urban sites studied between neighbouring acute sector providers, at least round the margins for new developments and certain specialties. The newly created and potentially powerful macro-purchasers may move from their early reactive role to more proactive strategies, seeking to reshape service configurations.

Health care can best be seen as in the very early stages of a long-term change process. The local quasi-markets studied are still unsophisticated in nature, as a new set of structures, processes, roles, relationships, and skills is still relatively unformed. Elsewhere (Ferlie *et al.* 1992), we have drawn attention to local variation in the rate of development of the purchasing function, and the importance of local prehistory and sources of leadership in explaining this variation. We would see these factors as at least as influential as market structure.

We should also remember that our data relate to the early 1990-3 period and that further development may already have occurred. Furthermore, our data are drawn from acute sector settings and the situation may be quite different in community and mental health services. However, we would speculate that the potential for competition in such services is if anything less than in acute services.

3.5. Conclusions and Discussion

Quasi-Markets in Health Care: an Initial Assessment

So how would we assess the effects of the introduction of the quasi-market? Our picture is drawn from the top of the organization, and the situation may appear very different at service level. Our data relate to indicators of organizational process, and we have little information as to changes in output, let alone outcome. It is also difficult to attribute cause and effect as many different streams of policy, not just the quasi-market reforms, may be interacting.

Nevertheless, we feel that our data are able to contribute to the wider debate. We consider first of all key evaluative criteria as outlined by Le Grand (1994).

Quality It was initially hoped that NHS contracts would be let on quality as well as cost and activity criteria. Some NHS localities have displayed a concern with service quality issues since the mid-1980s (e.g. the total quality management wave of the late 1980s), and the reforms represented an opportunity to build on this early work. The Patients' Charter initiative has reinforced this concern with quality nationally. A separate line of policy has facilitated the diffusion of clinical audit activity within a professional arena.

For more to happen locally, the organization needed a home for the quality issue. Where there was an executive director prepared to sponsor the quality issue (e.g. director of nursing), much attention was paid to the development of quality specifications in the contract. Generally, however, the finding was that cost and activity criteria were decisive in the letting of contracts, and that quality criteria were in the end of secondary importance.

Efficiency Some of the long-standing national pressures for increased efficiency (such as the Treasury efficiency index; national day surgery targets) have continued to push up activity levels since 1990, but are not part of the quasi-market system. Indeed such central planning may restrain the operation of pure market forces.

However, a number of the NHS trusts studied were making substantial efforts to cut their cost base and reduce their prices, by shedding staff and contracting functions out. Our conclusion is that NHS Trusts face harder budgetary constraints than the old units, and that this is now leading to some substantial internal reorganizations designed to achieve delayering and downsizing.

Another and less obvious aspect of greater efficiency is a switch of resources from interventions of unproven efficacy to those of proven efficacy. The national NHS R and D strategy launched in 1991—in a policy development quite separate from the introduction of the quasi-market—aims to achieve the spread of such knowledge-based practice. In the end, such R and D may inform macro-purchasers, but as yet, its effect has been marginal.

Choice and Responsiveness There was little evidence of enhanced patient choice as a result of the reforms. Within primary care, GP fundholders are expected to act as proxies for their patients, making contractual decisions on their behalf. The district health authorities were concerned about the financial consequences of unrestrained extra-contractual referrals, and an attempt to rein the numbers back or to convert them into more controllable cost and volume contracts.

There were continuing efforts to get waiting list times for elective work down, but this owed more to central ring-fenced funding than to the effects of the quasi-market.

Equity A continuing concern for equity was observable in some of the purchasing organizations studied, perhaps because of the influence of the public health tradition. Such personnel were often grouping around the 'health of the nation' agenda. There was sometimes a concern to ensure that non-fundholding GPs were not disadvantaged in terms of their ability to access trust services.

Such concerns were not so evident in the NHS trusts, where market logics were stronger. The trusts needed to respond to the demands of GP fund-holders, hence the emergence in some places of two-tier services. There was talk of expanding private provision within the trusts, although with few results as yet. We are worried about a possible loss of a concern with equity as a guiding value within the new-style NHS.

We would also add our own evaluative criteria of management capacity and professional involvement, where we believe that the reforms can be seen as more successful.

Management Capacity Since the Griffiths Report (1983), there have been continuing attempts to increase managerial capacity in the NHS (e.g. introduction of general management). Sometimes this was achieved at district level, but did not always filter down to the old unit level.

A major effect of the reforms has been to upgrade management capacity further down the organization, as the old units have gone out to trust status. In our view, this transition was not just marked by a shift of power to management, but also an enhancement of the managerial skill base.

A number of filtering processes can be seen as operating. Managerial names were vetted centrally, and internal candidates seen as too weak filtered out. There has often been a later process of reviewing middle management. The large acute sector trusts in particular have proved challenging and high profile propositions for ambitious chief executive officers. The trusts also have their own boards which can potentially give them strategic direction, unlike the old units. Cost, information, and human resource management systems have been overhauled and invested in. New skills such as marketing and communications have been developed for the first time.

Of course, all these developments have also pushed management costs up. Sceptics argue that costs exceed demonstrated benefits, and there are now signs of a backlash against these increased management costs. Our point is that the level of management capacity can generally be seen as higher in the NHS trusts than in the predecessor units.

Professional Involvement   Again since the Griffiths Report (1983), there have been continuing attempts to get doctors into management. This has often foundered on the career incentives facing doctors, whereby managerial experience is not seen to be as important as professional excellence. Within the NHS trusts, provision was made for the appointment of a medical director and director of nursing at board level. Often a clinical directorate structure was created below board level. These developments have resulted in the formation of a hybrid group of doctors and nurse managers, who undertake managerial as well as clinical tasks.

There have been strains where, for example, the medical director has tried to combine this role with acting as chair of the Medical Advisory Committee. Nevertheless, these roles do offer senior clinicians new board-level experience. They are expected to take a more corporate view and to tackle strategic issues of service configuration, finance, and human resource management. In our view, these new roles offer an important management development opportunity for these senior clinicians.

Quasi-Markets in Theory   Our theoretical purpose has been to characterize quasi-markets from a 'New Economic Sociology' framework rather than from the conventional viewpoints of micro-economic theory or 'the New Institutional Economics'. Three core ideas were advanced:

• that the quasi-market must be seen as a *relational* market. Clearly, the case study evidence suggested that this was not an atomized market but rather one in which a few powerful purchasers were in more or less continuing negotiation with a few powerful providers. Judgements were made on the basis of trust and reputation as well as on hard data. There were, however, some early signs of increasing social distance as traditional relationships came under pressure.

In South Shire, the negotiations between the two chief executive officers around the contract formed the core of the negotiating process. The relationship between the two parties was seen as continuing, perhaps even as indefinite. However, the view that the interaction process would include important processes of social exchange, undertaken so as to reduce uncertainty and to build trust, was not confirmed. If anything, traditional informal flows of information seemed to be drying up. Different cultures and value systems could be seen as emerging in the trust and in the purchasing organization, with very little staff movement between the two. This is consistent with a negotiative, rather than fully cooperative, approach to contracting.

In Mid-Shire, there was more evidence of competition emerging between the three acute providers. Nevertheless, this remained an inward-facing market, and external providers were not moving in. The district health authority was keen to maintain a cooperative (critics would say collusive) relationship with traditional providers. Here the pattern of district health authority–trust contact if anything improved with new personnel (admittedly from a very low base). Relations between key executives on the two organizations could be seen as cordial but not close.

- that the internal market is *socially embedded*. There was found to be a high degree of continuity in the personnel staffing the upper reaches of the health care organizations. There is then a small health care élite (but one which contains distinct clinical, managerial, public service, and quasi-political components) which displays considerable stability at the apex of these organizations. Long-term careers emerge and continue despite reorganizations.

Although the general picture is one of stability in social networks, there was also some change. Change was most evident in relation to the non-executive component of these local health care élites. There was a high rate of non-executive turnover, for instance, in Mid-Shire. There was an increased premium on the possession of business skills apparent in the appointment process. One question is whether new networks are displacing old ones, marking a shift from public service to more business-based élites. The chair performed an important trust–DHA-linking function in Mid-Shire.

A number of different social networks link the organizations studied. The professional network was the strongest, followed by the managerial network with (perhaps surprisingly) the links between rank and file non-executives being the weakest form of network. Far from representing an integrated and cohesive élite, rank and file non-executives were often surprisingly isolated from colleagues in neighbouring organizations. Often these 'foreign policy' functions fell to the chairs, with their quasi-political orientation.

• that the quasi-market is *institutionally embedded*. Much evidence was found to support this proposition and a social network approach by itself is too micro. The quasi-market is very much inward facing, regulated by higher tiers. Directives (e.g. junior doctors' hours) continue to cascade down from the centre. The practical expression of this institutional control can be seen in such features as the arbitration mechanism, designed to resolve disputes in the localities in the absence of a right to redress in the Courts. Rules concerning prices, rates of financial return, and productivity targets are all set centrally and transmitted downwards. There is a potential contradiction between the rhetoric of free markets and the heavy weight of a continuing regulatory apparatus.

Quasi-Markets and Organisational Change   In Chapter 2, the argument was advanced that the reform processes of the 1980s, with their reliance on top-down radical shock strategies and the exercise of political clout, at the very least opened the way to substantial organizational change. The previous pattern of public sector reorganizations as relabelling exercises may have come to an end as a series of complex and systemic changes were pressed down upon public sector organizations over a considerable time period.

The introduction of quasi-market ideas—across a wide range of public settings—represents a good exemplar of such a systemic change process outlined in Chapter 2. Complex in itself, it also triggered off further related changes (e.g. the development of cost and information systems to support the contracting process). Structural reorganization to accommodate quasi-market ideas has self-evidently been widespread as organizations have disaggregated into purchasers and providers. Change has also taken place to key work processes (e.g. the emergence of contracting) and to key non-executive director and executive director personnel at the top of these organizations. Some of the consequences have been unheralded and negative, such as the drying-up of informal information flows between institutions.

At the same time, the pace of change has so far been restrained in our case study sites, perhaps because of political sensitivity in the early period. Few new entrants have moved into the field, there have been no bankruptcies, and contracts have been relet at the margins. It is of course possible that the pace of change has accelerated since the end of fieldwork, since we were studying the early days.

In terms of the cultural change evident as a result of the introduction of the quasi-market, the picture is as yet mixed. The language has so far changed faster than the reality. The strong element of continuity still in the system has so far acted to restrain the development of a fully fledged market culture. The strength of the inheritance may erode over time, however, and the 1990 appointments to the new boards marked a significant influx of private sector personnel onto trust boards in particular (as we discuss further in Chapter 5). There are also signs of different subcultures emerging in purchasing organizations, acute trusts and non-acute trusts.

Even if the quasi-market in health care develops further, in our view it is unlikely ever to resemble neo-classical models of markets. This is not so much because they are relational and socially embedded in nature (although they are) given that professional service organizations in the private sector (such as law or management consulting) may share these market characteristics (Yorke 1990). It is more due to the esoteric and indeed ever-expanding body of bio-medical and clinical knowledge, the continuing powerful role of the medical profession (as we argue in Chapter 7), and the institutionalized nature of the quasi-market in heath care due to the political sensitivity of the sector.

Under these circumstances, the quasi-market in health care is likely to remain different from models of markets in the private sector, in realization as in conceptualization. We are justified in talking of a hybrid model which is certainly significantly different from the pre-1990 order but which will not simply converge onto private-sector models or cultures. This notion of hybrid forms will be developed throughout the analysis.

This argument is advanced in respect of the quasi-market in health care. It would be interesting to compare the evolution of the health care quasi-market with other quasi-markets (eg. social care; the BBC) to see whether the hybrid form holds in those sectors, or whether there is a more rapid convergence onto private sector models.

A PROCESS OF TRANSFORMATIONAL CHANGE?

4.1. From Change to Transformation

Introduction

In Chapter 1, we posed the question, is radical change occurring in the public sector, or is it a case of relabelling, not change? The data presented in Chapter 2 illustrated that health care has undergone sector-wide change which has altered the fundamental framework within which public health care is provided. One key aspect of these changes has been the creation of novel forms of organization in the new purchasing authorities. On the basis of this evidence, we concluded that significant changes were occurring in health care in the UK. Here we progress the debate and extend it to include a new question: can the changes which are evident be described as transformational? This chapter debates and explores the analysis of organizational change and questions how radical and widespread the changes are.

A considerable number of writers have, in recent times, referred to the phenomenon of transformational change in organizations (Dunphy and Stace 1988; Gersick 1991; Beckhard and Pritchard 1992; Romanelli and Tushman 1994; Blumenthal and Haspeslagh 1994). These authors have sought to argue that transformational change is a particular form of strategic change, radical in its impact. However, they have failed to adequately define the characteristics which delineate such transformational change from strategic change (though some such as Blumenthal and Haspeslagh (1994) and Romanelli and Tushman (1994) are addressing this particular issue).

Here we start from the premiss that transformational change produces more fundamental and pervasive outcomes than strategic change within a large-scale organization or sector. It is suggested that transformational change, like strategic change, affects a number of the major systems in the organization. In addition, it is a multilayered process affecting different levels of the organization and even the context of the organization's operation, simultaneously. This form of change has much in common with other examples of strategic change in the public and the private sectors (see, for example, Tichy 1983; Pettigrew and Whipp 1991; Hinings and Greenwood 1989; Pettigrew, Ferlie, and McKee 1992) but, it is argued, it also has a number of additive and distinctive characteristics. There is a lack of consensus among authors, however, as to how the indicators of transformational change may be defined. Broadly, transformation may be defined as achieving fundamentally changed outcomes within an organization (Dunphy and Stace 1988; Blumenthal and Hasplagh 1994). Alternatively, greater weight may be given to the processes by which transformational change occurs in an organization, emphasizing the speed of change and the role of crisis (Romanelli and Tushman 1994). Given this confusion, in this chapter we shall attempt to refine the definition of transformational change and in this section after discussion of the literature we will propose an operational definition to be tested against the empirical data.

In this chapter, we will postulate that there has been strategic change in health and in education, as the result of a number of major, top–down changes in the last few years and the essential theme of this chapter will be to explore the extent to which these changes can also be described as transformational in nature.

A slightly different comparative approach is adopted in this chapter compared to the preceding ones. Health and secondary education are selected for paired comparison because of the similarity of the change objectives set for each of these services. This approach allows an in-depth and comparative analysis of complex situations. A brief review of the contexts will set the scene.

Each service has undergone, prior to 1990, a lengthy period of change, driven by government initiatives such as compulsory competitive tendering in education and the introduction of general management in health. Similarly, each is now undergoing a shift to a quasi-market, introducing the concepts of competition and consumer choice into the provision of a previously public service. In each instance, the avowed intention of the government was to introduce greater efficiency and the gradual improvement of standards.

Here it will be argued that in health, the cumulative effect of these earlier changes and the impact of the NHS and Community Care Act 1990, has produced transformational change. In education, one fundamental piece of legislation was the Education Reform Act (1988), introducing the concepts of local management of schools, accompanied by the introduction of the National Curriculum and the chance to opt out into grant maintained status. Now the supporting legislation of the 1992 Schools Act and the 1993 and 1994 Education Acts means that the change process continues. It may be too early, as yet, to judge the longer term impact of this sustained and extensive process of top–down change in education.

There are other similarities. Like health, the education sector has a high proportion of professional staff. In both health and secondary education, the

boards have been restructured and given a new composition with the introduction of lay members as non-executive directors.

One of the key features of British organizational life in the 1980s was the
continuing experience of top–down pressure for change in both public and
private sector organizations. In the 1980s, the Thatcher Government consistently focused on institutional reform. In the public sector, local government,
the civil service, education, and health were all affected. There was an ongoing
process of privatizing organizations which had previously been in the public
sector, such as the water and gas utilities, and the telephone network. This
sustained process of top–down change raises interesting theoretical questions
about the nature of effective change processes in large organizations, whether
public or private. Glendon (1992) explores the notion of effective, power-
driven top–down change and challenges the view that effective organizational
change has to involve a level of commitment from those affected. Here the
opportunity is offered to analyse change processes in the public sector, as so
much prior research has concentrated on the private sector.

Theoretical Perspectives on Strategic and Transformational Change

Previous discussions in the literature have examined the nature of strategic
change processes in organizations. Strategic change, as opposed to incremental
change, has been a topic of relatively recent interest. It is relevant to note that
in a seminal text on planned change in organizations by Bennis *et al.*,
published in 1976, the topic of strategic change is not covered.

Earlier work on planned organizational change centred on changes at the
team, unit, or divisional level (Greiner and Barnes 1970; Mumford 1972; Partin
1973; Ottaway 1976). However, the increasing rate of change and the growing
recognition that major organizational changes had to be incorporated into the
strategic management processes of the organization, led to a greater emphasis
on a macro- or holistic-view of organizational change. The influence of the
Tavistock Institute's work on open socio-technical systems (Trist *et al.* 1963;
Herbst 1974; Rice 1963) combined with the earlier US laboratory-based
approaches (Lippitt *et al.* 1958; Golembiewski 1972) to give a more comprehensive understanding of organizational change (see Friedlander and Brown
1974). Early applications of these ideas underlined the complexities of large-
scale strategic change (Warmington *et al.* 1977).

Strategic change has been defined as a major change affecting one or more of
the main systems in an organization, such as the strategy, structure, technology, or control systems (Tichy 1983). He further emphasizes the multiplicity of
the political, structural, and control aspects of the processes required to
successfully achieve strategic change, comparing them to the intertwining
strands of a rope.

A number of studies have sought to illuminate the processes of strategic organizational change. Quinn (1980) describes strategic change as a process of logical incrementalism, involving both planned and evolutionary processes. He argues that strategic change can be effected in an incremental, cumulative manner. These data clearly challenge the rationalist, logical perspective of how change in organizations is managed. Pettigrew's (1985) study expands our understanding of the unfolding nature of strategic change, as well as offering a much clearer perspective on the time frames involved and the political dimensions of large-scale change. His study emphasizes the importance of external pressures and the role of crisis in initiating change in large organizations, illustrating the cocktail of internal and external pressures which produces strategic organizational change. Work by Nadler (1987), Mintzberg (1987), Kanter (1983), Pettigrew and Whipp (1991), all evidence the interest in the area of strategic change and explore the complexity of the issues involved in effective strategic change. One of the key factors pinpointed by these authors is the interlinking of differing arenas of management, for example, the importance of developing an organizational culture which supports and encourages change is underlined by Kanter. In similar vein, the need to link strategic intent with the implementation of changes is underlined as a critical success factor in the work of Pettigrew *et al.* (1992).

In examining the literature thus far, the distinction between incremental and strategic change can be drawn. Incremental change is relatively smaller in scale, producing change outcomes which are focused on one function or unit of an organization. Strategic change, on the other hand, is seen as effecting major subsystems and producing outcomes which impact across many parts of an organization. The timescale of strategic change is seen to be longer. There are areas of uncertainty, particularly relating to processes. One key question would be this: can cumulative, incremental change produce successful strategic change?

It will be noted that much of the research already quoted was carried out in the private for-profit sector and relatively little research has been done in the public sector. The work of Pettigrew *et al.* (1992) is one notable exception. Their findings illustrate that public sector contexts may require different approaches to effect successful outcomes. Similarly, Hinings and Greenwood's (1989) text drawing on work in the public sector in both Australia and the UK and Shortell *et al.*'s (1990) research on the US hospital system, underline the similarities and differences of managing organizational change in public, as compared to private sector, settings.

From a theoretical perspective, there has been interest in discriminating and describing forms of change. Attempts have been made to create typologies of change which elaborate the distinguishing characteristics of different types. As long ago as 1975, Golembiewski *et al.* offered an interesting typology which distinguished between alpha or incremental change (defined as change in some state along a constant scale which can be measured), as compared to beta change (which was defined as change in some state complicated by a changing measuring system). Levy (1986) offers a similar view, writing of first-order change as incremental adjustments that do not affect the organization's core and second-order change, which involves alteration of the system's basic rules.

Other writers have provided different models. Tushman and Romanelli (1985) describe discontinuous or framebreaking change, as when an organization passes through a period of punctuated equilibrium. It involves, they suggest, 'relatively short bursts of fundamental change (revolutionary periods)' (1985: 1141). Their specification of transformation is that it includes sharp and simultaneous shifts in strategy, power, structure, and control mechanisms. This model recognizes not only the scale of the changes involved, but also the importance of timescale and the speed of change as an aspect of more radical organizational change. Tushman and Romanelli (1985) have also drawn distinctions between reactive and proactive change, which responds to or foresees external pressures.

The development of these typologies and models provokes useful debate. Terms such as 'frame-breaking', 'metamorphosis', and 'revolutionary' are frequently used interchangeably. Many of them were not founded in empirical data and are thus untested. Discussing their model of punctuated equilibrium, Romanelli and Tushman (1994) themselves underline that: 'little research has explored the empirical validity of the model's basic arguments'. There have been some recent studies which sought to research major strategic changes in organizations and these provide test grounds for the validity of the distinctions often drawn between incremental and strategic change. The work of Pettigrew (1985) has already been cited. A more recent comparative study (Pettigrew and Whipp 1991) of organizations in different sectors underlines the importance of strategy and the judgements and choices made by senior management about what policies to adopt in specific circumstances. This research also illustrates the importance of intangible assets, invested in the people who make up the organization. These results are particularly interesting because of the common themes emerging between results from the private sector and work on managing organizational change in the health sector (Pettigrew *et al.* 1992). Similar themes emerge from the work of Kanter in the USA, first through her study of successful organizations (Kanter 1983) and then through her work on change in large-scale organizations (Kanter 1989).

Gradually through these empirical studies, the range and scale of different forms of organizational change is elaborated. One emerging theme, interconnected to innovation and competitiveness, is to define and understand how radical, fundamental strategic change is brought about in organizations. The terms 'transformational' and 'framebreaking' are being increasingly used to broadly distinguish a more fundamental form of change, but the variations in form are considerable. Child and Smith (1987) offer an example of transformational change from private sector manufacturing, stressing the lengthy period of reappraisal and recognition which preceded transformation. Grinyer *et al.* (1988) in researching company turnarounds in the private sector show the importance of a similar mix of external pressures and crisis in driving change, combined with internal strengths in senior management and sustained effort. Romanelli and Tushman's definition of transformation is tested (Romanelli and Tushman 1994) using data drawn from a sample of private sector firms. This article is significant in that it defines a set of criteria for assessing transformation. These are organizational strategies, organizational structures, power distribution, control systems, and organizational culture. Clearly the criteria are broadly defined and difficult to operationalize. The authors found that the information on cultures and control systems was inconsistent and incomplete. Moreover the article suggests that changes in any of these domains may indicate transformation, irrespective of whether they occur simultaneously. This would make the distinction between strategic and transformational change difficult to make.

The literature provides a variety of ideas with little precise definition of terms. There has been little empirical testing, so that the differences between strategic and transformational change remain unclear. For example, is it about the scope and depth of outcomes, or about a radical and revolutionary process which produces rapid change, or both? In the following section, in the light of our empirical data and the literature, we set out our proposed criteria for assessing transformation.

Defining the Reality of Transformational Change

From a preliminary analysis of the impact of the NHS and Community Care Act, it is clear that these changes have much in common with prior changes. It can be described as a top–down change, driven by political motives as well as by the need to shepherd resources and improve efficiency. So it has characteristics in common with some of those earlier changes. The data will illustrate that it has been difficult to operationalize parts of the changes, particularly in implementing purchasing. The legacy of past modes of operating have affected managers' abilities to alter their behaviour and systems from managing to purchasing. Maintaining a distant and contractual method of control has been a particularly distinctive change for some players. These themes repeat the results emerging from previous research in health care (see for example Pettigrew *et al.* 1992; Shortell *et al.* 1990). They are also reminiscent of issues in strategic change explored in the literature on the private for-profit sector, where the link between strategic planning and vision and operational reality is problematic (Mintzberg 1987; Kanter 1989; Pettigrew and Whipp 1991).

However, the changes resulting from the NHS and Community Care Act can be seen as having distinct features. The first of these is that the Act has created multilayered change impacting virtually simultaneously on a number of levels within the health service. The cumulative effect of this multilayered change process, it will be argued, is to create a change process of great force and scale. By virtue of these very characteristics, it has overcome some resistance and potential resistance. This is not to argue that radical or transformational change has been achieved in a planned and controlled way. The reality is more complex, with radical levers being used by government in the first instance and creating both intended and unintended consequences. The emerging strategy or pattern has been shaped by a plurality of interests and also by some redefinition on the part of government as the changes unfolded. The final pattern is still emerging and being amended.

In the education sector, a number of these themes and changes recur. (Glennerster 1991; Ranson 1993; Edwards and Whitty 1992; Barber 1994; Tooley 1995). The whole of the education sector, at secondary and tertiary levels, has undergone a complex and profound process of change over a period of years. Legislation has been introduced which also drives a top–down change process. (Milliband 1991; Keep 1991; Grace 1993; Evetts 1994). Combined with the introduction of greater parental choice in deciding on the school to which children will go and the advent of comparative league tables, these changes have had a significant impact. The question remains whether the education service is undergoing transformational change.

As already suggested, in much of the literature, terms like radical and transformatory are used interchangeably. In order to adequately address the question of whether transformation is occurring in health and education, one needs to identify the operational indicators of transformation. A weakness in much of the literature on organizational transformation is that it is general and does not define empirical assessment criteria for judging whether change on this scale is occurring. Equally in the literature on public sector restructuring, few criteria for assessing the extent of change have been established. In Chapter 2, we proposed six indicators of transformatory change, which we reiterate here to remind the reader:

1. the existence of multiple and interrelated changes across the system as a whole;
2. the creation of new organizational forms at a collective level;
3. the development of multilayered changes which impact below the whole system, at unit and individual level;
4. the creation of changes in the services provided and the mode of delivery;
5. reconfiguration of power relations (especially the formation of new leadership groups);
6. the development of a new culture, ideology, and organizational meaning.

Applying these six indicators it is possible to clarify some of the distinctions between transformatory and strategic change. At the broadest level, transformatory change is defined as producing multiple change outcomes, both horizontally across the organization and vertically up and down the layers of the organization. Specifically, transformation includes the creation of novel organizational forms and changes in the products–services of the organization. The breadth, scope, and radicality of the changes is greater than would be anticipated for strategic change. One would not anticipate that strategic change automatically included the generation of new organizational forms, for example. Furthermore, transformation, according to this definition, also involves the reconfiguration of power relations and the development of a new culture. With these indicators, we attempt to embrace the concept of 'frame-breaking' (Tushman and Romanelli 1985; Tushman *et al.* 1988) and second-order change (Levy 1986) which involves alteration of the system's basic rules. In the remainder of this chapter, these criteria will be used to interrogate the empirical evidence. Following on from the material already presented in Chapter 2 on the changes affecting the sector as a whole, this chapter will focus on the last four criteria quoted above. The next section will examine changes occurring at the unit level, first alluding briefly to the individuals who are at the strategic apex and secondly examining in greater detail changes to the intra-organizational structures. In Section 4.3, the focus will be on the impact of new specialist innovations e.g. new medical technologies and on the way in which service is delivered. The following section will look at individual roles and the reconfiguration of power relations. The last section presenting empirical data will examine the evidence on the changing culture of public sector organizations.

Part of the argument about the form and definition of transformatory change underlines the interlinkages between changes at different levels and parts of the system. The sections which follow draw artificial boundaries between different aspects of the changes purely for clarity of presentation.

In the final section, conclusions will be drawn about the extent and nature of change occurring in these two key parts of the public sector; that is, health care and education.

4.2. Multilayered Changes within Organizations

Changes at the Apex of Organizations

In putting forward the argument that transformational change can be better understood and defined by the application of assessment criteria, we have tried to stress in the criteria themselves the power of multiple level changes. In this section, the focus will be on empirical data on the extent and form of structural changes occurring at the unit or single organizational level and within the boundaries of the organization. These changes can only be under-stood and analysed when taken in the broader context of the changes to whole sectors already discussed in Chapters 2 and 3. There the discussion centred on structural changes which have led to the creation of whole new organizations, such as purchasing organizations, whilst here we shall focus on changes within the organizational boundaries.

In Chapters 2 and 3, it was noted that facets of the government's drive to alter the public sector involve the introduction of greater managerialism and the creation of a quasi-market. One specific aspect of this shift has been the system-wide introduction of the private sector board model to the strategic, corporate management of units. The study of the new boards in health care and of their operation has been a key focus of our work in this sector and will be analysed in later chapters in this book (especially Chapters 5 and 6).

Here a number of points concerning health care will be emphasized as a preliminary to the more detailed discussion of the education sector. The restructuring of the boards of purchasing authorities and trusts has meant not only substantially changed responsibilities, but as stated in Chapter 2, new membership. In particular, trust boards now have to be able to analyse their competencies and devise a strategy which will enable them to bid for contracts. All of these tasks represent new demands on senior managers, many of whom have always worked in health care. Chapter 2 also emphasized this shift from management by hierarchy to management by contract which requires an altered conception of management and an altered mode of behaviour. So the ground rules for management have changed dramatically.

By comparison with health care, in secondary education, the strategic apex of the organization has also undergone change. Schools have seen the introduction of a governing board, modelled on the private sector and having far wider powers than previously. In this example, however, the membership and composition of the board are different. School boards are led by an independent chair. Then they must contain representatives of the different stakeholders, the parents, the teachers, and the local community. The former two groups of representatives have also to be elected from the constituency they represent. Additionally, the board may co-opt other members usually for their specific expertise. Headteachers are entitled to a place on the board as corporate members, if they so chose. Thus a school board only contains one executive member, the headteacher, alongside a group of other directors, some there as representatives and others co-opted for their expertise.

School boards, like trusts, are facing a new set of demands. The establishment of a market or quasi-market in education has occurred. First, there has been the devolution of budgets to schools and local management of schools. Secondly, schools have been offered the opportunity to 'opt-out' of local authority control and become grant maintained. And thirdly, parents have been given freedom of choice to select schools for their children. Thus school boards are also facing the need to consider the strategic management of their school for the first time. Their relationship with their local education authority has also undergone some change, becoming more distanced and with the local education authority playing an increasingly enabling role, rather than one of direct line management. Most significantly, schools are managing their own budgets, and have new responsibilities for staffing, for a range of personnel decisions, and for the upkeep of buildings. In a recent change, schools will be allocated a budget for the inspection of the school. As part of devolved management, schools have to produce a school development plan showing how the school expects to cope with the future. As with the health sector, this makes new demands on the managerial skills of the board members, who also need to take a more strategic stance.

For secondary schools, the changes to the governing bodies have been a particularly significant development. Headteachers in schools have in managerial terms held a position of almost unprecedented power. Torrington and Weightman (1989) show in their research that compared with industrial managers, the power of the head is unparalleled. Now headteachers may be leading the school, and reporting to a governing body, some of whose members may have significant management experience. Whilst this change may be seen as a potential benefit, there are clearly many problems with the board model implemented in schools (Baginsky *et al.* 1991; Fergusson 1994; Shearn *et al.* 1995; Monck and Kelly 1992; Deem 1990). The first issue relates to time, experience, and training. The majority of members of school governing bodies are volunteers and are not paid an honorarium, so time to prepare for meetings and to train is at a premium. Secondly, parent and teacher representatives do not 'de facto' have management experience. Likewise, headteachers are usually from a professional teaching background and may have limited training as a manager. And yet the scale and complexity of the management task, particularly of budgetary responsibility, is now considerable. Finally, the research data shows (Baginsky *et al.* 1991; Shearn *et al.* 1995) that few board members have any comparable experience of sitting as a board member on a private sector board, so there is considerable confusion about the role of a board and of the corporate responsibilities of the individual member. They demonstrate at least five different models of practice in operation, all with different relationships between the headteacher and the board.

Comparatively, there are three key differences between the sectors in the impact of these changes at the strategic apex. First, the external demands on school boards from the establishment of the quasi-market in education are not so extensive as the demands on health boards. Schools are not fighting for contracts to produce income, but are still operating under a system of guaranteed central funding, based on pupil numbers. So there is an indirect market pressure, because if they lose pupils they lose income. Health providers are under direct market pressure and have to be able to secure contracts in order to maintain their enterprise. Secondly, the establishment of the market in education has been slower than in health care. Between 1988 and the time of writing, less schools than anticipated have decided to opt out into grant maintained status. By October 1990 there were forty-four, by July 1992 there were 217 (Times Educational Supplement 1993). Out of nearly 25,000 schools in England and Wales, there were under 1,000 grant maintained schools by April 1994 (King 1994).

As a result, early research evidence (Halpin *et al.* 1991; Fitz *et al.* 1993) shows that the impact of grant maintained status on the whole secondary education system has not been as great as anticipated. In health, the number of units which are not trusts is now very small. Only forty-four remained as directly managed units by April 1994 (Hospital and Health Services Year Book

1994). More than 90 per cent of hospital and community services revenue in England was spent in trusts by April 1994. Therefore the whole system of service is now based on contracts. Finally, the impact of the changes to membership at board level appears to be more profound in health than in education. There is a substantial shift towards a managerialist perspective, particularly in trusts. (Ferlie *et al.* 1993; Ashburner *et al.* 1993*a*). The combination of a full-time executive group, complemented by non-executive directors with largely business backgrounds (Cairncross, Ashburner, and Pettigrew 1991) accounts largely for this shift. On the other hand, school boards are much less dominated or led by expert managers. Professional headteachers have limited management experience to contribute from the executive side. Parent, teacher, and community representatives do not necessarily have management expertise, so the shift towards managerialism has been relatively slight. Indeed studies (Baginsky *et al.* 1991; Shearn *et al.* 1995) show that school boards are floundering in some instances with insufficient time, knowledge, and managerial expertise to cope with aspects of their role such as managing the budget.

Therefore one may conclude that whilst considerable change has taken place at the strategic apex of organizations in both health and education, the impact has been more substantial in health.

Changes to the Intra-Organizational Structures

The concept of a quasi-market as the basis for operation in the public sector not only introduces the need for a substantial shift in management thinking from management by hierarchy to management by contract, but also fundamentally changes the systems of management. As the basis for negotiating a contract, one has to define the service being offered, and the quantity and quality available at a set cost. Only then can a price for the service be agreed. Historically, in many parts of the public sector, even the precise definition of the service being offered was a novelty, whilst the reliable costing of specific services was rare. In this respect, the introduction of the quasi-market has had immediate, indirect impacts. In this section we will focus on just one of those: the consequent changes to the internal organization of units in health and education.

In the period immediately prior to the passing of the NHS and Community Care Act in 1990, those units, mainly acute hospitals, who had applied to become first wave trusts underwent a period of rapid structural change. In order to attain trust status, the hospital had to be reorganized on the basis of groupings around specific, defined services, which would become cost centres with devolved budgets. The period 1990-1 saw a rapid process of reorganization of units with the preferred structural model being that of the clinical directorate. For example, in one region by mid-1991, ten out of thirteen districts had established clinical directorates in all their acute units (Fitzgerald and Sturt 1992). Thus in a relatively short timespan, 77 per cent of all the acute units in the region had developed clinical directorates, though the devolution of budgets was largely incomplete. Only one district had had this structure in place for several years. What is particularly noticeable about this rapid restructuring is how externally driven the changes were. Prior to the White Paper *Working for Patients* which preceded the Act, the Resource Management Initiative had piloted a number of alternative models for organizing and structuring a health service with devolved budgeting (Disken *et al.* 1990). However, the effectiveness of these various alternatives had still not been assessed when the force of legislation engulfed the service, causing a largely untried and untested structure to be widely adopted.

One consequence of this choice of the clinical directorate model was that whilst it had been developed in the USA for acute hospitals, it was far less appropriate to community health and mental health services. Many of these latter services nevertheless felt pressurized into adopting the clinical directorate model.

The clinical directorate model is a subunit-level structure which is based on a service provided directly to patients. One of the early questions raised was how best to group and to define the boundaries of services. For example, historically, many clinical groups in hospitals were founded on the nature of the expertise being employed, rather than on the category of patient being treated. Thus some patients, such as the elderly, would traditionally have found themselves regularly moving between departments to see different specialists.

Research (Harwood and Boufford 1993) shows that the majority of clinical directorates are managed by a clinical director, frequently though not exclusively a doctor, managing on a part-time basis. The clinical director is supported by a management team, often consisting of a business manager and a staff manager. Clinical Directors are budget-holders, who then sit in a corporate capacity on the executive board of the hospital.

The clinical directorate structure and the management processes it supports represent a major shift from the dual management structure of general managers and professionals. One of the major criticisms of health service management, repeated over a number of years, was the separation of clinical practice decisions by doctors from resource decisions by general managers. This induced a situation where it was virtually impossible and certainly highly undesirable to impose resource limits on professionals. Now there is potentially greater coherence, because the clinical professionals who are responsible for the key decisions on service and thus spending are a part of the resource allocation process.

A second major change epitomized by this structure is the shift from individual, atomistic decisions to a team-based approach to managing the directorate. The clinical directorate operates on the basis of a business or service plan, upon which the contract will be agreed. The business planning process has to involve a more holistic analysis of the service, including staffing and costs. But the directorate is also managed by a team and to be successful, it is clear that the team has to work and to use complementary assets (Harwood and Boufford 1993).

As with all organizational structures, the clinical directorate structure is simply the skeletal framework supporting or inhibiting the systems and processes of management. In health, it is clear that there has been a dramatic change in the intra-unit structures in order to support management by contract. The structure adopted is based on care groups managed by a team. It involves the devolution of authority and budgets down to a lower level in the organization closer to the patient (or consumer). Finally, it is totally dependent on the inclusion of professionals in the management process for the first time. In many respects these changes may seem appropriate; certainly they would fit with the thrust of management thought and research about the more effective structures for managing a service organization. And yet these changes raise a series of issues and dilemmas.

Given the haste with which many health care organizations—from various sectors—made these structural changes, how is the effectiveness of the structure to be assessed? It is apparent that the imposition of a clinical directorate model in certain community health care locations conflicts with the locality management structures previously in place. The implications of operating within the clinical directorate structure are considerable, and demand the acquisition of new skills across a wide range of organizational members. Beyond skill acquisition, there are issues of attitude and the weight of history. Though the structures may appear, in the acute sector at least, to offer potential; this can only be realized with a major change in cultural values. To quote two specific examples, doctors have not traditionally given equal weight to the opinions of members of the nursing and paramedic professions. In the clinical directorate team management structure, they need to do just that. Another example would be the involvement of doctors directly in management decision-making and the resource allocation process. Many doctors do not have a high opinion of managers or management, indeed negative stereotypes abound on both sides (R. Stewart n.d., Elston 1991). Therefore they do not value becoming a manager and indeed some would see it as a betrayal of their profession (Fitzgerald 1994; Dopson 1993b).

In the education sector, the impact of the introduction of a market-based system on the individual school is markedly different. There is very little evidence to suggest that grant maintained schools have altered their organizational structures in any significant way. Research data (Halpin *et al.* 1991) suggest that grant maintained schools are characterized not so much by how different they are from local education authority schools of similar status and size, but by how alike they are. It is clear that in the early period between 1989–91, the schools which balloted for and were successful at attaining grant maintained status were a skewed group. The group contained well-above-average numbers of schools who were ex-grammar schools and also single-sex schools (Halpin *et al.* 1991; Fitz *et al.* 1993; King 1994). Nevertheless, this research provides no evidence to illustrate that they are adopting different structures or different kinds of management practices. They are distinguished by the manner and size of their funding. Two areas in which substantial changes are reported (Halpin *et al.* 1991) are in the relationships with the school board and in the area of reputation management. Reputation management is a demonstrable concern focusing on the outward-facing image presented by the school and its members to the public at large. It includes such actions as tightening up on the dress code for pupils, specifying how pupils should speak to staff and visitors, and improving the decorative order of the school buildings. These latter changes may be early evidence of a shift in management processes, if not in structures.

The key comparative question would seem to be why has the introduction of the quasi-market had a more significant impact on the structures of health care organizations, when compared with school organizations? There would appear to be two major factors to explain the differences. The first one is external to the school and is sector-wide. The development of the market in education has been a slower process than in health, starting in 1988 and still in 1994 only operating on a partial basis. Latest figures (King 1994) show that grant maintained schools represent only 3 per cent of all schools. It may therefore be argued that the market as such is not operating or is doing so only embryonically. Secondly, though budgets have been devolved, which is a substantial step for schools, there is no contracting process to act as the lever for change inside the school organization. Thus the school system, its organization, and its structures remain largely untouched by these changes.

4.3. Changes to the Technology and Delivery Systems

In putting forward our argument about the characteristics and criteria for transformational change, we have postulated the view that transformational change involves multiple processes of change from different sources occurring simultaneously. This section will discuss the impact of selected changes in the specialist technologies of the services, which in the continuing evolution of the knowledge base have continued to occur and are having a simultaneous and cumulative impact alongside the other changes already examined.

In health, we focus on two examples of significance. One is the development of non-invasive surgical technologies often referred to as micro-surgery, but in fact covering a wider range of alternative procedures than that. The second is the shift of care for patients with mental illnesses and learning disabilities from institutional care to community care. Neither of these changes can be said to have started at exactly the same time as the introduction of the quasi-market, indeed both predate this change. However, these long-term changes to the delivery and technological systems add to the pressure for major change.

Briefly, the advances in surgical techniques which have been gathering pace over the last ten years mean that many conditions which would previously have required a hospital stay can now be treated as day cases or with an overnight stop. Apart from the advantages which this gives to the patient in terms of lower risks from anaesthetics and less disruption to life, it has great cost advantages and allows many more patients to be treated. With such a combination of benefits to recommend it, it is hardly surprising that medical professionals and management alike have urged the wider adoption of such procedures (Russell *et al.* 1994) The impact of these advances has therefore been considerable and has meant the commissioning of new day surgery units and the closing of beds in acute hospitals.

The second technological advance is especially interesting, because it relates as much to changes in the social production of knowledge as to changes in 'hard' technologies such as drugs (though these do play a minor part). Much of the recent thrust of thinking in psychiatric care has argued that the institutional regime in large mental hospitals was not therapeutic for the majority of patients and was certainly unnecessary for most mentally handicapped people. The alternative idea was that care in smaller units in the community would be more appropriate and not create long-term effects, such as dependency. But such a policy whilst superficially simple, was difficult to implement as it involved the closure of long-stay, often large, institutions and the concurrent recommissioning of alternative smaller units. The management of these specific changes represents a substantial and complex management task, taking years for each unit involved (Ferlie 1990; McKee 1988). Whilst some policy-makers and government advocates had argued that the change would save money, in reality it was difficult to produce precise forecasts of the costs of the community care alternative, without knowing exactly what buildings and unit sizes would be established. Again the impact of this change is significant, changing the delivery of care to the mentally ill and support to those with learning disabilities.

Whilst these two selected examples, in common with many other advances, impact most significantly on the services provided to specific groups of patients they have been selected here because each of them has major capital implications and as such the impact of these changes has a chain effect with wider repercussions. These two examples, in combination, have instigated a massive and long-term reappraisal of the capital stock employed in health care. Large numbers of older hospital buildings have been or are being sold and quite different replacement units are being developed. The changes also have implications for the range and type of skills which are required to staff these new facilities. The justification for each change has been that patients will benefit and it will enable patient care to improve. Further evaluation is required to demonstrate that this is actually the case, particularly in the recommissioning of community based facilities for mentally ill patients. Lastly, all of these developments are occurring alongside the changes deriving more directly from the NHS and Community Care Act.

Comparing the situation in health with that existing in education, one might argue that education has never, over the last decade, been subject to the rate of technological change which has been normal in health care. Thus many of those professionals employed in secondary education have not been subject to and are not acclimatized to this rapid rate of technological change (Barber 1994; Hargreaves 1994). In a service which is delivered largely through the hands and presentation techniques of individual professional teachers, the impact of technology has not been nearly as great in the secondary education sector as it has, for example, in the post-experience education sector where the idea of open learning systems delivered mainly through computer-based training systems is commonplace. In primary and secondary education, the main external force for change in the delivery systems of learning to pupils has been the introduction of the National Curriculum. Whilst this has impacted on the specification of what is taught to some extent, some have argued (Armstrong 1991; Fergusson 1994) that it does not significantly change the true content of education. It can be manipulated and may either confirm or constrain good practice. More significantly, the National Curriculum specifies common standards and a common core curriculum which affects the total system of school management. It curtails the autonomy of headteachers and class teachers, limiting variation in what is learnt at a particular age and what children should have achieved as they pass from one stage to the next.

The argument put forward in the previous paragraph is not intended to imply that schools and the professionals who teach in them have not been placed under considerable pressure by the changes to the National Curriculum and the accompanying testing procedures. However, these pressures are largely ones of increased workload and inadequate resourcing for the changes. Research has shown (Coopers and Lybrand Deloitte 1988; Monck and Kelly 1992) that the available funding is inadequate to deliver the curriculum as intended. The constant pressure of shortage of resources does have an impact on the quality of the services provided and on the individual professionals, but the difference is that education staff have not been required to deal concurrently with large-scale technological change and innovation, in addition to change driven by a top–down government agenda.

4.4. Reconfiguration of Individual Roles and Power Relations

We now consider the changes which have occurred to key individual roles in health care and education and on the implications for power relations in these organizations. Attention will centre on selected roles, where change has had a significant impact.

We have already commented briefly in Section 4.2 on the changes in board composition at the strategic apex of health organizations. The interplay of executives and non-executives and the inclusion of particular functions within the board sets up a new dynamic. Associated with the structural changes in health organizations, outlined in Section 4.3, roles at the subunit level in the management of individual specialities have changed. These new roles also affect the dynamic of both the professional and the managerial political systems.

Tracing the implications of changes at the subunit level, it is evident that previously, most hospitals, community units, and mental hospitals or services were managed by a general manager with responsibility for the entire organization. Budgets were not normally devolved down to the specialities, though occasionally this was the case for support services, such as pharmacy and pathology. It was possible to track the costs of areas of care and to plan a budget. But spending was harder to manage directly, because it was largely incurred by clinicians, who did not report in a conventional line management relationship to the general manager. Clinicians worked as independent professionals, operating in a dual system where they had a clinical responsibility to a clinical head of speciality (or similar), whilst the administration and management of the whole unit was in the hands of a general manager. As discussed in Section 4.3, the changes which have now occurred include the internal restructuring of provider units. The role of clinical director has been created, as a new part-time management role, responsible for the running of a directorate. Despite their part-time nature, these are sizeable management roles. For example, research (Fitzgerald 1994) shows that clinical directors manage major budgets of up to £4.3m. The specification of the role of the clinical director is variable in different locations and still undergoing change (Harwood and Boufford 1993; Fitzgerald and Sturt 1992). In broad terms, there seem to be five main areas of activity and responsibility: these are strategic planning, setting quality standards, allocating the budget within the clinical directorate, developing the business plan, and supporting a customer orientation in all staff.

The significance of these roles lies in the fact that after a considerable history of failed efforts, clinicians have been drawn into the management process in substantial numbers. These new hybrid professional–manager roles represent an important bridge between the medical professionals and general managers. For the first time in many years, clinical professionals are directly involved in the decisions about how scarce resources should be deployed (many aspects of these professional roles will be discussed further in Chapter 7). They are also potentially in a far more knowledgeable position to deal with issues of performance and quality among professional colleagues. However, lack of management training, problems of motivation and work overload threaten the effectiveness of the clinical directors. The clinical management roles are also significant because most clinical directorates are managed by teams which include the director, a business manager, and possibly a staff manager. Such roles are frequently filled by people from different professional backgrounds, such as nursing or finance. Again, this represents a significant shift in approach, because it is clear that clinical directors cannot work successfully if the team members do not work together.

Further critical role changes have occurred in the purchasing roles in health authorities. As discussed in Chapter 2, the health authorities had to completely convert their operations from the line management roles they exercised in the past to become the purchasers of health care for a local population. This required the restructuring of the organization in response to these new demands, but also generated new roles unique to purchasing and previously unknown in health. This section will focus on two of these new roles: contracting and health needs assessment.

Purchasing organizations are responsible for defining, specifying, and agreeing contracts with health providers in both the public and private sectors. Because the system of resource allocation was previously centrally directed, there were few people in the health service who had skills in contracting, either in the setting-up and legal requirements of a contract or in the processes of negotiating contracts (Bennett and Ferlie 1994a; and 1994b). So in this instance, there was an immediate and urgent need to develop these skills or to acquire them in the market place. What is noticeable about the introduction and use of new and more commercial skills into an organization is that it challenges accepted ways of thinking and generates indirect changes (Whittington *et al.* 1994; McNulty *et al.* 1994).

The next example of the development of a new role is equally interesting, but quite different. In order to perform the new functions of purchasing health for the local population, there is for the first time the need to analyse the health needs of that population that is to examine and analyse demand. Again this represents a shift from a largely professionally led system, which had few mechanisms for accessing the views of users or would-be users. Now the district health authority has been given the responsibility of health needs assessment. This responsibility was allocated to the public health function in the district health authority, thus considerably enhancing the power and responsibility of that function. The director of public health is normally appointed to the board in most districts (Cairncross *et al.* 1991). Directors of public health had the daunting task of setting up systems to determine the health needs of the population largely from scratch. An even more difficult task is to determine priorities for health gain and care in a context of resource constraints.

The role of the director of public health has therefore changed dramatically in form, status, and focus. It is evident that this has created difficulties for individuals and for the professional speciality. Some individuals display concern about the nature of the current role and uncertainty about the managerial aspects of the role (Dawson *et al.* 1993). Given its prior history, the professional group faces problems in coming to terms with its newly acquired power base (Lewis 1987).

In health, therefore, it is evident that a range of key roles have changed in a significant way. These changes have impacted on power relations. First, in both purchaser and provider units, the introduction of non-executive directors with their external experience, has strengthened the managerialist perspective. (The detailed evidence underpinning this statement will be presented in Chapter 5.) Secondly, in trusts, there has been the creation of new professional management roles at board and speciality level. These roles can, and sometimes do, alter the relative power relations between the managers and the professionals. Professionals are involved in the key resource decisions and can have significant influence and power (Ferlie, Ashburner, and Fitzgerald 1993; Fitzgerald 1994; Elston 1991). These new powers are balanced against the increasing precedence given to managing within the contracts, which vests greater weight in the expertise of accountants and frames decisions. Purchasers have also experienced shifts of role and power, with considerable new influence moving towards the public health directorate.

In education, a more restricted process of change in individual roles has occurred, but is still ongoing. Within the school unit, the role of the headteacher has undergone the most substantial range of changes. First, the devolution of responsibility for the major part of the budget to schools under the local management of schools greatly extended the management responsibilities of headteachers (McGovern 1992; Broadbent *et al.* 1992; Marren and Levacic 1994). The role of the headteacher as the manager of the school system took a significant step forward, not just in terms of autonomy, but also in the greatly extended demand for management skills. Whereas in the past, the headteacher had been responsible for curriculum management and for key areas of staff management, the management role now embraces strategic planning, budgeting, resource allocation, and the entire system of cost control and monitoring. Grace (1993) emphasizes that the addition of these extensive management responsibilities impacts on the other, previously core, aspects of the headteacher's leadership role, such as pedagogical leadership and moral leadership. These points are reinforced by Foreman, who outlines the new demands of the headteacher's role in terms of planning, personnel management, pedagogy and curriculum development, and the management of change. As a result of his analysis he takes the view that role overload will become a major issue.

All of these responsibilities have to be exercised within the context of a new governing body, with a different composition and extended powers. Research indicates an uneasy relationship between many heads and their governing bodies (Baginsky *et al.* 1991; Shearn *et al.* 1995; Evetts 1994). Whilst many governing bodies had delegated certain powers to headteachers, these studies showed that there was considerable disagreement about what these powers were and a disturbing lack of clarity. In many instances, headteachers were operating in largely grey areas by default. Whilst it was clear that some headteachers found the advice and support of the governors, and the chair in particular, invaluable, others felt threatened or, to quote one description, 'like a pawn or a minion'. Earlier research by Jones in 1987 illustrated an even more negative picture with headteachers feeling unsupported and undermined by governors. In a similar vein, some authors (Grace 1993; Evetts 1994), speculate that many headteachers will see their acknowledged position as the leading professional threatened. However, empirical evidence from early pilot studies in Scotland (Munn 1991) does not support this concern. Governing bodies in the pilot were seen to be largely supportive of their heads, even questioning central government policy on their behalf.

Clearly the new responsibilities given to headteachers represent a major personal challenge to individuals and to the profession (McHugh and McMullan 1995). As in the case of doctors, few professional teachers have had any significant management training. But unlike the health care context, headteachers are more isolated in two ways. First, the composition of the boards of governors does not automatically mean that they are supported by executive and non-executive members who have relevant management and other professional expertise. Hemmings *et al.* (1990) provide evidence of the urgent need for governors to improve their knowledge of educational issues. But non-executives do not receive an honorarium for their work on the school board and it is therefore more difficult to insist that volunteers undertake periods of training. Nor do headteachers operate as part of a management team. Whilst team management systems are in place in many secondary schools and these provide a useful foundation on which to build, they are nevertheless part-time management teams with mixed levels of expertise. The situation in primary schools is worse with many headteachers managing in isolation.

The extension of the head's role to include financial control and responsibilities is by no means the whole story. As already mentioned, the headteacher has a changed relationship with the board of governors and with the local education authority. Additionally, each school has to produce a school development plan, which is an important strategic document intended to identify the longer term plans for the school. Leask (1992) demonstrates that school development plans also encourage the process of self-evaluation and review. Such processes are particularly important to quality as they facilitate improvement and progress. Whilst the means for producing the plan is not specified, it is clear that in practice headteachers will be expected to take a lead role. Indeed research results (Baginsky *et al.* 1991) illustrate that many plans are drawn up entirely by headteachers and taken to the governors for approval. Again this activity places different demands on headteachers who have previously been in a reactive role, often awaiting the outcomes of local education authority decisions.

In considering the headteacher's role in relation to the rest of the teaching staff, it is more difficult to analyse the extent of the changing relationships. As the headteacher takes on a wider portfolio of management responsibilities, a consequent increase in delegation down the hierarchy is to be anticipated. The evidence supports the argument that senior members of staff are spending increasing proportions of their time on management and administrative tasks (Helps 1994). The extent to which there is delegated authority in a school, for example, for staff development seems to vary widely. C. Day (1985) concluded that the degree to which teachers are involved in the school's decision-making correlates positively with their level of satisfaction with the school management.

A second major area of change in education is in the roles of staff within the local education authority. As discussed in Chapter 2, in a similar way to health authorities, local education authorities have moved from the direct management of a local school system into a purchasing and enabling role. Formula funding establishes the local education authority as a buyer of education services from its schools. It has considerable discretion in setting the terms of the contract. The local education authority can also regulate the internal market by determining the number and type of schools and the categories of pupils they can admit. In its second role the local education authority acts as a seller of specialist services to the local schools. Such services include building and grounds maintenance; educational psychologists; advisory teachers and financial administration such as payroll. Both these organizational roles and skills base require individual roles to change substantially.

Whilst the local education authority has always had an overseeing role, which included central planning of provision, this will now operate via the internal market as the means of control. Levacic (1992) argues that local education authorities are now adopting an M-form organization separating operational and strategic decision-making. On the one hand, this creates strategic visioning roles, which require strategic planning and management expertise. On the other hand, it creates a second set of roles which require the marketing and contracting of specialist services to purchasers. These roles demand marketing expertise and knowledge to specify the content and negotiate agreement on contracts. These are all entirely new skills which in some instances will have to be grafted on to specialist professional skills.

Comparatively, the range and scope of changes to roles and to power relations is seen to be more widespread in health than in education. Substantial change has occurred in both contexts, but there are critical variations. In health, a wider range of key roles have changed in both purchasers and providers, whilst in education many of the changes in the provider organizations have centred on the headteacher. If anything, this has served to reinforce the previous power structure and concentrate more power on an already powerful figure.

4.5. Changes to the Cultures of the Organizations

Organizational culture has been described as the 'glue' which holds the organization together (Schein 1983, 1985). As suggested in Section 4.1, many writers in discussing effective approaches to radical or strategic change stress the role of culture (Kanter 1983 and 1989; Tichy 1983; Nadler 1987).

The core argument proposes that longer term change in an organizational system will not be effected or sustained, unless the underlying values and belief systems of the members shift. This may be particularly true if the foundational logic of the system is changing, as when a public sector organization shifts to a market-based and more commercial mode of operation.

But culture is an ambiguous and loose concept, which is difficult to operationalize. Indeed, if one defines organizations as patterns of meaning, values, and behaviour (G. Morgan *et al.* 1983) then organizations are cultures. Pettigrew (1990) questions the utility of the term and the concept, and in particular questions the effect which management action can have on culture. Even in the relatively more simple and concrete definitions of culture, such as Schein (1985) and Smircich (1983), the different levels of visibility and analysis are acknowledged. These definitions emphasize that the visible manifestations of culture such as the portraits of past chairmen on the walls of bank boardrooms are only the outward signs of standards and values. The norms of behaviour and their enactment are another critical level of the expression of culture. But all of these are underpinned by the values held by organizational members. Meyerson and Martin (1987) distinguish three different views of culture which help to expose ambiguities and contradictions. They identify three paradigms: culture as an integrative mechanism; culture as characterized by diversity and differentiation; and finally, culture as ambiguity. Emerging from these debates, it is interesting to note that the second paradigm, culture as diversity, embraces and recognizes the existence of subcultures in many organizations.

In relation to our evidence concerning transformational change in organizations, it may be useful to suggest that more emphasis may need to be given to patterns of meaning and the cognitive frameworks in use, as well as to values, if we are to comprehend how organizations change fundamentally. Recent literature has pointed to the significance of cognitive frameworks and the mind-sets of organizational members, suggesting that effective transformation can only be achieved if these cognitive frames alter (Hinings and Greenwood 1989; Isabella 1990; Giola and Chittipeddi 1991; Bartunek, Lacey, and Wood 1992; and Bartunek 1993).

Finally, it is significant that much of the literature from the private sector has stressed the need for congruence between organizational strategy and culture if the organization is to compete successfully (Kanter 1989).

In reviewing the preceding themes in this chapter, the remainder of this section will focus on the cultural impact of these changes in health and education.

Within health care, there is evidence of slight shifts in the extent to which providers take account of the requirements of their consumers. For example, there is evidence of reputation management being taken more seriously with the increased use of public relations and press management to influence the image of the organization, as presented to the local public. Small, but significant, indicators of this are visible in the changes to signposting and car parks in many trusts. Less overt but equally significant were the growing number of trusts in the sample who had bought or retained specialist public relations advice. However, a much greater cultural shift is evidenced by alterations in the balance of power, intra-professionally. Overall, one of the most substantial cultural shifts that has occurred is in the professional hierarchies. Specialist consultants in provider units now listen to the requests and preferences of GP fundholders, because they are purchasers of health care, in a way which would have been considered extraordinary a few years ago. There has been a dramatic shift of power towards primary care. This is underpinned by the power of the GP fundholder as purchaser, but also by the changes in health technology towards less invasive techniques, the movement of mentally ill patients into the community, and the growing voice of advocacy groups demanding supported care at home. Culturally, this represents a major change to the power levers of the health care organization as a whole (Ashburner and Fitzgerald 1995; Elston 1991; Dawson *et al.* 1992 and 1993). In essence, attention shifts from the high technology and potentially technically interesting areas of medicine, which excite the professional interest of many doctors and moves towards the areas of high patient demand, such as care of the elderly. Gradually the values of the culture may change to accommodate this shift.

Alongside these changes are significant indicators of increased managerialism in all parts of the system. At the top of the organization, this shift in thinking and to a lesser extent in values is most apparent. First, there is a more proactive approach taken to the management of scarce resources (Harrison and Pollitt 1994; Elston 1991; Butler 1992; Walby and Greenwell 1994). Secondly, the information bases are improving and the bases for decisions are both sounder and more overt (Harrison and Pollitt 1994). The indicators of change are perhaps strongest if one examines the costing and specifications of contracts and the gradual improvement in the specification of quality criteria. The setting and monitoring of such standards impacts on the methods of service provision. However, improvements in data are still very limited when one examines assessment of local health need and priorities.

Increased managerialism can also be seen at the subunit level in provider organizations. The substantial changes in the management of clinical specialities is a prime example (Harwood and Boufford 1993; Fitzgerald 1994). The increase in managerial approaches has certainly led to shifts in the balance of power and activities between medical professionals and general managers. However, on balance we would not argue that this has been a simple one-way flow from professionals to managers. (These points will be reviewed in more detail in Chapter 7.)

Every bit as significant as the shift towards managerial perspectives and concerns has been the shift from management by hierarchy to greater management by contract. Many of the traditional line management relationships, for example between the district health authority and the hospital units, have been swept aside and replaced by a different, contract-based relationship. This is also true of inside provider units, with service departments such as radiography, developing internal contracts with the departments they supply. A contract-based relationship not only changes the nature and skills of management, but tends to be an overt and more open process of inter- and intra-organizational relationships. Management by contract has several effects on organizational culture, as it disrupts the established hierarchical power bases, opening up the possibility for new groups to step in. It may offer new information, which can be used as the basis for power and control, such as data on increases in demand. And finally, it challenges the informal networks of managers and professionals, by disseminating information more widely (Bennett and Ferlie 1994*b*).

In reviewing the situation in health, it is apparent that some cultural changes are evident, though still not well embedded. Many changes are driven by contracts and by at least the partial acceptance by managers and professionals that some changes were needed. There is no substantial evidence that competition and the market ethos are greatly valued. Nor is there much evidence to support the notion that patient or consumer choice has been increased (Glennerster *et al.* 1994; C. Williamson 1992; Walby and Greenwall 1994). Whilst others such as GPs and advocacy groups are vying for the position of patients' representative, patients cannot directly influence the purchase of health care. Consumers do not appear to be having any greater impact on the operation of the system than in the past, with a few marginal exceptions. Whilst there are indicators of a shift in power towards primary care and GP fundholders, this has not been followed by a substantial shift in funds or major alteration in the profile of contracts. The setting of contracts is still not driven by a comprehensive system of needs assessment in a locality. As a result, the community seem to have few leverage points into the system.

Comparatively, the picture in education is different. There is evidence here too of the school system beginning to adopt a changed attitude to the external world. There is clear evidence of reputation management, particularly in the grant maintained schools (Halpin *et al.* 1991; Glover 1994). One specific aspect of this is the rise in exclusions. Parffrey (1994) documents the substantial rise in exclusions, which she suggests are caused by anxieties over image and performance. Lee (1992) underlines similar concerns in relation to children with special educational needs.

The devolution of responsibilities to individual schools has led to a major shift of power away from the local education authority and towards the school (Levacic 1992; HM Inspectorate 1992; Ranson 1993). In this process, the headteachers appear to have gained the greatest increase in power (Evetts 1994).

One of the greatest differences between the education sector and the health sector is that parents are demonstrably exercising choice and schools are responding (West *et al.* 1995; Coldron and Boulton 1991; David *et al.* 1994). The publication of league tables, whilst controversial, may not impact directly on parents' choices of schools, but there is evidence that the local public reputation of the school influences choice. Parents are also represented on the governing bodies of schools and thus can have an influence on the decisions taken within the individual school. There is both greater access to information on the local school system and greater involvement by consumers (or their parents!). We would not suggest that all parents are satisfied with the degree of choice or the local education authorities' role (*Sunday Times*, 4 June 1995).

Within education, there is also evidence of increased managerialism, and a shift from line management to management by contract. The professionals in education are clearly affected by the changes to the system overall and many appear to feel driven by the external nature of many of the levers for change. Heads and classroom teachers report different degrees of satisfaction and concern (Marren and Levacic 1994) with the changes occurring within schools. The main reported concern of class teachers was that financial considerations predominate over educational ones. Within the school boundary, there is less evidence of changes to roles and structures when compared with health care. The professional hierarchy might almost be said to be reinforced by some of the changes. These data must be treated with caution. However, there is some embryonic evidence of internal restructuring now emerging (Penney and Evans 1995). This is that these changes are the result of the value contact in which teachers' work is being changed by the introduction of market forces. Within the school boundary, there is less change within the teaching profession than is seen in health care. The professional hierarchy might almost be said to be reinforced by some of the changes.

Overall, it is difficult to substantiate the view that, as yet, there has been a radical shift in values in health or education. One might conclude that there is less internal cultural change within the whole of the education system than within health. On the other hand, the consumer and the local community are attaining greater influence and leverage on the education sector and still seem to have achieved only minimal influence on health care. In the longer term this may prove significant. In health, there does appear to be an embryonic shift in cognitive frameworks. This is not a simple movement from concepts of a freely available public service to market-based goods or services. It is, rather, an embryonic reformulation of a public service, within a market economy.

In health care, data suggests that some managers and medical professionals are accepting the concept of a bounded and resource constrained service, whilst maintaining the need for equity, access, and public accountability. Many do not necessarily accept that an internal or regulated quasi-market can effectively deliver these aspects (Harrison and Pollitt 1994; Dopson 1993*b*; Dawson *et al.* 1992). In education, resource constraints appear less widely accepted within the education service. And whilst the concept of parental choice may be acceptable, many argue that the reality is choice for some, but not all parents. Thus, one sees debate about the core values of both services.

4.6. Conclusions

This chapter has taken the concept of 'top–down' change and restructuring discussed in Chapter 2 and extended it to incorporate a new question. Can the strategic change now occurring in the public sector be described as transformational change? The evidence presented in the earlier chapters certainly confirms that radical change is occurring, across the public sector. And in reviewing the organizational change literature at the beginning of this chapter, it was apparent that writers and researchers are increasingly referring to the concept of transformational change (e.g. Beckhard and Pritchard 1992; Romanelli and Tushman 1994). Yet the term and the concept are loosely defined and indeed descriptions of so-called transformational change were extremely varied in content. Blumenthal and Haspeslagh (1994: 101) in particular, draw attention to the fact that 'a consensus on what transformation is will not emerge until it is better defined and given a framework so that firms facing similar issues and circumstances can make meaningful comparisons'. Therefore to facilitate our assessment of the extent and radicality of change in health care and education, we proposed six indicators of transformational change in section 4.1. We have used these throughout this chapter to examine the evidence from research.

In analysing the extent to which transformational change is taking place in health and education against our chosen indicators, we would argue that there is much stronger evidence of multiple changes at interrelated levels in health than in education.

Comparing our assessments with the work of Blumenthal and Haspeslagh (1994), one may comment on several aspects. Their proposed definition of transformation is 'that to qualify as a corporate transformation, a majority of individuals in an organization must change their behaviour' (1994: 101). Whilst we would agree with their stress on behavioural change and acknowledge that structural or technological change of itself can achieve little, the definition does not assist us to understand the processes by which such behavioural change is to be achieved. Moreover, it is difficult, using this definition to distinguish between strategic and transformational change. Indeed the authors underline in their own typology of transformations, that different processes using different levers can lead to transformation. Their definition therefore still appears to need refinement. Our own proposed definition offers, we believe, a more comprehensive framework for identifying transformations.

Another issue raised by comparison of our assessments with the Blumenthal and Haspeslagh definition is the relatively narrow base of private sector examples upon which the latter is founded.

Our examples are drawn from the public sector which is essentially different, and produces a broader base for comparison. One key difference identified between the two contexts is the role of the senior management in driving for or facilitating a transformation. Whilst Blumenthal and Haspeslagh acknowledge that there are conflicting views on the role of top management in a successful transformation, they adopt a firm stance, stating 'In our view, strategic transformation requires strong leadership from the top team' (1994: 105). Our own evidence would support a more cautious position, with greater possibility of variation in differing contexts. In health care for example, the changes are externally driven by the government and the senior managers' and senior professionals' roles appear to be to convert and divert the reforms into a set of strategies which are capable of implementation.

Transformation, on our evidence, has not meant the total acceptance of the replacement of the old system by a market-based system, but rather a blend of old and new which produces something radically different. Transformation has occurred as a result of the multiplicity of forces for change, some driven externally, through the changes to quasi-market, but others driven by professional and technological change. Though directions have been set, they have sometimes been diverted, and unintended as well as intended consequences have resulted.

Another interesting comparative factor is the timescale taken to achieve transformation. Blumenthal and Haspeslagh indicate that transformation can take between two and ten years to achieve, depending on the approach adopted. We would argue that whilst their estimates of timescales match our own, factors such as the prior history of change and the context are as relevant as the processes used. The combined influence of prior history and context on the timescale for change has been highlighted previously by others writers (Hinings and Greenwood 1989; Child and Smith 1987; Pettigrew *et al.* 1992). We would suggest that our current research evidence reinforces the importance of these factors in understanding probable timescales for change. Indeed it appears that one distinguishing feature between the secondary education sector and the health care sector is that the latter has undergone a prior history of significant and sustained organizational change, which has prepared staff for the latest phase of changes.

We would therefore argue that transformation is under way in health and is partially complete. For completion, the changes to the organizational culture, in particular, need to be sustained and this will require, we believe, a longer period of sustained effort.

In considering the evidence from education, the relatively slower pace of change must be noted. There is not the same combination of multiple external and internal forces for change in this sector. Nor have the external changes been driven with equal vigour in education as in health. There is further recent evidence of the government backing away from some of its original intentions, with the reduction in testing on the National Curriculum and some movement in the refinement of the league table criteria. One might argue that the education professionals have fought a more vigorous defence of their position than the medical profession. However, this might be a hasty and unsubtle conclusion to draw, since there is evidence that medical professionals are successfully flexing their muscles and ousting some of the more macho managers and non-executives.

The data suggests that the external forces of consumer and local community may be having a more direct impact in education, than in health. In the longer term, this may produce radical change in education.

Across the examples, it is clear that professional battles are still very much alive. Professionals argue to maintain an autonomy which they see as their right, against the pressures of increased managerialism. Perhaps most interestingly of all there is equal turmoil within the professions, particularly within health, and the changes to intra-professional power positions are notable.

Overall, one of the critical unresolved issues to emerge from the data is the timescale and nature of cultural or behavioural change. The definition propounded by Blumenthal and Haspeslagh places behavioural change at the core of the definition of organizational transformation. And yet the estimation and assessment of when the majority of individuals have changed their behaviour is methodologically fraught. For example, does majority refer simply to numbers or is status an influencing variable? In the latter case, one moves towards the idea of changing a critical mass of people in the organization. Furthermore what kinds of changed behaviour count? Our own original set of criteria for assessing transformation included the notion of a change in the culture. This is also an ambiguous and loose term, which is difficult to put into operation. Indeed, in analysing our data, we are left with doubts as to whether the evidence we have found of changed behaviour and some changed organizational norms can be credited as complete or partial culture change. This analytical process has led to a reassessment of our proposed criteria for judging an organizational transformation. Drawing on the work of Giola and Chittipeddi (1991), Isabella (1990), and Bartunek (1993), it may be more accurate and precise to suggest that there has to be evidence of change in the cognitive frameworks or mind-sets of organizational members for a successful transformation. Such shifts may be easier to assess and to put into operation. The analysis could be based on more accessible data. These might include the ranking or weighting attributed to different criteria, such as cost versus patients' ease of access in taking management decisions. Where these criteria or their rank order were seen to shift in a consistent pattern over time, one might conclude that the cognitive frame of reference had altered. We would propose substituting the criterion of evidence of a significant and consistent shift in the cognitive frameworks in use, particularly by management for our previous sixth criterion of the development of a new culture.

Finally, the issue of alternative, effective change strategies for large organizational systems is reopened. The use of top–down, externally driven, or power-driven change strategies have often been characterized as less effective or less sustainable in the long term, except in response to crisis. Here in health and education, we see such strategies occurring and having significant impact. This raises many questions. About the relevance of contact, is it different in the public sector? About the role of sustained external pressure when linked to internal levers and seized by some internal stakeholders, is it an example of external pressures being hijacked? And finally, about the over simplification of top-down versus bottom-up concepts, is the minimum condition for successful strategic change engagement at several levels in the organization?

BOARD COMPOSITION: MANAGERS AND 'MAGISTRATES'

5.1. Introduction

The influence of the New Right on public sector reforms, as described in earlier chapters, has led to the introduction of the concept of market-based competition and the attempt to create a more entrepreneurial ethos, both of which are based firmly on models and ideologies from the private sector. A related and important element of public sector reform processes has been the transference of the private sector board model to the strategic apex of the new operating units and purchasing groups, as briefly described in Chapter 4. Previous forms of authorities with direct or indirect local authority influence and democratic accountability have been removed and the new board model introduced. Within the health service, this reform, unlike others, was not optional but statutorily imposed and has a number of major implications for the development of the new public management.

This chapter will look first at the increase in the number of non-elected bodies in the public sector with their implications for local democratic control. The new NHS authorities and boards are just one example, but a significant one, of this recent phenomenon. Secondly, it will examine the private sector board model which has influenced the new composition of NHS boards, with its clear implications for the growth of managerialism. It will consider how appropriate this model is for board effectiveness, corporate governance, and probity. The increasing power of executive and non-executive directors is one of the distinctive features of the new public management and can be seen to be both an objective and a means in the process of reform.

In examining the trend towards the introduction of non-elected bodies to run public services, it is essential to have information on who the board members are and how the process of accountability operates. In discussing boards, the issues of financial probity and corporate governance have come to the fore in both the public and the private sector. (*The Economist* 1994: Charkham 1994). Whilst these are key elements of a board's operations, it is essential also to emphasize the importance of assessing its effectiveness. The composition of the board is a critical element for all these issues. (Conyon 1994). Changes to the composition and membership of the new health authorities and trusts within the health service are a prime example of this process within the public sector, given the large number of new health service boards, the speed of development, and the high political profile and visibility of the NHS. Across England, Scotland, and Wales, over half of the forty biggest public sector spenders and largest organizations, run by non-elected bodies, are health service authorities and boards.

Section 5.3 will present data from our NHS study on who the members of these new boards are, their experience, motivation, and attitudes to the reforms and also look at the impact of these changes with regard to accountability and the growth of managerialism. Chapter 6 will develop this theme by looking at the role and effectiveness of the new boards and the influence of members at this strategic level. The concept of board effectiveness should lie at the heart of this discussion, given that the rationale of the White Paper *Working for Patients* (Cm 555, 1989), for changes to the composition of the authorities, was to make them more business-like.

5.2. The Growth of Non-Elected Bodies

Although the number of central non-elected bodies, or quangos, has declined since 1979, those which are regionally or locally based have greatly increased. This has resulted in a threefold increase overall, with over 2,300 bodies and 17,000 appointed members (Skelcher 1993). As the *Financial Times* (14 January 1993) stated, non-elected bodies now control more than a fifth of public spending. This includes running the health service, distributing funds to higher and further education, and dispensing legal aid. Bodies such as the Health and Safety Executive, the inner city development corporations, and the training and enterprise councils are closely interrelated with private sector organizations. Such activities are extending as schools and public housing projects are increasingly moving away from local authority control. A European Policy Forum Report (1992) argued that the UK's public services are increasingly being run by a new élite that cannot be held to account, raising the question of the accountability of the new-style organizations.

The first Thatcher Government was determined to reduce the number of quangos as it wished to limit the power of Whitehall and promote a free market economy and by the end of its term there were 500 fewer. Subsequently, new quangos were created in the shadow of the old. For example, as the seventeen English new town development corporations were wound up, new urban development corporations were set up. The Manpower Services Commission was abolished but its training functions were passed to more than eighty new training and enterprise councils and to local enterprise companies in Scotland. This was defended in guidelines issued by the Cabinet Office in 1985, which said that new bodies were acceptable if they were 'the most appropriate and cost-effective solution'.

Thus by 1990/1 non-elected bodies were responsible for spending £41.7 bn, three times the amount for 1978/9 and 20 per cent above the rate of inflation. Other reforms in process in the public sector can be expected to increase their number and spending levels further. Many of these new bodies are being created to manage public services as independent, competing organizations with no direct accountability, such as NHS trusts. Trusts now account for over 450 new bodies and if in addition, the Government's projection on schools opting for grant-maintained status is fulfilled, total numbers will be increased by a further 1,000.

Accountability and the democratic deficit are now central issues. J. Stewart (1992) has described the removal of a number of functions from local democratic control and has criticized the non-elected bodies as acting as a 'new magistracy'. Not only has control been removed from local authorities who are directly accountable to the local population but it is argued that these new bodies have no new form of accountability even to the users of the services. As the European Policy Forum argues, this leaves public services increasingly under the control of unelected boards whose members are answerable only to the ministers who appoint them and provide funds. At the centre, the fragmentation of parts of the Civil Service into agencies also reduces the direct line of accountability to ministers. Lord Bancroft, previously the head of the Civil Service, who resigned his post during the last Thatcher administration, speaking on Radio 4 (4 February 1995) identified the key question in the creation of agencies as the issue of accountability. He believed that the fragmentation of services had reduced what had been a direct line of accountability to a minister to a cat's cradle of confused and indirect lines. There is also, in Britain, no body of administrative law to regulate their activities. Similar bodies in the USA are required to publicize proposed policy changes and give opportunities for informed comment. The issue of account-ability will be developed further in Chapter 8.

The development of these public sector bodies has led to claims that the Conservatives have used patronage to appoint Conservative supporters to key positions. Baroness Denton, then junior minister at the Department of Trade and Industry, responsible for 804 public appointments, was quoted in the *Independent* (1993) as saying that she could not remember 'knowingly appointing a Labour Party supporter'. Analysis by the *Financial Times* (1993) of the chairs of the ten largest NHS and the thirty largest non-NHS bodies, shows that the only known political affiliation was Conservative. None of the top forty was a known Labour party member or Liberal Democrat. Whilst the appointment of thousands of people to the new health authorities and trusts in the early 1990s did not at that stage create a major controversy, a similar plan in 1994 relating to the creation of new bodies, with government-appointed members, to govern the police was met with considerable resistance from within the police service.

The *Financial Times*'s (1993) analysis showed that two-thirds of non-elected members were from business and industry. This marks a move away from appointing professional public sector managers. The preference for outsiders as opposed to public sector managers or professionals is also shown by the fact that the new health service bodies no longer have statutory places for health professionals with a representational role. It is not just a question of who the new members are but their level of influence. In education the most important quango until the 1980s was the Schools Council, which had reserved places for nominees of the teachers' unions, the local authorities, parent and employers' organizations, as well as for those of the Secretary of State. Despite the representational nature of its composition, schools and local authorities were not required to follow its recommendations. Now there are two bodies, the National Curriculum Council and the Schools Examination and Assessment Council, with considerable powers to define for all schools finer details of curriculum and ages at which children should attain certain basic skills. The members of these bodies are all appointed by the Secretary of State for Education with the potential that appointments will reflect the ideological views of the incumbent minister. The *Financial Times* survey confirmed that the chairs were not representative of the people for whom they provided a service: for example, only two were female and almost half had gone to public school.

Given the increase in the number and importance of non-elected bodies and their proliferation at the national and local level, it is important that the issues around the management of public services, the way in which members are recruited and appointed, and the characteristics of those members, are debated. The process of the selection of people to chair authorities and to become members of authorities is also important given their role in ensuring probity and accountability. Klein (1994) suggests that the criteria for selection should be made apparent to ensure that independence and a willingness when necessary to confront managers and ministers are the main qualifications rather than pliability and political correctness.

5.3. The Transference of Private Sector Models to the Public Sector

The process of appointment of members of non-elected bodies to run public services and its lack of openness, are only part of the debate surrounding the new boards. There is also the question of the efficacy of changes to board composition designed to empower managers and whether such private sector models are appropriate for the public sector. Klein (1994) questions whether it is possible to import more business-like methods into the NHS without at the same time weakening dedication to the collective interests of the service. He believes that the introduction of entrepreneurship and such features as performance-related pay run the risk of bringing with them self-seeking behaviour on the part of individuals. This raises the question of whether the private sector model can accommodate traditional public sector values or even continue to see them as important.

In considering further the debate of whether management skills are generic or contextually specific, as raised in Chapter 1, it is important to examine particular examples of the direct application of private sector structures into the public sector, such as the use of the private sector board model. Theories of management have as a central concern the different conditions within which management occurs. Thus organizations have been categorized in various ways, by sector, size, function, markets, and so on. Even within a single organization there is recognition that different functions may require different management styles. Many writers stress the fragmented and intuitive nature of actual management activity (Kotter 1982; Mintzberg 1973; Pettigrew 1987), where the variables in the wider context are of critical importance (Hales 1986). The sheer complexity and variation of what the private sector terms 'management' is encapsulated in what has come to be known as 'contingency theory' (that is, the form of management that emerges is that which is most appropriate to a given organizational context). Such a school of thought would be unlikely to recommend the direct transfer of models from one organizational setting to another. If private sector models and ideologies are to be used by public sector reformers to introduce more effective management into the public sector, it needs to be asked: which private sector models do they chose and why? The basic premiss that private sector models will lead to greater effectiveness also needs to be examined.

There is no one generic model of management identifiable within the private sector. At an organizational level the government reforms assume a very crude or oversimplified model of the private sector based upon concepts of markets and competition. These not only fail to acknowledge the high incidence of cooperation that exists between organizations, even direct market competitors, at other levels (such as product development) but also fail to understand the strengths of the planning model which are not replicated in the market model. Taking the specific instance of board composition, it needs to be determined to what extent this reflects reality or some ideal, and whether there is any evidence that a board of directors model could cope with the needs of the public sector or whether the outcome would be more business-like public services.

An alternative perspective on the transferability of management structures is taken by writers who see management approaches as being equally relevant for all organizations regardless of differences in context. Advocates of entrepreneurial management, like Kanter *et al.* (1992) and Peters (1992), maintain the relevance of this approach across the public–private divide. Du Gay's review (1993) of Osborne and Gaebler's book on entrepreneurial management in the public sector (1992) succinctly highlights the flaws in their arguments. Osborne and Gaebler have described an approach to introducing reform into the public sector which reflects the ideas behind this new entrepreneurial model. They see bureaucracy as the enemy of 'good governance' and the impetus for the change growing from customer demands for more choice, quality, and responsiveness. It must be remembered that a bureaucratic style is not found exclusively in the public sector and that it developed as an organizational form that was the most appropriate for the needs of a particular type of organization. Many private sector firms, certainly well into the 1970s, also displayed strong bureaucratic styles (Clegg 1990). Since then both the private and the public sector have been seeking to develop more flexible and responsive management styles. (Hedlund 1994; C. A. Bartlett and Ghoshall 1995; Ferlie and Pettigrew 1994a).

Osborne and Gaebler's ideas can be seen as compatible with the New Right ideology but they attempt to dismiss this comparison by suggesting that the American government's route to a more business-like public sector in the 1980s was very crude and only concerned with the achievement of markets and competition via privatization. This is an oversimplification and does not acknowledge that privatization was merely one of a number of means for achieving much broader range of objectives such as greater managerialism and less powerful professional groups. Thus in the NHS the process of the empowerment of management and the introduction of markets, which parallels the process of privatization carried out elsewhere, are seen only as mechanisms for increasing efficiency. They describe the privatization exercise as having been a failure and they present the entrepreneurial model as ideologically neutral.

The selection of entrepreneurial methods, as the means to achieve managerialism and control over professionals, cannot be presented as a socially or politically neutral decision. The advocacy of competition and markets is incompatible with collectivism and planning of services. For example, the feasibility of long-term planning for the provision of services with equity of access, quality and distribution cannot be assured in market conditions. In management terms the concept of entrepreneurialism includes decentralization and making people more responsible for their areas (that is, empowering them). However, as we have seen, a corollary to this empowerment is fragmentation and reduced accountability. What also needs to be assessed is the extent to which this decentralized empowerment is in fact a reality. What level of autonomy do the boards in the NHS have? The limited autonomy of trust boards has already been explored. How does this compare with the autonomy and the level of control over their organizations held by a private sector board?

To acknowledge that the public and private sectors have a number of basic differences but still insist that entrepreneurial ideas are as relevant in one sector as the other pays insufficient regard to the different types and levels of responsibility that public sector managers have. Most importantly they are there to serve the public interest and guarantee a defined level of service. J. Stewart and Walsh (1992) argue that these differences create specific conditions and additional requirements of managers which relate to notions of need, equity of treatment, and access to services. The positive features of traditional public sector management relate to the strengths of the bureaucratic style in ensuring a lack of corruption and patronage. Weber (1947) emphasized the irreducibility of the different spheres of the politician, the bureaucrat, and the entrepreneur and the consequent necessity of applying different protocols of management to them. Ackroyd *et al.* (1990) go further and argue that public services form a distinctive form of work organization. One key difference between entrepreneurial and bureaucratic action is that the entrepreneur is a guide or enabler rather than a doer. Not only does this encourage fragmentation but it creates problems of control, as the providers of services are moved away from regulatory bodies and thus direct accountability.

Whilst aspects of bureaucratic organization may require change to create a more flexible, responsive, organization, this need not necessitate its wholesale denigration. There are as many dangers endemic in an entrepreneurial culture as there are in a bureaucratic one. It is thus naïve to assume that models, personnel, or ideas from the private sector or of an entrepreneurial nature are inherently superior to anything in the public sector, since too little account is taken of the weaknesses of private sector models and the strengths of the public administration model that are being lost.

The argument that models from the private sector are not directly transferable to the public sector might in itself also be too simplistic. What needs to be distinguished more clearly are the areas where the public or private context might affect management approach and areas where it might not. Both types of organization are responsible for the management of resources and many operational issues are broadly comparable. Here there is a need to examine the value of various management techniques, which should owe no particular allegiance to either sector, but given the private sector dominance of management literature, may be seen to emanate from there. There are specific lessons and techniques which can be learnt across sectors but given the distinctions between the public and the private, these need to be applied selectively and be judged on appropriateness to the organization and its objectives.

There is a case to be presented that the changing nature of public sector work, the growth in size of public sector organizations, and the changing demands being made on them, would inevitably lead to the need for change. Gunn (1989) sees this process occurring primarily from within the old administrative élite rather than having been imposed from outside. The desirability of the development of public administration into public management is less of a contentious issue than is the means by which it is achieved. The balance of influence between external and internal forces will determine the eventual ethos and form that the new public management will take.

The Private Sector Board Model

Two of the defining features of the private sector model of board of directors are its responsibility for the governance of the organization and its account-ability to its shareholders. The existence of such a body is intended to ensure that the actions of senior managers are monitored and there are adequate levels of accountability. However, a major issue in the private sector is whether present board models are an effective and appropriate form of governance (Cadbury Report 1992; Conyon 1994). As with styles of management there are a diversity of models of operation in the private sector, which will be examined in more detail in Chapter 6. In selecting which model might be the most appropriate for the public sector, the key differences between the sectors again need to be considered. As J. Stewart and Rawson (1988) have pointed out, one major difference is the politicized context in which public sector bodies operate.

A full assessment of the effectiveness of private sector boards of directors is problematic given that the literature is still developing (but see Pettigrew 1992 for a recent review; also Pettigrew and McNulty, forthcoming). What exists in the literature is often information on their composition, together with self-reported views on roles and much that is prescriptive. Fitzgerald and Pettigrew's (1991) review of the literature concludes that there is no fixed pattern of board composition. The Company Act 1985 only requires a company to have two directors with their main duty being to prepare annual accounts. There is no distinction made between executive and non-executive directors and there is no legal requirement for the positions of either chairs or non-executives.

However, policy interest is increasing (Institutional Shareholders Committee 1991). Figures from Bank of England surveys (1985, 1988) show that the average size of a UK private sector board is nine and that non-executives formed 33 per cent of directors in 1983 and 36 per cent in 1988. On 58 per cent of boards the chair was an executive, usually the chief executive, in the organization. By comparison, data from the US shows that non-executives there form 74 per cent of directors and the average board size is thirteen. However, executive chairs still predominate at 80 per cent. Conyon (1994) reports recent innovations in UK corporate governance with an increased tendency to split the roles of chief executive officer and chair and the growth of audit and nomination committees.

In the UK, the Committee on the Financial Aspects of Corporate Govern-ance was set up with Sir Adrian Cadbury as its chair to examine the composition and workings of boards of directors. This followed several notorious scandals, such as Guinness, Maxwell, and BCCI, which exempli-fied well the inadequacies of current practices. The Committee made several recommendations; that the roles of chief executive and chair should be separated and by inference that the chair should be a non-executive; that the influence of non-executives be strengthened and that they should be independent, with no business or financial interests in the company. The Cadbury Report (1992) recommends that non-executives should be mandatory for quoted companies and that they must have audit committees with at least three non-executives on them. There is a strong trend towards the use of committees as subgroups of the board to promote specialization and greater involvement. One of the key issues here is where the power lies within the organization. A major impetus for the Cadbury committee was the level of power that resided in the chief executive officer–chair grouping, associated with the relative lack of power of the shareholders and the limited influence of the non-executives (Mace 1971).

In the private sector, were these recommendations to be followed, there would need to be a considerable shake-up of British boards. Conyon (1994) suggests that not all of Cadbury's recommendations are being fully implemented as 40 per cent of those companies which operated renumeration committees in 1993 had the chief executive officer as a committee member. Besides the high, though decreasing, percentage of chief executives who also act as chair, a survey by Korn Ferry (1989) showed that of the one-third non-executives, very few were independent, with 62 per cent being executive directors from the main board. The Cadbury Code also recommends that non-executives on the board should be of sufficient calibre and number for their views to carry significant weight in the board's decisions. The target is to create a board composed of a balanced membership of knowledgeable executives and high calibre, independent non-executives with relevant complementary skills. The Cadbury model has been followed by the NHS, with the separation of roles for chair and chief executive, equal numbers of executives and non-executives, and their independence from the organization. In this the NHS can be seen to have created a model which fulfils the Cadbury recommendations for financial probity, but there is still a question of whether such recommendations, even including those specifically relating to financial reporting, can strengthen sufficiently the non-executive role in ensuring probity. Issues relating to board operations and effectiveness will be discussed at more length in Chapter 6.

5.4. From Authorities to Boards

To understand the significance of the changes to the composition of health authorities, it is necessary briefly to consider their previous composition. Historically, there has always been tension and debate between different interest groups about who should be members of the bodies created to run the health service and how they should be appointed. Should appointment be in a personal capacity or as representatives of certain groups? It was Richard Crossman, the Labour Secretary of State for Health who introduced the principle of representative membership bringing in the tripartite composition of professionals, local authority representatives, and lay members. Later changes to the composition of authorities reflects the growth of managerialism. The underlying assumption of the 1990 Health and Community Care Act, with its removal of professional and local authority representatives and the introduction of an equal number of senior managers, is that there is a trade-off between managerial efficiency and the representation of different interest groups and that there was a need to tilt the balance towards greater management efficiency.

These changes were the least publicly debated aspect of the 1990 Act. As the earlier White Paper (Cm 555, *Working for Patients*, 1989) stated:

Chairmen and members of health authorities will continue to have a vital role in the management of the Service and will need to spearhead the changes that the Government is proposing in this White Paper. Because so much management responsibility is now delegated to local level, the Government has decided that the membership of authorities should reflect this new role. (para 8.2)

Thus the emphasis was placed on strengthening the role and influence of management. Thinking on composition may also have been influenced by research which was critical of the effectiveness of the previous style of health authorities. Much of this criticism focused on the tripartite composition as each group represented sectoral interest groups. K. Lee and Mills (1982) believed that this led to a lack of corporate identity, and P. Day and Klein (1987) wrote of the resulting role confusion. The attempt to combine management with representation was deemed to have failed.

One aspect of the role confusion or ambiguity analysed by P. Day and Klein and also by Ranade (1985), centred on the potential conflicts faced by members by being both the agents of the Secretary of State and also being expected to represent the interests of local people. This potential conflict remains. Other causes of role ambiguity are a consequence of poor management rather than composition. Central to this was the lack of clarity on role and objectives. P. Day and Klein contrast the uncertainty within health authorities with the clarity of goals and confidence of the members of water authority boards. The development of such a corporate identity was judged to be an outcome of their shared language of accountability which had emerged from common objectives and criteria on which performance could be judged.

The 1990 NHS reforms focused on composition as well as roles. Not only were an equal number of places on the board given to senior management but the emphasis in recruitment of the lay or non-executive members was on senior managers from business and industry. The loss of elected members weakened traditional channels of local accountability and health authorities could now be constituted with no medical representation. Health professionals included on family health service authorities were appointed on a personal basis and not as representatives, giving considerable added weight to the power of managers in relation to those of professional groups. This is critical at the strategic level given the increased importance being placed on these bodies by the Government as the spearhead of the reforms in primary care. Some of the key consequences of these changes are that the overall size of the authority has been almost halved, with non-executives limited to just five places. In addition, the emphasis on recruiting business people meant that the range of people serving from different backgrounds was reduced.

The process of recruitment has been described as operating through a system of patronage with all chairs, regional non-executives, and three of the five trust non-executives being appointed directly by the Secretary of State, whilst the regional chairs appoint two trust and all the district and family health services authorities non-executives. Our survey and interview data reveal that the main means of recruitment was word of mouth, with the regional chair carrying the greatest influence, within which the use of local business connections rated highly. In the two regions studied no attempts were made to advertise or to contact groups outside the personal realm of experience of existing chairs. To attract people from the private sector, the decision was made to offer non-executives an honorarium since private sector directors were paid. The objective was to create bodies significantly different from their predecessors. The language signified changes alone—from authorities to boards, from managers to executives, and from members to non-executives—signifying the intended shift of culture and values.

There remained, however, key differences between the operations of health authorities and boards in the NHS and those in the private sector. In private companies directors are accountable to the shareholders, whereas in the NHS they are accountable only to the Secretary of State. Company directors are financially liable, unlike their NHS counterparts, and the freedom of action of NHS authority and trust directors is severely limited in comparison with most boards since resources are politically controlled and allocated at a higher level.

Membership of Authorities and Trusts in the NHS

Research is still developing on the characteristics and attitudes on board members in both the private and public sectors. Private sector studies include Fidler (1981), Useem (1993), and Pettigrew and McNulty's (forthcoming) study of competition, attitudes, and behaviour of non-executive directors. Some studies of public and voluntary organizations have focused primarily on biographical details such as gender, ethnicity, age, local connection, and employment. Earlier studies within the NHS by both Ranade (1985) and Elcock (1978) were concerned with the motivation of members and role negotiation. Our survey has added an extra dimension, that of attitudes. This section will examine some of the data from our survey of members of health authorities and trusts carried out during their first year, under the headings of selection, private sector orientation, qualifications and skills, attitudes, motivation, and balance of composition.

The key variables for the analysis of the data were the percentages of new and experienced members, the percentage based within the private sector and the differences between the executive and non-executive members. The most striking finding with regard to the membership of the new district, regional, and family health authorities was that over 73 per cent of chairs and non-executives had previous experience as health authority members. For chairs alone the figure was over 90 per cent (Ashburner and Cairncross 1993). This high degree of continuity is similar to that found by Elcock (1978) following the 1974 restructuring, when he found that over three-quarters of the members interviewed were either employees or had served on the old management boards. By contrast on the first wave trust boards only 27 per cent of non-executives had previous experience on health authorities (Ashburner 1993*b*). The actual level of continuity of membership may in fact be of less significance than who has been removed from the authorities and which of the remaining lay members were selected to continue. Thus the difference can only be understood by examining exactly who the members of both sets of authority are.

Selection of Executive and Non-Executive Members

The key difference on the new-style authorities was the inclusion of senior managers. On regional and district health authorities there is a statutory requirement that the chief executive and finance director take two of the five places. On family health service authorities with the inclusion of the four professional members there is just one executive place for the chief executive. On trust boards this statutory requirement extends to include one doctor and one nurse, leaving just one position vacant. As noted earlier, there is no requirement for a medical or health-related professional to be on district or regional health authorities, and 20 per cent of newly formed authorities had neither. Most of the others had appointed their director of public health as an executive member. Given the role of health authorities in purchasing, it is notable that only half of all authorities had also appointed a director with responsibility for planning or contracting. In the first year of the reforms many district health authorities had not fully come to terms with their new role (Ferlie, FitzGerald and Ashburner 1993). One in five authorities appointed a director of quality but far fewer appointed a nurse. Human resource directors came off even worse with only 5 per cent of districts appointing them but a quarter of the regions doing so. Thus personnel and nursing are the functions least likely to be represented on health authorities. Many health authorities and trusts felt constrained being limited to just five executive posts and having to choose a subgroup of the existing executive team. Many had solved this by inviting a much wider group to actually attend meetings. Since at very few times during any of the research observation of meetings was a vote ever called, there was little to distinguish between the full members and those attending. One key consequence of this was that the executives invariably outnumbered the non-executives.

In the selection of non-executives the broad guidelines issued by the Department of Health, following the 1990 Act, were not radically different from those for the generalists in the past (Ashburner and Cairncross 1991) stressing that people should be selected primarily on their personal attributes. What these desirable personal attributes might be was not spelt out to see how these might be different to those required from the earlier generalists. Subsequent Department of Health guidelines also did not specify the criteria for recruitment but encouraged the focus of the search for non-executives to be in the business community, with the implication that it was private sector business skills that were being sought. It is significant that the precise objectives of these bodies and the desired characteristics of their members were not a focus for debate. Yet if previous criticisms of role confusion and lack of corporate identity were to be avoided there was a need for clarity of objectives. It is only after the organization's and the board's objectives have been clearly defined that the criteria for the non-executives can be specified. A Department of Health brochure at the 1989 CBI conference stated: 'If you have experience of large-scale organisations, you will be particularly welcome' (Rees 1990). This appears to represent a reinforcement of already existing trends rather than a total change of criteria. In the past, the generalist or lay members were in the minority, and without senior management members, such bodies could not be said to be managerialist in nature. In the regions where our studies took place the main focus in the search for new members was in local business groups personally known to the regional and district chairs such as the chamber of commerce. Despite this, in interview, the senior manager in one region responsible for interviewing potential appointees said that the main objective was to achieve a broadly based non-executive group.

Private Sector Orientation

The extent to which a broad base of non-executive members was achieved can now be examined. The majority of all non-executives across regional and district health authorities and trusts were employed in the private sector. In trusts and districts those based in the private sector comprised about two thirds of non-executive members, with the slightly lower percentage at regional level probably explained by their higher percentage of retired people. The self-employed non-executives interviewed, comprising, for example, accountants, solicitors, public relations consultants, and owners of their own businesses, were also all based in the private sector. (The figure for the family health services authority is inflated by the presence of professional members.)

The first-wave trusts had only a slightly higher percentage of non-executives

Table 5.1. Present or most recent employing organization by type of authority (chairs and non-executives only) (%)

| | Type of health authority | | | |
	Trust	Regional	District	Family Services
Private (service)	30	9	21	13
Private (manufacturing)	18	24	20	8
Self-employed	19	24	23	36
NHS	10	12	8	20
Other public	16	12	17	16
Voluntary	6	7	7	5
Other	2	12	4	3

Notes: components may not add up to 100 due to separate rounding.
n = 1,653.

employed in the private sector than did the health authorities. The differences between the continuing and new members shows that on health authorities more than two in five new members (41 per cent) are from the private sector compared with just over a quarter (28 per cent) of continuing members. This indicates that a significant percentage of continuing members were also employed within the private sector. This might represent an imbalance between those who were and those who were not invited to continue in membership. The overall percentage of non-executives based in the private sector is slightly higher than in the general population where it is 63 per cent (Jowell and Witherspoon 1985).

The percentage of non-executives from a NHS or public sector background was around a quarter in each type of authority with continuing members three times more likely to have a public sector background than new members. The importance of public sector experience must be recognized because regardless of the specific management skills private sector managers bring with them, as Lachman (1985) recognized, members from a public sector background may well be better able to recognize the implications of, and operation of, political influence.

That there is a stronger business element amongst trust non-executives than among those in other authorities was shown by the high percentage who are directors on boards in the private sector. Over two-thirds of trust chairs and almost half of trust non-executives were directors compared with half of authority chairs and a third of non-executives. Equally, in the health authorities less than five per cent of chairs and non-executives were on the board of companies employing 500 people or more, compared with 20 per cent of trust non-executives. This is a much stronger representation than that other public service settings such as polytechnic boards of governors, where less than one-third of the independent directors were directors with registered companies (Bastin, 1990).

Qualifications and Skills

The majority of all members have some kind of professional qualification and almost half have a degree. Chairs emerged as least qualified relative to other members but all groups were more highly qualified than the population at large where only 5 per cent had a degree or equivalent until the recent expansion of higher education (OPCS 1983).

There is little variation between the different types of authority. These findings show little has changed since Elcock's (1978) study of members in Yorkshire and Northern Regional Health Authority, where he also found that the majority of members held a university degree and a professional qualification. There is a lack of comparable data about the qualifications of private sector board members. This data suggests that health service boards have a high calibre of both executive and non-executive members.

When all members were asked what special skills they brought to the board the majority included those of management and leadership. Whereas 99 per cent of chief executives said management, so did 65 per cent of non-executives. The results were similar for leadership with 90 per cent and 52 per cent respectively. With regard to functional skills, a higher percentage of executives claimed skills in areas such as planning (67 per cent), contracting (40 per cent), computing (30 per cent), and all aspects of health-related and medical issues. For the non-executives it was the areas of personnel (43 per cent), finance (35 per cent), and marketing (26 per cent) where they were more likely to bring skills than were the executive. The figure for personnel skills can be accounted for by the lack of representation of personnel executives on many boards, but that of finance is more likely to represent a focus for recruitment amongst non-executives. It must be noted that in the early days of the reforms when our survey was carried out, the operation of the internal market had not become fully established and skills in areas such as marketing had yet to be addressed by many executives.

However, when asked about the attributes necessary for a non-executive,

Table 5.2. Members' qualifications by type of member (%)

	Degree	Higher degree	Management qualification	Professional qualification	Other
General manager/chief executive	50	23	56	64	5
Executive	55	31	28	85	2
Chair	42	15	23	56	8
Non-executive	49	18	18	64	7
Total	50	21	24	67	6

Note: n = 2,141

Table 5.3. Perceived key essential or very important attributes of non-executive members

	Chief executive	Executive	Chair	Non-executive	Total
Common sense and good judgement	94	94	93	91	92
Sufficient time for board business	85	86	84	82	83
An ability to work well in a group	68	73	67	67	69
Experience of management in business	26	32	43	38	36
Experience of management in public sector	19	17	17	23	21

Note: The survey asked the respondents to put attributes into the following categories: essential, very important, important, neither important nor unimportant, not important.

personal qualities were considered more important than specific skills or experience.

Business or management experience gained in the public sector was apparently less highly rated than that gained in the private sector. This was most marked in the trusts where 52 per cent thought that experience of management in business was essential or very important compared with just 23 per cent that thought the same for public sector experience. What is notable is that overall both were rated lower than other desirable attributes for non-executives. This is despite the very high level of management skills present on boards.

Attitudes of Executive and Non-Executive Members

What needs to be examined next is the extent to which the backgrounds of the non-executive members influenced their attitudes (Cairncross *et al.* 1991; Ashburner and Cairncross 1992). When asked if they agreed that trusts and health authorities should be modelled on private sector boards of directors, 72 per cent of chairs and 64 per cent of non-executives from across all types of authority and trusts said that they should. This contrasts with the responses of the executive members, where only 28 per cent of trust chief executives, 63 per cent of health authority chief executives, and 57 per cent of other executives agreed.

It is important to understand the extent of attitudinal differences between the executive and non-executive members if we are to begin to judge the extent to which the value systems of the non-executives from the private sector might begin to influence managers and management decision-making. If boards are to be the strategic apex of their organizations, then the attitudes of the non-executives will have an important influence on strategic policy-making. Non-executives from the private sector were more likely to agree that the NHS had sufficient resources to do a good job and were less likely to agree that the NHS provided good value for money, than were executives. When asked whether competition and the internal market were needed to make the NHS more efficient, only half of all executives in health authorities agreed compared with 87 per cent of chairs and 73 per cent of non-executives. Similarly, 97 per cent of chairs and 83 per cent of non-executives believed that the White Paper *Working for Patients* would result in better care for patients compared with 71 per cent of executives.

This difference in attitude between the NHS managers and non-executives may reflect the public–private divide. It also suggests that the pressure for greater managerialism is not just related to the empowerment of NHS managers but also to a desire for a change in attitudes and culture and the consequent need for the chairs and non-executive members to be the spearhead of the Government's reforms. What could be seen as an inbuilt bias towards the private sector, could also be seen in the preference for management skills acquired within the private sector over those from within the public sector as shown in the previous section.

Motivation

An examination of the motivation of non-executives should increase our understanding of the behaviour of health authority and trust members. Despite the emphasis on recruiting members with business experience, many non-executives and chairs also had public or voluntary service experience. Over 40 per cent had been or were governors of a school, college, or polytechnic. Health authority members were slightly more likely to have been involved in public service, with 15 per cent being councillors compared with 11 per cent in trusts. While it is interesting to note the continuing involvement of local councillors on the new health authority and boards, unfortunately it is not possible to say whether they cross all political spectra. Bastin's (1990) study of boards of polytechnics governors and colleges of higher education, where similar changes have occurred, found that local authority links also remained strong. In health authorities, 11 per cent of members were JPs compared with 9 per cent in trusts. This marks a slight decline when compared with Elcock's (1978) study of two regions. He found 55 per cent of members were school or college governors and almost 40 per cent were JPs.

Comparisons with Elcock's study also show a decline in the numbers of members involved in voluntary activities. In his study, over 67 per cent of members were involved in voluntary associations compared with 46 per cent in our study. Klein and Lewis's (1976) study of consumer representation found that 85 per cent of members of community health councils had links with voluntary organizations.

With so many active citizens amongst its members, it is clear that a commitment to public service is one component of motivation. Non-executives, however, rarely gave only one reason for joining the health authority or trust. Across all types of authority the main reason given was the opportunity to exercise skills and experience gained elsewhere (67 per cent). For health authorities members 86 per cent said that the payment of an honorarium was not a factor in their decision to accept appointment, but this figure was 46 per cent for those on trusts. This may reflect differences in attitude and expectations of the new non-executives, since on trusts over two-thirds were new to health authority work. On health authorities 90 per cent of those continuing said it was not a factor compared with 75 per cent of the new. This may be related to the expectation of payment of those serving on private sector boards or the requirement of some firms for recompense for their employees' time.

Balance of Composition

Appointments were made to the newly formed health authorities prior to the setting up of the first wave trusts. When the decline in the numbers of women and ethnic minorities compared with the old-style authorities became apparent, guidelines were issued about broadening the basis of selection to try to include more women and ethnic minorities. The new boards were clearly unrepresentative in many ways but these were the only two criteria selected for guidance by the Department of Health. This raises complex issues around what is meant by representation. Earlier guidelines had stressed that representation was not to be a factor in the role of non-executives. So are women and ethnic minorities on boards or authorities because they represent the wider community and are they therefore expected to represent the views of their group as part of their role? It is difficult to see that such a role is possible since there are no lines of accountability to the groups being represented.

Whatever the motivation for addressing the issues of gender and race, whether to forestall potential criticism or as a genuine attempt to broaden the basis of recruitment, the initial decline in numbers after 1990 was significant. The percentage of women on the new authorities fell from 35 per cent (King's Equal Opportunity Task Force 1990) to just 20 per cent on regional and 24 per cent on district health authorities. On trusts, where submissions were refused unless there were female appointees, women comprised 26 per cent overall, 28 per cent of non-executives, but just 6 per cent of chairs. Ethnic minority numbers have fallen from 3 per cent to less than 2 per cent across all types of authority. This outcome can be partly accounted for by the emphasis in recruitment of senior business people where there are very few women and ethnic minorities, and on the means of recruitment through overwhelmingly word-of-mouth contacts with the dominant influence being that of the regional chairs who at that time were all white and male.

Comparable figures for other parts of the public and voluntary sectors show that these figures are not untypical. Of the independent governors on polytechnic and higher education boards 20 per cent were women (Bastin 1990), the same percentage holding true for women local councillors (Widdicombe Report 1986), while Kearns's (1990) study showed that 30 per cent of housing association management committees were women. By contrast boards in the private sector are relatively devoid of women. A 1989 survey (Holton and Rabbetts 1989) showed that of the top 200 companies 89 per cent had no women on their boards. In 1991 only 6 per cent of members of the Institute of Directors, mainly from small and medium-sized firms, were women (Howe and McRae 1971).

The move towards the private sector board model disadvantaged women in three ways. Women formed a higher percentage of the previous members who were removed (Ashburner 1993*a*), and recruitment focused on senior business people and on the inclusion of senior executives who are also predominantly male. (The percentage would in fact have been even lower had it not been for the intervention of the NHS Women's Unit in the appointment of first wave trust non-executives.) The NHS is of course a signatory to the Opportunity 2000 campaign which has resulted in the setting of a 1994 target for 35 per cent women board members, which represents only a return to pre-reform figures. The significance of the decline in the number of women on boards and authorities lies in the differences in their backgrounds, attitudes, and approaches to their role from those of the male non-executives.

In most aspects of specific skills, board, and individual roles, our survey data suggested that women's responses did not differ from those of the men. This suggests that women have equal competence but they also displayed a different and wider range of backgrounds and skills. The main differences in women's contributions result from these different experiences and the different attitudes which these have produced, rather than anything which is intrinsic to their sex. Our survey data on the reasons why people became health authority members (Ashburner 1993*a*) showed that 23 per cent of the men, but 43 per cent of women, included in their motives 'to represent the interests of local people'. On trusts, 36 per cent of women non-executives felt it was 'very important' for their role to include that of being 'the voice of the community', compared to 20 per cent of men.

In our health authority survey, most motivation factors elicited a higher response from women than men. 'The opportunity to exercise skills and expertise gained elsewhere' was included by 57 per cent of men but 70 per cent of women. Similarly: 'it would be something you would be good at and this would be satisfying' was ticked by 38 per cent of men and 50 per cent of women. Women also placed greater emphasis on individual attributes such as common sense, ability to work in a group, and lack of bias. Important differences directly related to background showed that, without women non-executives, knowledge and experience at board level in areas such as mental health, disability, the elderly, nursing, and public health would be more limited. Women also had or made more time available for work related to their non-executive role. Only one-third of the men but half the women anticipated spending over forty days per year on board business (Ashburner 1993*a*).

It is important that those who set about increasing the proportions of women and ethnic minorities are clear about their reasons for doing so. This is necessary in order to avoid role confusion for those appointed and to make selection and recruitment easier. Although it is unlikely that in the move to recruit more women it is intended that they should represent women in general, the unintended consequences are clearly beneficial if a truly broader base, than just those from the private sector business community, is sought.

Summary of Research Findings

One of the key differences between the new-style health authorities and the new trust boards was that the former had developed from pre-existing bodies but the latter were completely new. Hence the marked difference in the level of continuity of previous members, with 73 per cent on health authorities and just 27 per cent on trust boards. Although members totally new to the health service were more likely to be employed in the private sector, a high proportion of continuing members were also. This was clearly one criterion for their reselection. The use of word-of-mouth in the selection of members, with the primary criterion being business experience, has led to a higher level of homogeneity in the backgrounds of non-executives. The increasing numbers of non-executives from the private sector, the decline in numbers of women and ethnic minorities, the trend of declining involvement in public and community activities, and the higher expectation of financial recompense amongst the newer non-executives suggests a change in the type of person being appointed. With the exclusion of professionals and local authority representatives, the potential for these bodies to develop a homogeneous private sector orientation becomes even stronger.

In combination with the inclusion of an equal number of senior managers, the contrast with the past becomes more marked. The most recent health service reforms, which mark a continuation of the policy to increase the level of managerialism, no longer rely just on the empowerment of managers within the NHS. As was seen from the differences in attitude towards the reforms, it was the chairs and the non-executives who were the group most strongly in support of the reform process.

5.5. Conclusion

The changes in the composition of NHS boards and authorities have had important consequences both for the issue of local accountability and for the continuing increase in the level of managerialism. They are also an important element in the development of the new public management.

There is a need to unpick the implications for the governance of the public sector of the continuing trend away from representative to non-elected bodies. As has been seen from an examination of what is occurring in the health service, not only has any direct form of local accountability been removed but so has the broad base of the membership. If the appointment of members is on the basis of political support for the policies of the government of the day, then a much stronger force from within the public services will be working towards these ends. This factor, as in the case of the NHS, might help to militate against any resistance on the part of management, and enhance the potential impact of the reforms.

One of the objectives behind changes to the composition and structure of health authorities and boards lay in emulating the private sector board to make them more business-like. This was partly to distance them from the image of the old-style authorities as rubber stamps. If the new authorities and boards retained a modest role and very limited impact, then the question of composition would not be so critical. If, however, they can be seen to be more influential and performing a strategic role, then the question of who is on the board is critical. A notably different style of management or attitude towards the health service at this strategic decision-making level would exert a strong force for change. What is evident from the research evidence so far is that changes to the composition of boards in themselves are not sufficient to ensure effectiveness. The high level of homogeneity of non-executives has meant the loss of a broader base of experience, which would ensure that a wider range of views and options were voiced. The next chapter examines how this homogeneity manifests itself in the operations of the boards and develops this discussion by considering the implications of boards composition and operations for probity as well as effectiveness.

It may be that board composition may represent an area where the private sector may usefully learn from the public sector. For all its faults, the NHS has moved to adopt many of the recommendations of the Cadbury Code. Even some of the weaknesses we have highlighted in NHS boards—narrow selection criteria; closed élite networks; class, gender, and ethnic homogeneity; the erosion of a public service mentality by a cash nexus; and the undervaluing of certain skills—need to be vigorously confronted in the private sector as well (Pettigrew and McNulty, 1995). For example, where selection is through informal patronage rather than an explicit merit-testing process, non-executive directors may find it more difficult to negotiate a position of independence *vis-à-vis* the chair.

We suspect that the issue of board composition will not go away and that further reorganization is likely. It is to be hoped that policy will be informed by the expanding body of research findings which are now available.

How does the evidence so far presented contribute to our understanding of the new public management? The board model introduced to the health service was closer to that suggested by Cadbury than to any models common within the private sector. Even so, the Cadbury Report was written in response to failures within the private sector models and not as one appropriate for use in the public sector. In relation to structure and composition it is more clearly a private sector model than a hybrid, since it lacks even a token attempt at downwards accountability. What therefore needs to be considered is what differences there are in the role, values, and operations of the private and public sector boards. These are addressed in Chapter 6. As with any models or processes transferred from the private sector, it is important to ensure that it is appropriate, to avoid any weaknesses and to ensure that any strengths of the public system can be retained.

THE BOARD: FROM RUBBER STAMP
TO STRATEGY-MAKER?

6.1. Introduction

Have the changes to the composition of boards in the public sector, as exemplified by those in the health service, had a significant effect upon the way that such boards operate? One conclusion from Chapter 5 was that changing the structure and composition alone would not necessarily make boards more effective. Similarly, Charkham, in his analysis of private sector boards in five countries, concludes: 'No type of structure ensures the competence of individuals or effective group dynamics but some obviously help more than others' (1994: 331). How decision-makers on boards interpret their roles and how they operate as a group are key to board effectiveness, but the empirical data from the private sector on what happens within board meetings is still developing (Pettigrew and McNulty's (1995) study goes beyond the conventional focus on structure and composition to discuss the winning of power and influence). This chapter will present primary data, derived from direct observation of eleven boards in health care, over periods of between twelve and eighteen months. Taking the board's role in the strategy formulation process as an important indicator of its level of effectiveness, we will explore the foundations for, and the processes of, effective strategy formulation.

The main changes to composition of boards in the health sector have been the inclusion of senior management and the importing of predominantly private sector non-executives. This represents more than simply a change of name from the old lay members or generalists, but the creation of a new non-executive role similar to that within private sector boards. In acting as directors rather than representatives of a particular group, the objective is to move away from the pre-1990 rubber stamp model. The reference to earlier health authorities as being merely rubber stamps (Ham 1989) emphasizes their secondary role in approving decisions that had been taken elsewhere, by managers or clinicians. As managers were not members of the authority, their role was restricted to that of reporting to the authority and seeking ratification for their actions and plans. The phrase has become somewhat of a cliché, with the implication that all such authorities were ineffective. This weakness is seen as based upon what P. Day and Klein (1987) have described as the role confusion of individual members and authorities as a whole. There was a wide range in the members' backgrounds and interests, and the problems faced in trying to arrive at a consensus reflected this lack of corporate identity. To have a wide range of views expressed at authority meetings might seem a strength. However, the weakness was that each group of members was acting on the basis of the interests they were representing. This representative element of members' roles was thus removed in 1990 to increase the focus on the development of a corporate body. Such moves to reduce the diversity of health authority members may well increase the potential for consensus but might also reduce the range and quality of the debate.

What needs to be assessed is the extent to which private sector models have influenced not just structures and personnel but the way that boards define their role and their modes of operation. A key element in board effectiveness is often seen as the extent to which they are developing a strategic role. In order to understand how a board's role relates to strategy there is a need to examine the processes within board meetings, what issues are brought to the board, the role and influence of the non-executives (Pettigrew and McNulty, 1995) and the way in which private sector experience is balanced with the needs of the public sector. If it can be shown that boards in the public sector are becoming more strategic then the significance of the 1990 changes in composition becomes greater.

A move to a more strategic, influential, public sector board would have implications not just for the efficiency or effectiveness of the organization itself but for its role in the implementation of government policies. This would have particular relevance given the increase in the numbers of non-elected bodies within the wider public sector and the evidence presented in Chapter 5 that support for the health reforms was stronger amongst non-executives than executives. Strategy is formulated within an organization's structural and cultural framework and is an explicit or implicit statement of values. Understanding how these might be affected is important in the development of an analysis of the extent and depth of change as a consequence of top–down pressure for reform.

However, the concept of effectiveness, as applied to boards, needs to go beyond ensuring that the organization has strategic direction and is managed effectively, or that wider policies are implemented, but must also include additional issues of probity and accountability. It was only after the financial scandals in Wessex and the West Midlands, discussed later in Chapter 8, that the issue of probity came to the fore in the health service, and new central guidelines were issued. There has been an equal lack of attention to the issue of board accountability in its widest terms, with the only formal accountability being upwards. Charkham (1994: 4), establishes the two basic principles of good corporate governance as first, that management must have the freedom to drive the enterprise forward but secondly that it must exercise this freedom within a framework of effective accountability. If the public sector is to model itself on the private, then enough should be known of the model's weaknesses and strengths in order to avoid the former. The issue of accountability will be discussed at greater length in Chapter 8.

This chapter develops the themes of the previous chapter but moves further to an examination of the roles, processes, and practices of authorities and boards. It will begin with an analysis of how boards in the private sector operate and how they define their roles. This will be followed by an analysis of our research data in which we can identify some prerequisites for effective strategy formulation. Important elements include: control of the agenda, the stage of policy development when it comes to the board, the extent to which options remain open, and the decision-making frameworks that are in operation. In this, the data also provide an analysis of the contributions and influence of the executives and non-executives. In drawing conclusions, we observe that a better understanding of the strategy formulation process, and of how effective boards are in their various roles, have implications for boards in both the public and the private sectors. Finally we will re-examine the concept of the public sector board as a hybrid organizational form.

6.2. Private Sector Boards

Board Roles

The board of directors is seen as representing the strategic apex of the organization with responsibility for leadership. Despite their obvious importance there is still not enough known about how boards operate within the private sector (Pettigrew 1992) or what makes them effective. Much of the literature on the role of boards is prescriptive rather than descriptive and what research that exists often uses indirect reporting methodologies. However, a recent study by Lorsch and MacIver (1989) was based upon extensive empirical evidence from directors in the USA. This identified the main functions of boards to be the overseeing of the management of the company, review of the company's performance, overseeing its social responsibilities, and ensuring compliance with the law. This accords closely with Trickers's (1984) earlier definition, based on UK boards, which suggested three main board activities: establishing strategic direction, monitoring and evaluating performance, and participating in executive action. Pearce and Zahra (1991) argue that powerful boards are associated with superior corporate financial performance.

These lists are predominantly inward looking. J. Pfeffer (1972), on the other hand, acknowledged that boards could also have an important role in facilitating relationships with external organizations as well as a ceremonial function. Such roles will have a particular relevance for public sector bodies in their interface with their clientele and community, particularly for those with the core purchasing functions where there is a need to establish the level of need. Kovner (1974) in his study of hospital boards in the USA stressed the importance of the outward-looking roles of these boards.

As the review of existing literature shows, boards have a number of roles but most of the lists, including that of Lorsch and MacIver, do not specifically include a strategic role. As FitzGerald and Pettigrew (1991) suggest, the lack of a prescribed role in strategy formulation may be due to the fact that boards do not necessarily plan or initiate strategy but do influence the decision on what option to take. More recent literature, by contrast, does emphasize strategy as the principal function of the board (Charkham 1986; Zahra 1990). A survey by the Institute of Directors (Coulson-Thomas and Wakelam 1991) suggested that in the future boards would spend less time on monitoring and more on initiating processes for change. They regarded strategy as important because of the ever-growing complexity and competitiveness of the business environment.

Other research suggests that the board's role in strategy formulation is far from clear (Andrews 1982; Mace 1971). Although based on earlier research, both writers suggest that there is more rhetoric than reality with regard to the strategic role of the board. Without access to the operations of boards it is not possible to say whether the prescribed strategic role actually develops. There is also a danger that an overemphasis on just one role at board level might not necessarily be conducive to overall effectiveness. Wommack (1992), for example, believes that the board's role in strategy should be restricted to the review and analysis of management proposals. Fama and Jensen (1983) also separate these two roles and categorize them as 'decision management' and 'decision control'. They see the former as the role of management and only the latter as the responsibility of the board.

Any ambiguity in practice between these two roles may well be due to the preponderance of executive rather than non-executive directors on most private sector boards, as discussed in Chapter 5. What this highlights, however, is that boards do need to discuss and clearly define their strategic role and to distinguish it from the management role. The importance of this becomes clearer when the specific role of non-executives in ensuring probity is considered.

A study of board roles by Molz (1985) identified seven types of delegation to management and their subsequent implications for the level of control of the board. He notes the growing influence in the private sector of managers over their boards and that the majority of boards delegate away the major portion of their decision-making authority. He sees the lack of power of the board, and of the non-executives in particular, as a critical factor in the accountability of the board and their presentation of the various stakeholders, in a similar way to that described by Charkham (1994).

A key factor in the question of board control was identified by Molz as the balance of effort between their role in the monitoring of past events and their assessment of future strategy to enable corrective action to be taken. Of the seven types of board described by Molz, there were two which most closely resembled the roles of health authorities and trusts and both displayed a higher level of strategic control at board level than was judged to be the norm in the private sector. Such a lack of control by the board has a clear implication for its effectiveness.

This still leaves boards with the decision of how to treat their strategic role, especially the balance between formulation and evaluation. The importance of board involvement in the formulation of strategy is that it may help to clarify organizational objectives and priorities but the problem is that such involvement may affect the board role of independent evaluation of management and the strategic plan. The importance of the independent evaluative role is also central to any form of accountability and falls primarily on the non-executives.

The study of behaviour in the boardroom thus represents an underdeveloped field. Pettigrew (1992) argues that the study of how boards function will represent a major priority for management analysts over the next five years. He characterizes the problem in terms of how managerial élites behave within organizations. Within the narrower field of the public sector, we also need to broaden the theoretical agenda out from the old members' literature, which often focused on board composition or the development of member typologies, and display a greater concern with questions of élite formation, the distribution and use of organizational power, the nature of influence processes, and patterns of decision-making.

The disconnection between the current corporate governance debate and the more scholarly approaches is curious because there is a long tradition of work in the area of managerial hegemony, or the superior power of the governed, which might be usefully accessed (starting with Berle and Means 1933; then on to Zald 1969; Mace 1971; Lorsch and MacIver 1989). This literature implies that—at least outside rare moments of crisis—executives use their full-time role, superior technical knowledge, richer information flows, and selection of pliant non-executives to control the organization. The public and shareholders are seen as passive, unable to organize sufficiently to challenge the managerial élite.

Other studies have subtly qualified or undermined this managerial hegemony thesis. Herman (1981) argues that management (the chief executive officer and the executive directors) control the firm, but in the context of a varying set of constraints and latent powers of stakeholders such as outside members of the board, shareholders, and creditors. Shareholder activism has revived during the early 1990s, as seen in the acerbic 1995 British Gas AGM, when senior management faced a barrage of public criticism over spiralling pay.

Kosnik (1987) has argued that the managerial hegemony position is often assumed, yet the empirical evidence in support of this theory is sparse. Certainly, two alternative theoretical approaches are available. For agency theorists (Jensen and Meckling 1976; Fama and Jensen 1983) the board is an alternative monitoring device that helps to control corporate management (the agents) to further the interests of the principals (the shareholders). It is assumed within agency theory that effective boards will identify with shareholder interests and use their experience in strategic decision-making and control to exert leverage over any self-interested tendencies of corporate management.

A second and critical sociological tradition (Wright Mills 1956) argues that advanced capitalist societies are dominated by a small but tightly integrated power élite which control key positions in society and whose interests conflict with the vast majority.

While class theorists accept that there may be divisions within the power élite, these are seen as relatively slight and as being overridden by integrating mechanisms which create a tendency to class-wide unity (Mizruchi 1992). Useem (1984) argues that there exists among leaders of the largest firms an inner circle whose multiple board membership enables them to view the world in terms of the long-term interests of business as a whole.

We need to distinguish carefully between local and national élites, and as far as appointments to NHS boards are concerned members of local élites may predominate over national figures. We also need to investigate how powerful non-executives really are. Class theory assumes that non-executives are indeed powerful, as ambassadors of wider class interests. However, this power-based explanation of why it is that individuals seek board status has been questioned by Zajac (1993) who has put forward alternative explanations based on prestige, friendship, or pleasure in the process. Élite theory may then operate with a very crude theory of motivation.

The Non-Executive Role

Charkham (1994) stresses the importance of independent non-executives, as only board members really know if the board is functioning properly and the acid test is whether the non-executives are strong enough to say no when they feel they must. As he says, the role 'requires skill, tact and courage which overfamiliarity and personal friendship must not weaken', as accountability of management to the board is the bedrock of the system. The great majority of boards are dominated by executives. As the figures presented in Chapter 5 showed, less than 10 per cent of directors on British boards are independent and of the 38 per cent in non-executive roles, 62 per cent came from the main board of the company. This reduces the possibility that independent non-executives have the opportunity or influence to ensure accountability or probity or to influence strategy.

The PRO-NED guidelines (1987) for non-executive directors do not apparently challenge the status quo as they suggest that their main role is to be 'advisory and supportive', adding later that they have responsibility for 'helping make sure that the executive leadership functions as it does'. This does not place a very strong emphasis on monitoring and sees the non-executive in a complementary role to management rather than one in which the relationship might ever become confrontational. The Institute of Directors' Guidelines stress three main aspects of the non-executive's role: widening the horizons within which strategy is determined, monitoring management performance, and ensuring ethical and legal conduct.

Other research points to the relative lack of power of non-executives. Lorsch and MacIver (1989) found in the private sector in the USA that non-executives' powers and effectiveness were constrained by limited information, knowledge, or expertise; the power of the chief executive; the power of group norms; lack of consensus on goals; and limited time. This was despite their greater numbers (74 per cent of directors). Correspondingly the influence of non-executives was enhanced by having the confidence to express their views and ideas, knowledge and information about the matter under discussion, control over the agenda and the discussion process, cohesion on the board (which required time) for discussion to be achieved. The chair also performed a crucial role in managing the meetings and the non-executive contributions. One conclusion that can be drawn from such data is that the essence of a board's effectiveness lies with the non-executives.

An important private sector study which has focused on the influence of the non-executive or part-time member is that of Pettigrew and McNulty (1995). They look at some of the conditions, processes, and abilities which contribute to the development and exercise and power and influence by some part-time board members. They see this as being shaped by the structure and context of the board's operations as well as the legal, institutional, and social framework which helps to mould directors' interpretations of board conduct. The third key element is the willingness of board members to use the power resources that they have.

Their interim analysis shows that the influence of part-time members peaks in time of crisis and transition and that non-executives find it easier to challenge an item brought to the board than to initiate changes of direction which challenge the perspectives and attitudes of corporate management. Such factors are important in ascertaining the influence of non-executives when they might have different cultural influences to the executives.

The Deficiencies of the Private Sector Model

A major problem in the private sector is seen as the lack of regulation. The 1985 Companies Act requires all quoted companies to have at least two directors but the creation of a board and the position of chair are not actually required by law. Legally, the term 'non-executive director' is not recognized, as all directors have the same level of responsibility and outsiders, whether independent or not, are not a necessity. The inclusion of non-executives is only mandatory on audit committees. The Cadbury Report (1992) suggests that non-executives should be mandatory on boards of quoted companies and should be of sufficient calibre to carry weight in the decision-making process.

A second identified weakness of private sector boards as recognized by Charkham (1994), is the strain placed upon non-executives who share an equal level of responsibility but without the time and knowledge of the executives and without any formal powers. He compares the British system unfavourably with that of Germany where there is a dual board system: an executive board and another called a supervisory board which comprises shareholder and employee representatives. The latter has formal powers since the executive board is required to inform and consult the supervisory board.

In his analysis of corporate governance in five countries, Charkham (1994) concludes that although the UK has some excellent boards, the limited legal requirements mean that it also has some of the worst. He feels that the cooperative and supervisory roles of the non-executives are simply not consistent, that accountability was often nominal rather than real, and that, as in the US system, there was the possibility that a powerful chief executive could dominate the board. Some of the best boards he identified, regardless of country of origin, were those based upon a collegiate system. He believed that the absence of access to information as of right allowed poor governance to continue and that the real problem for the USA and the UK was that many people did well from the present system and were therefore reluctant to change it.

The UK model of boards of directors does not immediately strike one as the most effective form to follow. It may well give the balance of power to management but as Charkham (1994) has so clearly shown, the empowerment of management is not necessarily the same as, nor does it necessarily lead to, more effective boards. The overpowerful chief executive and the dominance of the executive are instead identified as weaknesses in the system when it comes to ensuring accountability and probity. The model of the board chosen for the health service follows the recommendations of the Cadbury Report (1992) more closely than do most private sector boards. Non-executives not only comprise six of the eleven places but all are independent of the organization. Also, the positions of chair and chief executive are separated and the position of chair is always taken by a non-executive. A key difference, however, is that far from the chair being first among equals, as in the private sector, in the NHS its appointment is by the Secretary of State. Given the inability of the non-executives to remove them, they may emerge potentially as very powerful figures.

The conclusion that the empowerment of management is not necessarily related to the effectiveness of the board and can indeed be counter-productive is important. Taken with our earlier conclusion that changing the structure and composition of the board by itself would not lead to greater effectiveness, the issue of how a board defines its role and set of interpersonal relationships becomes the central focus. What is the optimal division of labour between the executives and non-executives, and how can it be achieved? Along Molz's (1985) continuum of roles, delegation by the board to management is the main feature of the first three types, which are those common in the private sector. The next three types involve the board retaining control, one of which is that of strategic control, where the board's role moves beyond monitoring to involvement in strategy formulation, thus enabling the board to set priorities and tangible objectives.

6.3. Strategy Formulation as a Process

In understanding how boards operate and how effective they are, the extent to which a strategic role is being developed has been taken so far in our analysis as a key element. In analysing the data on board processes it is imperative that we explore what is meant by strategy and its relevance for board performance. The previous section has shown that not all prescriptions for board roles include a strategic role but that more recent literature identifies this as a primary board role (Charkham 1986; Zahra 1990; Pettigrew and McNulty 1995). While the extent to which the board should engage in strategy formulation may be disputed, in many cases such a strategic role will be expected.

This section will review some of the ideas and issues emerging in the literature on strategic management and, in combination with those on boards and change, develop a framework within which to analyse what we have found in our study of health service boards. Much of the literature on strategic management has an outward-facing perspective which has been strongly influenced by rational planning and marketing concepts (Asch and Bowman 1989; Greenley 1989; Thompson 1990). The literature on strategy formulation is more varied, ranging from rational planning approaches, through evolutionary and emergent approaches to the dustbin view of strategy. Whittington's (1993) review of the strategy literature suggests four different perspectives. The first, classical, approach is formalistic, rational, and analytic (Chandler 1962; Sloan 1963; also Porter 1980) with a presumption that organizational decision-makers can make explicit choices about direction. It is often highly top–down in nature, with leadership seen as residing in the chief executive officer. Implementation is seen as a discrete and relatively unproblematic phase, coming only after the earlier phase of explicit and conscious formulation (see Mintzberg's (1990) critique of the classical model).

The second approach is the evolutionary approach, arguing that markets and competitive processes will by themselves lead to the selecting-out of inefficient providers. Indeed, developing a long-term strategy can be counter-productive:

expensive to generate and difficult to modify. Population ecologists such as (Hannan and Freeman 1988: 25) argue: 'organisational selection processes favour organisations with relatively inert structures, organisations that cannot change strategy and structure as their environments change'.

The third approach is the processual approach, which takes a more sceptical view of the role of markets (Whittington 1993) than population ecology. But strategy is not seen here either as an explicit or highly rationalistic process, but as much more emergent (Mintzberg and Waters 1985) in nature. This is partly because of the cognitive limits on rational choice (Cyert and March 1963) or the role of cognitive frameworks (Weick 1979; Argyris and Schon 1978; Johnson 1987) in mediating the receipt of external information. Strategy-making may also be seen as a shared and collective process rather than as an individualistic and top–down decision (Pettigrew and Whipp 1991). Strategy formation and implementation blend into each other, and at each stage the strategist should be aware of the micro-politics of the organization (Pettigrew 1973; Pettigrew 1985; Pettigrew *et al.* 1992).

The final approach can be described as the systemic model, which assumes that the rationales underlying strategy are peculiar to particular sociological contexts (Whittington 1993). Decision-makers are embedded (Granovetter 1985) in social and institutional webs which generate culturally specific forms of rationality. Less attention is accorded to the limits of cognition than in the processual model. The focus of analysis also shifts from the individual organization to the social and institutional setting.

In our view, research originating from an organization behaviour tradition on the initiation and implementation of strategic change has produced models of the change progress which have moved from rational, staged models to more iterative, contingent, multifaceted models (see Greiner 1977; Quinn 1980; Tichy 1983; Lovelady 1984*a* amd 1984*b*). Effective change implementation may require attention to be paid to leadership, micro-politics, communication, and the process of generating commitment. The implementation of strategic change can in reality be seen as untidy, iterative, and risky.

In essence, while rational analysis and explicit moments of choice may play important roles, the strategy process must in our view be seen as containing other important aspects: intuitive choices, power negotiations, the emergence of a group consensus, and aspects of non-decision-making (Bachrach and Baratz 1963) whereby certain items are excluded from the agenda. Strategy formulation and implementation should not be seen as linear, staged processes but as ones which involve iteration. Both processes are limited by imperfect communication of information, in terms of transmission and receipt. Communication will also always be clouded by the numerous and different interpretations of the stakeholders.

It may be helpful, as an heuristic device, to break the notion of the strategy formulation process into a number of behavioural items which require consideration (see also Pettigrew 1985). The following represents a long list of candidate items for potential analysis:

- issue-spotting;
- preventing and suppressing issues;
- encouraging issue development;
- challenging old assumptions and articulating new ones;
- providing new data and perspectives;
- providing new forms of analysis for strategy;
- shaping decision-making;
- making strategic choices.

We now present some data from our study of boards in health care. These data are organized around three key themes which reflect many of the items listed above:

- setting the agenda (both operational and strategic);
- decision-making processes;
- how boards form strategy.

Each of these perspectives defines radically different degrees of influence for organizational members, especially senior management. There have been relatively few empirical studies of strategy formulation to illustrate what actually happens in organizations and which model is used in which situations, or proves most appropriate. One longitudinal study by Grinyer and Norburn (1974) which included direct observations and real time data showed how the classical approach overemphasizes choice and underemphasizes the role of informal communications in strategy formulation.

A more general problem with the literature is that it is rooted in the private sector and by analysing public sector organizations the frame of reference can be broadened. As yet, a dynamic theory of strategy has not been developed nor has the core question of what makes one organization more successful than another, been answered. In our search for the essence of what makes a board or organization effective, we need to know whether strategy makes a difference. Is it just conventional wisdom that there is a need for strategy or is there real evidence?

Recent research evidence would seem to support the case that strategy can make a difference to performance, perhaps undermining the radical scepticism of the population ecologists. In studies of what makes an organization competitive, Kanter (1983 and 1989) has emphasized the need for an organization to seek a balance or fit between the strategy and the environment; and to ensure the strategy adopted matched with the culture and structure of the organization. Pettigrew and Whipp (1991) have highlighted a series of factors which collectively define and discriminate between organizations which compete effectively and those which were less effective. This included as a variable the strategic choices made by senior management. If strategy is a critical variable in success then it can be seen as the mechanism whereby management can make sense of and translate its judgements into a direction and ultimately, if the strategy is implemented, into actions. These five factors associated with high firm performance can be defined as:

- environmental assessment: the move from technical and specialist data collection to become a collective open learning system;
- leading change: change leadership which can involve action by people at every level of the business;
- linking strategic and operational change: the process had both as intentional but also as emergent character;
- human resources as assets and liabilities: treating human resource management as a strategic concern; coping with the linked analytical, educational, and political dimensions of the process;
- coherence in the management of change: the ability to manage a series of interrelated and emergent changes at once.

Research on the health sector in the USA (Shortell *et al.* 1990) further underpins the importance of strategy. In a comparative study of the strategies adopted by large hospital systems in the USA they demonstrate that the strategic choices made by senior management were one of the key factors in success. They also demonstrate that in the hospital context these strategies have to be produced using collaborative processes which involve the professionals, the clinicians in particular, if they are to be successfully implemented. In a British study of strategic change in the health service, Pettigrew *et al.* (1992) show that those districts that were the most effective at implementing change maintained a consistent strategic direction over time, despite the competing demands of their environment. In terms of strategy, Pettigrew *et al.* (1992: 227) found data and clear thinking helped frame strategic thinking.

Perhaps analytical considerations represented necessary conditions, while sufficient conditions related to processes of negotiation and change. Here the starting-point was critical: a broad vision seemed more likely to generate movement than a blueprint. Such broad visions were found to have significant process and implementation benefits in terms of commitment-building and allowing top–down pressure to be married with bottom-up concern.

In our view, conceptual separation of strategy formulation from strategy implementation is counter-productive in understanding them both as part of a single process. For example, Quinn's (1980) view of logical incrementalism incorporates an iteration from formulation to implementation and back again. In this way responses to environmental pressures can feed back into the formulation process and produce a more coherent strategy. Mintzberg (1987) also depicts the formulation of strategy as far from a rational process and more of a craft process involving iterations and adjustments. This includes an acknowledgement of the use of intuition in reaching judgements about appropriate choices. The complexity of the process is stressed by Hart and Banbury (1994) who argued that organizations could be mapped as possessing different levels and types of strategy-making capability. Interestingly, they demonstrate that organizations which simultaneously use multiple strategy-making modes out-perform those using only a single mode.

6.4. Board Processes

In studying the processes within board meetings, an understanding of what can be judged effective depends upon the purpose of the board, its role and objectives. Department of Health guidelines prior to the formation of the new authorities and trusts did not specify their specific roles or purpose. There are fundamental differences between the purchasing role with its links into the community and the need to assess the whole range of health needs, when compared to an acute trust with its provider role and hierarchical structure or to a community trust with its different focus and dispersed workforce. That there was a lack of thought to how the roles of each type of board differed, is evidenced by the uniformity of their composition. The White Paper *Working For Patients* (Cm 555, 1989) anticipated mainly acute units going for trust status and set the composition formula to suit them, which perhaps resulted in many community and ambulance trusts having to include additional executives to cover their key senior personnel. The needs of a health authority board with its external focus on purchasing strategy and the identification of health needs are clearly very different from those of more inward-facing and operational hospital-based trusts.

Empirical evidence from the observation of eleven different post-1990 NHS boards for periods between twelve and eighteen months, plus in-depth interviews with all board members (see Appendix), is presented to enable an insight to be gained into how these boards operate, what involvement they had in strategy formulation, the contributions of different members, and how all of these factors can develop over time. Data on members' perceptions of their own and the board's role comes from our two national surveys of all health authority and all trust members carried out during their first year of operation.

During the first months after establishment, there was some ambiguity amongst both executive and non-executive members as to what their precise role was (Ashburner and Cairncross 1991). This was more notable on district and regional authorities where there was more emphasis on policy interpretation and purchasing than on operational factors, with which members from the private sector were more familiar. During the period of observation, very few of the boards studied put any time aside during or between meetings to address the issue of defining the board or individual roles more precisely. As the issue of probity came to the fore in 1993, several of the study boards were beginning to address these issues and introduce more formal training sessions. Guidelines from the Department of Health on probity and corporate governance emerged in 1994. As clearer terms of reference have been established, this has also enabled boards to define their role more precisely and to focus any recruitment of new members on those skills or background that are seen to be most appropriate.

At the outset of the study the assumption was made that the main objective of changes to the authorities was to enable them to become more strategic decision-making bodies. This was based upon the White Paper (Cm 555, 1989) objective that boards should become more business-like in nature and extrapolation from what private sector boards were assumed to do. Boards had to address the question of what their specific role and involvement in strategic and operational issues was. Without a definition of purpose, there is nothing for the board to measure its performance against. Criticisms about the lack of effectiveness of the old-style authorities, centred on their composition, abound but, as has been shown, composition is only one of the variables potentially affecting effectiveness and impact.

Foundations of Board Effectiveness

Our analysis of the processes which occur at board meetings are based upon a number of prerequisites which need to be established first. These include the format of meetings, regular attendance by all board members, the amount and timing of available information, and the skills that individuals bring to their roles. This data is presented at more length elsewhere (Fitzgerald 1992; Ashburner and Cairncross 1993; Ashburner 1994*b*).

The survey revealed that the overwhelming majority of boards met formally once a month and that meetings were subdivided in a variety of ways between public and private or confidential. This happened less frequently in trusts which were statutorily required to meet in public only once a year. The meetings held in public tended to repeat the private agenda omitting items deemed confidential and adding others that were viewed as positive for public relations. This part of meetings emphasizes the boards' outward-looking role but was seldom a forum for open discussion on the early stages of policy or strategy formulation.

Each board had, to varying degrees, set aside time in board meetings or arranged extra meetings to discuss certain issues in more depth. One district authority held informal meetings once a month whilst others held them as and when they were required, with only one regional health authority calling an extra meeting within the first year. The trusts tended to substitute informal meetings for board meetings two or three times a year. In some authorities there were no subgroups, whilst in others several had been set up, usually to address specific functions such as marketing and issues such as complaints. Subsequent to the research each board has been required to set up an audit committee, following the Cadbury recommendations, and most have also set up a remunerations committee, as is common in the private sector. The role played by informal meetings and subgroups was not specifically addressed by the research but clearly these can play a critical role both in the level of involvement of the non-executives in debating issues in more depth and in their general education.

In the case study boards there was a very high level of attendance and this can be seen as a significant development. This consistency of attendance at meetings along with the high level of homogeneity amongst non-executives led to individual members expressing strong feelings of corporate identity. This was conducive to the development of open debate in the private parts of meetings, although the homogeneity could also result in a limited range of viewpoints being expressed. High attendance also ensured greater knowledge of the agenda and the history of prior discussions on a topic. A recurring theme in the presentation of the data on board processes is the level of individual and board development that occurred during the period of the research.

Whilst the standard of data and its presentation varied between boards, there was no evidence from the interviews that members felt dissatisfied with the available data. There were a number of examples of the format, presentation, and timing of information to the board being regularly discussed, with adjustments and improvements made based on members' feedback. Whilst most boards had some form of secretarial support, this did not allow for executive summaries to be made of often bulky reports. Non-executives were aware that they could request any additional information should they require it.

The study produced extensive data on the backgrounds of both the executive and non-executive members and about the processes adopted to select and train them (FitzGerald 1992; Ashburner and Cairncross 1993; Ashburner 1994) to which only brief reference will be made here. There are two major observations. First, on the whole, executives had considerable experience of management in the NHS, usually at a senior level, before appointment to the board. The possible exceptions to this are the professional members who did not necessarily have prior management experience. Executives, including medical professionals, had functional or specialist experience but few of them had prior experience of serving as a member of a corporate board.

Secondly, the non-executives were predominantly from a private sector background but within this there was considerable variety in relation to their level of experience. As with the executives, many had a functional specialism but many were not knowledgeable about the health sector, before joining the board. By their own assessment and on independent judgement, the learning curve for a member with no prior experience in health is at least one year. A proportion of non-executives also had no prior experience of board membership.

Setting the Agenda

A board's freedom to frame strategy is influenced by the organization's position and interlinkage with other organizations. In the case of the private sector this will include relationships with parent companies, whilst in the NHS it includes relationships with other tiers and the Department of Health. Decentralization of management has given greater autonomy to individual units to manage their internal affairs but the broader policy base within which they must operate is set by the Department of Health. It is within these parameters that individual boards can set their strategies. One of the key issues which relates to both the content and process of board activities is the formulation of the agenda.

Our examination of board processes involved an analysis of the content of meeting agendas and the time spent on each item. The main questions that need to be addressed are what items are brought to the board and what is the balance between operational or for-information items and those involving strategic decision-making. Related to these is the question of the stage in the decision-making process at which items are brought to the attention of the board. This indicates the need to open the strategy box in terms of both process and content, as discussed earlier. These are critical factors in the non-executive's ability to monitor or influence executive decisions.

Setting a board agenda presupposes an awareness of the type of items that come within the remit of the board to address. In the early months of the case study boards' operations, setting the agendas was the responsibility of the chief executive who therefore implicitly made these decisions. At the time of interview none of the chief executives could clearly explain the boundary between what was or was not an issue for the board. Most said that it was an intuitive assessment based upon what they felt to be the main information they believed the non-executives should have and the main issues facing the organization. Those boards in the study set up in the first year of the reforms did not discuss the type of issue that should be brought to board meetings and specifically what the balance between operational and strategic issues should be. Trust boards set up in later waves benefited from the learning process undergone by earlier boards and like the third-wave trust in the study, did specifically address these issues. On all the boards studied, as board processes developed, different ways of composing the agenda emerged, with both executives and non-executives able to add items when they wished to.

There were widely differing practices with regard to the number of items on the agenda (Ashburner *et al.* 1993*a*). For example, over an eighteen-month period, one regional health authority's agenda averaged twenty-six items whilst the other averaged just thirteen. District health authorities tended to have the most crowded agendas as they tended to combine public, private, and confidential parts into one meeting, and one regularly had over thirty agenda items. The trusts tended to cluster around nine to eleven items per meeting. Meetings could last anywhere between two and four hours but the majority took about three hours. Only one board had split their agenda by type of item, those for information, discussion and approval. The pattern of time spent on different items was broadly similar between boards with the majority of items (70 per cent) being dealt within five minutes or less and key discussion items taking anything from twenty minutes to an hour. The time spent on finance, for example, averaged ten minutes at district health authorities and over fifty at trusts.

The analysis of the data has identified the balance of discussion between operational and strategic items, the differences between boards, and how these changed over the period of the study. The survey of members identified what they saw as the most important roles for the board. Five were judged to be important or very important. First was the obligation to meet the health needs of the community, second was judging priorities with regard to spending, and third was determining the strategic objectives. Fourth was ensuring that standards of care were defined and fifth, the monitoring of the organisation's performance. Here there is a clear recognition of both the strategic and monitoring roles.

In contrast to members' expectations, the majority of all meetings related to items for information and operational issues. A key operational issue, vital for the monitoring of performance, was finance, and this uniquely appeared on every agenda and at many meetings was the item that took the greatest proportion of time. Finance could equally be presented as a strategic issue since the implications of limited funds and unlimited demands would have a fundamental effect on any strategy.

There were substantial differences in the balance of agendas across the range of boards studied. The regional health authority meetings contained the fewest items of strategy and there were rarely policy items that required a decision. When policy was made it was in reaction to events where policy was obscure or non-existent. One example of this was when a policy decision had to be made on whether GP fundholders could set up a company and purchase services from themselves. The primacy of the monitoring role at region and the uncertainty of their role in the internal market, might account for their limited strategic role.

At district level, there was a limited number of strategic items on most agendas; on average only one or two. Not all of these led to discussion or decisions since they were ongoing issues where external negotiations or consultation was required before a decision could be reached. Taking a comparative sample of six meetings from across the different sites, the items discussed were, in one district, the health investment plan; in another the placement of a special unit between two competing provider units; and in the third, whether three acute units should seek trust status together. On other occasions specialized purchasing decisions were debated, for example, on whether funding would continue for IVF treatment.

Family health services authorities tended to have a higher percentage of agenda items involving policy or strategy, but this did not result in any greater number of actual decisions being required at meetings. In one, an important strategic item was the question of the joint working between the family and the district health authorities, in the process of developing joint purchasing. As has been noted, the development of purchasing units has meant that smaller district health authorities especially have needed to merge to achieve a viable size. In such authorities this has been a predominant strategic issue.

Trust boards differed from other boards in the extent of their strategic role. Although the actual number of strategic items was still relatively few, they did occupy a greater percentage of the discussion time and were more likely to result in a decision. This more strategic role developed in trusts may be related to their newness and being unhampered by traditional authority precedents or to a clearer understanding among the directors of the operational provider role, which more closely parallels a private sector service organization.

There was evidence of greater involvement in strategy over the period of the study, especially in the trusts. Regional health authorities have undergone radical restructuring and are now executive outposts rather than the first line of management. Districts still show the widest variation in their progress towards a strategic purchasing role, which is partly attributable to the disruption caused by the merger process.

Decision-Making Processes

There are a number of key influences on board processes which have a direct bearing on how effective the board will be strategically and in relation to probity. The level of influence of each of the groups on the board will be examined with an analysis of the contributions made at the board meetings observed during the study.

The questions of when items are first presented to the board and the degree of choice open to the board in the formation of policy are important dimensions in understanding the board processes. If items are brought to the board at a late stage in the decision-making process, not only does this mean that the non-executives have had less time to become familiar with the issues, but also that they have had less opportunity to contribute in the formative stages. It is also more likely that the range of potential options will have been reduced, and at the extreme, only one course of action is put to the board for approval. This would be an echo of the old-style boards and their role in rubberstamping executive decisions. This highlights one of the ways that the board process can be influenced.

The question of timing of presentation of issues to the board, as described above, is one way that the executive can control or influence board operations and this can be broadened to include items which may not ever reach the board agenda. Whereas this might be seen as a direct attempt at control, an indirect form of control is one which we have termed 'funnelling'. At a two- to three-hour meeting held just once a month there is only time for a limited number of items. How this selection or funnelling process is decided upon is critical. Although the chief executive usually had the main responsibility of drawing up the agenda, in some authorities, and especially the trusts, the chief executive would consult the board chair. Since many chairs had a greater involvement in the organization than did other non-executives, there would be less likelihood of key strategic items being omitted or not brought to the board until near the end of the decision-making process.

As with many of the criteria which are essential for the effective operations of the board, such practices that enhance its operations are dependent on the discretion and personalities of individuals. In this the roles of the chief executive and chair are crucial as is their interrelationship (R. Stewart 1991; Ferlie *et al.* 1995). The extent to which the chief executive and/or the chair dominated the meetings varied considerably between boards. The natural consequence was that where the chair and chief executive were less dominant, the contributions from other members increased and the scope of the discussion broadened. Certainly as non-executives gained in knowledge and experience they were more prepared to contribute to discussions. They were also more likely to ask for particular items of relevance to be placed on the board's agenda which could potentially broaden the scope of the meetings.

It is not just funnelling that can restrict debate at board level. How the chair chooses to conduct the meeting and the extent to which other members are allowed to speak is very important. Another important factor is how the chief executive presents his or her report which can be crucial in the extent to which items are open to discussion or closed. In most of the case study sites both chairs and chief executives encouraged participation and contributions from all members. In only one site, a district health authority, did the combination of dominant chief executive and a weak chair have the outcome that far fewer broad-based discussions took place at meetings. In another, it appeared to be the deliberate management strategy of the chief executive that items on his report were carefully worded to avoid giving recommendations for decision.

On the board the chief executive is technically an equal member with the other members, unlike at management meetings. Most executives in interview, however, said that the hierarchical relationship might constrain their contributions at board meetings, whereas in an apparent contradiction, they would be more inclined to speak their mind fully at management meetings. Executives have the advantage over non-executives in that they have many other meetings to discuss issues and work through differences. There was thus a tendency for the executive to bring issues to the board once there was a level of consensus or, if there were differences, for these not necessarily to be expressed.

The survey of members showed that non-executives acknowledged that the executives had the most influence on the process of decision-making. One-third of members also said that much of their work could still best be described as rubberstamping management decisions. This response was more heavily weighted towards new members, and was less common on trusts. More interesting, though, was the response of executives who generally agreed with the statement that they would not put proposals forward if they thought that the non-executives would find them unacceptable. This is one indication of how non-executives can exert an influence, but we need to examine the extent of their direct influence.

During the period of the study there were only a few examples where it was clear that the views of the non-executives had outweighed those of the executive in the process of making a specific decision. In one trust the non-executives successfully reversed an executive proposal that there would be no new signposts and in one district the non-executives succeeded in changing the balance of spending to ensure a greater amount went to mental health. To examine the influence of the non-executives, we need to analyse members' contributions to meetings.

The common thread between all case study boards was the tendency for executives, especially in the early days, to limit themselves mainly to the reporting role and to answering questions and for the non-executives to question on points of clarity and to offer opinions. The type and extent of contributions cannot be generalized by role or background as these were more dependent upon individual personalities.

Non-executives and executives alike could be divided into those who limited their contributions to those areas where they had specific responsibility or knowledge and those who contributed on most issues. The former pattern of contributions was often influenced by background or the basis upon which members were appointed. Most notable here were the non-executives on regional health authorities who were appointed as family health services authority chairs, the university appointees on all boards, and to a lesser extent the practitioner appointees on family health services authorities.

There were some differences between types of authorities with the most limited level of discussion occurring at regional health authority meetings. This may have been influenced by several factors, from the lack of strategic items on the agenda to the less clearly defined non-executive role which resulted in the lack of engagement with authority business of some of the non-executives. This is exemplified by one non-executive who after nine months on the authority where community health council (CHC) minutes were presented monthly, asked what a CHC was. At district level the non-executives were more likely to question the executive but they seldom challenged the executive. At both these types of authority the executives were more likely to dominate the meetings.

The composition of family health services authorities with just one executive produced a different pattern of contributions. Attending executives spoke very little except to present reports or answer questions. Despite their non-representational role most practitioner members spoke only to their own area and some were very quiet. On both family health service authorities the nurse member was the most successful at developing a generalist role. The discussions therefore were dominated by the lay non-executives, who were, individually, the most successful at contributing over a wide range of topics. In one family health services authority there were frequent challenges of the chief executive officer and chair. Even though the chief excutive officer was the only executive on the board, members still felt that they had the greatest effect both on proceedings and outcome.

On the trusts it was notable that executives were comparatively new to their corporate roles and appeared more willing to open up debate with the non-executives, even to the point of actively seeking advice. In two trusts the opinion was expressed by the chair that the non-executives were 'keeping the executives on their toes'. Although both of these boards had one non-executive who was very quiet, debates were relatively lively, and although some non-executives were willing to challenge the executive, this was always on detail rather than on the underlying assumptions or philosophy of the decision. The norms of politeness and consensus still predominated. So although items that had a clear strategy implication were discussed, the extent of non-executive contribution was marginal. During the period of the research, as the experience and knowledge of the non-executives grew, so did the extent and quality of their contributions.

The non-executive role has been shown to be a critical factor in the effectiveness of boards in the private sector (Pettigrew and McNulty, 1995) and it is no less important in the public sector. It is, however, problematic to assess the overall effectiveness of the role of the non-executives in the formulation of strategy or in monitoring and ensuring probity.

We therefore concluded that the formulation of strategy often occurs as an implicit rather than an explicit process and few decision points could be traced. The emergent nature of decision-making before the recommendation to the board stage is reached means that it is essential for non-executives to raise items at an early stage and for executives to keep the board informed or involved throughout. For this the board is again totally dependent on the executive.

One factor that makes it difficult for the non-executives to monitor the executive is the emphasis placed on their supportive role which places them in a role complementary to management. This, plus the tendency of many boards to allocate specific roles to non-executives, draws them more into the operational management role, and makes it more difficult to retain an independent overview. Charkham (1994) stressed the incompatibility of the cooperative and supervisory roles.

How effectively members are able to carry out these roles is dependent upon a number of factors which are in the remit of individual boards to address but which are not necessarily recognized in the formal structure and mechanisms for accountability. These behavioural and processual issues include the timing of data, what is put on the agenda, how much information the non-executives are given, and how open the chair and chief executive allow the meeting to be. As the non-executives gained in knowledge and experience, we found that the number and quality of their contributions increased but this by itself cannot ensure their ability to play a full and effective role.

How Boards Form Strategy

In drawing together the data on the extent of the non-executive influence on strategy and its development over the period of the research it was possible to classify four different levels of involvement. Level A would be a continuation of the pattern of contributions on the old-style health authorities, in which non-executives essentially acted as rubber stamps. Although some questions of clarification may be asked, executive recommendations tend to go through with little real debate. At level B, the non-executives can be seen to be more probing, questioning proposals that come from the executive even to the point of sending them back for reconsideration. The important point here is that the non-executives are still not involved in the development of strategy. At level C there would be a substantial non-executive involvement in deciding strategic options and at an early stage in the process.

In these instances it is likely that any given strategy will pass through a staged series of discussions, with non-executive directors involved in several of the stages. At level D, the board debates and delineates a vision of strategic priorities for a future period of time. The non-executive directors are involved in shaping this vision, which underpins medium term statements of strategy. The shape of the vision and the timescale for its achievement may be flexible, but its assumptions form the foundation for prioritizing strategic developments.

Localities may move from one level to another through time, although moving on from Level B may be complex, hard work. Two factors will be essential: having non-executive directors in post who have the experience, expertise, and confidence to move from Level B to C and D and having executives who genuinely want the non-executive directors to make this transition. It should be noted that the use of the levels model is only a device and does not imply determinism or that movement is only in one direction.

In our case study sites, our analysis showed that by the end of the research period, there were no sites at Level A. The majority of the sites were at Level B, with Trusts showing greater signs of movement to Level C. At the end of the period of study (i.e. mid-1993) one trust had virtually achieved Level D. Two trust sites and one district health authority could be seen as beginning at Level B and progressing to Level C. Interestingly, in the case of the district health authority this progress was severely hampered by the loss of several, experienced non-executive directors for a variety of reasons, within a six-month period. The board then had to go back through a new learning phase, which caused rapid regression in the strategy-making capacity of the board.

This section has discussed a wide number of variables which all have an influence on board effectiveness and it is the cumulative effect of these which is significant. The starting-point for any board which wishes to address these issues needs to be an open discussion of what the role of the board is in relation to that of management and the boundaries between issues which are the prerogative of managers and those which should come to the board. If this process is allowed to emerge by default as a result of custom and practice then this allows much greater power to the executive. Whilst some of the study boards became set in their ways, others remained open to the process of self development.

6.5. Concluding Discussion

This chapter has shown the importance of the board processes in determining how great an impact the board will display with regard both to managerial issues in the formulation of strategy and to corporate governance in the monitoring of the executive and ensuring probity. The private sector-style boards which are being introduced into the public sector are becoming more important managerially when compared with the old-style authorities. The reformulation of the authorities into boards was seen as part of the general drive to increase managerialism but given that the main weakness of private sector boards is their dominance by management, it is crucial that the process is understood and the type of board that is most appropriate for the needs of the public sector is chosen.

When we talk of boards being 'effective', we mean 'effective' in relation to a range of board roles. An increased effectiveness in one area may detract from another. As we said in Section 6.1, one of the definitions of good corporate governance is the ability to balance the needs of all the key stakeholders. A decision should be made by the board to decide on the extent to which it delegates control to management. An involvement in strategy formulation can be seen as important but it is necessary to balance this with the need of the non-executives to retain an independent stance to enable them to evaluate both the executive and the strategy. It is critical that the need for accountability and the representation of key stakeholders does not become secondary to organizational success factors now that the only formal accountability is to the Department of Health and success is judged predominantly in financial terms.

The decision-making process that occurs at board level can be seen only one stage in the total strategy process. Our observation of boards in the health service has shown the iterative and emergent nature of the decision-making process and how it often occurs as an implicit rather than an explicit process. Few explicit choice points could be identified and decision processes were often collective and consensual in nature. It was often difficult to disentangle policy formulation and implementation.

Going back to the initial strategy typology generated by Whittington (1993), the first point is that our characterization of the strategy process is at marked variation in almost every respect to the classical model portrayed by the rational planners.

Nor did the evolutionary model fit with actors' perceptions of what was important to them. Board members nearly always assumed that the possession of a coherent strategy was a competitive advantage particularly essential to the management of organizational change and that it would lead to superior performance, contrary to the sceptical views of the population ecologists. 'Strategy chatter' was widespread. Whether this widespread perception is objectively valid is difficult to test in the absence of a different kind of efficiency study than was possible here. However, unlike private sector markets, quasi-market forces by themselves are unlikely to be allowed to weed out inefficient providers. The quasi-market was shown to be relational and as socially and institutionally embedded. Thus reconfiguration based on considerations of strategic planning (as in the case of the London hospitals) (Tomlinson Report, 1992) is more likely to operate as an instrument of change than quasi-market forces.

Some disengagement of individuals and organizations from the national, social, and institutional context (against Granovetter 1985) was also evident as increased emphasis was placed on the autonomy and future of the single organization such as a NHS trust. The organizational field of the public sector is becoming more loosely coupled in nature. To what do actors owe loyalty and their identity? We suggest that national reference points such as the college or occupation have perhaps declined in importance, while the micro-identity of the organization has increased.

In our judgement, the processual or emergent model of strategy is the perspective most validated by our data. This has important consequences for tying strategy-making and organizational development activity more closely together. Within this perspective, strategy involves building on internal core competences, not simply repositioning the organization in response to market signals (Whittington 1993). Key competencies are not traded on the market but have to be built up within the organization (Grant 1991). What matters, therefore, is the slow and patient building-up of such core competences (Hamel 1991) based on intangible assets such as learning levels, the attitude to experimentation, the ability to manage change, and levels of tacit and esoteric knowledge (Pettigrew and Whipp 1991). The harder edge is that it is through carefully acquiring such strategic competencies that organizations increase the probability of high performance.

The centrality of the non-executive role has been recognized and it is necessary to identify the factors which might impede the ability of non-executives to contribute to board decisions and to monitor and hold executives to account. An important conclusion is therefore the need to develop the non-executives to increase their knowledge and confidence; to ensure they act in an independent and, if necessary, challenging way; and to recognize the need for continuity to given them time to develop their role. This needs to be matched by the conscious development of the board and the specification of its precise role.

A key conclusion is that the research evidence suggests that the boards studied were progressing towards being more strategically oriented, albeit at different speeds. The influence of the board on the strategy of the organization means that the composition of the board is likely to have an effect on the content of strategy. The predominance of private sector non-executives and the consequent level of homogeneity could therefore become a strong force for cultural change and the backing of government policies. Other factors that will have a bearing on this are the extent to which the non-executives, whatever their background, apply policy decisions and their expertise in relation to the needs of the organization rather than in a narrowly prescriptive way. This chapter has identified the prerequisites for an effective board and has developed an analysis of the processes of strategic decision-making which should inform our understanding of management control at the strategic apex of an organization, whether it be in the public or the private sector.

Another important theoretical implication is that our data add to other studies which cumulatively suggest that the managerial hegemony or rubber stamp thesis is too crude and has been somewhat overstated. Our evidence of a greater involvement by the non-executive directors and the board in strategic process in the NHS trusts (all acute in our sample) than in the district, regional, or family health authorities is also interesting.

Within the private sector, Lorsch and MacIver (1989) suggested that non-executives may move centre stage in moments of crisis, with the reconfiguration of the power relationships which had held in routine conditions. Pettigrew and McNulty (1995) add to this the observation that non-executives find it easier to say no—to exercise negative influence—than to initiate changes of direction which challenge the perspectives and attitudes of corporate management.

It was possible for non-executive directors to win positive influence, however, but this required a much stronger power base and more political will and interpersonal skill. Power sources included relevant expertise and experience; power derived from internal or external power figures (such as the chair); using the authority of representational roles; and most crucially the flows of experience and informal information which arose from relationship- and network-building in and outside the boardroom.

Within the NHS, R. Stewart *et al.* (1989) had similarly suggested that the old district health authorities possessed a negative boundary-setting role. Ranade (1985) also pointed to an interesting subgroup of pre-1990 members who acted strategically in a more proactive way.

Since the 1990 reforms, we concluded that the non-executive directors on the boards studied were successful in negotiating a more active role in the strategy process than the managerial hegemony thesis suggested. While their involvement was partial, vulnerable to turnover, and perceived as moving on from a very low base, nevertheless this is a significant development. One explanation is that for all the criticisms of the 1990 reforms, these did attract senior, experienced, and skilled personnel who are self-confident and powerful enough to begin to challenge the domination of senior management.

As old problems decline, new ones emerge. Has the pendulum swung too far in favour of an appointed non-executive élite and is there sufficient opportunity for other groups such as professional staff to contribute to the development of strategy? Is the organization sufficiently accountable to the wider groups of stakeholders, the patient, and the community? These issues are taken up in the following two chapters. The notion that boards and authorities must be either democratically accountable or managerially effective also needs to be challenged. This misconception that the two factors are mutually exclusive has arisen first because historically each view has been associated with opposing political views, and secondly because the reforms designed to increase managerialism mistakenly assumed that this would also increase organizational effectiveness.

Managerial effectiveness and democratic accountability could be compatible. If management models and measures are viewed as tools, then they can be seen as value-free and neutral. They can be used for whatever ends management and the government choose. What makes them value-laden are the measures chosen and how they are brought in and used. There has in our view been too simplistic a reliance on what have been seen as private sector models and practices. Whether in fact an unheralded hybrid model is now emerging remains an intriguing possibility. Before a definitive view can be taken, however, it will be necessary to consider the question of the accountability (discussed in Chapter 8) of these boards.

PROFESSIONALS AND THE NEW PUBLIC MANAGEMENT

7.1. Themes and Issues

In this chapter, we address a number of interrelated themes focusing upon the fluctuating position of professions and professionals in the changing public sector.

Three broad themes will be explored in this chapter. The first theme relates to the impact of competition and the quasi-market on the professions and on professionals. The second theme centres on the changing character of the management processes within organizations and examines the argument that greater managerialism has impacted adversely on the professions. The third theme focuses on individual professionals. It provides an analysis of the role of professional managers, as a new hybrid form. This theme examines these processes of development and the subsequent issues raised for professional managers, their colleague professionals, and their colleague managers.

In what ways are these themes important to our understanding of the new public management? Chapter 1 addressed the issue of the extent to which the management of the public sector could be described as a distinctive process of management. There are a number of facets to this debate and here we shall centre on those which relate to professionals.

First, the public sector can be characterized as a service sector consisting distinctively of public service organizations. Much attention has therefore been given to the ethos and values of public service and accountability which are said to be distinctive aspects of public sector organizations in shaping work processes (Ranson and Stewart 1989; J. Stewart and Clarke 1987; J. Stewart and Walsh 1992; J. D. Stewart 1986). 'It has been argued that it is dangerous for organisations in the public sector to adopt uncritically, values pursued by private firms. The public service ethic is not to be regretted.' (J. D. Stewart 1986). Secondly, one may analyse the characteristics of these constituent organizations. One distinctive feature of public sector organizations is that they are highly professionalized (Hood 1991; Pollitt 1990; J. D. Stewart 1986; Local Government Training Board 1987; Harrow and Willcocks 1990). Public service values combine therefore with the values and standards of the professions to create a complex pattern of influences. Have the escalating pressures on the public sector resulted in an erosion of traditional professionalization? How has the professional character of the public sector, previously upheld as a distinguishing characteristic, been affected?

In this introduction, we suggest a number of ways in which these unfolding debates relate to professional work in the public services. An immediate scan of the impact of the new public management across a range of professions makes it clear that it is varied. As Crompton (1990) has pointed out, many of the occupational groups traditionally described as professions have derived considerable advantages from the shift to market forces. She points to the rapid expansion of the professions of accountancy and law, in both the public and the private sectors. It is clear that changes to the structure and management of the public sector have exerted new work pressures on the teaching profession, in higher, secondary, and primary education. These pressures have had a variety of impacts (Johnes and Cave 1994; Keep 1992).

From the wide-ranging debate about the changing nature of public management, introduced in Chapter 1, we identified four variants of the new public management. It is clear as Davies *et al.* (1993) point out, that the new public management is not a homogeneous set of practices across the public sector. A specific unresolved debate centres on the definition of 'new public management' (Gunn 1988; Harrow and Willcocks 1990), and whether it includes as a central tenet a shift towards managerialism and the empowerment of management. If this empowerment has occurred, has it taken place at the expense of professionals? Scott (1985) disputes the early theorists' ideas that professionalization and bureaucratization are opposing forces. He sees them as companion processes and like C. Davies (1983) argues that they can work well together. Here we seek to argue that the picture, both at the collective and at the individual level, is complex and cannot simply be portrayed as a unidimensional shift of power from professionals to managers.

These arguments suggest there may be differential impact of the top–down changes currently under way across the public sector. The combined force of the quasi-market and the shift to greater managerialism is having a complex impact, with some losers and some gainers. The empirical evidence presented in this chapter will suggest that there is no clear-cut pattern, and we cannot safely conclude that the new public management has had uniform, adverse impacts on the professions. Part of the explanation for these differences may lie in the pace of change in different organizational contexts.

Another and more fundamental part of the explanation may lie in the nature of professional expertise and its association with a set of conditions which no longer exist. The question of whether the concept of a 'profession' and of a 'professional' remains valid will be addressed in the next section.

Overall, this chapter will seek to examine, in more detail, the relative positions currently of management and the professionals in the public sector. Data will be presented to illuminate the debate and illustrate the changing relativities over time. These data are drawn from several of our studies in health care, but particular references will be made in this chapter to a specific study of a cohort of doctors who were taking on management roles and undertaking management training (Fitzgerald 1994*a*, and 1994*b*). One caveat is necessary: as this cohort in its entirety accepted management posts willingly and undertook management training, they should be seen as a skewed sample.

In Section 7.2, we explore the theoretical and conceptual background to some of the current debates concerning professionalism and professionals.

In Section 7.3, we focus on the first main theme of the chapter which examines the thesis that the introduction of market-type mechanisms represents a threat to the traditional power bases of the professions (McKinlay 1988; Hafferty 1988). The nature of these potential threats will be analysed and tested against the impact of market mechanisms in the public sector. There are a number of interrelated questions posed. First, whether the quasi-market has affected all professions uniformly. Secondly, what has been the impact of the fragmentation of the system into competitive business units on the exercise of a profession's collective power. Thirdly, whether competition in the market-place will generate competition and conflict within a profession with individuals having to compete with colleagues on grounds of competency. This form of internal competition undermines the principle of collegiality within a profession. Lastly, to what extent has the introduction of a contract-based system created pressures towards quantification and quantifiable standards, which may distort the values held by professionals about quality service and cause conflicts (consideration of this final issue will be merged with the discussion of the second theme set out below).

In Section 7.4, the discussion centres on our second theme. This theme traces the effects on professionals of the gradual introduction (Metcalfe and Richards 1984), through a series of initiatives, of managerial standards and controls, with a consequent move away from the older definitions of administrative management. The rise of the manager in the 1980s and of managerial standards of performance has led to conflicts about priorities between professionals and managers. The process of change in the public sector has brought about consequent changes in professional–management boundaries. This section will be based on data concerning the historical basis of professional power and the arguments about professional dominance, de-professionalization, and/or proletarianization (Elston 1991; Friedson 1984, 1986, 1987; McKinlay and Stoeckle 1988; Oppenheimer 1973; Haug 1973, 1975) which will be reviewed in the next section.

The chapter will challenge the simplistic view that the professionals have lost out to managers. Closer scrutiny suggests that there has been a complex and interactive process of adaptation by both managers and professionals in some parts of the public sector. In this theme, data on the changing roles of individuals holding management positions will be utilized to argue that the roles do not fit the stereotypes, nor do individual incumbents exercise power in isolation but rather through collaborative and team-based decision-making.

The final theme is the focus for Section 7.5 and relates to the impact of the multiplicity of changes on individual professionals. Issues include the implications of creating and defining the roles of new professional managers. We propose that these roles should be seen as new hybrid management roles. Becoming a hybrid generates its own problems: for example, how to train and socialize individuals into the new role. Finally and most importantly such individual role changes affect interrelationships with other professional colleagues and other managers.

To elaborate these themes, the chapter will draw on original data from a number of our studies within the health care sector, and contrast the emerging picture with that occurring in other parts of the public sector and in other newer professions.

7.2. Key Concepts in Relation to Professionalism

To enter into the debate about the impact of the quasi-market on professionals and the changing boundaries between professionals and managers, one must appreciate the historical concept of a professional and a profession. It is important to differentiate here between the collective, that is the profession, and the individual, that is the professional. One continuing source of confusion in the literature is a failure to distinguish the unit of analysis. The concept of a professional has always been an ambiguous one, described by Becker (1970) as a folk concept. Profession, in these terms, was in the eye of the beholder.

Nevertheless, there are a range of theoretical perspectives which could be used to discuss the concept of professionalism and core concepts in that debate. Here three key perspectives will be alluded to: the functionalist perspective, the interactionist perspective, and the theory of closure. The functionalist tradition sets out to define the binding and distinguishing features of a profession (Parsons 1951). The interactionist perspective on the other hand sees the professions as part of a broader and general classification of occupations, with differences of degree rather than kind (Abbott 1988). Closure theory (Collins 1979; Parkin 1979) focuses on the strategy adopted by groups to achieve closure and control, and thus links with managerialist perspectives. Across these various perspectives, there are some commonly agreed characteristics of a profession (Abbott 1988; Asburner 1994a; Elston 1991; Friedson 1986; and McKinlay 1988). For example, there is a body of expert knowledge over which the profession exercises a degree of control and, in the purest form, a monopoly of practice. The profession sets standards of training and controls entry to the group. Once professional membership has been achieved, members of the profession relate to each other on a collegial basis. Within a profession, individuals—as the holders of specialist expertise—expect to exercise a degree of autonomy over their work and their work processes. Some of the ambiguity regarding definitions can be attributed to a confusion of levels and focuses of analysis. Murray *et al.* (1983) provide a useful distinction between the 'outward' and 'inward' faces of a profession. Throughout this chapter, there will be a clear differentiation between discussion of the profession as a collective whole and a focus on the individual professional.

The core focus of this text is the changing nature of public management. This chapter is particularly concerned with changes in the relative power positions of managers and professionals. Therefore two key concepts upon which attention will be focused are the extent of professional dominance over other arenas and the degree of autonomy exercised by the professional.

The concept of professional dominance refers primarily to the collective dominance of the profession over other related professions and over patients (in the case of the medical profession) or consumers (Friedson 1970; Haug 1973; Haug and Lavin 1983). Though historically the processes of change in the public sector are still largely unresearched, there is a measure of agreement about the dominance of the medical profession and its ability to fight off and reject unwanted changes. In the current context this makes the medical profession a particularly interesting case for study. The education professionals, on the other hand, appear to have been less successful in dominating policy in education and have been left with mainly defensive tactics.

Professional autonomy can be conceptualized at the individual and the collective level and refers to the various forms of autonomy exercised over the content and conditions of practice. Elston (1991) reviews the classifications of autonomy proposed by Friedson (1970), Ovreteit (1985), and Schultz and Harrison (1986) and concludes that three main forms of autonomy may be distinguished. These are: political autonomy, the right of the profession to make policy decisions as the legitimate experts; economic autonomy, the right of the profession to determine remuneration; and technical autonomy, the right of the profession to set its own standards and control performance. As Elston (1991) points out, the debates are hampered by inadequate conceptualization of the concepts of dominance and autonomy. This exacerbates the inherent difficulty of assessing changes in the distribution of such an elusive quality as power. Here, we shall argue that indicators of change in relative power positions can only be accessed by detailed, longitudinal studies which immerse the researcher in the unfolding events and their interpretations by the participants. Readers should see Pettigrew (1973) for an example of this kind of research which explored the changing balance of power between two different specialist occupational groupings.

Clearly, our understanding of what constitutes a profession is influenced by history and context. To understand the current situation of professions, one must contextualize them in the economic and social changes of which they are a part. Abbott (1988), McKinlay (1988) and Hafferty (1988) have all argued that the professions can only be understood as part of a dynamic system in a social environment.

To exemplify the importance of this statement, let us return to the earlier paragraph, in which we identified the core characteristics of a profession from the literature. It was suggested that a profession is based on an identifiable body of knowledge. However, it can be demonstrated that even this supposedly concrete attribute is culturally defined and bounded. In the UK and the USA, great stress is placed on the rational and scientific nature of medical judgements and decisions. Yet, as Payer (1988) illustrates, such medical knowledge is highly culturally influenced. Her study demonstrates the wide variations in medical thinking across the UK, USA, France, and Germany.

She questions how the science of medicine can be so different, when the patients are genetically similar. In a thought-provoking (and highly amusing text), she documents the differences of clinical thought: for example, low blood pressure will be treated with eighty-five drugs and hydrotherapy in Germany, but would entitle the sufferer to lower-life insurance rates in the USA and be accounted healthy. For completely different reasons, it is interesting to compare the position of the Soviet doctor to his/her European and US counterparts. Field (1988) illustrates that the status of the Soviet doctor in society is much lower than in the West and the degree of autonomy negligible. Nevertheless the Soviet doctor maintains a very dominant position over the patient.

Clearly some of the accepted attributes of a profession may be debatable and may vary over time and space. Whereas historically the body of medical knowledge may have been easier to codify, this may no longer be achievable with newer areas of knowledge. Similarly the accepted position, power, and status of a professional may be seen to have been won over time, within a particular societal context. It is apparent that in defining a 'profession', generalized concepts have been developed on relatively narrow comparative foundations.

Elston (1991) underlines that US developments are applied to the UK with little consideration for their validity. It seems to have been assumed that if evidence of de-professionalization (and/or proletarianization) has been detected in the USA, then such a trend will be replicated here. This makes little allowance for key differences of context, for example the greater dominance of doctors over other clinical groups in the UK. Our study supports the view that the position of professionals in the UK is developing in different ways to the USA and the result may be a rather different pattern of dominance and autonomy. Larkin (1988) has emphasized that historically the position of the medical profession in the UK in the past has been State-supported. It will be interesting to examine the extent to which this will continue in a market-based system.

Given the nature of the criticisms and debates in the literature about the concept of a profession and a professional, it is clear that these are not unambiguous or absolute concepts. Some writers have argued that professions would be better understood as part of a broader typology of occupations. Abbott (1988) argues for a relative interpretation of the concept, with greater research interest focusing on the permeable boundaries between the established professions and other groups.

Another strand of research raises similar queries. Scarborough (1995) argues that the critical issues of today do not focus narrowly on the position of professionals, but relate to the management of expertise more generally. His arguments are based in an analysis of the trends and structural changes in employment evident in the post-industrial or post-modern society. Many writers have postulated that firms will be increasingly dependent on experts or knowledge workers for competitive advantage (Bell 1973; Prahalad and Hamel 1990; and Senge 1991). Parallelling these changes, there is an explosive increase in newer bodies of knowledge with their own specialists and experts. Many of these newer areas of expertise have not developed along the lines of the older, historically established professions; despite a similar foundation in the ownership and control of a body of knowledge. One explanation is that the social and political conditions are now different and to establish the boundaries of a body of expertise and group control over boundaries and entry standards would be impossible and unacceptable. This argument rests on the view that social and political conditions are not conducive to the creation of new professions.

Crompton (1990) after an extensive review of the literature, concludes that professions are better understood as a mode of control than as an occupation. This is useful because it centres interest on boundaries, control and status, and defensive tactics during periods of change and helps to explain behaviour at the collective and the individual levels.

Already these debates call into question the relevance of the concept of profession today. Is it merely that the concept itself is ambiguous and in a dynamic environment the boundaries of the definition shift? Or is the issue a more fundamental one: that the professions themselves are an outmoded form?

An alternative argument which adds to the scepticism focuses primarily on the nature of expertise and the underpinning technologies, which tend to make the communication of knowledge more open and transparent. Gibbons *et al.* (1994) present a thesis concerning 'the new production of knowledge', arguing that we are witnessing a profound shift in the forms of knowledge production, from what is described as Mode 1 to Mode 2. When Mode 1 dominated, knowledge and its problems were defined and accumulated by professionals in universities and similar institutions; they were largely based on disciplines and had to comply with agreed principles.

In Mode 2, it is postulated, knowledge is produced in context, by differing configurations of human resources, through heterogeneity, and across disciplines. The authors point to a number of reasons which combine to account for this trend. This line of argument has radical implications for academic disciplines and for professions. It leads to the conclusion that professions as occupational groupings are a historical anachronism and that there will be no further professions created. It also suggests that the mode of operation of the individual professional and professional values, such as self-regulation, may be difficult to sustain.

From the arguments discussed so far, one might conclude that the idea that professions are innately different from other groups of experts may be questionable. However, it is clear that over the period of their history, professions have established ways of doing and behaving. Some of these have common elements across several professions but some are unique. The established professions condition and socialize their members in powerful ways. Raelin (1985) presents an interesting account of these methods of conditioning, utilizing them as the foundation for the argument that they increase the probability of professionals' resistance to management control. He argues that there are five features of professional culture (into which professionals are conditioned), which lead to conflicts with management. Raelin's work underlines that the debates about professions and professionals can only be understood if one incorporates values into that debate, alongside questions about the body of expertise, modes of control, and behaviour.

At the core of much of the current debate is an argument about how best to control and manage expert labour. This includes professionals as well as newer specialisms, since organizational professionals constitute 75 per cent of all professional employment (Raelin 1985). Essentially, this argument can be framed as professionalism versus managerialism. The question is which of these alternative approaches produces the most effective results or whether the current demands, particularly in the public sector, require a different management approach?

7.3. The Impact of Competition and a Quasi-Market on Professionals

A Quasi-Market and Change to a Market-Based Framework

In Chapter 3, above, and in earlier work (Ferlie 1992, 1994), we have debated ways of conceptualizing a quasi-market and of understanding its operation. Currently, the theoretical model which appears to offer the best fit with the emerging evidence is to conceive of the market-place as a relational market. This view sees the market as less atomistic and the key players as active. Conceptualizing a quasi-market in this way, one would expect to see a number of core characteristics, such as social embeddedness and institutional embeddedness. In this section, selected evidence emerging on the operation of the market in the public sector will be reviewed. Since many parts of the public sector offer professional, specialist, human services, it is anticipated that patterns of social relations, particularly professional networks, will influence the market. It is apparent that reputation and information on reputation, frequently transmitted via personal recommendation, is critical in establishing a market position in professional services. Thus reputation can be described as a key intangible asset having peculiar relevance in a professional market.

The general trends in organizations across both the private and the public sectors towards strategic business units, small corporate cores, and flatter, more flexible organizations have been documented by many writers (Handy 1990; Peters 1992; Kanter 1989; Ferlie and Pettigrew 1994*b*). A feature of this trend is the shift from management by hierarchy to greater management by contract. This has been one of the major aspects of the changes imposed on the public sector. However, it is interesting that whilst there has been much comment on the nature of the changes, there has been so far only limited research on the processes of market-driven change or on their impact on professionals (Whittington *et al.* (1994) is one example). There have been a number of studies of specific organizations or services (e.g. Greenwood *et al.* 1990; Hinings *et al.* 1991; Dawson *et al.* 1992; Winch and Schneider 1992; and Ferner *et al.* forthcoming) but the majority of these feature professions in the private sector. From the limited data available, it is possible to extract some tentative indicators of common issues across a range of professionalized contexts. These include the problems of developing effective strategic leadership at the top of the organization; the need to include professionals in senior management; and the changing role of middle managers.

These indicators are supplemented by a model developed by Whittington *et al.* (1994) based on a broader comparative study of change in professional services in the public and private sectors. Such data provide bench-marks against which the findings from the present studies in healthcare and evidence from other sectors can be aligned.

The Impact of Competition and the Quasi-Market across the Professions in the Public Sector

In looking across the public sector, it is apparent that the introduction of market concepts has impacted differently on the various parts of the public sector. By focusing on selected examples, the range of responses can be illustrated.

In the field of local government, the process of contracting-out services, compulsory competitive tendering as it was initially described, has been in place since the 1980s. Whilst this process had a profound impact, it is only recently that contracting-out and market-testing has penetrated to the professional areas of service provision. The majority of the original services opened to external competition were based on manual skills, such as cleaning, catering, transport, and refuse collection. Only recently have similar changes been introduced for services such as architectural services. Moreover, the analysis is complicated by the fact that professionals dominate senior management positions in local government and it is therefore difficult to isolate the impact on professionals. The evidence which exists suggests that professions have differential responses to the changes. Harrison and Nutley (1993) demonstrate that engineers welcomed compulsory competitive tendering and market-testing believing they were well equipped to exploit the benefits. The full impact of these processes on professional areas may be still to be felt in the future.

In another part of the public sector, the Civil Service, the impact of market forces on professionals is even more embryonic. As Richards (1993) points out, a lot has happened and a lot has not happened. The Ibbs Report (Efficiency Unit 1988) and the advent of Next Steps agencies was intended to devolve responsibility, but to quote one agency chief executive: 'If "freedoms" are synonymous with "shackles", then I have them to the extent that prisoners can hobble in leg irons.' Dopson's (1993*a*) work on middle managers in the HMSO indicates, despite some enthusiasm, there is limited evidence of any substantive impact on the middle levels in this organization. A further confirmation of the as yet limited rate and pace of change within the Civil Service is provided by the research of Colville *et al.* (1992) on the Customs and Excise service. They report on seven pilot experiments which they researched between 1989–90. In their conclusions, they suggest that such experiments have changed the context for change and prepared the foundation, thus creating greater receptivity to change. The suggestion is that in the next round of changes, now under way, the results will be more substantial and possibly more radical.

The situation in health care and in higher education, on the other hand, is substantially different. First, the quasi-market has been introduced across the whole health sector, rather than specific functions being subject to compulsory competitive tendering or market-testing. This has produced radical change across health care, as was demonstrated in earlier chapters. For the medical profession, it has meant adapting not only to changed structures, but also accepting the legitimacy of purchaser and client demands on their activities. In higher education, a degree of competition always existed between institutions. This has been encouraged in a variety of ways, including the conversion of all institutions at degree level into universities, and the introduction and publication of league tables on both research and teaching quality. Additionally, the pressure on resources forces higher education institutions to compete for external funding. This has led to a search for alternative sources of funding, to the extent that for some universities, direct government funding now represents only a proportion sometimes less than 50 per cent of total funding (*Independent* 1995).

In higher education, there has also been increasing consumer pressure from research grant providers and from course participants, creating pressure to perform to expectations in both these areas. So here, in health and higher education, the market is having a major impact on the professionals. The extent to which these influences alone limit the autonomy of professionals, or simply set higher and more transparent standards of quality in research and teaching activities, is arguable.

For the secondary education sector controlled by the local education authority, seeking private funding has not been an option. As demonstrated in Chapter 4, for many schools, the main impetus to opt out of local authority control and become a grant maintained school was the opportunity to control their own spending and to gain additional resources. In the analysis in Chapter 4, we suggested that the market was impacting at the periphery of a school's functions, for example in the management of public relations. Our examination also proposed that the role of the head teacher had been radically affected both by the introduction of the market and by the new relationships with the boards of governors. Overall, however, the main group of professionals, the schoolteachers, have seen greater work pressures come from constrained resources rather than the new public management.

In some other parts of the public sector, professions have certainly been profoundly affected by change, but it is arguable whether it is market-based change. Goodsir (1993) argues that the police have all the characteristics of a profession in terms of expertise and autonomy, but that in this case the collective power of the group is being eroded by the importation of specialists, who are often civilians.

Similarly, dramatic changes have occurred in the librarian profession, but these have been the result of the advent of information technology, replacing and obliterating the specialist expertise base of the occupation. Davies, *et al.* (1993) and Davies and Kirkpatrick (1993) show that librarians are now searching for a replacement professional role.

Flood (1993) presents data on the massive expansion of the legal profession in the private sector. These data are interesting in that they provide an excellent illustration of the attack wrought on a profession by structural changes in professional firms and the commercialization of the services. For example, old-style law firms with six to ten partners identified with clients' interests and offered a personalized service to clients. Firms with 1,000 members cannot do this. This example demonstrates that some of the structural and commercial pressures experienced in the public sector are broader trends affecting the private as well as the public sector. Whilst the transference of these pressures may be seen emerging in the new public management, they are not exclusive to it and may be a pervasive attribute of current organizational life.

It is evident that, to date, the quasi-market has produced greater impact on professionals than the introduction of compulsory competitive tendering or market-testing. Even the impact of the quasi-market has varied across the professions, with some gainers and some losers. Later in this chapter, we shall examine some examples of the processes of change in more detail, to assess how these results were achieved. It is also clear that other forces have impacted on some professions, for example new technology. More particularly, in many examples, other trends and influences are in evidence, such as constrained resources and the pressure towards value for money and efficiency. It is the complementary pressures of greater managerialism and enhanced market forces which are impacting on professions within public sector organizations.

Implementing a Quasi-Market: Fragmentation of Units

In this section, we move into a more detailed level of analysis of the processes of change as they occur within specific parts of the public sector, particularly health care. The focus is on the impact of the first stage of implementing a quasi-market, the splitting of purchasers from providers and the setting of contracts. This process has shifted a national, integrated public health system towards a far more fragmented and less centrally planned system.

What impact does this fragmentation of the systems have on the professionals who work in them? At the national level, the medical profession has never been completely united. Whether the maintenance of a united front and the exercise of collective power will be made more difficult by a scattered membership is unclear. The breakdown of consensus about the role of the State in health care may mean a reduction in the medical profession's privileged position in policy-making at the centre. Current evidence suggests that the BMA continues to wield considerable power, nationally, on topics which generate high feelings, such as performance-related pay or night-time call-out for GPs. What is certain is that the pattern of collective power will be different. The data below vividly illustrates the internal shifts of power within the professions.

In health care, there have been substantial alterations in the relative power of different sections of the profession. The split between purchaser and provider has underpinned the passing of more power into the hands of GP fundholders and public health specialists, as purchasers. To quote one consultant in an acute trust: 'I think the market in health care is developing. The GP fundholders are the key, though small in number at present (i.e. September 1992), they are having a large effect. I think their big demands will be restrained by the increase in numbers of fundholders.' In what was previously a provider-led service, it was virtually unknown for acute specialist consultants, for example surgeons, to consult GPs on the kind of secondary service they would like the hospital to provide. There is now widespread evidence of changed behaviour in this regard, with hospital-based consultants initiating contacts with referring GPs and responding to GPs' priorities.

Public health specialists have demonstrated a mixed reaction to their potential new powers (Dawson *et al.* 1993). In some instances, public health directors see themselves as having a critical role to play in developing a health care service which meets local needs. The following quote, from a director describing their role within the district health authority board, illustrates this view:

My role within the health authority and the board is a balancing act between the local population and its health needs, the medical profession and management. I think it is essential to take a pragmatic view of health needs assessment and really concentrate on what we know and things we can improve, like teenage pregnancy rates. In the absence of thorough long-term data we have to take decisions on how to apply resources, as best we can.

In other instances, as Dawson *et al.* (1993) illustrate, professionals are uncertain of their role and some feel inadequate and ambiguous about adopting a managerial orientation.

In higher education, the picture more closely mirrors that in health care, with the service moving from a provider-led service towards a purchaser or consumer-led service (Johnes and Cave 1994). In secondary education, some members of the education profession seem to be trying, albeit reluctantly, to break away from local education authority control, but there is as much evidence of responding to parent and consumer choice, as to the autonomy offered by decentralization.

At the unit level, the relationships between units in healthcare have changed. The district no longer forms a collective organizational boundary and indeed the boundaries and shape of many districts have been changed by mergers between district and family health authorities. This has disrupted long standing relationships between senior clinicians and senior managers. Concern has been expressed as to how the market will be regulated. It remains to be seen whether the new regional office or the district as purchaser can maintain an overall service strategy. At this broader inter-unit level, it could be argued that the collective autonomy of the medical profession over policy may be weakened. Whereas, previously, there existed an agreed and representative medical advisory machinery to examine and influence capital and service development across a range of providers in a locality, this role now lies with the director of public health and the board of the district health authority.

The fragmentation of the system of health care into purchasers and more autonomous, decentralized provider units has had an effect on the existing interrelationships between professionals and managers. There has been a shift in the relative power of different subgroups in the medical profession. Nevertheless, despite the formal operation of a contracted service, there is evidence that informal dependencies and past relationships persist. One example of this in practice is in a speciality-like community or child health services, a complex health care context in which care is delivered in close cooperation with a range of other agencies, including primary care and social services. To quote a specialist in this field:

I see a very constrained market. It continues to be controlled by the providers and unless there is a massive expansion of the district health authority, they will be dependent on the data provided by the units–but we do only offer advice and they may not listen. But we would kick up a fuss if they didn't. . . .

This quote typically shows the nature of the dependencies existing within a relational market and the influence of past relationships of trust.

In another example, heads of service from different acute hospitals in a district had a professional network and regularly met to discuss issues of common interest. With the advent of trusts and competition, this meeting was no longer felt to be appropriate and indeed there was evidence of less information-sharing across units. However, the director of public health, who was held in esteem, continued to hold informal speciality meetings with clinicians from different trusts.

It could be argued, tentatively at this stage, that the collective political autonomy of the profession to influence health policy at the regional–inter-unit level may be somewhat impaired.

Implementing a Quasi-Market: Competition Between Professionals

One of the threats resulting from the implementation of a market in health care proposed by Hafferty (1988) was that it would introduce internal competition between professionals. In the UK, this would represent a profound change in relationships within the professional group, because with a hitherto diminutive private health sector, the extent of competition for patients has been relatively small, when compared with the USA. One might argue that competition encourages the identification and marketing of the distinctive competencies of a particular service and thus undermines the collegiality of the profession. Collegiality is based on the premiss that once qualified to a professionally set standard, all practitioners are 'equal'.

In health, there is a general belief that competition is increasing. One consultant offers this view: 'Competition is already fairly evident. They are beginning to fight each other in some specialisms. I don't think that is healthy.'

There is growing evidence at the strategic board and also at the speciality level that professionals are adopting an increasingly rigorous approach to defining the nature and quality of the services on offer. In part, this is driven by the purchasers, and the specification of services which they adopt. Again the quality measures are frequently influenced by the directors of public health. However, there is also data to illustrate a proactive approach, particularly at the speciality level, with individual clinicians seeking to carve out a market niche for their service. To quote one clinical director discussing the strategic plans for the service:

We have had two awaydays and worked out what we are good at and have worked out a strategic plan for the next five years. Our key objective is to be one of the top ten units in the UK. We have already started a two-year quality programme . . . We have started to refine and define the criteria for identifying the top units: it involves a scoring system based on costs, quality and the effective outcomes of treatment. We are using standards from other countries, e.g. Holland, to bench-mark our standards.

This quotation provides ample evidence of a clinical manager rapidly learning to understand the concept of the market and how to position a service for long-term survival. It is also notable that in the current absence of satisfactory data to assess quality adequately, the response is to set about developing such a database. The medium-term results of these actions will certainly be to expose some clinical services, which are not of equivalent standard. Indeed, the publication of league tables has already begun this process of discrimination.

Within other areas of the medical profession a more ambivalent response to competition has been displayed. Public health specialists with a chequered history of development and less security in the status and credibility of their specialism, have continued to display confusion between the advisory and management aspects of their roles (Lewis 1987; Dawson *et al.* 1993).

GP fundholders are in many instances still coming to terms with the degree of business management involved in running a practice as a small business. However, early data show that GP fundholders are more likely than district health authorities to shift their contracts to another provider (Glennerster *et al.* 1994).

In education, it is clear that the introduction of a market has affected the strategic behaviour of governing bodies and of individual professionals. In some respects, the impact of the consumer or their parents as proxies, appears to be more direct in education than in health. The impact of league tables, however inaccurate, can be seen to influence decisions by schools. Hence the rate of exclusion of disruptive or truanting children has increased (Lee 1992). Heads are striving through the prospectus and open days to identify the particular merits of their establishment. Reports in the press documenting the shorter lengths of service of headteachers show that governing bodies are now more likely to use exam-result league tables as the grounds for dismissing headteachers.

In concluding this section, it is evident that the introduction of competitive mechanisms, such as compulsory competitive tendering, or of a quasi-market represent differing variants of the overall process of introducing competition through markets in the public sector. As might be anticipated, these processes impact differently on the respective organizations and quasi-markets appear to have produced greater and more fundamental change. Where quasi-markets have been established in health and in higher and secondary education, again the speed and depth of change varies. There is evidence to show that the fragmentation of units has led to a lack of cohesion among professionals, broken some historical links and caused embryonic competition between professionals. However, there is also support for the view that many of the same players remain in key positions and that established professional networks and ties can continue to operate across boundaries, though weakened in some instances.

7.4. Changing Management Processes and the Impact on Professionals

Professionals and Boards

As the previous section has shown, the implementation of a quasi-market has impacted on the existing interrelationships between professionals in different units. Within units, the impact of the changes to a market framework has been profound and complex. One of the research problems therefore is that a detailed, longitudinal and processual methodology is required to uncover the interdependencies and their impacts. At this level of analysis, the combined impact of the quasi-market and increased managerialism are interwoven. Management by contract has led to the specification of volumes and standards of service. This trend has greatly exacerbated the already strongly experienced pressures towards increased efficiency and value for money (characterized in Chapter 1 as NPM Model 1). This point underlines the argument that the quasi-market and managerialization can be viewed as joint forces for change. In health care, one clinician perceives the future thus: 'The old days of the clinician and "his" practice will go and it will become a corporate responsibility. There will be increasing restrictions on clinical practice, not just, anything goes.' The ambivalence of this individual's attitude to these changes is portrayed in the quote.

At the strategic level, every organization in health care has undergone significant change. As was seen in Chapters 5 and 6, every trust and district health authority is now headed by a board consisting of an independent chair and five non-executive directors and up to five executive directors. A place is reserved for a medical specialist on the boards of trusts and in the first round of appointments, most district health authorities elected to have a public health specialist on the board (Ashburner and Cairncross 1993). On the one hand, this gives clinicians access to the most senior and strategic decision-making fora. The evidence from our research in health care (Ferlie *et al.* 1992; Ferlie, Asburner, and Fitzgerald 1993; Asburner, Ferlie, and Fitzgerald 1993*b*) demonstrates that the medical directors in trusts and public health directors in district health authorities are exercising considerable influence on boards. The data pinpoint the role of medical director as a key pivotal role. Medical directors have a critical input to the development of the service plan, because they can make refined judgements about the areas of distinct professional competence which exist in the trust. To quote one medical director talking about his role:

My job is to take equal corporate responsibility as a member of the board: to advise the trust on medical matters; to assist in the setting of contracts, and the development of patient care in the areas of our own special expertise (i.e. our current specialities) and to act as a support and guide to clinical chairs.

The newly constituted boards have provided evidence of an improved level of debate and questioning from the non-executive directors in particular, as demonstrated in Chapter 6. But there remains an issue about independence and the need for a balance of views among board members. Several of the boards studied had developed a culture of either compliance or of limited debate, with aversion to conflict. In several examples, the challenges to this bland consensus in the group have come from a professional. 'I sometimes think that we do need the radically different view, the challenging position that says "well hang on, you are going to completely disadvantage this geographical area", not necessarily going along with the position guided by the chairman. It is often my role to do that' (director of public health). Indeed, in a minority of boards, they have been allowed to take on the role of licensed dissenter. Such dissenters had a securer base within the system, more self-confidence, and a more subtle approach to the raising of issues of concern than other clinicians lower down the formal hierarchy. It is clear from our analysis that a professional base may provide the foundation for an effective dissenting role at board level.

The setting of a strategic direction for service organizations in the new market place is not straightforward. Progress in developing strategic direction and strategic decision-making has on the whole been faster in the trust provider units than in the boards of the purchasing district health authorities. (For early evidence of this see Ferlie, Ashburner, and Fitzgerald 1993; Ashburner, Ferlie, and Fitzgerald 1993*a*.) This is due to a complex set of factors, but most significant is the novel nature of a purchasing organization. Overall, even with the addition of outside private expertise, the boards in health care have found it difficult to generate an innovative service strategy. One component of this has been the lack of strategic management expertise of clinicians, but also of many senior general managers. This finding mirrors the data provided by Whittington *et al.* (1994) which emphasizes the struggle being experienced in both health and R and D organizations to assert strategic control over their operations.

An interesting direct comparator to the health care board is the school or new university board of governors. The movement to a more market-based framework has not induced the same degree of change in schools, as has occurred in health care. As discussed in Chapter 4, headteachers have the right to sit as a governor, if they so wish. A study (Baginsky *et al.* 1991) of a sample of locally managed schools illustrated that in 80 per cent of the cases the head had exercised their right to sit on the governing board. Alongside their responsibilities for the management of the school budget, the board also has new powers to select and dismiss staff. From the professional perspective, these changes may be seen as a mixed blessing. Clearly, the head has a significant forum for the exercise of influence within the governing board. Because of the nature of his/her professional job responsibilities, the head is the only professional member of the board who can speak knowledgeably about the management of the school. As with the medical professionals on health boards, the extent of the heads' professional influence will be determined by their competence in the management arena. Early results from pilot studies (Thomas 1988; Baginsky *et al.* 1991) have shown that heads can exercise a high level of influence over the board, with the potential for great power being invested in one individual. There are no other executive members of the board and the other professional members are there in a representative capacity and may have limited knowledge of budget and management issues.

Professionals' Roles within the Management Process

Within individual units in health care, the market model has induced new and more devolved structures of decision-making and control, particularly within provider units. The majority of provider units are now trusts and have established a system of clinical or speciality groupings based on a clinical service. Critically, these services are managed by a clinical director, or equivalent title which constitutes a new role. The incumbents of these posts are virtually all clinicians, who have agreed to take on part-time management responsibilities. Harwood and Boufford (1993) show that in their survey, 75 per cent of the directorates studied had doctors in the post of clinical director. Most clinical directors are budget-holders and are responsible for budgets ranging between 1.9m and 4.5m (Fitzgerald 1994). Such posts offer an opportunity to have a significant influence on the development of a service and to shape practice.

The research data on clinical directors and their activities (Harwood and Boufford 1993; Fitzgerald 1994; Fitzgerald and Sturt 1992; Cowling and Newman 1994) shows that they are engaged in a variety of tasks which are crucial to service delivery and to the development of the service. Many clinical directors face the need to manage substantial and often multiple changes in the provision of services. Examples would include the rationalization of services from a number of different sites; the development of new modes of service delivery, such as day-case units; the reduction in hours of work of junior doctors; and the introduction of quality standards and systems of monitoring standards.

Some specific examples will help to illustrate these complexities in context. One clinical director describes the rapid expansion of his/her area of responsibility:

I have been the head of the speciality for eight years. Originally, this speciality was going to be a clinical directorate on its own. Then the clinical director of anaesthesia resigned and I was asked to take it on. Then theatres were added. So I was left reeling with the shock of this growing area. It had gone from the manageable to the unmanageable. Also I had a business manager who was not good. . . . I am a clinician and my long-term objectives are to improve patient care, not keep hospitals open or save the government.

Another description states: 'As a theatre manager, I am developing an internal contract with surgical users, but I am frustrated by the lack of reliable information. Also I am managing a major change caused by the rebuilding programme in theatres.'

Another aspect of the establishment of the new structures is that clinical directors are working closely as part of an interdisciplinary management team. This brings doctors into close daily contact with managers, nurses, and other para-medic professionals, not in a hierarchical forum, but as colleagues in a team. Such contact can and does change attitudes. One clinical director said:

I have debated and thought about the split of duties, but it is very difficult. I have made a change now and got rid of a business manager and now I have two nurse manager grades. One manages the nurses and does the operational management and one is responsible for information technology and does long-term strategic planning. I have also employed a secretary/administrator who also does projects and is working up to a higher administrative post.

Clinical managers can therefore be seen to have gained an increased arena of power for the professional. The implementation of a market framework in healthcare and the concomitant changes to structures and roles which this has entailed, has led to significantly higher professional involvement in the management process at both strategic and operational levels within units. Thus for senior management, the movement to a market-based system may involve some sharing or loss of control to professionals.

Again one sees a different pattern if one compares with education. The later stages of the changes to a more market-based framework in secondary education include the voluntary adoption of grant maintained status by schools, thus freeing them completely from the control of the local education authority. As mentioned in earlier chapters, this process has been variable. It may therefore be that the impact of these changes is not yet visible. Within schools, there has not been the same degree of change and restructuring as has been evident within the health sector. Some grant maintained schools are recruiting persons with managerial expertise, such as bursars and marketing managers, but these roles are usually additive to the current structure. There is no evidence of the creation of important new professional manager roles, such as the clinical directors. The process of grafting on new areas of management expertise is similar to the developments seen in GP fundholders, with the advent of practice managers and in colleges of further education, with the employment of marketing managers. The deeper cultural changes required to underpin the incorporation of this expertise will take longer to emerge (Fook and Watson 1992).

The overall effect of changes in management processes on professionals is difficult to assess. The simplistic view that managers have always gained power, roles, and authority from professionals is not borne out by data from our detailed, empirical studies. These emphasize the complexity and variety of the changes which are occurring, differing on a number of dimensions, in different parts of the public sector. At the organizational level, some of the changed structures and new professional manager roles offer opportunities for professionals to exercise considerable power in senior decision-making forums. Professionals are seen adopting these roles, adapting to them (sometimes reluctantly), and becoming involved in the management process. Also at the organizational level, it is evident that the systems of management are being altered. Many of the key changes in systems have been externally driven by the government, as in the case of costing systems or the Patients' Charter. Whilst the intention behind a change such as the Patients' Charter may be impeccable, its implementation is not. What it serves to demonstrate is an externally driven process which resets managerial priorities. This removes control and decision-making from both managers and professionals. The example of the Patients' Charter illustrates the setting of inappropriate targets which removes judgement from the professionals and distorts the service. As one clinician in a cardio-thoracic unit stated:

In order to fulfil the Patients' Charter and see the required number of patients on time and minimize waiting times, I stick rigidly to the schedule. All this means is that if a patient with more complicated symptoms than anticipated, presents themselves for first appointment, they will probably be asked to come back for a second appointment. Whereas in the past I would have dealt with them immediately and caused a delay to the outpatients clinic. I do not think this helps patients.

In a different way, the process of contracting and external government pressure to produce 'league tables' of trusts has provided impetus to the development of medical audit systems. In many acute and community specialities, medical audit was already well developed prior to the NHS and Community Care Act (obstetrics could be a prime example). However, the requirement to have demonstrable systems of medical audit is now much more widespread. One reason for this appears to be that doctors clearly maintain control over the whole of the medical audit process. S. Harrison and Pollitt (1994) define the issue as one of control. Medical audit is one quality arena in which the standards and the assessment are controlled by the doctors. This increasing awareness of the need for self-regulation, in order to avoid external regulation is now also apparent in primary care. It represents a process of actively embracing known 'professional' standards, to maintain the arena of control.

In the case of higher education, the introduction of clearer and more transparent standards for research and teaching again may superficially seem eminently sensible. In reality, selecting appropriate criteria for the judgement of research and teaching performance is not straightforward. As in health care, the criteria selected distort behaviour and judgement. In education, there is the additional problem that performance management and the pressure for improvements in performance can only be exerted negatively, through threats and penalties. There are no rewards to offer and staff are already poorly paid, comparative to the private sector. Such managerial pressure removes the one incentive of autonomy, previously open to the academic.

In terms of these changes to management systems, the evidence suggests that priorities are being shifted through such systems, which focus greater attention on financial and quantifiable targets. This process accords greater weight to a managerial perspective and increasingly constrains autonomy.

7.5. Individual Professionals, Professional Managers, and Hybrids

Clinical managers represent an extreme example of specialists moving into a corporate or general management role. Such conversions of specialists to generalists are not uncommon. As people move up an organizational hierarchy, it is frequently the only way to obtain further promotion. However, in most instances the specialist has had some prior experience of management and possibly management training. For doctors, neither of these things may be true. As a profession, medicine is academically orientated. Qualifications, research, and publications are all valued and indeed play a major part as promotion criteria for senior posts. Doctors' perceptions of management and what management entails are coloured by the frequently held view that managers are not well qualified and that management is easy to learn. Moving into a clinical management role however, entails accepting a major challenge in terms of new tasks, novel tasks for which the individual is not necessarily well trained. It also involves working more closely with managers on a management agenda, which some medical colleagues may not accept as legitimate. Clearly the issue of appropriate and timely training is critical to operating successfully as a clinical manager. The combined evidence from a number of studies (Fitzgerald 1994; Dopson 1993*b*; Harwood and Boufford 1993; and Cowling and Newman 1994) suggests that where doctors are carefully selected for clinical management roles (and not pressed into service), they can readily benefit from management training and particularly from the opportunity to learn with managers from other sectors.

The remainder of this section will draw more heavily on our study of a cohort of doctors who were assuming management roles (as mentioned in Section 7.1).

Fitzgerald (1994) illustrates that the overwhelming reaction of the cohort members to their management training was positive. One feature of the training which was especially welcomed was the opportunity to mix with managers from other sectors. Participants stated: 'The NHS is very parochial in its approach and I found it a real eye-opener to meet with managers with broader perspectives;' 'One of the most important aspects of the programme was sharing experience with people outside the NHS.' The evidence also illustrates that such clinical managers rapidly absorb their learning and start to apply it in their work context.

The clinical manager role needs to be understood as a new hybrid role. The creation of this role should not replicate a copy of a general manager role, nor should it be seen as a purely liaison role. Uniquely, clinical managers can potentially combine in-depth clinical knowledge and credibility with management expertise.

In Section 7.4, above, we saw that many clinical directors have sizeable change management agendas, as well as being expected to run services against a dynamic background. The evidence also suggests that clinical managers are grasping some thorny problems, in relation to clinical colleagues and dealing with issues which have been allowed to fester up to now. One clinical manager argues: 'I have now been able to tackle barriers between professionals in the NHS and the course has pointed up the validity and relevance of this. I have gained a new language and communication with other NHS professionals and an enhanced awareness of professional differences.' Specific aspects of their management experience will be explored here. First, clinicians describe embarking on the resolution of problems sometimes of long standing, in relation to clinical colleagues. These are issues relating to differential levels of performance among colleagues, as well as inequitable distribution of workload. Up to the present, clinical freedom has meant that few general managers have dared to deal with these issues. These problems of performance may be broached via the processes of medical audit. Problems of workload and the distribution of work are currently highlighted by the need to alter junior doctors' hours of work, but this also provides a lever to address this issue more generally. Significantly, it appears that there are some indicators here that issues of professional performance and professional standards are being addressed and handled by clinical managers.

It is notable that in the clinical directors and medical directors, we see the creation of a new cadre of professional managers. Equally significantly, in operating in their management capacity, we see them using professional values as the prime drivers of some of their management actions. The practical result of this is that difficult and intractable quality issues are being addressed.

In the research, clinical managers focused on an important second aspect of their management experience, namely the nature of their relationships with other doctors and colleagues. They drew particular attention to the fact that one of the most difficult aspects of adopting a clinical management role was maintaining good relationships with colleagues. They stated that where they were experiencing problems in their management roles, such problems were frequently linked to poor-quality relationships with colleagues, either medical or management. All the clinical managers recognized that they were playing a critical boundary role between management and the remainder of the medical professionals. They perceived part of their role as translating ideas from one forum to the other. Many members of the cohort acknowledged the importance of sitting on the boundary between management and medicine and not identifying totally with either. Frequently, remarks underlined the vital importance of a medical background and a current medical practice for maintaining credibility with medical colleagues. The following quote typifies these views: 'Being a careful sort of chap, I will continue my clinical work. I think you lose credibility if you stop and knowing what is going on is important . . . And then I really enjoy my clinical practice.' With the objective of maintaining credibility in mind, several members of the cohort commented on the importance of not exhibiting too much missionary zeal on management topics, as this might have a dysfunctional effect on some colleagues.

Whilst many clinical managers experience support from their colleagues and from management, there are some who see themselves as separated and on occasion isolated from clinical colleagues. The extent of this isolation varies considerably from one location to another. In some instances, it is merely a question of language and communication. Clinical managers have to exercise care in employing management terms, which may not be understood by medical colleagues. The following quote exemplifies the view: 'I do feel at a distance, mentally, from most of my colleagues. I have to frame what I say to colleagues in an acceptable form. I cannot use the language that I have in common with managers, of cost and resources. Over the course of the last year, I have changed quite a lot.' The most common response from the cohort participants illustrated more difficult, but not intractable relationship issues. Below a couple of the clinical managers describe their situations:

Some colleagues also are a barrier to adopting a new style. They are not an overriding problem, but I do feel that they do not understand my approach or what I am trying to achieve. I am hoping to overcome this by example, so that over time, as the results show up, it will change.

There are a few negative attitudes from some colleagues–ie. consultants–which is to be expected. I had expected scepticism, but this is why I did not come back (from management training) all gung-ho. It comes down to raising awareness in the team and I have this as a long-term objective. One will always have less enthusiastic colleagues.

In a minority of examples, clinical managers are subjected to a degree of downright hostility from some colleagues, as in the case of one clinical manager who was publically called a traitor by a colleague of long standing. Such pressure causes considerable stress.

In the medium term, the willingness of consultants to accept a clinical management role may be influenced by these events and pressures. To quote one medical director: 'If I decide to leave this role, it will be because of the isolation and the sense of distance from colleagues' (this quote is drawn from a setting where both professional colleagues and managers were, on the whole, supportive).

The problems of professional relationships illustrated here represent major barriers to the recruitment and retention of high quality, experienced clinical managers.

In exemplifying and discussing their changing collegial relationships, many clinical managers also focused on improving work relationships, as a priority task on which they were currently engaged. In their analysis of the areas of learning gained from participation in management training, improved understanding and skills in handling interpersonal relationships were regularly mentioned. For example, one clinical manager stated: 'I am using the course learning in the way I am dealing with difficult people . . . This helps in dealings with junior doctors and consultants. I have learnt how to say "No".' On the whole, the responses of cohort members to their training were highly positive. The topic area of interpersonal relationships, in particular, was seen as one of the key areas of management development.

In their relationships with management colleagues, the data demonstrate two interesting factors. First, the boundaries and divisions of management activities between specialist–professional managers and general managers are blurring. Secondly, the members of this cohort had reasonably positive relationships with general managers.

In terms of the first factor relating to the tasks of clinical management, these individuals are regularly working alongside both general managers and other professional managers such as nurse managers and paramedic managers. This daily, detailed involvement and the processes of team-working mean that the boundaries between general management and clinical management become blurred. Particularly at the most senior levels, it is clear that active and knowledgeable clinical directors and medical directors expect to be involved in all management decisions, but with a specialist part to play.

To quote one medical director:

I think I have persuaded X [the chief executive officer] that we should be involved. I keep asking if the consultants are involved. We have consultants leading, with heavy support from good managers. . . . My role as medical director is to advise the non-medical managers and the chief executive officer. I have just spent three days away, discussing the organization structure and other developments.

It is notable that in discussing their interpersonal relationships, the cohort members quote fewer instances of problems with management colleagues, than with medical colleagues. However, this finding should be treated with extreme caution. As already stated, this cohort is skewed, since it contains only clinical managers who have willingly accepted their roles and individuals who have undertaken management training. It appears that management training generates increased confidence, as well as improving the ability of clinicians to contribute to the management process. On the whole, these dual effects draw these clinical managers into more productive and less conflictual relationships with general management colleagues. Other research data, however (Dopson 1993*b*) demonstrate that the majority of interviewees in the sample of clinical managers: 'were reluctant to enter management and did so for one or more of the previously quoted reasons, or were bullied into it, or it was a case of "muggins turn next".' It cannot therefore be assumed that these more positive findings on clinical manager–general manager relationships can be generally applied.

In concluding this section, it is apparent that taking on a medical director or clinical director role is a difficult and arduous task. Many of the incumbents are overworked, but reluctant to abandon their clinical practice. These new hybrid management roles offer the potential for considerable influence to professional managers. To achieve this, however, the roles need to be creatively defined and support has to be moulded to suit different needs. There is evidence that this can be done, but there is also evidence that many locations are not so well advanced. All the available data supports the view that management training is beneficial if not a necessity, but again overall, only a minority of clinical directors have been offered training.

7.6. Conclusions

Overall, the empirical data presented in this chapter, in relation to the changing role of professionals in the public sector, lead toward some interesting and challenging conclusions. Whilst the data on the implementation of a market framework in other parts of the public sector, such as the Civil Service, is still embryonic, initial analyses provide grounds for reflection and re-evaluation of some current received views of the position of professionals within the new public management.

The conclusions to this chapter will be presented in four sections. The first three will review the themes emerging at differing levels of analysis by focusing initially on comparisons across all the professions, then on specific professions such as the medical profession, and finally on the individual professionals. The fourth and final section highlights new themes emerging from the data presented in the chapter.

Professions in the Public Sector: Loss or Gain?

At the meta-level of analysis, scanning across the professions which are most strongly represented in the public sector, the impact of the market appears to operate at two levels. Where the process of introducing elements of competition and market principles has been approached via compulsory competitive tendering and market-testing, to date, the effect on professionals is limited. This may be partly accounted for by the issues of timing and the progression of these systems from manual to technical and professional areas of activity. Nevertheless, where a quasi-market has been introduced across a whole sub-sector, as in health and education, it is apparent that the market changes have had a far greater and more direct impact on professionals. It may well be that by directing their attention to one profession, some commentators (S. Harrison and Pollitt 1994) are led to the conclusion that market forms are uniform and having similar effects across all parts of the public sector. It must also be acknowledged that it may be too early to judge the long-term impact of processes like market testing. As writers like Colville *et al.* (1992) and Dopson (1993*a*) comment the processes of change are slow in the Civil Service and appear to have reached only an early stage in relation to professional services.

Overall, one cannot sustain the argument that all professions in the public sector have lost power, influence, and autonomy as a result of the introduction of a quasi-market or the impact of increased managerialism. The forms of the market are not uniform and the impact on different professions is highly variable. Some professions, such as accountants, have risen in influence and in numbers during the change period.

The Position of Individual Professions and Professionals?

Focusing more closely on the individual professions themselves, again variations in reaction and therefore in the impact of the changes is in evidence. Thus some engineers in local government react to the market as a relatively welcome opportunity, which they feel equipped to exploit. Some of them identify with practices in the private sector. Other professions, such as the teaching profession, demonstrate more negative and defensive reactions, as the professional associations resist the government's proposals.

In the specific case of the medical profession, one can find evidence of mixed reactions and adaptation. In terms of the professional bodies, such as the BMA, there was initial opposition to the government's reforms which was not sustained over a long period. It is evident that on specific topics the BMA is prepared and capable of strong opposition, as for example on performance-related pay for doctors. The impact of the market and increased managerialism are inextricably mixed and where they combine, as in health, the profession has experienced higher levels of change and greater external control.

One of the most striking features of the impact of the quasi-market on the medical profession is the dramatic shifts of power, intra-professionally, between specialities. There are data to illustrate that the provider-led service of the past has altered to a more purchaser and GP fundholder-driven service. Thus general practitioners have gained considerably in power *vis à vis* their colleagues in the acute specialities. The current evidence of changed behaviour may also produce more substantial long-term effects within the profession, for example, making careers in some specialities appear more attractive in future.

In terms of the individual professionals themselves, the picture is complex. There are some losers, some gainers, and some adapters. Overall, the most noticeable characteristic is adaptation. While the primary professional socialization remains in place, there is evidence of some professionals deliberately developing more managerial skills and knowledge over time, with real shifts in self-image and identity taking place, but this does not mean that professionals are being transformed into surrogate general managers.

In addition to the intra-professional changes mentioned in the previous paragraph, there is substantial evidence of changes which shift power towards professionals. Particular examples would be the creation of clinical directorates within provider units and the establishment of new roles such as that of the medical director, the clinical director, and the director of public health. All of these changes involve medical professionals in decision-making processes and positions of influence in new and significant ways. We would not wish to argue that these changes are unproblematic or that all the processes work efficiently. It is apparent that the potential of these changes is not always being realised, or the implementation places great strain on some individuals.

To balance the evidence of gains in power, there are also data which indicate a shift of power and control away from individual clinicians. Here the evidence relates mainly to the introduction of externally driven (or imposed?) standards, which act as controlling devices. One particularly public one, which has already been quoted, is the introduction of the Patients' Charter. However, there are many other examples, such as the implementation of business planning systems, the development of budgeting systems, and the review processes for medical staff. Arguably any of these systems, well used, could work in favour of the medical profession. Nevertheless they represent an increased systemization of health care services, the sharing of information across a wider professional and managerial body, and constrain the organization and provision of care by professionals. It is important to note at this point that even when further managerial systems have been introduced, these changes have frequently been externally driven and not proposed by the managers themselves.

Re-examining the themes of professional autonomy, dominance, and control discussed at the beginning of the chapter, in the USA, a number of writers have postulated the view that to some extent medical professionals have lost autonomy and power (Haug 1973; Haug and Lavin 1983; Friedson 1984; McKinlay 1988; and Hafferty 1988) since their mid-twentieth-century apogee.

Assumptions have been made that the same trends would become increasingly apparent in the UK. Yet both Haug (1988) and Friedson (1987) have returned to the arguments to question, in different ways, the accuracy of the thesis even in the USA. Reviewing the data emerging from our research and from other studies in the UK, it is clear that the picture here is complex. The description which best fits the data is not one of de-professionalization and loss of power, but of professional adaptation. This explanation of events is substantiated by the mixed evidence of gains and losses already presented.

Detailed analysis of the specific areas of autonomy, identified by Elston (1991), further reinforces this conclusion. The medical profession has never had large-scale economic autonomy in the UK since 1948, so there has been no significant change there.

In terms of political autonomy, this resides at the collective and at the individual levels. The negotiating position of the BMA in relation to the government remains strong. One might argue that gradually over time, the profession has wrought a shift away from the appointment of the more outspoken, anti-doctor chair apparent on some of the early post-1990 health authorities and trusts. At the region, professionals maintain influence over the planning and coordination of health care. It can be argued however that the break-up of the old district professional advisory machinery has reduced the influence of professionals at this level of coordination. At the individual level, doctors now have control and influence over key budgetary decisions, which enhances their political autonomy. More broadly, the new powerful positions of medical director and director of public health provide for influence into strategic fora, which both create and enact policy. Cumulatively, the medical profession would appear to have gained more political autonomy than it has lost.

The third area of autonomy defined for professionals is technical autonomy and this is a crucial area of control. The introduction of league tables of performance for trusts and the extension of managerial systems of control combine to tighten the boundaries of the technical autonomy of the professional. They can clearly be seen to act as constraints on behaviour. It is evident that individual doctors feel irritated at these changes. But one must raise the question here (often raised by professionals themselves) about what legitimate areas of technical autonomy are? Technical autonomy is not professionally defined as autonomy to act as one wishes. Many of the responses in the area of increased technical control have interestingly come from within the profession. We have noted that medical professionals have been the prime drivers in the development of clinical audit systems, and have sought to actively develop and control the quality of clinical practice. One might argue that these developments represent an acknowledgement by the profession that the self-policing of quality standards needs improvement and that greater transparency of standards is now expected. Another response from within the profession is that control over performance standards, within provider units now lies with clinical managers and not with general managers. Both of these developments can be interpreted as different means adopted by the profession to maintain control within the boundaries of the profession and even to extend that control, if possible. Against this, as NHS trusts increasingly compete in the quasi market, they may well become dependent on innovative, clinical product champions (see Bennett and Ferlie's (1994a) analysis of the role of clinical change agents in the development of new service systems for HIV/AIDS in the 1980s) for new products and services. The reputation of innovative clinicians becomes a prime intangible asset which will affect the trusts' business performance.

Finally, there is very little evidence in the UK of arenas of the doctor's professional activity being ceded to other professions unwillingly. There is even less evidence, despite the rhetoric, that the shift to a quasi-market framework has given any greater influence or control directly to consumers. Therefore the dominance of the medical profession over other professional and para professional groups and consumers in the UK appears largely intact.

One specific development alluded to in this chapter has been the creation of new hybrid professional manager roles. Here we draw attention to the fact that some of the restrictions and standards of behaviour for medical professionals are being created by the new professional managers themselves. In setting overt quality standards and exerting influence to uphold those standards, they are making transparent already existing professional standards of performance, which in the past may have been implicit. It also creates pressure for uniform conformance to standards which may not have been the case in the past.

All in all, one cannot substantiate the view that there has been a unidirectional shift of power from professionals to managers in health care in the UK. The evidence is complex and sometimes contradictory, demonstrating both losses and gains in different areas and at different levels of analysis. We would argue that the most accurate interpretation is that in a changing context, the profession can be seen as altering within its boundaries, for example, between specialities and adapting in novel ways. Against the core criteria of professional autonomy, the medical profession appears to be maintaining its position. Ironically, over the longer term, the greatest threat may come from within. Competition for patients is still embryonic in the UK when compared to the USA, but there is evidence of its development in a few areas. Competition between professionals will increase the strains on professional collegiality and may cause frictions which will impair collective action by the profession as a whole.

Novel Emerging Themes

Additional novel themes emerge from these data which might form the basis for further research. The creation of the new hybrid professional manager roles is in itself an interesting phenomenon. First, the evidence suggests that with the appropriate training and support, hybrid professional managers can be developed with a powerful combination of professional expertise and managerial competence. Most significantly, our data suggest that management training does not transform professionals into surrogate general managers. Instead, professionals retain their past professional and caring values, which they now apply in the management fora also. In reality, this can lead to the exercise of professional, accountable management. The hybrid is visible in other parts of the public sector (Clarke and Newman 1993; Clarke *et al.* 1994) and may be seen as a part of the development of the new public management, converting and altering processes and forms of management from the private sector to an adapted public sector form. This theme will be explored in greater depth in Chapter 9. Secondly, the professional manager offers a new approach to the management of professional staff. In the older established professions, there has been unwillingness to accept and resistance to the right of non-professionals to supervise the work of professionals. The embryonic evidence from our research suggests that professional managers are prepared to investigate and actively manage issues of professional performance. In terms of the implications of these findings for the management of expert staff more generally, it is important to research further the conditioning factors which lead to the successful development of hybrid managers. Finally, there are many interesting issues surrounding the relationships of professional managers to their colleague professionals and to other general managers. The hybrid sits on the boundary between managers and professionals, forming an important bridge. But the position can be an uncomfortable one, isolating the individual from both groups. The hybrid both represents the professional agenda and embodies its disciplining by the managerial one. This leads one to question the stability and sustainability of the role.

A final theme to emerge from the findings is the question of the survival of the old professions. Given the broad trends towards the rapid development and exchange of newer areas of expertise (Scarborough 1995), it is questionable whether the original autonomies attached to the ideal-type definition of a profession could survive. It is apparent that in the UK at least, some of these characteristics, such as economic autonomy, are largely defunct. One might argue that quite apart from the implementation of the quasi-market, the professions would have needed to adapt to survive at all. For example, whilst the exercise of technical autonomy may still be acceptable, its practice, it may be argued, needs to be more open and transparent, for continued acceptance. At the collective level of the profession, this may mean adopting more open and demonstrable systems of self-regulation. For the individual professional, it may involve more change. Will the credibility of professionals be sustained if they do not develop greater openness and tolerance and responsiveness to client expectations?

THE QUESTION OF ACCOUNTABILITY: NEW FORMS OR A DEMOCRATIC DEFICIT?

8.1. Introduction

Chapters 1 and 5 have already touched on the question of the accountability of restructured public service organizations and that discussion will be developed further in this chapter. A contest between alternative notions of accountability is evident, and is a key aspect of the current debate around the rise and nature of the new public management.

In Section 8.2, we review the growing public and policy concern evident concerning accountability mechanisms in the public services. Section 8.3 outlines a number of alternative models of accountability, including novel market-based accounts which can be seen as of growing significance in the 1980s. Also in Section 8.3, these models will be tested against empirical data derived from our study of NHS board members (see also Cairncross and Ashburner 1992*a* and 1992*b*, for an earlier analysis). The question of whether the new purchasing organizations will really develop as 'tribunes of the people' is addressed in Section 8.4. We conclude in Section 8.5 that the lack of robust models of accountability in the public services now gives rise to considerable concern, and that this may represent the Achilles' heel of the new public management movement.

8.2. The Growing Debate

Accountability in the Public Services

Ensuring effective accountability is of course also an important and topical question in the private sector where recent experience has shown the existence of problems. Current private sector themes include: how to ensure the accountability of the directors to the shareholders; how to guarantee probity; and how to respond to the wider social and ethical responsibility of business.

There is, however, still a sense that public organizations legitimately face even more stringent accountability tests, for reasons that will be explored shortly (see Ranson and Stewart (1994) for a more extended discussion). Sometimes this is assumed—particularly by writers operating from a public administration tradition—almost as a self-evident truth. Perhaps we need to dig a little deeper into why this emphasis on accountability in the public services should be so strong. The key question is: should restructured public service organizations (e.g. NHS trusts, training and enterprise councils, New Universities) still be seen as rightfully subject to traditional public service notions of accountability?

On the one hand, these organizations have adopted some of the character-istics and culture of private sector firms and may be directed by senior personnel with a private sector background. The rhetoric is often one of unleashing entrepreneurial potential, getting away from the Weberian bureau-cratic vices (or indeed virtues) of due process and standard treatment. They can thus be seen—in this view—as a public–private hybrid or as a quasi-firm, very different from the standardized Welfare State agencies they have replaced. In this model, improved performance matters more than process and excessive concern for accountability is seen as getting in the way of results.

In our view, however, these organizations remain essentially 'public' in important senses of the word. They legally remain within the public sector, and as such are bound by a separate legal regime (for example, disputes over NHS contracts are settled through an arbitration mechanism devised by the Secretary of State with no right of access to the courts). Property rights have continued to be generally public rather than private in nature (although this is changing with the growth of private capital, for example, in the NHS). They deliver public services largely funded through taxation and the price mechanism is poorly developed. Some of these organizations can impose consumption on users (notably the criminal justice system, social care services, the Child Support Agency) who therefore cannot be seen as customers exercising choice. Public services continue to have a 'rescue function', providing service to low income users who could not afford to pay market prices. Goods such as education and health are frequently seen as 'merit goods' rather than 'private goods', so that society is alarmed if individuals' consumption falls below an accepted minimum level (such as hypothermia and the elderly).

So restructured public service organizations should still be seen as essentially public in nature, despite the move to more private sector-style forms of organization. Thus it follows that they can rightfully be expected to face tough accountability tests.

Increased Concern about Probity in the Public Services

There is rising concern that the traditional mechanisms used to ensure the accountability of public services—along with their supporting organizational culture—have been eroded as a result of recent organizational restructurings, with consequent loss of traditional standards of probity.

The early 1990s have been marked by a resurgence of interest within both private and public sector organizations in the linked themes of corporate governance, probity, and accountability. This growth of interest can be seen in part as a highly topical reaction against evidence of serious breakdowns in probity at the top of a number of important organizations during the 1980s.

As discussed earlier in Chapter 5, this is not solely a public sector phenomenon. In the City, weaknesses in the standards of financial reporting and accountability have been highlighted by such spectacular recent cases as BCCI, Maxwell, and reports of spiralling directors' pay (Conyon and Leech 1994; Conyon *et al.* 1994). Concern was such that the Cadbury Committee was set up and its report (Cadbury Report 1992) outlines how it is that the independent function of chairs and non-executive directors on the boards of corporations can be strengthened.

When assessed against Cadbury, the post-1990 system of corporate governance in key public services such as the NHS can be seen as highly progressive in character, with provision for a high proportion of non-executives, a non-executive chair, and few interlocking directorships.

Within the public sector, however, there is none the less disturbing evidence of important failures of corporate governance and indeed of loss of probity, dating from the mid 1980s. For example, serious incidents in the NHS have been investigated by recent Public Accounts Committee (PAC) reports. Its investigation into the failure of the West Midlands Regional Health Authority to exercise effective control over its regionally managed service organization concluded: 'we consider that there was a series of failings at all levels of management, and that there was a serious failure by members of the RHA, and in particular their Chairman, in their duty to secure the accountability of regional management' (PAC 1993*a*: p. vi). The role of the district auditor, rather than that of regional health authority members, in getting this information into the public domain was a noteworthy feature of this case.

A similar enquiry into the failure in Wessex Regional Health Authority to control the introduction of its information technology strategy found that the former regional general manager had been a strong driving force. Nevertheless, the report also concluded that regional health authority members had allowed themselves to be kept at arm's length and that: 'even if such a large share of the blame can be attributed to a single individual, the following conclusions suggest that fundamental changes are needed in the management and accountability arrangements at RHAs' (PAC 1993*b*: p. iii).

The NHS Management Executive has now issued advice which should lead to a further strengthening of corporate governance systems (e.g. authorities have been advised to set up audit committees and to keep a register of members' interests).

Nevertheless, the PAC is now so concerned about a spate of recent incidents across the public sector—not just in the NHS—that it has now issued advice that there need to be strong and effective systems of control and accountability, underpinned by responsible public service values (PAC 1994), to ensure probity in public services. Its underlying concern is that the old public sector culture, seen as a guarantor of probity, has been seriously undermined by the rise of what it sees as the more entrepreneurial values apparent within the new public management. This may be a somewhat overstated and idealized view (there have been well publicized and long standing probity problems in public sector organizations such as some inner London boroughs), but still provides grounds for real concern.

The Democratic Deficit and the 'New Magistracy'

While the introduction of the new public management certainly highlights important problems in ensuring the effective accountability of public services, some would argue that these are in fact of long standing and derive from the growth of large-scale, specialized government over a much longer time period.

Thus P. Day and Klein (1987) argue that accountability problems arise because the modern Welfare State has become a mass service delivery state. Not only has government grown in scale and complexity, but there is increased reliance on expertise and professionalism in service delivery. Within this complex institutionalized and professionalized web, individual citizens find increasing difficulty in holding service providers and decision-makers to effective account.

P. Day and Klein distinguish between political and managerial dimensions of accountability. Political accountability is about those with delegated authority being answerable for their actions to the people, whether directly in simple societies, or indirectly in complex societies. Here the criteria of judgement are contestable, and reasons, justification, and explanation of behaviour have to be provided. It is through these accounts that citizens make judgements about whether decision-makers have acted honestly and wisely.

In contrast, managerial accountability is about making those with delegated authority accountable for carrying out agreed tasks according to agreed criteria of performance. Fiscal audit would be a good example of a mechanism designed to ensure such managerial accountability. Management by objectives techniques or individual appraisal systems offer other levers for assessing managerial performance against an agreed set of tasks. Managerial accountability can be seen as much more confined and bounded in nature than political forms of accountability.

Traditionally, ministerial accountability to Parliament was seen as the ideal type of political accountability. However, with larger scale and more complex departments, it became increasingly unrealistic to expect ministers to take personal responsibility for actions done in their name. Softer notions of accountability such as ministerial answerability for departmental actions began to emerge.

A continuing decline of Parliament's ability to scrutinize the behaviour of the executive led to a number of policy innovations in the 1960s and 1970s designed to rebuild overloaded channels of accountability. In terms of political accountability, a much expanded Parliamentary Select Committee system was created. As far as enhanced managerial accountability was concerned, new forms of scrutiny and of administrative audit were created (the ombudsman, complaints boards). In the 1980s there was a further extension of financial audit systems, as bodies such as the National Audit Office and the Audit Commission expanded in role.

The 'New Magistracy' Arrives

Periodic opportunity for election is a long established mechanism for ensuring public accountability. There is then traditionally a democratic base to the notion of accountability in the public services, either through direct election (as in local government) or through nominated boards (as in the NHS) which historically have included elected local representatives.

An important aspect of the new public management has been the introduction of widespread changes to the governance systems which are now apparent across a wide range of public agencies (e.g. urban development corporations, the new universities, NHS trusts and authorities, training and enterprise councils, the current introduction of independent members to police authorities). There has been a general decline in the role of elected members and of staff representatives and an increase in the number of individuals formally appointed for their personal skills and qualities. Critics claim that they have also been appointed on covert political criteria. The marginalization of elected representatives represents a major change in governance systems and may require the development of new models of accountability.

Recent survey evidence (Skelcher and Davis 1995) of the characteristics and attitudes of non-executive board members in eight types of local appointed bodies suggests:

- just over half the respondents hold a position on more than one local appointed body. It is not unusual for some board members to hold four or more positions simultaneously;
- personal contact is identified as the most common and favoured means of recruitment;

- there is a tendency for boards to appoint individuals with similar backgrounds and characteristics to existing members.

But also

- Board members see their role as transcending party political agendas. They feel strongly that they are independent of any political party;
- Public duty or a desire to serve the community is the factor most frequently mentioned by respondents as motivating them to accept an offer of an appointment.

Traditional forms of accountability are seen by J. Stewart (1992, 1994) as coming under strain with the growth of these local non-elected bodies since such government lacks the legitimacy of a direct democratic base. They further overload the already fragile doctrine of ministerial accountability. Given the lack of democratic legitimacy, these organizations may paradoxically find it more difficult to take the controversial or unpopular decisions for which they were created (this may be why purchasing organizations in health care have been slow to develop explicit rationing).

Whilst the appointment of thousands of people to the new health authorities and trusts in 1990 did not create a major controversy at that stage, a similar plan in 1994 relating to the appointment of independent members on police authorities had to be modified in the light of public and police resistance. These concerns about standards in public life were recognized in the appointment of the Nolan Committee, which recommended a much more explicit process of appointment to local bodies. Interestingly, appointments to NHS trusts proved the single most controversial area covered in submissions to Nolan.

So recent reorganizations of the public services have been seen as impoverishing traditional concepts of public accountability (Weir and Hall 1994) and as leading to the rise of a 'new magistracy' (J. Stewart 1992) whereby there is a shift of power from elected representatives to non-elected nominees. Local government takes on an increasingly marginal role and an increasing 'democratic deficit' is heralded (Bogdanor 1994). The new institutions are seen as leading the way to an appointee state which is neglectful of local community interests. For example, the London Docklands Corporation has been widely criticized for being unresponsive to its local population in its regeneration strategy. While downwards accountability is eroded, upwards accountability if anything strengthens (for example, the construction of stronger line-management hierarchies in the NHS or the new universities).

It is, however, interesting that the reformed governance system of schools presents a very different model from that generally apparent elsewhere, with continuing representation from parents, staff, and local community figures.

The Composition, Role, and Behaviour of Non-Elected Élites

Amongst these critical accounts, however, there is sometimes a too rapid move from presenting often unsystematic data on élite composition to unargued inferences about élite behaviour. For such critics, the most important distinguishing feature about accountability in the new public management is that effectively there is none:

since 1979, the NHS has been transformed into a series of quangos directed mostly by businessmen with Conservative leanings, usually selected more for their professional position than for their identification with the local community. No body of administrative law has been developed to regulate their activities. Equipped with a mission statement of effectiveness and efficiency, they have been freed from the constraints of formal accountability to those who use the NHS and pay for it through taxes. (N. Pfeffer and Pollock 1993)

Weir and Hall (1994: 15) similarly argue that this new non-elected élite operating within the public sector will typically behave as a creature of central government:

members of the New Magistracy continually assert their independence of government in media interviews. This is assumed to be a public good, though the exercise of independent powers by unelected bodies would subvert the basic principles of democracy. The reality, however, is that Extra Government Organisations (EGOs) possess scarcely any independent room for manoeuvre. They have specifically been created, or adapted, to act as dependent agencies within parameters of policy and resources set by government.

This critique reflects the common public perception that public services are now directed by a small, cohesive, politically correct (i.e. right-wing), *nomenclatura* which staffs the appointee state, effectively out of democratic control. Power has shifted to the higher echelons of the party-state apparatus, with a small number of key individuals holding multiple board-level positions in the new-style public sector.

Typically these accounts present little behavioural data on how this élite really makes decisions, and whether there is consensus or conflict within the élite. Crude theories of motivation are apparent, which assume that these local élites act essentially as marionettes, transmitting central instructions downwards.

This debate could be usefully informed by the more general controversy between élite theory and pluralism (Mizruchi 1992), which offer very different accounts of the distribution of power and the nature of decision making in advanced capitalist societies. Élite theorists would argue that while there may be conflict over day-to-day issues, there is in the end a tendency to higher order unity amongst the élite. Pluralists, by contrast, might argue that the appointee state is in fact composed of a number of loosely coupled sub-élites (political, managerial, professional, academic, public service) which may be in negotiation, even conflict, with each other. Any assumption that these sub-élites possess a tendency towards higher order unity (in this case overarching support for the broad new public management programme) needs empirical testing and could well be unsafe.

It can also be argued that while there may be weak formal mechanisms for accountability, these may be powerfully supplemented by informal senses of accountability (such as an internalized conception of duty). Little contemporary empirical data on these élite members' informal senses of accountability have been adduced, despite previous research in this area (P. Day and Klein (1987) concluded that a sense of upwards accountability at that stage seemed weaker among NHS authority members than their sense of downwards accountability). Of course, such statements are only reports of intentions and are more powerful when linked to data on action: how powerful are these senses in practice? Nevertheless, this line of argument alerts us to the need to get beyond crude and mechanistic accounts of personal motivation and to explore a broader range of possible models, motives, and mechanisms.

We conclude this section by stating that the question of the accountability of restructured public service organizations is now correctly perceived as of major significance. In our view, such bodies should still be regarded as public organizations and as such rightfully face tough accountability tests. While there is increasing concern that such organizations are not effectively accountable, rigorous empirical and behavioural data which could illuminate these questions are scarce.

8.3. Alternative Models of Accountability

Given the centrality of the accountability debate, it may be helpful to make explicit some of the different models of accountability currently implicitly in use. Within the private sector, Molz (1985) has similarly attempted to generate a typology of different roles played by the board of directors. He developed a continuum of models, reflecting the involvement of different stakeholders, ranging from a narrow managerial model of control to a much broader model of social control, where the board of directors escapes managerial domination and interacts with, and learns from, society outside. The point is that there are very different models of accountability on offer, all of which have different implications for the distribution of power and also for organizational design.

In our postal surveys of NHS board members, we asked two questions in relation to senses of individual and corporate accountability (see Cairncross and Ashburner 1992*a* and 1992*b*). The results from health authority members and NHS trust directors are summarized in Tables 8.1.–8.4.

These survey data suggest first of all the multiple senses of accountability which often co-exist in a confusing manner. They also illustrate a substantial sense of upwards accountability to the Department of Health and Secretary of

Table 8.1 *To which groups do you consider yourself accountable as a health authority member (%)?*

	General manager	Executive	Chair	Non-Executive	Total
Local community	58	60	58	67	64
Chair	89	68	14	61	60
Patients	44	47	55	59	55
Health secretary	35	25	51	36	38
Department of health	27	25	44	29	30
General manager	4	62	4	15	23
Health authority staff	16	26	15	23	22
Taxpayers	10	7	12	9	9
Others	1	—	—	—	—

Note: n = 2, 141
Source: Cairncross and Ashburner (1992a: 20)

Table 8.2 *To which groups do you consider the health authority as a whole accountable (%)?*

	General manager	Executive	Chair	Non-Executive	Total
Local community	63	74	62	70	69
Health secretary	61	68	42	68	65
Patients	50	53	52	63	59
Department of health	29	51	48	68	59
Health authority staff	10	26	16	25	23
Chair	11	18	14	15	15
General manager	2	5	3	12	9
Taxpayers in general	14	6	10	6	7

Note: n = 2,141
Source: Cairncross and Ashburner (1992a: 21)

Table 8.3 *To which groups do you consider yourself accountable as a trust director (%)?*

	Chief executive officer	Executive	Chair	Non-Executive	Total
Chair	76	73	8	71	65
Patients	48	59	68	61	60
Local community	25	37	45	54	45
Health secretary	40	29	82	48	44
Trust staff	28	54	29	37	42
Chief executive officer	—	79	3	10	35
Taxpayers	36	27	58	30	32
Purchasers	28	24	47	31	30
Department of Health	33	29	37	26	29
Others	4	6	3	54	5
Don't know	—	—	—	1	—

Note: n = 376
Source: Cairncross and Ashburner (1992c).

Table 8.4 To which groups do you consider the trust board as a whole accountable?

	Chief executive officer	Executive	Chair	Non-executive	Total
Health secretary	64	80	63	75	75
Local community	60	68	61	60	63
Patients	56	59	63	66	62
Purchasers	52	53	63	66	62
Department of Health	52	60	50	56	57
Taxpayers	36	47	42	44	44
Trust staff	32	47	34	43	43
Chair	20	29	18	14	20
Chief executive officer	8	11	11	8	9
Others	4	6	3	54	5
Don't know	—	—	—	2	1

Note: *n* = 376.
Source: Cairncross and Ashburner (1992c).

State. Within the local board group itself, 71 per cent of NHS trust executive directors reported a personal sense of accountability to their chair which may in turn be associated with a reluctance to challenge the chair in board meetings.

More qualitative material derived from our interview work can help us examine respondents' accounts in greater depth, and to try to assess the hierarchy of these senses of accountability (what happens, for instance, when the Secretary of State advocates one course of action, but the local community the opposite?).

Accountability Upwards

This model represents classical public administration doctrine. Ministers are responsible to Parliament for the delivery of nationally organized services and will resign where there has been gross error. Parliamentary questions and debate represent key instruments of scrutiny, with the result that information flows upwards from the services to the minister's private office for ministerial briefing. It might be thought that under these circumstances ministers would enjoy a monopoly of expertise; however, specialized pressure groups also lobby to get their pet topics parliamentary time, briefing sympathetic MPs and testing ministers' command of the subject. Specialized House of Commons Committees also represent fora for parliamentary scrutiny of the Executive and in particular the PAC, armed with local auditors' reports, keeps a watchful eye on probity and value for money. Senior civil servants (e.g. the Permanent Secretary) act as accounting officers who report to the PAC, again ensuring an upwards flow of financial information.

In terms of the concept of democracy in use (Gyford *et al.* 1989; Leach 1990), this approach implies the familiar model of *representative democracy* in which candidates (usually from organized political parties) present themselves at elections on the basis of an agreed manifesto. Those elected, however, are seen as representatives and not as delegates.

In this model, local decision-makers within the public services act essentially as agents of the Secretary of State who wields considerable appointment powers. Their accountability is upwards to the minister and Parliament rather than downwards to their local communities. The scope for local strategy making is therefore limited as the key task is rather to implement national policy.

This model has long been attacked as unrealistic, given the complexity and scale of modern government and the limited time and expert knowledge available to MPs. Recent moves to more decentralized government, to decision-making through market forces and the contract, and the creation of Next Steps agencies (all key features of the new public management) make it even less convincing. Recent controversies over the Child Support Agency and the prison service have exposed the difficulty of drawing a line between policy and operations and of deciding who should be held accountable for errors of judgement.

If concern about inadequate public accountability persists, one option would be to move back to strengthening lines of accountability upwards, for example, by increasing the role of Parliamentary Select Committees. This would, however, require major reversals of policy towards managerial decentralization, and result in even stronger information and reporting requirements upwards.

Turning to empirical data, P. Day and Klein's (1987) earlier study of the sense of accountability evinced by health authority members concluded with a paradox. According to received doctrine, health authority members should aim to combine a sense of accountability upwards to the Secretary of State with sense of responsibility downwards towards their district. Those expectations are shared by critics who assume that appointed rather than elected members will look upwards rather than downwards.

P. Day and Klein's findings, however, suggested that most health authority members did not accept this definition of their role. Members were more concerned to fulfil their responsibilities towards the district, whether it was called the community, the people, or the patients. Only a few members even mentioned their formal accountability upwards and then as a lower priority to their general feelings or responsibility downwards. Except as a source of funding, central government authority was seen as irrelevant and members did not consider themselves in danger of reprimand or sacking, unless for some financial irregularity.

However, our post-1990 NHS data indicates a stronger sense of upwards accountability than was apparent in this earlier data. This may appear paradoxical given the rhetoric of devolved management. In part, it reflects the arrival of executive directors on the Board, with their experience of working in a hierarchically based mode to the chief executive officer. Public health directors, however, sometimes reported a split sense of upwards accountability, reflecting their right of direct access to the authority: 'I am accountable to the district general manager for the majority of things—but for some general areas of professional advice I am accountable to the authority' (director of public health).

Moreover, alongside proclaimed moves to more decentralist modes of management, there has also been a less obvious move over the last five years towards a vertically integrated and line-managed organization within the NHS (e.g. reconstitution of regional health authorities as regional offices; tighter national efficiency targets).

While NHS board members interviewed in our study felt individually accountable to a variety of people and institutions, the line of formal accountability was often perceived as linked to the appointment process and who had made the appointment.

In one trust, most executive directors reported a feeling of accountability to the chair or the chief executive officer. Another chief executive officer felt personally accountable primarily to his chair, and to a much lesser extent to the other non-executives, to the NHS chief executive and his agents, and remarked 'I suppose I feel some accountability to the local population.' He felt that the strength of the accountability mechanism was best tested by the two questions: who can fire you? who can cause you to be fired?

If purchasing organizations really are to develop as 'tribunes of the people', then one might expect them to be marked by a strong sense of downwards accountability and a weak sense of upwards accountability. Even in these organizations, we found that the sense of accountability often remained in an upwards direction.

For example, the executive director of a district health authority responded, when asked about the direction of accountability:

To the Secretary of State via the regional health authority. There is no doubt in my mind at the end of the day that is the position. The region has such power over our resources that one cannot afford to get into a position where you are doing the opposite of what region wants you to do.

A district health authority member, perhaps surprisingly, replied: 'I really always see myself as accountable to the chairman and district general manager for what I am doing.'

Another district health authority member argued: 'I am accountable to the chairman: it is too grandiose a view to talk of being accountable to the population as a whole.' A non-executive ot the regional health authority also saw his accountability as straight to the Secretary of State as his appointer. He felt that he shared his responsibility for delivering 'what is required by the government of the day' with the regional general manager.

Accountability to Staff

An alternative model is that board members should be held accountable to staff, either generally as good employers or more specifically as representatives of particular occupational or professional groupings. Such ideas were of increasing importance in the 1970s, often linked to the rise of the industrial democracy movement, including arguments for worker representatives on the board. However, after 1979, such proposals for increased staff representation on boards were rarely implemented and policy moved in quite a different direction. Staff and professional representation on the boards of public service organizations has indeed often been weakened as a result of recent reorganizations.

The sense of accountability to staff amongst board members was found to be relatively weak in our NHS interview data, and indeed much more active human resource management policies were emerging in some sites which were being imposed on staff by top management.

However, surviving professional members sometimes talked of a continuing sense of accountability to their professional college. This could pose a sharp dilemma for senior doctors who took on the role of medical director in NHS trusts, as their managerial and their professional roles and responsibilities could collide.

The family health services authorities, in particular, still contained representatives of professional groupings which represented yet another basis of accountability:

I think that the family health services authority should be accountable to the community it represents, and that's a hard one, and it is possibly my and other lay members' role to do that. I think it needs to have some kind of accountability to the professions that feed into it, there are the four basic professions. I think there has to be accountability nationally. I think there has to be accountability for the areas in which it relates to other authorities. So there is quite a lot of basic accountability there. (family health services authority member)

It remains to be seen whether these professional representatives of the family health services authority will continue to have places on the bodies likely to be created when the family and the district health authorities merge in 1996 or whether a board of directors model will be brought in, based on the earlier district health authority experience.

Accountability Downwards

This third concept of accountability relates to accountability downwards where there are a number of different approaches. The first model is one of *participatory democracy* (Gyford *et al*, 1989; Leach 1990; Ranson and Stewart 1994), where there is a widening of the scope for political activity in the public services and an extension of consultative and cooperative processes between representatives and local people. The process of information transmission and influencing is two-way rather than simply one-way from the organization to the local population. There is devolution of influence (perhaps even of some control) through devices such as decentralized (and democratized) service delivery, the promotion of cooperative ventures, user voice and encouragement of voluntary action. Participatory democracy is, however, seen as an adjunct to representative democracy and usually not as a replacement for it.

This perspective links with the work undertaken within the community development tradition (Hambleton 1988), for example the creation, support, and involvement of user groups such as tenants associations. Within the health service, patient advocates and advocacy groups have also been emerging sometimes armed with an ideology of consumerism, more willing to challenge traditional professional forms of domination and indeed knowledge (e.g. services for women provided by mainly male doctors).

C. Williamson (1992) analyses the growing consumer movement which can be seen as a long-term social and intellectual trend evident over the last forty or so years, and its application to health care settings. This raises the question of the distribution of power between professionals, managers and consumers. Here she highlights the emergence of specialist roles ('*consumerists*') among consumer groups. Such people undertake more general work around the sharing of knowledge and experience than is possible at individual consumer level, together with the identification and advocacy of oppressed and suppressed interests amongst consumer groupings.

A very different model of *delegate democracy* is also possible (Leech 1990), where in a party-dominated system power is shifted from elected representatives to the wider grouping of party members. Office-holders are seen as party delegates who are expected to abide by party majority decisions, are mandatable and recallable by party bodies. Such a model of delegate democracy was favoured by the Labour Left in the 1980s, but seems to have vanished almost without trace in the management of the public services by the early 1990s.

There are then various options for reinvigourating downwards accountability in the new public management. One would be to introduce direct elections to each local body. Another would be to restore local authorities' nominating powers to these boards. In health care, a proposal has been made to transfer purchasing responsibility to local government (AMA 1993):

it could be argued that the clearest case for a major local authority role was in the District Health Authority whose involvement as a provider will be largely replaced by a role as a purchaser, determining local needs—a governmental role for which local accountability is required. (J. Stewart 1994: 32)

Turning to our interview data, there were a number of statements reported to us by respondents in our case study localities which indicated a prima-facie concern to ensure continuing downwards accountability in the post-1990

NHS—the weakness rather was that there were no mechanisms to ensure that this concern was put into practice.

In one trust studied, the application document's statement of benefits to patients included a reference to the ability 'to provide management which is both more local and locally accountable'. It was stated that the trust would 'work systematically to find out the views of GPs and patients about our services and make improvements'.

The trust board here reported a strong sense of accountability to patients and staff, rather than to the purchasers:

This is an independent organization. There is a line of political direction informally through the chairman and there are certain statutory responsibilities, but independent organizations are not managerially accountable in that way. (trust director)

the accountability is really to the patients, the institution, and the place. It is about the service here; that is, what makes us comfortable or uncomfortable about what is going on, not particularly about whether we are going to upset the Secretary of State. (trust director)

More so than the executive directors, the non-executive directors in one NHS Trust recognized their formal accountability to the Secretary of State, but tended to regard it as secondary to other forms of informal downwards accountability. For example, the chair felt legally accountable to the Secretary of State but also reported:

I could not care a hang about the Secretary of State. I am accountable to the people who actually work within the institution and the patients. If I fail, I fail the people who work here and I fail the people who are our customers. That to me is far more important than failing the Secretary of State.

In one health authority, another non-executive director reported a similar hierarchy of accountabilities: 'I am accountable to the patients, to the people of (the locality), they appoint me to work on their behalf. Then I am accountable to the board of the health authority.'

In one trust, a community director reported a strong sense of downwards accountability, in part due to her long career in the field locally:

Well, I have been asked to be the trust representative for the community health councils who I know anyway and I have known for years. I was a community health council member once before I went on the area health authority. I think there is just a role for somebody who lives in the area, who has lived a long time in the area, who people know to be involved with the health service and who listens to people, and who meets a lot of people, as I do when I go to my own doctor's surgery.

In a family health services organization, however, one member found it difficult to see how accountability to the community existed in any direct sense and that much depended on the behaviour and attitudes of members:

I think the family health services authority as a whole is accountable to the region and the Department of Health. How far one is accountable to the local community is a much more difficult question. We are not elected, we do not go out and take the hustings and discuss our policy. What one does, I think, is try and keep one's ear to the ground on issues, the more visiting and things like that one can do, the more one can become aware of what is happening on the ground and better one can feel one is actually helping to identify how the service is better in this particular area and therefore in an indirect way one is being accountable to the local community. But it is difficult to say that one is accountable to anyone. One could argue that perhaps one is accountable to the chair.

However, one needs to ask: what mechanisms are there in place to support this informal sense of downward accountability? In practice, there appears no formal mechanism to ensure the accountability of NHS trusts downwards to the community apart from the AGM and any meetings in public or meetings with the community health council. The degree of access accorded to the community health council in relation to the board decision-making process may be an important indicator of the degree to which the board faces downwards to its local community. Public meetings may be another indicator but here health authorities and NHS trusts are generally holding fewer meetings in public than before 1990. Some Directors of the Trusts studied were highly sceptical of the value of meeting in public, arguing that it inhibited free and frank discussion.

Market-Based Forms of Accountability

> but doesn't the public sector lack that essential spur which makes it imperative for the private sector to give good service, i.e. doesn't it lack competition and consumer choice? Yes, but there is no reason why greater competition cannot be generated within the public service itself. Choice in the health service depends on information about waiting times, about assessment of hospitals, about medical performances. Choice implies the ability to change doctor more easily and to choose to go to consultants whose waiting times are shorter. This can in effect bring more competition.
>
> (Griffiths 1988: 202)

> understanding customers will thus be one of the most characteristics of a competitive council—and one of its most difficult tasks. 'Clients' need to be treated as 'customers', services need to be provided for the public rather than simply to it.
>
> (Audit Commission 1988)

Not all agree, however, that the new public management has eroded the accountability of public services. Indeed the New Right's model of market-based accountability stresses the empowerment of users as customers. It deliberately marginalizes the exercise of political forms of accountability through intermediate institutions (such as local authorities) which are seen as captured by vested interests and thus cannot be trusted to act as good proxies for their citizens. The political system is here seen as failing to provide an effective mechanism for the exercise of accountability.

The New Right critique of the expanded Welfare State (see Dunleavy 1991) argues that State apparatus produces an oversupply of public services, funding more and more services out of taxation when they would be better provided through the market. Public sector bureaucrats naturally seek to expand their departmental budgets, along with the power and prestige of their agencies. They are allied with closed iron triangles of sectional vested interests (e.g. professionals, particular pressure groups, election-wary politicians) which together compose a collusion system in which resource levels are constantly bid up, along with the burden of taxation on the public.

Group leaders are here seen as able to insulate themselves from the opinions of group members. The New Right would argue (see Dunleavy's critical review, 1991: 39) in particular that 'altruistic' élite groups acquire influential positions intermediating between Welfare State agencies and their clients. Both 'poverty professionals' and 'Welfare bureaucrats' share a common interest in bidding up resource levels and maintaining complex programme rules and regulations which only they can understand.

Supporters of this model argue that recent organizational changes yield a democratic gain, through making services directly accountable to their clients and removing distorting intermediaries. As William Waldegrave argued, (quoted in Weir and Hall 1994: 12):

the key point is not whether those who run our public services are elected, but whether they are producer responsive or consumer responsive. Services are not necessarily made to respond to the public by giving our citizens a democratic voice, and a distant and diffuse one at that, in their make up. They can be made responsive by giving the public choices, or by instituting mechanisms which build in publicly approved standards and redress when they are not attained.

Here accountability is seen not so much in terms as citizenship rights but consumer rights. Public services are to become more directly accountable to their customers. Central to this model has been an attempt to shift power from producers to consumers, by breaking up monopoly providers or, where this has not been possible, to bring in new forms of regulation such as the setting of service standards and provision of compensation when these are not achieved.

Associated with the emergence of this market-based model have been a number of other linked developments. During the 1980s there was increased attention paid to the empowerment of individuals as consumers of public services. The Griffiths Report (1983) placed a central role on the development of a consumer mentality in the NHS: on acquiring information on the needs and expectations of users and acting on it. As the 1980s wore on, a wider stream of work on quality initiatives (e.g. total quality management programmes) and customer care programmes became established throughout the public sector, for example in social security and local government (Griffiths 1988). Privatized corporations such as British Airways were held up as exemplars in the quality field for the rest of the public sector. There has also been a growth in market research and the use of techniques such as focus groups to gather more systematic information on the behaviour and preferences of users of public services.

More recently, the Citizen's Charter initiative (1991) has also extended the accountability of public sector providers to their users through the setting of performance targets. Such initiatives in effect act as a form of regulation of monopoly public services (just as the monopoly utilities privatized in the 1980s were also subjected to regulators). Standards are set by the regulator and redress provided if they are not met.

There is also continuing stress on the publication of more information to enable users to make informed choices between providers: the recent controversy about league tables of school performance provides a good example. Inspection procedures are also being strengthened and a stronger lay perspective introduced (e.g. clinical audit).

Power (1994) draws attention to the explosion of audit systems throughout the public services, which he sees as constituting a new mode of accountability within the public services based on private sector experience. The result is that the accountant has risen in power in the public as in the private sector. Quantified, simplified, *ex post* forms of control have increasingly displaced other and more traditional forms of control (such as informal professional dialogue).

Another form of market-based accountability is that of management through contract. Providers are to be held accountable to their purchasers through the agreed contract. The contract of course represents the preferred mode of transacting in a liberal economy and has been imported into the new public management as a means of organizing relations in disaggregated organizations. J. Stewart (1993) questions this use of contracts in the public services, arguing that it erodes accountability (particularly at case level) and limits public learning. There is some evidence that contracting may lead to the drying-up of informal information flows between organizations (Bennett and Ferlie 1994) which might stimulate such learning.

Reviewing such initiatives, Prior *et al.* (1993) argue that there is an implicit theory in use which can be summarized as follows:

- that use of competition and market mechanisms will provide greater choice, ensure quality, and achieve value;
- that extending the range of providers will increase choice;
- that providing information and setting standards will ensure accountability;
- that providing information, ensuring independent inspection, and setting standards will enhance quality and value;
- that the main management change required to ensure quality and achieve value is the provision of incentives for performance.

Critique of the Market-Based Model

This market-based model can be criticized for operating with a loose and misleading conception of the 'customer'. Who is the customer in the quasi-markets which have been created in key public services? Only rarely do individual users act directly to make choices (parental choice of school might offer one example, although even here choice is heavily constrained). More frequently new intermediary proxies have been created (e.g. health authorities as macro-purchasers; GP fundholders as micro-purchasers), on the assumption that they will reflect customer views in their purchasing decisions. This is an entirely unproven assumption which is in urgent need of empirical testing.

To what extent can patients or clients of public services rightfully be described as customers? Consumption can be imposed, for example, through the social control functions of the criminal justice system or the child protection work of social services. The choice of language may reflect no more than the current hegemony of ideas derived from the field of marketing within restructured public services. In an ideal typical market, such customers would have knowledge about a range of products or services, a degree of market power, and the capacity to make choices between providers. Does this accurately describe the situation facing users of public services?

Critics of the New Right model also argue that it operates with restricted notions of citizenship. While Pollitt (1988) accepts the need to make public services more user-responsive, he argues that there is also a need to consider questions of citizenship and of collective action at the strategic level. Public sector versions of consumerism are required where the concept of the citizen-consumer suggests additional values such as equity, equal opportunities, representation, and participation not apparent in more cosmetic 'supermarket' models.

These critical concepts have been influential in the development of a model of 'public service orientation' (J. Stewart and Clarke 1987) which tackles some common themes as, but also distinct from, private sector notions of consumerism. Ranson and Stewart (1994: 232) argue that these New Right notions of market accountability fail to take into account the need for decisions to be tested by citizens in the realm of public discourse: 'it has to be recognised that effective performance at all levels cannot escape from the values to be realised in the public domain. Effective performance cannot be achieved if justice is denied, citizenship ignored and equity confounded'. Hambleton (1988) also criticizes market-led models of accountability. These have difficulty in dealing with the needs of groups of users, given that many services are provided on a collective rather than an individual basis. Secondly, consumer choice within newly constructed quasi-markets often seems more apparent than real: for example, users may find it extremely difficult to negotiate an extra-contractual referral if they want access to a non-contracted provider in health care. Thirdly, it is a moot point whether providers are more able to influence customers through, for example, more sophisticated marketing strategies, than customers are able to influence providers. In practice, consumerist ideas may fail to reduce the disparity of power between the users and providers of public services.

Despite these criticisms, clearly novel market-based forms of accountability have been influential at central policy-making level in the early 1990s. Yet turning to our interview data, our local respondents hardly ever talked about market-led forms of accountability. Indeed, it was difficult to identify coherent accounts of what such forms of accountability might look like in practice. This suggests a worrying disjunction between models being developed at the centre and a lack of understanding of these models among decision-makers in the localities.

Self Accountability: Answerability to Own Conscience

The four models already reviewed can all be seen as externally located. Here we turn to an alternative model with an internal reference point: a sense of conscience. In P. Day and Klein's study (1987), respondents' answers often stressed weaker notions of answerability rather than stronger notions of accountability through a revocable mandate. Answerability to one's own conscience would fall into this category of response.

Some respondents in our study reported no sense of formal accountability but rather a strong sense of informal accountability to their own consciences for behaving ethically (duty-driven). This concept of accountability is not to be dismissed out of hand: some of the respondents could certainly be seen as examples of Douglas Hurd's 'active citizens' (hyperactive, perhaps, in some cases) with developed social consciences. A strong spirit of public service survived and was reported to us in interviews, although the test of the strength of conscience was whether a non-executive would ultimately be prepared to resign on a point of principle. We are aware that these interviews represent no more than self-reports, and that there may well be a contradiction between what board members say they would do and what they actually do.

Some of the respondents we interviewed very much saw themselves as autonomous self-starters throughout long and often successful careers, and these were personal qualities which they brought to the NHS:

I must be accountable to the Secretary of State who is the person that set me to do the job. Ultimately I feel responsible to myself and I have always been that sort of person— I am in control of what I do, I set my own targets to make the family health services authority aware of the community out there (family health services authority member).

Technically, accountable to chairman of region . . . But I feel my responsibility is mainly to myself, to the public to whom we have to deliver health services. This sounds rather pompous, but to myself, the public and my staff and if my nominal superior does not like it, well, then it is too bad (chair).

How strong are these reported informal senses of accountability? Critics would argue that they are simply rhetoric and window-dressing as directors of quangos have no reason to be concerned about what the public thinks of them (Pfeffer and Pollock 1993). There are two acid tests of this sense of accountability to one's own conscience. First, will members be prepared to speak out, even when in a minority on the board? Other data (Ferlie *et al*, forthcoming 1995) illustrate the tendency of the board to group-think, and show the difficult role played by the dissenter on the board.

The second indicator is the extent to which members are prepared to resign (or, more weakly, not seek reappointment) on a point of principle. For some, this may be difficult as it would mean giving up the payment now received by health authority members. For a few members and more especially chairs, given the wave of executive downsizing and delayering, health authority membership may serve as a remunerated and high status form of employment after redundancy, and one which they might be loath to give up.

We found very few examples in our case study sites of members resigning on a point of principle. This suggests that while informal senses of accountability are apparent, they may be difficult to operationalize in practice.

Confused or Multiple Senses of Accountability

As our survey data indicated, many respondents reported multiple senses of accountability. P. Day and Klein (1987) found that authority members used a clutch of words interchangeably, sometimes giving multiple versions of accountability. We found similarly that some interview respondents struggled with the whole concept of accountability for their actions and would give confusing or even contradictory accounts. The lack of clear thinking in such a central area is of major concern for all those who wish to see the development of effective forms of corporate governance in the public services.

Some respondents were still coming to terms with the notion of accountability for the first time in their careers. For some businessmen, a role in the NHS represented an important change from their private sector experience and the notion of accountability was still a foreign one:

I suppose in a sense we are accountable to what: the region? ... I feel the word accountability is a fairly odd one. When you run a small business for so long, the only people I was accountable to were the customers and the tax man, otherwise if you wanted anything done, you got it done (non-executive member).

I think we are accountable to the chairman as far as I understand. What that means in practice I have not the slightest idea. We do not actually do anything we are accountable for. We do not make decisions, we do not report back to anyone (non-executive member).

Some NHS board members reported multiple senses of accountability which ran in several directions simultaneously. One regional health authority non-executive, for instance, felt that that authority was accountable to the Department of Health in financial terms, but also responsible to patients and the public not to waste money, and also as accountable to the staff, who would produce a better service in a good working atmosphere.

A district health authority member replied, even more confusingly:

Ultimately, of course, we're accountable to the patients. But if you are talking about concrete accountability, I can't go out and say to the patients 'how am I doing?', but I am accountable to the patients through the work we all do on the health authority. I suppose that is through the chairman, through the regional health authority. If we do something which disadvantages our patients, then we should be accountable and I think the only way it would come would be through the region.

The presence of such confusion, and of overdependence on the chair, may make it difficult to ensure effective systems of corporate governance on these boards. Certainly it suggests that more development or training work may be urgently required, even at this very senior level.

To summarize Section 8.3, we have here outlined a typology of different senses of accountability as reported to us by post-1990 NHS board members. Informal senses of downwards accountability and of answerability to one's conscience had survived. When compared to the P. Day and Klein (1987) data, however, we surfaced more accounts of upwards accountability, perhaps reflecting the move to a more tightly managed and vertically integrated NHS or alternatively the arrival of more hierarchically minded executive directors on the board. This shift runs counter to the recent rhetoric of increased devolution and decentralization. There were very few reports of accountability to staff. Market-led models of accountability were evident by their absence at local level. Confused or multiple accounts were also common, as they had been in the P. Day and Klein study.

8.4. Purchasing Organizations: Will They Really Develop as Tribunes of the People?

User-Empowerment and New Purchasing Roles

Alford's (1975) analysis of the politics of decision-making in health care distinguished between three main interest groups: a dominant professional grouping, a challenging managerial grouping, and a repressed community grouping. His analysis raised the question of the distribution of social and organizational power in the health care arena in a sharp and direct way.

In the 1980s the balance of power in health care swung from professional to managerial élites to a greater degree than many had expected. This suggests that the distribution of such power was not entirely fixed but could be reshaped over time. Power had, however, merely been passed from one élite to another. In the late 1980s a growing rhetoric of user empowerment was noticeable. To what extent has a further shift from professional and managerial élites to wider community interests been occurring? This raises the further, and often unexplored, question of how it is that groups of users influence the decision-making process. While there are an increasing number of studies of user needs and preferences, often they have been organizationally naïve and have not considered how it is that users can influence the decision making process. What, in other words, are the mechanisms which can ensure user influence within health care organizations?

As indicated in Chapters 1 and 3, a key feature of recent public sector reorganizations has been the separation-out of purchasing and providing roles (e.g. health care, social care, market-testing within Whitehall). Within health care, purchasers are intended to take account of the needs and wishes of local users in setting contracts, and indeed to act as 'champions of the people' (Salter 1993). In our view, these new purchasing organizations do offer the potential (to put it no higher than that) to ensure more effective user participation in decision-making. Nor has this potentially critical role always been sufficiently recognized by those who criticize the 'democratic deficit' of the new public management, as their critique often focuses on provider organizations.

Within the new public management, the purchasing and providing arms may well be developing two quite different roles, orientations, labour-markets, and cultures. Some would argue that while providers may be expected to display a more business-like orientation; strong notions of equity, need, and community participation may remain within the purchaser culture. Where the purchaser is powerful, these aspirations may be reflected in the contracts they draw up with providers.

Certainly recent central policy guidance has stressed the need for health care purchasers to involve local people in the formulation and implementation of purchasing plans:

If health authorities are to establish a *champion of the people* role, their decisions should reflect, so far as practical, what people want, their preferences, concerns and values. Being responsive to local views will enhance the credibility of health authorities but, more importantly, is likely to result in services which are better suited to local needs and therefore more appropriate. There may of course be occasions when local views have to be overridden (e.g. on the weight of epidemiological, resource or other considerations) and in such circumstances, it is important that health authorities explain the reasons for their decision. (NHS Management Executive 1992a)

Purchaser organizations in health care are also being advised to construct interorganizational 'alliances for health' (NHS Management Executive, 1992b), where a traditional command and control model of management gives way to a model based on negotiation and persuasion. Partners in such alliances are not only seen as sister statutory organizations (especially district health authority, family health services authority, GP fundholders, and the social services department) but also voluntary organizations or community groupings. Health authorities are expected to develop more active and sophisticated mechanisms for public consultation.

In this optimistic view of the new order, purchasers take increased account of the needs and wishes of local users in the setting of contracts, indeed acting as 'tribunes of the people'. As organizations, they escape traditional 'provider capture', and also central political and managerial control, responding to the needs and aspirations of their local communities.

While there may have been a genuine intent in some quarters to shift the balance of power from professionals and managers to users collectively, there are also many countervailing forces remaining within the system (e.g. the imposition of national top–down targets; pressure to manage bad news and controversy; the continuing rise of management as a new power élite). The mechanisms for performing these new downward-facing roles have so far been unclear and it remains to be seen whether pleas for greater user involvement are rhetorical or real. Recent policy analysis (Heginbotham and Ham 1992) highlights the multiple and contradictory pressures on purchasing organizations, and user involvement may be sacrificed at moments of tension and crisis.

Using data derived from a linguistic analysis of community care plans drawn up by health and social care agencies, Schofield (1994) concludes that even at the level of rhetoric the plans of health care purchasers continue to be dominated by a medical, or at least a public health, model of needs assessment. They are resource- and efficiency-driven, and take a purchasing for outcome approach.

The perspective of the social services departments, by contrast, was found to reflect much more deeply rooted shifts in role and philosophy towards a more client-based perspective. Unlike health care, clear routes of local accountability are often defined within the social services department plans.

However, Ranson and Stewart (1989) note a number of organizational trends apparent in public sector organizations which may facilitate such a shift to participatory democracy and real user involvement: delegation of budgets to localities; greater use of outreach workers, and the creation of local neighbourhood offices. Aided by new forms of information technology, decentralization may be occurring in public as well as private sector organizations (Hambleton 1988). Within local government during the 1980s, there were interesting experiments with devolved financial management or area-based planning. Hambleton cites examples from across the political spectrum: the Labour Left in Islington; the Liberal party in Tower Hamlets, and the Conservative party in Cambridgeshire.

There is still some scepticism about the extent to which purchasers will be able to work as tribunes of the people. Nevertheless, these new purchasing organizations mark an important break with previous structures, roles and behaviours (Romanelli 1991) and may still develop more of a downwards facing and user orientation. Certainly they have often been underexamined in the accountability debate, which has been skewed towards provider organizations.

The Purchaser–User Interface: Some Evidence from Health Care

So purchasing organizations can be seen as a new organizational form still at an early stage of development (Ferlie *et al.*, 1994). This purchasing role is both new and different and is a key strand to the new public management. However, more work may well be needed on the purchasing role. The danger is that the pace of development was at least initially faster on the provider than the purchasing side (Parston *et al.*, 1991; Ham and Matthews 1991). While hospitals and community units elected to become trusts, districts did not always elect to become purchasing organizations and some have been slow to make the transition. The decision of the Department of Health to earmark significant sums nationally to accelerate the development of purchasing is seen by some (Ham and Spurgeon, 1992) as a signal that purchasing organizations are now receiving greater policy attention.

The Growth of Needs Assessment

In our study, we collected case study data from three different district health authorities which have been evolving into purchasing organizations (Ferlie *et al.*, 1994). The assessment of the needs of the local population represents a central role for these new purchasing authorities, but one which has been historically underdeveloped. The driving force for the development of such work has often been an expanding public health function. A key question is how much influence the public health function—represented through the director of public health usually as an executive director—has at board level.

In one district, the newly appointed director of public health can be seen as an influential executive director, sometimes playing the role of a licensed dissenter in relation to health policy. The directorate's annual report is a key strategic document which goes to the authority, but discussion in the round observed was not of a fundamental or probing nature.

A public health forum has been meeting in this district since 1990 to feed into needs assessment. This is a collection of many organizations, including the community health council, family health services authority and social services. Better links have also been established with GPs. An experiment in locality planning was being developed in one market town.

In a second district, the needs assessment function has also gone to the public health directorate, which is headed by a young, energetic, director, following the retirement of the previous post-holder. The director of public health is an influential executive director who works closely with the chief executive officer. The director of public health advocates community-based values, and was influential in lobbying for more social policy expertise among the non-executives to complement finance based skills. The director's annual report is seen as an important input into purchasing strategy, and as providing a clear strategic view of how the purchasing process should develop. There is an expressed concern to respond to the concerns and views of local users, as well as to develop an epidemiological perspective.

This district has also recognized a need for a much more sophisticated communications strategy. Public relations consultants are being used to develop new forms of communication with the public, such as leaflets in GP surgeries. As well as imparting information, this also helps establish expectations in relation to targets for health gain.

The third district's 'Strategic Principles' (1990) recognized that: 'The district health authority's role is to assess and identify the health needs of the residents, to promote health and to secure appropriate services and treatment to meet the identified needs.' The authority sees itself as having an advocacy role in relation to the needs of the population, working in close cooperation with other agencies, and is pledged to speak out where necessary. There is a strong commitment to promoting the health of the population, looking at social, environmental, and economic, as well as medical, factors. The authority has a long-standing commitment to the Healthy Cities Project and a large-scale consultation exercise, involving local voluntary organizations and the use of outreach workers. There is also a subproject on needs assessment and planning, which is seen as a major aspect of the development of the purchasing role. Reports on needs-assessment work are regularly made to the authority. One problem, however, is that other agencies are taking time to understand the new purchaser role of the district health authority.

The Development of Locally Sensitive Purchasing

The development of locally sensitive purchasing is also emerging as an increasingly important theme. Central guidance (NHS Management Executive, 1992a) suggests that public consultation and demonstrable local accountability are indicators of best practice in purchasing. The culture in local government, more than in the NHS, seems to be supportive of attempts to establish mechanisms of local consultation with interesting developments being reported in the social care sector (Wistow and Barnes 1993).

Health care, on the other hand, is experiencing a shift of power to GPs and GP fundholders, but has limited prior experience of locality management and substantive public consultation. Murphy (1993) illustrates that in these circumstances a variety of models of locality purchasing are being developed in health care. In particular, some centre on the GP, while others intend that users or community leaders should play a more central role. Most importantly of all, interest is fuelled by the expressed intention to involve vocal and articulate consumers. Elston (1991) highlights the range of reasons which account for this trend, citing active consumerism, criticisms of professional self-regulation and a consequent decline in trust in professionals, and a greater sense of personal responsibility for health. In some sectors (e.g. mental health), there may be conflict between the views of GPs and of local user groups.

How are Purchasing Organizations to be Held Accountable?

However, the extent of accountability of purchasing boards in health care can currently be seen as weak. Indeed there is much confusion as to whom a purchasing board is accountable and for what. Typically, smaller scale District Health Authorities have been grouped together into very large scale purchasing consortia, with the consequent danger of increased remoteness from the population.

If accountability is upwards, then the effective operation of this account-ability must be scrutinized. The parameters on which effective purchasing might be judged are underdeveloped and there is poor data to support judgements about performance. Short-term financial criteria may well crowd out longer term and more diffuse strategic criteria. Democratic criteria may well disappear altogether. Even if poorly performing purchasers can be reliably identified, it is not obvious what action is indicated.

If purchasing organizations, by contrast, are indeed going to emerge as tribunes of the people, then this implies substantial downwards account-ability to the population. Yet how is this to be exercised? There is a danger that purchasing organizations will emerge as remote and top-heavy bodies unless real thought is given to the development of locality-purchasing organized around natural community boundaries (which may not necessa-rily be the same boundaries as those of groupings of GP fundholder practices). We still have to ask: where is the user? Is it sufficient for the new purchasing organizations simply to hold meetings in public or should they be developing much more adventurous strategies (NHS Management Executive, 1992a) for acquiring information and demonstrating downwards accountability? Our evidence suggests that purchasing organizations still have a long way to develop before they can claim to be effective champions of the people.

8.5. Concluding Discussion: The Need for More Robust Models of Accountability

In this chapter, we have tried to unpack what might be meant by the term 'accountability' in recently restructured public service organizations. We argued that such organizations can rightfully be expected to face stern tests of accountability and noted recent concerns about the erosion of traditional channels of public accountability. We outlined a variety of different models, including new variants of market-led accountability.

Weak and Confused Mechanisms of Accountability

The mechanisms of accountability observed in our study were in our view weak and confused. Initially the 1990 NHS reforms can be seen as eroding traditional channels of public accountability (e.g. removal of local authority nominees; fewer public meetings). Given the argument that more business-like organizations required a looser regulatory regime, new forms of market accountability and accountability to the purchaser through the contract emerged instead at national level. However, it was noteworthy that a sense of market accountability was only rarely reported by interviewees, suggesting that such market-based models have only had limited impact locally.

We argued that alongside these formal mechanisms may lie informal senses of accountability. Our data suggest there is still a strong sense of informal downwards accountability reported by NHS members. There were also a number of reports of accountability to one's own conscience, although the link with action was untested in our study.

However, there was also a stronger sense of upwards accountability reported than we expected given the earlier P. Day and Klein data (1987). Perhaps this reflects the strengthening of the line hierarchy which has been evident in the last ten years and which may be shifting senses of the accountability mechanism on the non-executive as well as the executive side.

A number of respondents gave weak, confused, or indeed contradictory accounts, even when they had been in role for a considerable period of time, essentially replicating the earlier P. Day and Klein data. When compared, for instance, with the clarity found about the financial role and responsibility of board members, there seemed an alarming vagueness in relation to reported senses of accountability. Any hope that the 1990 reorganization would result in a crisper and agreed sense of sense of accountability does not seem to have been fulfilled. J. Stewart *et al.* (1995) put forward proposals for enhanced downwards accountability which need not necessarily involve local democratic control. Codes of practice and more transparent appointment procedures could for example be introduced. The local authority or the public at large could be given to right to recall, if backed by a referendum, as a means of introducing an element of contestability, especially into the workings of purchasing organizations.

Purchasing Organizations and User Involvement: Still Early Days

We have argued that purchasing organizations are underanalysed as an organizational form and that purchasing may be evolving as a distinct and novel branch of the new public management with its own set of tasks, culture, and values. There is here at the very least the potential for the development of a more participatory form of user involvement which could inform the purchasing function.

In our view, interesting experiments are now occurring, but little real impact is as yet apparent at the strategic core of the organization. These innovations may also be concentrated in a small group of leading-edge authorities. Freemantle *et al.*'s (1993) study of variation in the rate of development of the purchasing function concluded: 'the concept of health needs assessment is proceeding haltingly where other conditions are favourable, but has been abandoned beyond a ritual activity for the public health function where conditions are relatively unfavourable.' Sceptics argue that such experiments will remain at the margin of purchasing organizations which in reality will continue to put priority on achieving top–down and efficiency-led targets. Strong downwards accountability is unlikely to be achieved when there is such lack of clarity as to whom a purchaser board should be held accountable, and for what.

This chapter has noted the rising level of concern apparent about the accountability deficit within new public management organizations. We concur with much of that concern and in our view further action is required. More thought needs to be given to the development of more robust models of accountability and to ensuring that these models are owned by local boards and individual board members.

CONCLUSION

9.1. Introduction

Following on from a set of empirically informed chapters, this final chapter moves back to a higher level of analysis. We hope to have established that new public management style reforms, taken as a whole, represent a major attempt to restructure the public services, changing the nature of their organization and management. These reform programmes contain multiple strands with effects at system, group, and individual role levels alike. This is therefore an important and wide ranging phenomenon which is worthy of a broad analysis. What has been learnt about the rise and impact of the new public management? Is the new public management a monolithic ideology or can different variants be discerned which are competing for attention? What are the implications for the development of management theory in relation to public service organizations?

Section 9.2 of this concluding chapter will return to the key overarching themes introduced in Chapter 1 and which have been elaborated further in the course of the book. In Section 9.3, we highlight novel concepts and findings which have emerged in the course of the analysis. Section 9.4 will consider the implications for the development of new public management theory. It will finally outline some additional topic areas where further research into changing forms of organization and management in public sector organizations could now usefully take place.

9.2. Recapitulation of the Key Themes

What is Still Distinctively Public?

Contrary to the superficial rhetoric sometimes apparent, Chapter 1 argued that the UK public sector did not wither away in the 1980s. While its economic functions were curtailed, it continued to finance, and in large part to deliver, a wide range of core social policy functions (such as health and social care, education, criminal justice, and social security). The proportion of the UK GDP devoted to government expenditure has hardly changed since 1979, remaining at the 40–5 per cent level during this period, as indicated in Chapter 1.

While the intent of securing radical reductions in public expenditure is proclaimed from time to time by Treasury ministers, past experience indicates a wise scepticism. As soon as the Treasury succeeds in reducing expenditure on one social programme, expenditure in another programme unexpectedly mushrooms (the 1993 implementation of the care in the community initiative which tried to cap admissions to long-term residential care through giving more responsibilities to social service departments represents a good recent example). So the public sector still exists, is of very substantial scale and scope, and (in our opinion) is unlikely to shrink radically. This further raises the question of the optimal form of organization and management for this strategically placed sector.

This is not to say that there has been no change evident in the public sector since 1979. On the contrary, Chapter 2 indicated that maintenance management has given way to the self proclaimed management of change. There have been recurrent top–down and power-led efforts to secure change (although we also argue that this change process has resulted in some unintended as well as intended consequences) across the public services. Although the rate and pace of change varies from one service-setting to another, nevertheless the general pressure for change is constant. For example, a continuing commitment to building up managerial roles in the public services has been evident since the early 1980s.

There has been a substantial transfer of private sector models and concepts into public sector organizations in an attempt to make them more like firms. The importing of the management of change discourse into public sector organizations is in itself part of this wider process. It may be that in the future the public purse will continue to finance a wide range of services, but that provision will be delivered through a variety of private, voluntary, and informal providers.

However, relatively few of these providers may be private sector firms in the classic sense. Public sector management or worker buy-outs may be an important mechanism whereby such organizations are created, as may the construction of companies where managers report to a board on which public sector personnel are well represented. This raises for the first time in this chapter the question of intersectoral blurring and the new forms of organization and management emerging. These are themes which will be developed further throughout this concluding chapter.

Some have seen new public management-style reforms as trying to move the public services 'down group' (Dunleavy and Hood 1994); that is, making the public sector less distinctive from the private sector taken as a family grouping of organizations. In essence, other organizations converge on the model of the private corporation as the preferred organizational form, reducing intersectoral variety. The likely success of this mimetic process—whether it will 'stick' in the long term—must be related to the generic–sectorist debate reviewed in Chapter 1. The key question is whether management tasks in public sector organizations should be seen as essentially the same as, or as different from, management tasks in the private sector. If we conclude that difference is at least as important as similarity, then the likely long-term success of a such a simplistic cloning process could be regarded as slight. Rather than stabilizing at a discrete end-point, change is likely to beget further rounds of change as one disequilibrium succeeds another.

Elsewhere, we have argued (Pettigrew *et al.* 1992: 13) that there are both differences and similarities evident between the two sectors which need to be disaggregated in detail. Up to the mid-1980s the dominant problem in terms of management practice and theory was one of parochialism and isolation within the public sector. There was a too ready presumption of difference. Since the mid-1980s the problem has been the overmechanistic transfer of practice and concepts from the private to the public sectors. There is here too ready an assumption of similarity.

In this second set of circumstances, useful theories are likely to be those that can take account of intersectoral difference as well as similarity. Indeed, theories which do not do this may be positively harmful and misleading, resulting in attempts to impose change which fail to root and which have subsequently to be unpicked.

For example, in Chapter 3 we argued that public sector quasi-markets should not only be seen as socially and relationally embedded, but also as institutionally embedded. Conventional neo-classical models of markets fail to take adequate account of all three of these concepts, and even private sector-based relational models do not fully address the institutional element apparent within public sector quasi-markets.

Here we would argue that it is important to reiterate the continuing, distinctive features of public sector organizations. The primary or core purpose of public service organizations is to provide a service, not to make a profit. Furthermore, the definition and boundaries of this service are set by government, through a democratic process. Public sector organizations are not free to change or choose their primary purpose, as private sector organizations are to some extent (although in practice they may often be characterized by strategic inertia rather than strategic choice, see Pettigrew 1985). Nor can they select their market and only deliver their services to some users or consumers. Most public sector organizations are still publicly funded, (though it is interesting to note that non-traditional sources of income are expanding, for example in higher education (Hocking 1991), and that some universities such as Warwick have now achieved a position of 50 per cent self-generated funding). Finally, public organizations are in the main, highly professionalized organizations employing groupings such as doctors, teachers and social workers. It is this *combination* of characteristics which still makes public sector organizations distinctive.

This continuing sense of difference is epitomized in the current debate about accountability, or the lack of it, in recently restructured public organizations. As P. Day and Klein (1987) argue, accountability in public arenas rests on an ability to provide persuasive accounts. Novel models of management in the public services then require new forms of justification to users and citizens. Recent attempts to move the debate from a focus on accountability to a stress on performance, or to develop market-led models of accountability, have not so far been convincing to much of civil society and leading commentators (e.g. Bogdanor 1994; J. Stewart 1992) who must also be seen as important opinion-shapers in this field.

The failure to depoliticize core public service functions is evident as there continues to be intense public dislike, media coverage, and political action around, for example, attempts to develop explicit rationing in the NHS. While rationing was supposed to represent an early task for purchasing authorities, many of them have moved extremely cautiously in this field, except at the margins (e.g. IVF).

Beyond Relabelling: Top–Down and Power-Led Organizational Change

Nevertheless, we concluded that current reorganizations—at least on the basis of the NHS evidence presented—may represent far more than first-order change or a relabelling exercise. This is curious in itself because in the light of widespread professional opposition to the reform proposals, the organizational development literature—with its stress on the need for effective strategies to include participation, collaboration and commitment (Buckingham *et al.* 1975; Beckhard and Harris 1977; Mumford 1981; Schein 1985)— would have predicted the failure of such a top–down and power-led strategy.

So the conventional organizational development literature may be of limited use in explaining this new set of conditions. Often highly normative in tone, this literature also typically operated without developing concepts of power, or considering the role of power élites and the emergence of dominant forms of ideology. This literature was also slow to develop a theoretic discussion of a fuller range of organizational change strategies and their effectiveness in different contexts and purpose (but see Olmosk 1972; Lovelady 1984a, 1984b; Wilson 1992). There is in general a normatively driven reluctance to discuss whether sustained autocracy may deliver change more effectively than participation.

Public sector reform programmes have in the past been seen as yielding only modest long-term change (Alford 1975; Hunter 1980; Fry 1981), yet in the 1980s the pattern appears to have changed significantly. This finding may undermine the institutionalist perspective (Meyer and Rowan 1977) that the adoption of a new organizational structure may be seen as a legitimation device to maintain outside support and funding rather than a signifier of underlying change to values and purpose. Values are here decoupled from structures.

We feel that we are now seeing more than tactical behavioural compliance (but see Laughlin *et al.* (1992) for an alternative view at a more clinical level of analysis), and strong evidence was presented in both Chapters 2 and 4 of a process of transformational change getting under way, as viewed from board level in health care (more so than in educational settings). There was found to be strong evidence of change on five of the six indicators proposed, and only in the admittedly key sphere of cultural change (which might be expected to be most problematic) (Meek 1988) was there more mixed evidence of significant movement as yet. Securing such cultural change may require not only change to value systems but also to cognitive mind-sets (for example, actors may over time cease to conceive of the NHS as a comprehensive free public service and begin to conceive of it in other terms). The potentially powerful role of organizational élites, such as the NHS board members studied here, in shaping dominant value systems has been explored by Hage and Dewar (1973) and Hinings *et al.* (forthcoming) in other studies.

Why might this perhaps surprising conclusion be the case? Why has a top–down and power-led change strategy succeeded in delivering change if even unintended as well as intended consequences have been evident? We here outline a number of possible explanations. Sustained commitment from the very top (in this case political leadership) has long been seen as an important factor even in the organizational development literature, as identified by Beckhard and Harris (1977), and this finding has been confirmed in studies of strategic change in both the private sector (Pettigrew 1985; Pettigrew and Whipp 1991) and Whitehall (Metcalfe and Richards 1990). In this case, the central Department of Health has had powerful levers of appointment at local level, and can clearly influence the composition of the tiny public sector élites studied here who have, if anything, gained in power as a result of the reform process. They are the agents as well as the objects of reform. The localities thus relate to a powerful centre based in Whitehall which has acted as a powerful and consistent sponsor of the reform programme.

Nor should we ignore changes in the realm of ideas. Non-market-based ideologies were in retreat throughout UK society during the 1980s, and maybe in the end these broader ideological shifts were too strong even for the last redoubts of non-market values in the public sector as a process of ideological colonization took place (Laughlin *et al.* 1992). Some public sector managers present themselves as neutral and as non-ideological, looking up to follow current central direction: 'we must accept political realities'. At the same time, such managers typically gained from the reform process, and so were unlikely to go to the stake for any critical beliefs. Ideologically based resistance from some strategically placed subgroups within the public sector may have been weaker than perhaps expected.

Professional groupings were often split into winners (e.g. GP fundholders) and losers (e.g. consultants), so that their opposition was fragmented and diluted. Contrary to initial predictions, some medical professionals seemed to enjoy working in more market-like settings (Ashburner 1994a) and quickly adapted to the new order. The relationship between professionals and quasi-markets is nuanced and complex (McNulty *et al.* 1994), with winners as well as losers.

We also need to consider whether a distinctive and more sophisticated central implementation strategy has characterized the post-1990 period. This might help explain why it is that the pace and scope of local change seems to have accelerated. Implementation theory can be usefully accessed here, particularly the well-established literature on the failure to implement the complex and ambitious social policies and programmes launched by 'big government' since the 1960s (Pressman and Wildavsky 1973; Bardach 1977).

Conventionally, the study of the implementation process has been focused at two different levels (macro-implementation and micro-implementation) (Dufour 1991: 2–3). In rather over-normative terms, the distinction between the two has been drawn in the following terms:

the central government must execute its policy so as to influence local delivery organizations to behave in desired ways; we call this the macro implementation problem. In response to central actions, the local organizations have to devise and carry out their own internal policies, we call this the micro implementation problem (Berman 1978: 164)

In the UK, Dunsire (1978), Barrett and Fudge (1981), Lewis and Wallace (1984), and Hogwood and Gunn (1986) have worked on problems of macro-implementation and the design of implementation strategies more likely to last, while others such as Hunter (1980), Haywood and Hunter (1982), and Ham and Towell (1985) have stressed the emergence of micro-implementation gaps in health care: 'There is mounting evidence that governmental and DHSS preferences on priorities are not always accorded precedence locally' (Haywood and Hunter 1982: 159). This question of the local 'implementation gap' has also been considered by Hardy (1985) and Dufour (1991) specifically in relation to the hospital closure programme. Their analyses tended to focus on questions of micro-implementation, taking national policy as a given and highlighting the role of local forces, leadership capacity, and tactical skill as determining the pace of change in the locality. A similar focus on micro-implementation at local level was observable in our earlier work (Pettigrew *et al.* 1992).

In our current analysis, we deal with both the micro- and the macro-level factors which explain the distinctive outcome of the post-1990 organizational change processes within key public services.

While a few studies in the 1980s (Korman and Glennerster 1990) considered the interrelationship between implementation processes occurring at different levels of government, an ability to move between tiers of analysis in this fashion is now of enhanced importance given the changed behaviour of the centre in devising its implementation strategy.

A Novel Macro-Implementation Strategy

In the late 1980s and certainly after 1990, the centre has developed a more active and also sophisticated macro-implementation role in trying to scale down the implementation gaps which the literature had clearly identified in the 1970s and early 1980s (Pressman and Wildavsky 1973; Hunter 1980; Barrett and Fudge 1981; Barrett and Hill 1984). This can be seen as an important area where there is evidence of organizational and governmental learning taking place, in response to analysis of previous implementation failures.

Macro- and micro-levels of implementation have been joined in closer dialogue, but this is a process which has been essentially led from the top (top-led but bottom-fed). Much more attention has been given to devising an implementation strategy centrally as well as to the initial formulation of policy. Indeed, substantial process and implementation advantages may accrue if policy takes the form of a broad vision rather than a detailed blueprint (Pettigrew *et al.* 1992). Central strategy becomes more emergent and less formally stated at the beginning of the implementation process (Mintzberg and Waters 1985).

Unusually in both public and private sector settings (see Pettigrew 1985, for an analysis of the effects of the relatively limited tenure of the chairman of ICI in restricting change there), a consistent and coherent series of top–down reforms has been evident in the NHS since the early 1980s, building on each other piece by piece and creating greater receptivity to change at local level. This strategy may well have been emergent rather than planned, but with the benefit of hindsight has had important enabling effects. Without the introduction of NHS general management in 1986, for example, it would have been very difficult to move on to the creation of NHS trusts. The construction and progressive tightening up of a vertical managerial line across the whole NHS since the mid-1980s can be seen as an important and novel implementation resource available to the centre.

After 1990 the centre within health care adopted a clear project management function in relation to sponsoring the reform programme within the localities. The macro-implementation strategy can be seen as including the following features:

- a broad vision rather than a detailed blueprint at the beginning of the process;
- the provision of a visible focus of central leadership within the Department of Health both at ministerial level and overall project management level, to drive through key changes; use of tried and tested external advisers (e.g. Sir Roy Griffiths);
- the creation of new intermediate tiers in 'greenfield sites' (the Outposts)

seen as uncontaminated by the old regional cultures; setting intermediary tiers clear targets in relation to trust and GP fundholder status;

- a more proactive communications policy 'selling' the reforms;
- parachuting key personnel from the centre into high profile localities (e.g. Guy's); energizing and resourcing such allies;
- sponsoring a programme of development projects which could quickly be held up as role models nationally; building up coalitions locally and support networks centrally (e.g. first wave trust chairs);
- identifying and intervening in 'receptive' sites (e.g. first wave trusts) before moving on and diffusing the intervention to less receptive contexts;
- establishment of early successes (first wave trusts and GP fundholders; formation of district and family health services authorities) which helped signal that there was no going back.

Highly unusually for institutional reform programmes, the implementation of the health care reforms became a major and sustained political and managerial priority over a five-year period.

Nor does such a macro-implementation strategy seem to be a one-off within health care since similar implementation tactics were evident in the surprisingly rapid implementation of the Next Steps initiative within Whitehall. Gray and Jenkins (1995: 38) conclude 'as a programme of change, therefore, the Next Steps initiative appears to have made a significant impact where previous efforts have failed'.

The implementation strategy used in this case similarly included: a broad vision rather than a blueprint; the identification of a strong project management team at the centre; an active communications policy, selling the idea to journalists and academics as well as civil servants; identifying and intervening in a small number of receptive local contexts originally before diffusing the idea to more difficult settings.

We also stress that a strong element of unplanned change has been apparent, with the emergence of unanticipated consequences and unexpected organizational forms. The change process cannot be characterized by a simple and intentional 'planned change' model but seems to develop a complex logic and a momentum of its own.

We suggest it is not that the pre-1990 NHS is being replaced by a pure commercial model, but rather by a new form which combines traditional public service values and a greater business-like orientation. The final balance or mix between these two orientations is not yet clear neither is its theoretic and analytic status (as will be addressed later on in the chapter). However, it is unlikely that there will be a complete clear-out of the old public sector values and culture. Even at the initial 'unfreezing' (Lewin 1948) stage, we found few private sector radicals on our NHS boards studied, but rather many of the directors imported from the private sector continued to proclaim their belief in a tradition of public service within the NHS.

It was sometimes also evident that existing personnel reshaped and reinterpreted the top–down agenda, regrouping (for example) within purchasing organizations where considerations of need and of equity remained important or colluding to restrain the development of quasi-market forces. Such personnel do experience and make change, and do so in significant ways, but not always in the manner perhaps anticipated at the beginning of the process.

Changing Roles and Relationships

The new public management's effects at a group and individual, rather than at the system, level were explored in Chapters 6 and 7. Clearly, managerial groupings and individuals have often gained in power at local level as a result of NPM reforms. Chapters 5 and 6 pointed to the arrival of executive directors on NHS boards in 1990 and the importing of many non-executive directors with management experience in private sector organizations as twin examples of this process of managerialization. At lower levels, a growth in the number of business management and accountancy posts was also evident in our case study sites (see also Table 1.3 for national trend data on management posts).

However, we suggested that the dynamics and power shifts apparent within the new public management may be more complex than commonly supposed. Non-executive directors, for instance, might be powerful within institutions (indeed Chapter 6 argued that post-1990 NHS boards were moving towards a more strategic role than apparent hitherto), yet we found that their cross-institutional networks were typically weaker than those both of managers and of clinicians. The concept of an active, integrated, non-executive director network functioning across institutions suggested by élite theory (Mizruchi 1992) was not supported by our data. Indeed, some non-executive directors complained about isolation. To balance this argument, we should also say that there is evidence of a shared background across much of the non-executive director population, but this similarity does not seem to lead to sustained social or business contact across organizational boundaries.

Nor does our evidence support the idea of a simple and one-way process of de-professionalization (Haug 1973, 1975, 1988), but suggests a more subtle and complex picture, with some professions and professionals gaining, some adapting and some losing ground. The relationship between the greater market forces characteristic of the new public management and the extent of professional autonomy and reward is also not clear-cut: some doctors with established reputations are potentially well placed to benefit from the development of market forces.

There are also important shifts apparent within professions: for example, public health can be seen as a rising function within medicine because of its new strategic role within purchasing organizations. The introduction of GP fundholding was widely seen as shifting resources and power away from hospital consultants and towards GPs.

New and blurred roles were also appearing at individual level, where practising professionals took on substantial management responsibilities. In different ways, GP fundholders, clinical directors, and directors of public health can all be seen as exercising such hybrid roles where there is enhanced attention paid to management responsibilities. These developments at individual-role level in many ways parallel those at organizational level and reinforce the need to develop a theory of hybridization. In such roles, the primary socialization is into the professional role, with a secondary development into a managerial role. If such developments continue, then these multi-skilled groupings of professionals may succeed in reclaiming some of the territory ceded to the rising cadre of general managers in the late 1980s.

The Strategic Apex of Public Service Organizations

In organizational terms, one way of conceiving of the new public management is as the unbundling of large vertically integrated public sector organizations into a flotilla of quasi-autonomous organizations. The strategic apex of these devolved organizations assumes greater significance as it operates with an enhanced range of delegated powers and can potentially be seen as a major power source, reshaping the local organization along strategic lines.

Chapters 5 and 6 examined the composition, governance, and strategic impact of the post-1990 NHS boards as an exemplar of this wider process. Despite the importation of a private sector board of directors model, these boards can still be seen as containing some continuing public service traditions. In terms of structure, NHS boards can be seen as highly progressive when assessed against the recommendations of the Cadbury Report. Such boards are enjoined both to monitor probity and to contribute to strategic direction as two key tasks.

In terms of board composition, our data suggested that the characteristic dangers of NHS boards had perhaps moved from overfragmentation and sectionalism to those of group-think and overhomogeneity. We advocated a more balanced approach to board membership where different views could be exposed and debated. This in turn raises the question of more active approaches to board development and team-building, if such debate is to be seen as constructive rather than destructive.

Strategy development was found to be an important function for these boards. We argued that these boards typically approached strategy development in a processual and iterative way, rather than through formalistic exercises in rational planning. Strategy-making was often highly emergent in nature (Mintzberg 1987). We also argued that the rubber stamp or managerial hegemony thesis (Mace 1971; Herman 1981; Lorsch and McIver 1989) can be seen as somewhat overstated and explored why there had been at least some shift of power to the board as a decision-making group, and hence to the non-executive directors within those groups. The movement appeared to be greatest in the more contained NHS trusts.

Chapter 8 argued that the failure to provide robust models of accountability represents the Achilles' heel of current approaches to the new public management. It is for this reason that we criticized the NHS boards as failing to defend the important tradition of public accountability. These organizations are still perceived by civil society as essentially public sector organizations, and hence alternative models (such as market-based accountability) derived from private sector settings fail to persuade. Given that our non-executive director respondents often found it difficult to articulate a coherent account of accountability, we concluded that this was an area where more policy attention needed to be concentrated.

9.3. Novel Concepts and Findings

These initial themes introduced in Chapter 1 were found to be a useful way of organizing the data at a higher level of abstraction than the single empirical chapter. However, we can also ask what new findings, concepts, and theories have emerged in the course of the analysis? How has our analysis developed since the initial outline in Chapter 1?

Relational Markets

A core theme within this analysis of the new public management has been the characterization of quasi-markets in the public sector. Chapter 3 not only presented primary data from the NHS, but also developed a novel theory, rooted in a 'new economic sociology' framework, rather than the more conventional viewpoints of micro-economic theory or the 'new institutional economics'.

It was there argued that the quasi-market at least in health care must be seen as a *relational* market, where a few powerful purchasers were in more-or-less continuing negotiation with a few powerful providers. Judgements were made on the basis of trust and reputation as well as on hard data. There were, however, some early signs of increasing social distance as traditional relationships came under pressure.

The quasi-market was also found to be *socially embedded*. There was found to be a high degree of continuity in the personnel staffing the upper reaches of local health care organizations. There is then a small health care élite (but one which contains distinct clinical, managerial, public service, and quasi-political components) which displays considerable stability at the apex of these organizations. Long term careers emerge and continue despite reorganizations.

The professional network was found to be the strongest across organizational boundaries, followed by the managerial network with (perhaps surprisingly) the links between rank and file non-executives representing the weakest form of network. Far from comprising an integrated and cohesive élite, such non-executive directors were often isolated from colleagues in neighbouring organizations.

Although the general picture was one of stability in social networks, there was also some change, particularly in relation to the non-executive component of these local health care élites. The question here is whether new networks are displacing old ones, marking a shift from public service to more business-based élites.

The quasi-market was also found to be *institutionally embedded*. Much evidence was found to support this proposition and a social network approach by itself is too micro-analytic a perspective. The quasi-market is very much inward facing, regulated by higher tiers. Rules concerning arbitration, prices, rates of return, and productivity targets are all set centrally and transmitted downwards. There is a potential contradiction between the rhetoric of free markets and the heavy weight of a continuing regulatory apparatus. Continuing interventions by Civil Servants require rapid responses from chairs, senior executives, and others, diverting attention from local priorities.

Transformation through Top–Down and Power-Led Change

In our original thinking in Chapter 1, we introduced the concept of top–down and externally driven change, which may now be occurring throughout the public sector. As the analysis progressed, our attention shifted to examining the extent and radical nature of the changes under way, particularly in health care. The issues emerging from the data have both substantive and processual elements : are the change processes under observation processes of organizational transformation? Can a largely top-down change strategy produce strategic change? At what point and using what criteria should this be seen as going beyond strategic change to transformatory change? From a processual perspective, have specific mechanisms been adopted which can be related to the enhanced scale and scope of change? We have already considered the adoption of a more sophisticated macro-implementation strategy, and in this section we move on to consider the question of organizational transformation.

In our initial exploration of these issues, although the term 'transformation' was increasingly employed in the literature (Child and Smith 1987; Gersick 1991; Tushman and Romanelli 1985; Romanelli and Tushman 1994), there appeared to be few attempts at a precise definition of it. Therefore, in Chapters

2 and 4, we set out some criteria for defining transformational change, based on prior (Romanelli and Tushman 1994; Blumenthal and Haspeslagh 1994) and emerging empirical data. These criteria focus the analysis on the variety of levels at which change was occurring and the interlinkages between these levels. In drawing up these criteria, our attention is focused on the concept of multilayered change, as well as on multisystem change or change which impacts on a variety of systems. Previous definitions of strategic change (Tichy 1983; Pettigrew 1985) emphasize that such change extends across a range of major subsystems of the organization, such as the product–service subsystem, financial subsystems, and structural subsystems. Our criteria suggest that transformational change extends beyond this definition of strategic change to embrace multilayered, multisystems change, including the alteration of power bases and a substantial shift in the culture of the organization.

The next question is whether such a process of transformation is indeed now occurring in the UK public sector? There is a danger of premature generalization given our as-yet tentative definition of the term 'transformation' means that further detailed empirical analysis is still required. Such generalizations operating across the very different subsectors of the public sector also need to be tested, because the influence of history and context on the progress of change initiatives has already been established. We suggest the evidence of transformation in the health care sector is now significant. Change is apparent at a number of levels, permeating downwards from the top. These planned changes are reinforced by service and technological changes which have other origins and might be described as bottom-up or outwards-in. In health care, the evidence is as yet weakest when one considers the crucial area of culture change. Demonstrating cultural change is difficult and it might be anticipated that the time frame for cultural change would be the longest. It remains a complex judgement to make, but our data suggest some evidence of adapting values during change. For example, the acceptance by many GPs of the new role of GP fundholders and of some consultants as clinical and medical directors may, if sustained, lead to a change in their consciousness, so that managerial and market-type values rise in importance *vis-à-vis* traditional professional values. Of course our data are limited and require further elaboration, but these are important arguments to pursue further. We would propose that a key way of focusing further on the definition of transformation is to consider whether the changes have as yet involved a shift of organization mind-sets. Has the predominant definition of the ideal type of health service shifted? For example, have many members of the NHS moved from a view of the service as 'health care totally free at point of service' to some more bounded definition of what can be available?

Superficially our data suggest that top–down change can produce transformation. This may be the case, but we also suggest that the changes have not always gone in the intended direction. One key reason for apparent success and for the continued forward movement of the change process is that it has been reinterpreted by different stakeholders to serve other purposes.

The outcome of change may not then be to transform the organization from a public to a private-style efficiency driven organization, but rather to produce a new and perhaps hybrid form. At the organizational level this may result in the emergence of individually, more efficiency minded organizations which however retain some continuing public sector values and standards, as part of their core culture. However, caution must be expressed as to whether these changes will produce an overall saving and greater efficiency across the NHS as a whole, since a market basis of operation carries with it the possibility of higher management and overhead costs, along with interorganizational fragmentation.

Within other parts of the public sector, the picture is quite different. Taking the specific comparator of education, the evidence of multilayered, multiple system change is not as significant nor as comprehensive. There are data to support the view that major and radical changes are occurring in education, but the evidence for transformation, according to our criteria, is insufficient in that sector at this point in time. The extent to subsectoral variations in the pace and scope of change may then be significant.

Boards and Board Effectiveness

Our consideration of board effectiveness has taken into account that the definition of an effective board includes the need for a demonstration of accountability, as well as managerial efficiency. The lack of formal mechanisms for any level of accountability, other than to the centre, is a weakness in any public sector organization, where issues of equity, as well as accountability for public expenditure, remain paramount. The new structure and composition of NHS boards reflected the growth of managerialism, which has occurred at the expense of previous systems of accountability, however imperfect. Our critical analysis of private sector boards (Lorsch and McIver 1989; Fitzgerald and Pettigrew 1991; Charkham 1995) noted the dysfunctional effect of an overdominant executive, particularly if the roles of chairman and chief executive officer were combined. Even with a more independent and influential group of non-executives in the health sector, there remained the potential for an imbalance of influence.

The composition of NHS boards becomes more critical as they gain influence within their organizations. However, when we look at how effective boards are, it is not composition alone, but also board processes, that are the determining factors. In observing a number of boards in action, over lengthy periods of time, we have developed an analysis of both the foundations for board effectiveness and the factors contributing to effectiveness (Ashburner *et al.* 1993*b*; Ferlie *et al.* forthcoming). We would suggest that the essential, basic foundations for board effectiveness are individual members with the requisite knowledge and skills to contribute, regular attendance at meetings, and the giving of adequate and timely information. Beyond these basics, the balance of board composition and the role of non-executive members is central. It is important to ensure a balance between the involvement of non-executives in managerial problems and their independent role of monitoring and ensuring probity. The dominance of the executive can only be challenged by the board explicitly addressing the issues of the board's role and also the non-executives' roles. As a result there is a need to develop the individual board members to increase their knowledge and competence, but there is also a need to develop the board as an entity.

The formulation of strategy was identified in the literature as one of the significant indicators of a more effective board (Charkham 1986; Zahra 1990; Pettigrew and McNulty 1995) and the research has produced insights into the strategy formulation process. The decision-making which occurs at board level can be seen as only one stage in the total strategy formulation process and the processual model of strategy (Whittington 1993) was validated in our data rather than more rationalistic and formalistic models. The overall success of this process may be determined by the type and timing of the issues brought to the board, by the quality of the data available to the non-executives, and the opportunities they are given to contribute.

It is evident that involvement at an earlier stage in the formulation of strategy allows greater potential for genuine influence by non-executives. All our boards had moved beyond the old rubber stamp model and we concluded that the old managerial hegemony model (Mace 1971; Herman 1981) was too crude. In a minority of the boards observed, usually NHS trusts, the whole board was involved in a process of setting the strategic framework within which specific strategic decisions were to be taken. This process appeared to offer the greatest potential for coherent strategy-making.

Boards in the NHS are closer to the Cadbury Report's (1992) ideal than most boards in the private sector, but the model was not designed for public sector organizations. Although the types of accountability appropriate for public and private sectors differ, in principle it is essential for both to be accountable. The new board model could be seen more clearly retaining a public management culture and orientation if the mechanisms for account-ability to stakeholders other than the Department of Health were to be developed further.

The Analysis of Hybrid Organizational Forms

As suggested in a previous section, unplanned as well as planned change may now be evident within public service settings (Ashburner *et al.* 1994). Complex social action, namely attempts to re-engineer such large and complex organi-zations, may well have important unanticipated consequences, as Merton (1936) famously argued in his critique of synoptic socialist planning. It would be surprising indeed if the post-1990 reforms were to be an entirely orderly and predictable change process, especially as they involve ambitious attempts to intervene in the cultural sphere.

Notions of blurred and hybrid forms have been progressively introduced in the manuscript, both at organizational and individual role level. The concept of organizational hybrids is beginning to emerge in organizational analysis. Sternberg (1993) argues that in the American context the hybrid organization, combining government and business, is increasingly dominant. Decisions will be made through a variety of fora that are neither public nor private (such as university–industry collaboration, military–industrial cooperation). What is the ideological base of such hybrids? The conventional explanation might stress sectoral tension: the desire to privatise public activity or the desire to increase public intervention in the private sector. Sternberg suggests that such hybrids can instead be based on a coherent and shared post-liberal ideology, an ideology of partnership which seeks to direct important sectors of a capitalist economy collectively—in the public interest—but through privatized means. Similar processes of intersectoral blurring are explored by Emmert and Crow (1987) in respect of R and D labs.

Mintzberg's (1989: 265) discussion of the process of combination in his typology of organizational archetypes introduces the notion of hybrids which attend to different forces without letting only one dominate, thus adding to the range of organizational responses. Mackintosh *et al.* (1994) suggest public sector reforms can be understood—their example was taken from the university sector but the trend is wider—as creating a new form of hybrid organization. By hybrids, they mean organizations which both provide tax-supported services and rely on income from the commercial market. However, they do not see such hybrid forms as stable or coherent, but rather as operating on a dual logic, driven by quasi-market pressures on the tax-supported side, and by private market pressures elsewhere. The organization may split into two, as pressures to segregate the commercial side quickly develop.

Within transaction costs theory, there is also an interesting discussion of hybrid forms of governance, generally seen as organizational arrangements situated between markets and hierarchies. A number of points arise. Are such hybrid forms a 'heterogeneous assemblage of ill assorted objects' (Garrette and Quelin 1994) or can a small number of discrete hybrid forms be uncovered? How can these hybrid forms be classified in relation to previously established organizational forms? Thus Powell's (1991) discussion of network forms of organization clearly distinguishes them from alternative market and hierarchy-based forms as three ideal types. Bradach and Eccles (1991), by contrast, suggest that as transaction costs theory has developed, so the initial clear-cut distinction drawn between markets and hierarchies has broadened to the recognition of a myriad of alternative organizational forms.

The development of a theory of hybrid organizations may well be associated with the building of a typology of parent and hybrid forms. Typology-building is a key analytic activity within social science (Weber 1946; Miles and Snow

1978; Mintzberg 1979, 1983; Porter 1980, 1985). However, typology construction is a complex and demanding activity (Doty and Glick 1994) and a number of questions arise. Are the categories in the typology mutually exclusive and exhaustive? How do they address theory? Are the derived inductively or through a priori theory? To what extent can they be seen as ideal types?

The four models generated through a review of managerial theory and a knowledge of current public sector reform programmes in Chapter 1 represent our initial attempt to offer a typology. We could identify three coherent paradigms or archetypes (Greenwood and Hinings 1993), associated with specific value bases, derived from private sector management models and one from public sector management. Alongside these four original ideal types, we now speculate that at least one (possibly more) hybrid forms may be emerging as subspecies in the classificatory system. We return to the implications of this line of argument for future enquiry in the last section of the chapter.

Professional Roles

The public sector remains highly professionalized. The new public management is having an undoubted impact on professionals largely through the increase of managerialism, but there also is wide variability. This is accounted for by the need to consider the combined effect of managerialism and the introduction of a quasi-market. Professionals experience the most profound impacts where the entire sector has had market mechanisms introduced, as in health and education, and where this change is combined with an increase in managerialism.

Despite the rhetoric, there is no strong evidence that in the UK the shift of power as a result of the new public management-style changes is unidimensional, inevitably from professionals to managers. The picture is more complex. The changes occurring in the public sector certainly have resulted in shifts of power, but the evidence also suggests many processes of adaptation (Elston 1991; Walby and Greenwell 1994; Harrison and Pollitt 1994; Ashburner and Fitzgerald 1995). As a result, some professionals have gained, some have lost and some have changed. Directors of public health, medical and clinical directors, GP fundholders, and innovative clinicians who launch marketable new products can all be seen as gaining subgroups. Overall, the evidence is that professionals are under pressure and that an individual's work may, in some, but not all instances, be more constrained. Some of these pressures could be described as self-generated, given that a profession argues that its standards of quality are self-regulated, but such processes of self-regulation are not perceived by users to be transparent. Some other pressures on professionals are generated by broad social trends such as consumerism, masked in management speak. In many other instances, however, professionals can be seen adopting new powerful roles, exerting influence in different fora and responding skilfully to changed circumstances. The question emerges of how collegial the relationships remain between the professional–managerial groupings (e.g. medical directors) and the wider grouping of professional colleagues.

A key and interesting aspect of this process of adaptation is the growth of new individual hybrid roles such as clinical directors, as we discussed earlier. Within health care, there was strong evidence of the development of a range of new professional–manager blurred or hybrid roles. These roles are positioned at critical points in the organizational structures of both purchaser and provider organizations. It is clear that the formal responsibilities and power of these roles, if well exercised, would provide the incumbents with positions of considerable influence. Our empirical evidence suggests that in the trusts the role of medical director is, in reality, an important position of power and influence, but also that the holders of such roles could be subject to powerful cross pressures.

This is not to suggest that there are not many difficulties in learning, developing and managing such a part-time role. In purchaser authorities, on the other hand, we found less widespread evidence of public health directors with the skill and the will to exert influence from their role. Whilst the evidence suggests that these are powerful professional hybrid roles, the question remains as to whether such hybrids are stable in the longer term?

In terms of the operation of the hybrid role, one of the most interesting, if embryonic, results to emerge from the research is the nature of the relationship between the hybrids and their professional colleagues. On the negative side, it is clear that some professional managers feel isolated and may experience stress because of the negative attitudes of colleagues towards their management work (Dopson 1993*b*; Fitzgerald 1994). On the positive side, it is apparent that professional managers feel well able to deal with hitherto intractable problems of quality and professional performance.

9.4. The New Public Management in Theory

The empirical analysis developed throughout the book repeatedly suggested important differences as well as similarities between management tasks and processes in private and public sector settings. Context is important at the sectoral level. This is not a new observation but reinforces previous work which argues that it is within particular sectors that one finds patterns of values, structures, and systems (see Tolbert and Zucker (1983); Hinings and Greenwood (1988) for local government; Nelson, (1988) for law firms; and Hinings *et al.* (forthcoming)) for sports organizations. Within such sectors strategic recipes (Child 1988; Johnston 1987) emerge. We thus focus on the sector rather than the individual public service organization as the key unit of analysis, as we would argue that public service settings can be broadly seen as a family of organizations that contain important similarities and are experiencing common pressures. Accordingly, developments which we have analysed in depth in health care settings may have resonance for other public service settings.

So the sectoral context needs to be accounted for in analysis (Pollitt 1990; Ranson and Stewart 1994). Thus the distinctive role of government as a legitimate sponsor of mandated reform programmes within the public sector was highlighted in Chapter 2. The differences between markets in the private sector, even relational ones, and the more institutionally embedded quasi-markets of the public sector were highlighted in Chapter 3. The special accountability requirements of management in public sector settings were discussed in Chapter 8. The organizational system within the public sector is not confined to influence from the executive aim of central government and local public service organizations, but is also open to influence from active components of civil society which themselves are generating critical forms of organizational and managerial discourse. Commentators (J. Stewart 1992; Bogdanor 1994; Weir and Hall 1994) help crystallize growing public concern. Subsequently, rising issues are then taken up by the legislature (PAC, 1994) or an active judiciary (Nolan, Scott), whose recommendations trigger off a further round of counter-reforms.

However, we also argue that there may be cross-sectoral points of learning which can be explored between private and public sector organizations, so long as these comparisons are drawn in a sophisticated rather than a mechanistic way. Public sector management writing can be legitimately criticized for being insular and atheoretical. Even defenders of a highly distinctivist view of the public sector, such as Ranson and Stewart (1994), recognize the need to develop a theory of public sector management. So interesting conversations can be started across the sectoral divide, as long as the outcome of such dialogue is left open rather than taking a deterministic view that the public sector can always learn from best practice in the private sector in a unilinear fashion.

How can these two apparently rather different arguments be reconciled? In our view, public sector organizations can best be seen as lying on an extreme end of many organizational spectra (e.g. large size; large number of occupational groupings; heavily professionalized; heavily politicized; service organizations where quality is both important and difficult to measure; non-market-based forms of operation), but should not be seen as intrinsically of an entirely different order from private sector service organizations. Both the Fordist corporation and the bureaucratized Welfare State agency (and their successor forms), for example, can be seen as products of a similar broad historical and cultural context, at least when assessed against the very different organizational forms apparent in Far Eastern or Mediterranean societies (Clegg 1990).

Nevertheless, we conclude that those managerial theories, such as the theory of general management or the generic board of directors model, which do not recognize important intersectoral differences lack validity. While such theories were of enhanced popularity during the 1980s, their mechanistic adoption may result in unintended or counter productive consequences. If imposed from above (at least within a relatively open system), they are unlikely to take root, especially if they are reinterpreted from within or if active components of civil society agitate against them. The growing accountability debate is a good exemplar of this failure to root, fuelled by critical writers and commentators. (Bogdonor 1994; J. Stewart 1992; Weir and Hall 1994; Power 1994).

The result of such a mismatch between general managerial ideology and the sectoral characteristics of particular work organizations may either be further rounds of organizational change in a search for a new equilibrium which does not materialize or (more likely in our view) a continuing process of ideological reinterpretation with a move back to theories which display a greater awareness of the distinctive public sector context.

Returning to the variants of the new public management outlined in Chapter 1, this analysis suggests that Models 1–3, all of which are essentially derived from private sector management practice, are by themselves inadequate and require adaptation to a public sector context. NPM Model 4's advantage ('public service orientation') lies in its sensitivity to the distinctive public sector context. However, in our view, the public service orientation model veers too far in the presumption of difference. It heavily relies on political science notions (such as citizenship), and does not adequately explore the nature of public sector organizations as organizations. In its theoretical base, academic links with organizational theory remain undeveloped.

An implication of our analysis is that the value systems of public sector managers may well continue to differ in important ways from those of private sector managers. Non-market-based values, in particular, may be expected to be more prominent amongst groups of public sector managers. These are questions which are amenable to empirical study. Do these intersectoral differences in value systems really exist? Is there a more variegated pattern evident within the public sector (e.g. differences between provider and purchaser organizations)? Which managerial ideologies and writers are perceived as influential by public sector managers?

9.5. Future Research Agenda

For management scholars, therefore, we start by asserting that the public sector remains an important site of analysis, despite a pattern of recent neglect by the discipline. Sometimes the field of management studies has assumed that private firms (Ferlie (1992) develops this critique) represent the only organizational form of legitimate scholarly interest. While such studies of private companies are of great importance, they need to be complemented by a broad range of other studies, not just of public sector organizations, but also of other organizational forms, such as voluntary sector organizations, where some similar managerializing trends have been evident (Butler and Wilson 1990). More informally based modes of organising (e.g. the analysis of social movement organizations in Bennett and Ferlie (1994*a*)) are also of interest. If sectoral blurring continues to increase, so the study of new public–private hybrid forms will become more significant, and indeed public services will be financed and delivered through mixed models.

Given an agreement that the study of the public sector is of strategic importance within management studies, what are the more specific questions which now arise?

The Significance and Scale of the New Public Management

The overall significance and scale of development of the new public management described in this book is still unclear. One possibility is that it is only a short-term managerial fad (Abrahamson 1991) which will soon blow itself out, to be followed in its turn by still newer models. The new public management can in this scenario be seen as a limited managerial bubble with little enduring significance, on a par with total quality management or business process re-engineering change programme initiatives.

A second view is that we are only a little way into what may be a very long-term change process in public service organizations, as quite new management templates emerge and consolidate themselves. How extended is the life-cycle of this new template likely to be? Dunleavy and Hood (1994) speculate that the new public management movement may prove influential over a far longer time period than commonly assumed. Sometimes administrative reform ideas do not come into full effect until long after their original introduction, but subsequently persist and are then difficult to dislodge. They cite the example of the 1854 Northcote Trevelyan Report on the Civil Service, originally dismissed as far-fetched and as Chinese-inspired, but which consolidated itself into a public sector orthodoxy by the end of the nineteenth century which in some ways lasted until the 1980s, when it came under challenge from the new public management.

In this book, our primary data has been presented from post-1990 NHS settings, although this has been complemented with secondary material drawn from other public services, such as education. We hope to have substantiated the argument that new public management-style reforms have been evident across the public sector, and are not confined to one service such as the NHS.

We are aware that more comparative analysis would be helpful. We need more detailed comparisons between the experience of the different public services within the UK to establish whether a general pattern of change is apparent across the different public sector settings (e.g. Whitehall, police services, housing) and whether new forms of service delivery are emerging which cross conventional sectoral divides. Is a different range of actors apparent in a variety of settings? In this analysis of health care in England, the implementation chain can be assessed as consisting of a Whitehall department, its regional machinery, and upward-facing boards at local level. Is a more independent regional–national (Scotland, Wales) presence now emerging in some sectors? Are localities 'managing up' directly to Brussels and trying to bypass Whitehall?

We also need to assess the scale and significance of the new public management movement identified here. Can settings be identified which have not been subject to such pressures for reform, but which have enjoyed a different pattern of insulation? Do these reform programmes deepen over time, developing an internal momentum? What happens to the new public management when institutional reform moves down the political agenda, or if there is a change in central political direction?

At this point, the study of the implementation process re-emerges as of key interest. While the earlier 1970s literature often sought to acknowledge and explain growing local implementation gaps (e.g. Hunter 1980), the post-1990 period, not just in the NHS but also in Whitehall, has instead been characterized by the attempt to reduce implementation gaps (Gray and Jenkins 1995), orchestrated by a more sophisticated and interventionist centre.

A more specific study of the post-1990 central implementation strategy, both in health care and other settings, would be of great interest in the further development of implementation theory in what appear to be a changed set of conditions. At first glance, there appears to have been a concerted effort to engage in policy learning. To what extent was movement dependent on earlier layers of facilitating change, such as the introduction of general management? How did the centre drive the change process down into the localities? How were key personnel parachuted into the localities and how did they form supportive teams around them? What were the resource requirements of this change process? Where was most movement secured, where least, and what explains this variability? Is such a pattern consistently evident across reform programmes in different public sector agencies? Is there evidence of a similarly changed pattern of macro-implementation in private sector corporations trying to implement complex strategies for change?

Implications for Generic Organizational Theory

Future work should continue to examine the implications of new public management phenomena for the development and testing of more generic organization theory. As already indicated, we would criticize the extreme distinctivist position held by some public service orientation-style writers, and would be interested in developing further the implications of recent developments in public sector for more meta-level bodies of organizational analysis. Here we consider evidence of increasing organizational variety, which tells against currently dominant population ecology and institutionalist perspectives.

Against the predictions of institutionalists and population ecology theory (Meyer and Rowan 1977; Powell and Di Maggio 1991) our case study data indicate substantial variety within the organizational populations studied. Partly this related to varying patterns of historical evolution. While some organizations studied had clearly been through a major transition to a new model and had experienced radical and system-wide change (if not yet a full organizational transformation), in others operating within the same organizational population the pace of change had been much more incremental and probably had not altered core aspects of the organization (such as culture). Within organizations in the same population, some had made a transition, while others had 'got stuck'.

For example, the transition from family practitioner committee to family health services authority status in 1990 had been a radical change in some localities, but no more than a relabelling exercise in others. The result was the creation of two organizational subgroups (the first the old administered and professionalized bureaucracy; the second more actively managed and with a less regulated and more facilitative culture) which now displayed very different patterns of leadership, roles and relationships and culture. If the pressure for change continues, and the slower group catches up and goes through more radical change, then this subgroup variation may reduce in time. However, if pressure for further change is now contained, then the differences now apparent between the two subgroups may take on a permanent status.

NHS trusts, also, were generating distinctive and individual organizational personalities. Strong ideologies of organizational autonomy quickly arose ('you are master of your own ship'), often reflecting long and difficult local histories. Past relationships were sometimes seen as a negative role model, something to escape from, rather than as a source of useful models of practice.

In one case-study trust, loyalty to place and to what was seen as a historically prestigious and very special institution was a prime motivator for seeking trust status. In another trust studied, headed by a chief executive officer from a human resource management background, strong and distinctive attempts to create a developmental culture evident quite different in tone from command-and-control general managerial ideology. We here argue that there is evidence of organizational variety increasing rather than decreasing, reflecting a move within the new public management to greater devolution, less standardization, and greater local flexibility.

If these early findings that organizational heterogenity is more evident than isomorphism are sustained in other studies, there are some interesting theoretical implications. They run contrary to influential population ecology models (Di Maggio and Powell 1983; Hannan and Freeman 1988) which argue that organizations change essentially to become isomorphic with pressures emerging from their environment. The degree of organizational variation is seen as highly constrained by these evolutionary pressures. A process of isomorphism takes place which can be seen as 'the constraining process that forces one unit in a population to resemble other units that face the same set of environmental conditions' (DiMaggio and Powell 1983: 149). Often such isomorphic pressures are seen as emanating from the State.

The population ecology model has already been subject to some qualification. For example, Slack and Hinings's (1994) empirical study of isomorphism amongst a cohort of Canadian sports organizations concluded that while over time there was an increase in the degree of organizational homogeneity over time (a shift to a more professional bureaucratic type), key high impact systems (such as underlying values and beliefs; volunteer control over decision-making) had not substantially changed. There is thus a sequencing of change issue—some systems and organizational elements change earlier than others, but the systems most resistant to change are of core importance.

Our data supports this sequence of change argument. While system-wide change was found to be occurring on five of the six criteria of organizational transformation, the picture in respect of the key sixth criteria (organizational culture) was still mixed and the degree of movement seen could not yet be seen as decisive.

Another question to emerge from our data is whether the assumed trend to greater organizational isomorphism, at least within the public sector, needs to be questioned in the light of changed circumstances within the political economy. After all, it is the assumption of the controlling and influential State which remains central to population ecology as a source of isomorphic pressure.

Until the 1980s it had been argued in the rather different field of the economics of the firm that markets typically give way to hierarchies; now it is asked instead why it is that hierarchies give way to markets (Williamson 1975 and 1985).

Has the assumed trend to organizational isomorphism similarly gone into reverse? Within the private sector, the hitherto dominant paradigm of the large corporation has been challenged by the rise of new ways of organizing such as the large firm–small firm linkages, worker and manager buy-outs, cooperative and network-based forms of production (Ferlie and Pettigrew 1994*a*). Nor should we assume that the public sector is solely populated by Weberian bureaucracies. After a long period of continuing growth, the central state itself has been seeking to downsize, to become less standard, more flexible, and more locally diverse. The result may be a long-term switch from decreasing to increasing organizational variety.

Characterizing Hybrid Organizational Forms

The discussion in Section 9.2 outlined the growing body of literature now emerging on organizational hybrid forms, given evidence of increased inter-sectoral blurring. But the notion of a hybrid only makes sense in relation to the two prior forms from which it has emerged. An important task then is to build a typology of NPM models and variants. In Chapter 1, four models were outlined which together made up an initial typology and in this concluding discussion we seek to push the notion of hybrids further.

An important question is to establish how many hybrids are empirically occurring. A typology based on four ideal types could theoretically produce up to six hybrids. Further work is needed to assess the extent and significance of the hybrid forms empirically occurring. Another question is whether such hybrids can be seen as sustainable and coherent in the long term or as no more than a temporary transitional phase. In assessing the extent of such coherence, the emergence of an accepted value system and language, at least as held by dominant power élites, is often taken as a key indicator. Thus Clarke (1994) writes of the new managerial discourse associated with the rise of the new public management, which he sees as cutting across old professional discourses and offering a sharp new language of the customer. Our data of course indicate a more nuanced picture than this sharp dichotomy.

Hinings and Greenwood's (1988) discussion of organizational design archetypes similarly focuses on underlying interpretive schemes, similar to the concept of paradigm. This discussion of movement between archetypes highlights four tracks:

- inertia: most organizations can be expected to gravitate to a design archetype and remain there for a lengthy period;
- 'aborted excursions': after limited or temporary movement, as there is regression back to the original archetype;
- reorientations or organizational transformations where radical movement takes place between one archetype and other;
- unresolved excursions: there is here sustained movement from a coherent archetype without attaining a reorientation. Incomplete decoupling occurs without completed recoupling, leading to failed or resisted attempts at reorientation. As a result, an organization remains in an intermediate category over a long period of time.

In their later work, Greenwood and Hinings (1993) further argue, and present UK local government data in support of their case, that organizations over time will typically move from incoherence to coherence. The notion of hybrid forms has not been fully explored in much of the recent organization change literature which has concentrated on the perhaps rare examples of organizational transformation and specifying the conditions in which such transformation was more likely to occur. Perhaps as a reaction against the incrementalist-dominated literature of the 1960s and 1970s, the conventional 1980s model was often that long periods of incremental change were interspersed by periodic moments of system-wide, paradigmatic, or frame-breaking change (Miller and Friesen 1984; Pettigrew 1985; Tushman *et al.* 1988; Johnson 1987; Hinings and Greenwood 1989). However, the concept of an organizational hybrid does not equate to Greenwood and Hinings's (1988) conception of an unresolved excursion, or continuing contest between two or more existing bodies of organizational and managerial discourse. Of course, there are circumstances in which unresolved excursions do occur, for example, in the resistance sometimes displayed in mergers and acquisitions by the losing culture to acculturating to the dominant culture of the other organizations (Sales and Mirvis 1984).

In other cases, by contrast, a synthesis between the two existing archetypes may occur and a new form emerge which contains elements of both but at the same time expresses them in different forms. We need to know more about how such new hybrid forms, (or should they be termed hybrid archetypes?) emerge, and develop. Such processes of creation of a new archetype have not so far been adequately covered in the literature on design tracks (Hinings *et al.* forthcoming).

Of particular interest is the ideology and value system which emerges to underpin such novel archetypes. Can a coherent ideology in fact be discerned? Who acts as ideology carriers, and are such ideologies contested or resisted lower down the organization? How does the hybrid ideology relate to the two prior ideologies from which it has emerged as a synthesis?

The literature on organizational transformation of the 1980s (Pettigrew 1985; Johnson 1987) sometimes invoked the notion of paradigm shift, the cognitive moving from one internally coherent model to a second. Is this notion of a managerial paradigm somewhat too fixed? Following Rorty (1991), Tsoukas (1995) suggests that sets of beliefs should be seen in somewhat looser terms as webs. Such webs are constantly being rewoven to reflect new experiences, either on an incremental (first-order) or substantial (second-order) basis. Such processes of reweaving are continuous, emergent, and uncertain. Achieving equilibrium in the web (i.e. coherence) is the most important task for an actor. There is a human desire to ensure that beliefs and desires are coherent, to be able to convince ourselves and others that the stories we tell as a result of responding to new stimuli fit already espoused stories. Such fits are not achieved automatically, but actors need to reweave their webs in order to manage tensions and contradictions.

Transformation and Top–Down Change Processes

Fascinating issues for further research arise from our findings with regard to the change processes being observed, their significance and sustainability, and the determinants of successful change.

Further comparative research is necessary to explore in greater detail whether and in what circumstances top–down, power-led, or externally driven change can be more successful than expected in organizational-based models. The evidence from health care suggests that such strategies can produce radical and transformational change, but partly because stakeholders highjack the changes and produce unintended consequences. Research in other public sector settings (Glendon 1992) argues that power-led change can be surprisingly successful even in more hostile settings. Is this only true of public sector organizations where employees have been long accustomed to political dictate and learnt to adapt? Or is this also true in private sector organizations, and if so under what conditions?

Another aspect of these findings which engenders a wide range of further questions is the issue of initiating and implementing radical and transformational change successfully. To propose just a sample of research questions: how does one define transformation (Blumenthal and Haspeslagh's (1994) definition might be compared with our empirically derived criteria)? How do the criteria proposed in this text stand up to empirical testing in other organizational settings ? If it can be demonstrated that an organization has undergone transformation, how can this be related to indicators of success? Are, in other words, such transformations beneficial? Given that, we have questioned the timescales involved and whether the hybrid organization which we describe is no more than a transitional state, the issue arises of how long the transformation can take. Pettigrew's (1985) study of a rather more limited exercise in strategic change in ICI suggests timescales can be long. After fifteen years of sustained top–down new public management-style reform effort, while there had clearly been movement on structural, system, and role indicators, our assessment was that the degree of cultural change evident was still mixed and equivocal.

International Comparative Work

In much the same way as we viewed critically the lack of sophisticated and empirically based comparative analysis of the public and private sectors in the UK, so the same argument may be propounded at the national level. Sustained international comparative work is of key importance. Some high quality comparative work has already been undertaken between the UK, USA, and Australia (Pollitt 1990; Zifcak 1994), but UK scholars need to move further, beyond their usual pattern of insularity.

The brief review of international developments possible in Chapter 1 suggested that new public management movement may be particularly strong in Anglo-Saxon countries, although even here there are important inter-country differences in the rate and pace of movement. New Zealand, in particular, stood out as a radical outlier where the pace of change had been fastest. Given that much learning can often be generated by extreme circumstances and policy dramas, what are now seen as the benefits and disadvantages of the New Zealand approach? Has the rate of change continued to be rather slower in the USA, given the pattern of checks and balances which thwarts attempts at radical reform?

We also need to beware the dangerous and ethnocentric assumption that the rest of the world is converging onto the Anglo-Saxon model. Indeed, some of the Continental Western European material cited suggested that widely different models from the new public management may also be being adopted. A more sustained comparative analysis of developments in public sector organization and management in these Continental Western European systems (especially key countries such as France and Germany) would now be extremely helpful to plot the range of models being developed internationally.

Over the last fifteen or so years, public sector organizations in the UK have been placed under sustained top–down pressure for change. Contrary to previous literature, we have argued that there is now evidence of significant change occurring at local level, albeit sometimes in unanticipated ways. The change process has contained an important emergent element as pressures have been reinterpreted at local level and hybrid organizational forms have emerged. The task now is to trace the nature and consequences of this change process on a more sustained and long-term basis and to compare the British experience with those in other countries.

Appendix

RESEARCH DESIGN AND METHODOLOGY

....

Aims and objectives

The New Health Authorities project was funded by the NHS Training Directorate (1990–3), with the support of the National Association of Health Authorities and Trusts. The three primary aims of the study can be defined as follows:

1. to study the composition, formation, behaviour, and impact of the restructured post-1990 health authorities;
2. to consider the implications of this data for organizational and management development;
3. to use this data to contribute to the academic literatures on decision making at board level and on the changing nature of public sector management.

The team contracted to produce twelve 'Research for Action' papers published by the NHS Training Directorate which distilled some of the early findings and lessons for practitioners. Longer term and more academic work was also undertaken, of which this book manuscript represents the final stage.

The project consisted of two distinct data modules: two postal surveys, and case study work.

Postal surveys

Two national postal surveys were undertaken to gather basic descriptive but also some attitudinal data across the population as a whole. The first survey of all regional district and family health services authority members in England (1991) attracted a very pleasing response rate of 69 per cent, evenly spread by Region and type of member. Full results are reported in Ashburner and Cairncross (1993).

This was followed by a second survey of all board members on first wave NHS trusts. A pleasing response rate of 62 per cent was achieved, although the response rate for non-executives was substantially higher than that for chief executive officers (Cairncross and Ashburner 1992).

Case-study work

We were also concerned to gather more qualitative information on board roles, relationships and processes. Here the basic methodology used has been that of the longitudinal and processual comparative case study (see Pettigrew, McKee and Ferlie 1988; Pettigrew *et al.* 1992). This methodological approach allows for the analysis of retrospective change, real time analysis, and prospective or anticipated change. Historical antecedents and the chronology of change are considered vital. The design choice has been to conduct intensive analyses of a relatively few cases, rather than a more superficial analysis of a larger number. Such are the complexities of the host systems that a large number of superficial analyses would be in danger of missing key components of the explanation.

Clearly a variety of data sources has been used in these case studies. Archival material was often used in the early stages, sensitizing the researcher to the key questions and supplying a chronology of change. Site visits were also undertaken to get a 'feel' for the issues.

Semi-structured interviews were taken with all board members and key other stakeholders (e.g. senior clinicians not on the board, community health council representatives who were taken as a source of public 'voice'), giving a total of about twenty interviews per site or 220 overall. As different team members took on lead on particular sites, a jointly agreed pro forma was constructed and used across all sites to ensure consistency.

A novel feature of this study was the degree of access achieved to board meetings, both part 1 (in public) and part 2 (in private) over a long time period (up to eighteen months). Few researchers studying board-level decision-making have secured access to the boardroom, and we regard this access as a strength of the methodology adopted in this study. The longitudinal element was also vital in enabling us to track how these groups developed over time. When compared to our previous work (e.g. Pettigrew *et al.* 1992), there is thus an enhanced importance accorded to observational work and rather less stress on interviews.

Case-study sample

Eleven case study sites were selected within two regions, chosen so as to form a nested hierarchy of interlinking organizations within a region. We also wanted to cover a range of different health care organizations. These were the two key selection criteria employed.

The sample thus consisted of two regional health authorities (one in a Thames Region and one in the North); two family health services authorities; three district health authorities; and four acute NHS trusts. Of these four trusts, two were first wave, one second wave, and one third wave. There were no community or mental health trusts included in the sample, as it was felt that this would lead to an overfragmented sample given the relatively small number of localities to be studied.

Research team process

This project took the form of team research rather than individual scholarship. Team meetings were important in moving towards a consistency of approach and a common pro forma. Once these pro formas had been agreed, individual researchers took the lead in particular localities, but reporting back to the group. Participating sites were also offered individualized feedback at the end of the project. While we wanted the research to be useful to sites (hence the 'Research for Action' label), we were careful not to move into action research, as in our view this would have led to a loss of objectivity, role confusion, and the possibility of being 'captured' by one faction.

Initially analysis and writing concentrated on the individual cases, quickly followed by cross site policy and practitioner themes. The Research for Action series provided the main vehicle for disseminating such analyses, aided by a series of articles in the *Health Services Journal*. At the end of the project, however, the question of longer term and more academic analyses became more important. This book should be seen as the culmination of this process.

REFERENCES

Abbott, A. (1988), *The System of Professions: An Essay on the Division of Expert Labour* (Chicago: University of Chicago Press).

Abrahamson, E. (1991), 'Managerial Fads and Fashions', *Academy of Management Review*, 16/3: 586–612.

Ackroyd, S., Hughes, J. A., and Soothill, K. (1990), 'Public Sector Services and their Management', *Journal of Management Studies*, 26/3: 603–19.

Alford, R. R. (1975), *Health Care Politics* (London: University of Chicago Press).

Alvesson, M., and Berg, P. (1992), *Corporate Culture and Organisational Symbolism*, (Berlin: Walter de Gruyter).

AMA (1993), *Local Authorities and Health Services* (London: AMA).

Andrews, K. R. (1982), 'Responsibility for Corporate Strategy', in 'Board of Directors, part 2', *Harvard Business Review, 1977–1981* (Boston: Harvard University Press).

Aoki, M., Gustafsson, B., and Williamson, O. E. (1990), *The Firm as a Nexus of Treaties* (London: Sage).

Argyris, C. and Schon, D. (1978), *Organisational Learning: A Theory of Action Perspective* (Reading, Mass.: Addison Wesley).

Armstrong, D. (1991), 'Quo Vadimus' National Prescription or Entitlement Curriculum', *Forum*, 34: 22–3.

Arrow, K. J. (1963), Uncertainty and the Welfare Economics of Medical Care, *American Economic Review*, 53/5: 89–121.

Asch, D., and Bowman, G. (1989), *Readings in Strategic Management* (London: Macmillan).

Ascher, K. (1987), *The Politics of Privatisation: Contracting Out Public Services* (Basingstoke: Macmillan).

Ashburner, L. (1993a), 'Women on Boards and Authorities in the National Health Service', *Women in Management Review*, 8/2: 10–16.

——(1993b), 'The Composition of NHS Trust Boards: A National Perspective', in E. Peck, P. Spurgeon (eds.), *NHS Trusts in Practice* (Harlow: Longmans).

——(1993c), *FHSAs: Authorities in Transition* (Research for Action Press Paper, 8; Bristol: NHS Training Directorate).

——(1994a), *The Professions of Medicine in the Post 1990 Reformed NHS* (Working Paper; University of Nottingham).

——(1994b), 'The Composition of NHS Trust Boards', *Health Service Management Research*, 7/3: 154–64.

——and Cairncross, L. (1991), *1990/1991 Health Authorities in Formation* (Authorities in the NHS, 3; Bristol: NHS Training Directorate).

————————(1992), *Members: Attitudes and Expectations* (Research for Action, 5; Bristol: NHS Training Directorate).

————————(1993) Health Authority Members: Continuity or Change?', *Public Administration*, 71/3: 357–75.

————Ferlie, E., and FitzGerald, L. (1993*a*), *Boards and Authorities in Action* (Authorities in the NHS, 11; Bristol: NHS Training Directorate).

————————————(1993*b*), *Leadership by Boards in Healthcare* (Research for Action, 12; Bristol, NHS Training Directorate).

————————————(1994), *Organisational Transformation and Top Down Change: The Case of the NHS* (University of Warwick: Centre for Corporate Strategy and Change).

————and Fitzgerald, L. (1995), 'Beleaguered Professionals: Doctors and Institutional Change in the NHS', in H. Scarborough, (ed.),*The Management of Expertise*, (London: Macmillan).

Audit Commission (1988), 'The Competitive Council (Management Paper, 1; London: Audit Commission).

Bach, S. (1994), 'Managing A Pluralist Health System: The Case of Health Care Reform in France', *International Journal of Health Services*, 24/4: 593–606.

Bachrach, P., and Baratz, M. S. (1963), 'Decisions and Non Decisions: An Analytical Framework', *American Political Science Review*, 57: 641–51.

Baginsky, M., Baker, L., and Cleave, S. (1991), *Towards Effective Partnership in School Governance* (Slough: NFER).

Balazs, I. (1993), 'The Transformation of Hungarian Public Administration', *Public Administration*, 71 (Spring/Summer), 75–88.

Ball, S., Bowe, R., and Gewirtz, S. (1994), Schools in the Market Place: An Analysis of Local Market Relations, in W. Bartlett, C. Propper, D. Wilson, and J. Le Grand (eds.), *Quasi Markets in the Welfare State* (Bristol: School of Advanced Urban Studies).

Bank of England (1985), 'Composition of Company Boards', *Bank of England Quarterly* (June) 255–6.

————(1988), 'Composition of Company Boards', *Bank of England Quarterly* (May), 242.

Barber, M. (1994), 'Power and Control in Education 1944–2004', *British Journal of Educational Studies*, 42, 4: 348–62.

Bardach, E. (1977), *The Implementation Game: What Happens After a Bill Becomes a Law* (Cambridge, Mass.: MIT Press).

Barley, S. R., and Kunda, G. (1992), 'Design and Devotion: Surges of Rational and Normative Ideologies of Control in Managerial Discourse', *Administrative Science Quarterly*, 37: 363–99.

Barrett, S., and Fudge, C. (1981), *Policy and Action* (London: Methuen).

Barrett, S., and Hill, M. (1984), 'Policy Bargaining and Structure in Implementation', *Policy and Politics*, 12/3: 218–39.

Bartlett, C. A., and Ghoshal, S. (1995), 'Changing the Role of Top Management: Beyond Systems to People', *Harvard Business Review*, 73/3: 132–42.

Bartlett, W. (1991), *Quasi Markets and Contracts: A Markets and Hierarchies Perspective on NHS Reform* (Bristol: School of Advanced Urban Studies).

————(1993), 'Quasi Markets and Educational Reforms', in J. Le Grand and W. Bartlett (eds.), *Quasi Markets and Social Policy*, (London: Macmillan) 125–53.

————and Le Grand, J. (1994), 'The Performance of Trusts', in R. Robinson and J. Le Grand (eds.), *Evaluating the NHS Reforms* (London: King's Fund Institute), 54–73.

————Propper, C., Wilson, D., and Le Grand, J. (1994) (eds.), *Quasi-Markets in the Welfare State* (University of Bristol: School of Advanced Urban Studies).

Bartunek, J. M. (1993), The Multiple Cognitions and Conflicts Associated with Second Order Organisational Change, in J. K. Murningham (ed.), *Social Psychology in Organisations: Advances in Theory and Research*, (Englewood Cliffs, NJ: Prentice Hall).

————Lacey, C. A., and Wood, D. R. (1992), 'Social Cognition in Organisational Change: An Insider–Outsider Approach', *Journal of Applied Behavioural Science*, 282 (June), 204–23.

Bastin, N. A. (1990), 'The Composition of Governing Bodies of Higher Education Corporations', *Higher Education Quarterly*, 44: 3.

Bauer, M., and Cohen, E. (1983), 'The Invisibility of Power and Economics: Beyond Markets and Hierarchies', in A. Francis, J. Turk, and P. Williams, *Power, Efficiency and Institutions*, (London: Heinemann Educational Books).

Baumol, W. J. (1982), 'Contestable Markets; An Uprising in the Theory of Industry Structure', *American Economic Review*, 72: 1–15.

Becher, T., and Kogan, M. (1992), *Process and Structure in Higher Education* (2nd edn., London: Routledge).

Becker, H. S. (1970), 'The Nature of a Profession', in H. Becker, (ed.), *Sociological Work* (Chicago: Aldine).

Beckhard, R., and Harris, R. (1977), *Organisational Transitions: Managing Complex Change* (Reading, Mass.: Addison Wesley).

————and Pritchard, W. (1992), *Changing the Essence: The Art of Creating and Leading Fundamental Change in Organisations* (San Fransisco: Jossey Bass).

Bell, D. (1973), *The Coming of Post-Industrial Society* (New York: Basic Books).

Benefits Agency (1994), *Annual Report, 1993/4* (London: HMSO).

Bennett, C., and Ferlie, E. (1994*a*), *Managing Crisis and Change: The Organisational Response to HIV/AIDS* (Buckingham: Open University Press).

————————(1994*b*), 'Management by Contract in the NHS: Rhetoric or Reality?', paper to the ERU Conference 'The Contract State: the Future of Public Management', Cardiff.

Benington, J., and Stoker, G. (1989), 'Local Government in the Firing Line', in N. Buchan and T. Sumner (eds.), *Glasnost in Britain* (Basingstoke: Macmillan).

Bennis, W., Benne, K., Chin, R., and Corey, R. (1976) (eds.), *The Planning of Change* (3rd edn., New York: Holt Reinhart).

Berle, A. A, and Means, G. C. (1933), *The Modern Corporation and Private Property* (New York: Macmillan).

Berman, P. (1978), 'The Study of Macro and Micro Implementation', *Public Policy*, 26/2: 157–85.

Best, G., and Ham, C. (1989), 'Goodbye Rubber Stamp Image', *Health Services Journal*, 20 (Apr.).

Blumenthal, B., and Haspeslagh, P. (1994), 'Toward a Definition of Corporate Transformation', *Sloan Management Review* (Spring), 101–6.

Bogdanor, V. (1994), *Local Government and The Constitution* (Kensington Town Hall: Solace).

Boston, J. (1987), 'Transforming New Zealand's Public Sector: Labour's Quest for Improved Efficiency and Accountability', *Public Administration*, 65 (Winter), 423–42.

————(1992), 'Assessing the Performance of Departmental Chief Executives: Perspectives from New Zealand', *Public Administration*, 70 (Autumn), 405–28.

Boudon, R. (1989), *The Analysis of Ideology* (Cambridge: Polity Press).

Bradach, J. L., and Eccles, R. G. (1991), 'Price, Authority and Trust: From Ideal Types to Plural Forms', in G. Thompson, J. Frances, R. Levacic, and J. Mitchell, *Markets, Hierarchies and Networks* (London: Sage), 277–92.

Brazier, J., Hutton, J., and Jeavons, R. (1990), *Analysing Health Care Systems: The Economic Context of the NHS White Paper Proposals* (Centre for Health Economics, University of York).

Broadbent, J., Laughlin, R., and Read S. (1991), 'Recent Financial and Administrative Changes in the NHS: A Critical Theory Analysis', *Critical Perspectives on Accounting*, 2: 1–29.

———*et al.* (1992), 'It's a Long Way from Teaching Susan to Read: Some Preliminary Observations of a Project Studying the Local Management of Schools', in G. Wallace (ed.), *Local Management of Schools* (Bera Dialogues, 6; Clevedon: BERA).

———Laughlin, R., Shearn, D., and Dandy, N. (1993), 'Implementing Local Management of Schools: A Theoretical and Empirical Analysis', *Research Papers in Education*, 8/2: 149–76.

Brunsson, N. (1982), 'The Irrationality of Action and Action Rationality: Decisions, Ideologies and Organisational Action', *Journal of Management Studies*, 19/1: 29–44.

———(1989), 'Administrative Reforms as Routines', *Scandinavian Journal of Management*, 5/3: 219–28.

Buckingham, G. L., Jeffrey, R. G., and Thorne, B. A. (1975), *Job Enrichment and Organisational Change: A Study in Participation at Gallagher Ltd* (Epping: Gower Press).

Burke, C., and Goddard, A. (1990), 'Internal Markets: The Road to Inefficiency', *Public Administration*, 68: 389–96.

Butler, J. (1992), *Patients, Policy and Politics: Before and After Working for Patients* (Buckingham: Open University Press).

Butler, R. J., and Wilson, D. C. (1990), *Managing Voluntary and Non Profit Organisations* (London: Routledge).

Cadbury Report (1992), *Report of the Committee on the Financial Aspects of Corporate Governance* (London: Gee Publishing).

Cairncross, E., Ashburner, L., and Pettigrew, A. (1991), *Membership and Learning Needs* (Research for Action, 4; Bristol: NHS Training Directorate).

—————(1992*a*), 'Out of the Bunker', *Health Services Journal* (12 Mar.), 20–2.

—————(1992*b*), 'Just Trust Us', *Health Services Journal* 14 May), 20–2.

—————(1992*c*), *NHS Trust Boards: The First Wave; The First Year* (Research for Action, 6; Bristol: NHS Training Directorate).

CEPP (1994), *Evaluation of TQM Projects in the NHS* (London: Brunel University).

CSO (1993), Economic Trends: Annual Supplement (London: HMSO).

Challis, L., Day, P., Klein, R., and Scrivens, E. (1994), 'Managing Quasi Markets: Institutions of Regulation, in W. Bartlett *et al.* (1994), 10–34.

Chandler, A. D. (1962), *Strategy and Structure: Chapters in the History of the American Industrial Enterprise* (Cambridge, Mass.: MIT Press).

Charkham, J. (1986), *Effective Boards*, (London: Chartec, The Institute of Chartered Accountants)

———(1994), *Keeping Good Company: A Study of Corporate Governance on Five Countries* (Oxford; Oxford University Press).

Child, J. (1969), *British Management Thought* (London: Allen & Unwin).

———(1988), 'On Organisations in Their Sectors', *Organization Studies*, 9: 13–19.

——and Smith, C. (1987), 'The Context and Process of Organisational Transformation: Cadbury Ltd. in its Sector, *Journal of Management Studies*, 24/6: 565–93.

Clarke, J. (1994), 'Capturing the Consumer: Consumerism and Social Welfare', Open University, paper given at the ESRC Seminar 'Conceptualising Consumption Issues', University of Lancaster, Dec.

——and Newman, J. (1993), 'Managing to Survive: Dilemmas of Changing Organisational Forms in Public Services', in N. Deakin and R. Page (eds.), *The Costs of Welfare* (Aldershot, Avebury).

——Cochrane, A., and McLaughlin, E. (1994), 'Mission Accomplished or Unfinished Business? The Impact of Managerialisation', in J. Clarke, A. Cochrane and E. McLaughlin (eds.), *Managing Social Policy* (London, Sage).

Clegg, S. (1990), *Modern Organisations* (London: Sage).

Cm 555 (1989), *Working for Patients* (London: HMSO).

Cm 849 (1989), *Caring for People* (London: HMSO).

Cm 1647 (1991), *Custody, Care and Justice: The Way Forward for the Prison Service in England and Wales* (London: HMSO).

Cm 1456 (1991), *Prison Disturbances: April 1990* (Report of an Inquiry by the Rt Hon Lord Justice Woolf (Parts 1 and 2) and His Honour Judge Stephen Tumin (Part 2))(London: HMSO).

Cmnd 7615 (1979), *Report of the Royal Commission on the National Health Service* (the Merrison Report) (London: HMSO).

Cohen, M. D., and March, J. G. (1974), *Leadership and Ambiguity: The American College President* (New York: McGraw Hill).

Coldron, J., and Boulton, P. (1991), 'Happiness as a Criterion of Parents' Choice of Schools', *Journal of Educational Policy*, 6/2: 162–78.

Collins, R. (1979), *The Credential Society* (New York: Academic Press).

Colville, I., Dalton, K., and Tomkins, C. (1992), 'There's More to Dancing than Knowing the "Next Steps": Experimenting with Change in the Civil Service', paper to the British Academy of Management Conference, University of Bradford.

Common, R., and Flynn, N. (1992), *Contracting for Care* (York: Joseph Rowntree Foundation).

————and Hurley, D. (1993), 'Contracting for Care: Further Developments', paper prepared for the National Council of Voluntary Oraganizations Conference, University of the South Bank, London.

Conyon, M. (1994), 'Corporate Governance Changes in UK Companies between 1988 and 1993', *Corporate Governance*, 2/2: 87–99.

——Gregg, P., and Machin, S. (1994), *Taking Care of Business: Executive Compensation in the UK* (University of Warwick: Centre for Corporate Strategy and Change).

——and Leech, D. (1994), 'Top Pay, Company Performance, and Corporate Governance', *Oxford Bulletin of Economics and Statistics*, 56: 229–47.

Coopers and Lybrand Deloitte (1988), *Local Management in Schools*, (London: HMSO).

Corby, S. (1994), 'How Big a Step is "Next Steps"? Industrial Relations Developments in Civil Service Executive Agencies', *Human Resource Management Journal*, 4/2: 52–69.

Coulson-Thomas, C., and Wakelam, A. (1991), *The Effective Board: Current Practice, Myths and Realities* (London: Director Books).

Cowling, A., and Newman, K. (1994), 'Turning Doctors into Managers : An Evaluation of a Major NHS Initiative to Improve the Managerial Capabilities of Medical Consultants', *Human Resource Management Journal*, 4/4: (Summer), 1–13.

Crompton, R. (1990), 'Professions in the Current Context,' *Work, Employment and Society* (Special Issue) (May), 146–66.

Cyert, R. M., and March, J. G. (1963), *A Behavioural Theory of the Firm* (Englewood Cliffs, NJ: Prentice Hall).

Czarniawska-Joerges, B. (1989), 'The Wonderland of Public Administration Reforms', *Organisation Studies* 10/4: 531–48.

Dahl, R. (1961), *Who Governs?* (New Haven: Yale University Press).

David, M., West, A., and Ribbens, J. (1994), *Mother's Intuition? Choosing Secondary Schools* (London: Falmer Press).

Davies, A., and Kirkpatrick, I. (1993), 'Face to Face with the Sovereign Consumer: Service Quality and the Changing Role of Professional Academic Librarians', paper given to the ESRC Professions in Modernity Series.

————————and Whipp, R.(1993), 'Management and Professional Change in the Public Sector', paper given to the Professions in Management Conference, University of Stirling, Dec.

Davies, C. (1983), 'Professionals in Bureaucracies: the Conflict Thesis Revisited,' in R. Dingwall, and P. Lewis (eds.), *The Sociology of the Professions* (London: Macmillan).

————(1987), 'Viewpoint: Things to Come, the NHS in the Next Decade', *Sociology of Health and Illness*, 9/3: 302–4.

Dawson, S., Mole, V,. Winstanley, P., and Sherval, J. (1992), 'Management Competition and Professional Practice: Medicine and the Marketplace,' paper given at the Knowledge Workers in Contemporary Organizations Conference, University of Lancaster, Sept.

————————————————(1993), 'In or Out of Management? Dilemmas and Developments in Public Health Medicine', paper given to the Professions and Management in Britain Conference, Stirling University, Aug.

Day, C. (1985), *Managing Primary Schools* (London: Harper and Rowe).

Day, P., and Klein, R. (1987), *Accountabilities: Five Public Services* (London: Tavistock).

Deal, T. E., and Kennedy, A. A. (1981), *Corporate Cultures: The Rites and Rituals of Corporate Life* (Reading, Mass.: Addison Wesley).

Deem, R. (1990), 'The Reform of School Governing Bodies: The Power of the Consumer over the Producer?', in J. Flude and M. Hammer (eds.), *The Education Reform Act 1988: Its Origins and Implications* (Lewes: Falmer Press).

Department of Health (1994), *HPSS Statistics* (London: HMSO).

Di Maggio, P., and Powell, W. W., (1983), 'The Iron Cage Revisited: Institutional Isomorphism and Collective Rationality in Organisational Fields', *American Sociological Review*, 48: 147–60.

Dingwall, R., and Strong, P. (1985), 'The Interactional Study of Organisations: A Critique and a Reformulation', *Urban Life*, 14/2: 205–31.

Disken, S., Dixon, M., Halpern, S., and Shocket, G. (1990), *Models of Clinical Management* (London: Institute of Health Services Management).

Dopson, S. (1993*a*), 'Are Agencies an Act of Faith? The Experience of HMSO', *Public Money and Management* (Apr./June), 17–23.

————(1993*b*), 'Management: The One Disease Consultants Did Not Think Existed', Paper to the Professions and Management in Britain Conference, University of Stirling, Aug.

Doty, D. H., and Glick, W. H. (1994), 'Typologies as a Unique Form of Theory Building: Toward Improved Understanding and Modeling', *Academy of Management Review*, 19/2: 230–51.

Downs, A. (1967), *Inside Bureaucracy* (Boston: Little Brown & Company).

Dufour, Y. (1991), 'The Implementation of General Practitioner Maternity Unit Closure Proposals in Hospitals', PhD Thesis, University of Warwick: Centre for Corporate Strategy and Change.

du Gay, D. (1993), 'Entrepreneurial Management in the Public Sector', *Work, Employment and Society*, 7/4: 643–8.

Dunleavy, P. (1991), *Democracy, Bureaucracy and Public Choice* (London: Harvester Wheatsheaf).

——and Hood, C. (1994), 'From Old Public Administration to New Public Management', *Public Money and Management* (July/Sept.), 9–16.

Dunphy, D. C., and Stace, D. A. (1988), 'Transformational and Coercive Strategies for Planned Organisational Change: Beyond the OD Model', *Organizational Studies*, 9/3: 317–34.

Dunsire, A. (1978), *Implementation in a Bureaucracy* (Oxford: Martin Robertson).

The Economist (1994), 'Watching The Boss: A Survey of Corporate Governance', 29 Jan.–4 Feb., 62–79.

Education, Department of (1992), *The Implementation of Local Management in Schools: A Report by HM Inspectorate 1989–1992* (London: HMSO).

Edwards, T., and Whitty, G. (1992), 'Parental Choice and Educational Reform in Britain and the United States', *British Journal of Educational Studies* 40/2: 101–17.

Efficiency Unit (1988), *Improving Management in Government: The Next Steps* (London: HMSO).

Elcock, H. (1978), 'Regional Government in Action: The Members of Two RHAs', *Public Administration*, 56/4: 379–97.

Eliassen, K. A., and Kooiman, J. (1993), (eds.), *Managing Public Organisations: Lessons from Contemporary European Experience* (London: Sage).

Elston, M. A. (1991), 'The Politics of Professional Power—Medicine in a Changing Health Service', in J. Gabe, M. Calnan, and M. Bury (eds.), *The Sociology of the Health Service* (London: Routledge).

Emery, F. E., and Trist, E. (1965), 'The Causal Texture of Organisational Environments', *Human Relations*, 18: 21–32.

Emmert, M., and Crow, M. M. (1987), 'Public–Private Cooperation and Hybrid Organisations', *Journal of Management*, 13/11: (Spring), 55–67.

Enthoven, A. (1985), *Reflections on the Management of the National Health Service* (Occasional paper, 5; London: Nuffield Provincial Hospitals Trust).

European Policy Forum Report, (1992), *Accountability to the Public* (London: European Policy Forum).

Evetts, J. (1994), 'The New Headteacher: the Changing Work Culture of Secondary Headship', *School Organisation*, 14/1: 37–47.

Fama, E. F., and Jensen, M. C. (1983), 'Separation of Ownership and Control', *Journal of Law and Economics*, 26: 327–49.

Farnham, D. (1993), 'Human Resource Management and Employee Relations', in D. Farnham, and S. Horton (eds.), *Managing the New Public Services* (Basingstoke: Macmillan), 99–126.

——and Horton, S. (eds.) (1993), *Managing the New Public Services* (Basingstoke: Macmillan).

Fergusson, R. (1994), 'Managerialism in Education', in J. Clarke, A. Cochrane, and E. McLaughlin (eds.) *Managing Social Policy* (London: Sage).

Ferlie, E. (1990), *Understanding Change in Psychiatric Services: Whose Change Agenda?*

Whose Organisation? (University of Warwick: Centre for Corporate Strategy and Change).

——— (1992), 'The Creation and Evolution of Quasi Markets in the Public Sector: A Problem for Strategic Management', *Strategic Management Journal*, 13 (special issue) (Winter), 79–97.

——— (1994), 'The Creation and Evolution of Quasi Markets in the Public Sector: Some Early Evidence from the NHS', *Policy and Politics*, 22/2 (Apr.), 105–12.

———Fitzgerald, L. and Ashburner, L. (1992), *The Challenge of Purchasing* (Research in Action, Paper 7; Bristol: NHS Training Directorate).

——— ——— ——— (1993), *Board Teams: Roles and Relationships* (Research for Action, Paper 10; Bristol: NHS Training Directorate).

——— ——— ——— (1994), 'The Creation and Evolution of the New Health Authorities: The Challenge of Purchasing', *Health Services Management Research*, 7/2: 120–30.

——— ——— ——— (1995), 'Corporate Governance and the Public Sector: Some Issues and Evidence from the NHS', *Public Administration*, 73/3 (Autumn), 375–92.

———Cairncross, L., and Pettigrew, A. (1993), *Understanding Internal Markets in the NHS*, in I. Tilly, (ed.), *Managing The Internal Market* (London: Paul Chapman), 69–81.

———and Pettigrew, A. M (1994a), *Managing Through Networks: Some Issues and Implications for the NHS* (University of Warwick: Centre for Corporate Strategy and Change).

——— ——— (1994b), *The Nature and Transformation of Corporate Headquarters* (University of Warwick: Centre for Corporate Strategy and Change).

Ferner, A., Edwards, P., and Sisson, K. (forthcoming), 'Coming Unstuck? In Search of the Corporate Glue in an International Professional Service Firm', *Human Resource Management*.

Fidler, J. (1981), *The British Business Elite: Its Attitude to Class, Status and Power* (London: Routledge & Kegan Paul).

Field, M. G. (1988), 'The Position of the Soviet Physician; the Bureaucratic Professional, *Millbank Quarterly*, 66 suppl. 2, 182–201.

Financial Times (1993), *Financial Times* (14 Jan.).

Fitz, J., Power, S., and Halpin, D. (1993), 'Opting for Grant Maintained Status', *Policy Studies*, 14/1: 4–20.

FitzGerald, L. (1992), *Board Development* (Authorities in the NHS, 9; Bristol: NHS Training Directorate).

——— (1994), 'Moving Clinicians into Management: A Professional Challenge or A Threat?,' *Journal of Management in Medicine*, 8/6: 32–44.

———and Pettigrew, A. (1991), *Boards in Action: Some Implications for Health Authorities, Authorities in the NHS* (Bristol: NHS Training Directorate).

———and Sturt, J. (1992), 'Clinicians into Management: On the Change Agenda or not?,' *Health Services Management Research*, 5/2 (July).

———Ashburner, L., and Ferlie, E. (1995), *Strategy Making on NHS Boards* (University of Warwick: Centre for Corporate Strategy and Change).

Flood, J. (1993), 'The Governance of Law: Professions in the Management of professions,' paper to the Professions and Management Conference, University of Stirling.

Flude, M., and Hammer, M. (1990), *Opting for an Uncertain Future: Grant Maintained Schools*, in (eds.), *The Education Reform Act 1988: Its Origins and Implications* (London: Falmer Press), 51–72.

Flynn, N., and Hurley, D. (1993), *The Market for Care* (London: LSE).

Fook, N., and Watson T. (1992), 'Culture, Environment and Survival in Further Education Colleges', paper given to the British Academy of Management Conference, University of Bradford, Sept.

Ford, D. (1990), *Understanding Business Markets* (London: Academic Press).

Freemantle, N., Watt, I., and Mason, J. (1993), 'Developments in the Purchasing Process in the NHS: Towards an Explicit Politics of Rationing?', *Public Administration*, 71 (Winter), 535–48.

Friedlander, F,. and Brown E. (1974), 'Organisation Development', *Annual Review of Psychology*, 25: 313–41.

Friedson, E. (1970), *Professional Dominance: The Social Structure of Medical Care* (New York: Atherton Press).

——(1984), 'The Changing Nature of Professional Control', *Annual Review of Sociology*, 10: 1–20.

——(1986), *Professional Powers: A Study of the Institutionalisation of Formal Knowledge* (Chicago: University of Chicago Press).

——(1987), 'The Future of Professions', *Journal of Dental Education*, 53: 140–44.

Fry, G. (1981), *The Administrative 'Revolution' in Whitehall* (London: Croom Helm).

——(1984), 'The Development of the Thatcher Government's "Grand Strategy" for the Civil Service: A Public Policy Perspective', *Public Administration*, 62: 322–35.

Fudge, C., and Gustafsson, L. (1989), 'Administrative Reform and Public Management in Sweden and the United Kingdom', *Public Money and Management*, 9 (Summer), 29–34.

Fulton, Lord (1968), *Report of the Committee on the Civil Service*, Cmnd. 3538. (London: HMSO).

Garrette, B., and Quelin, B. (1994), 'An Empirical Study of Hybrid Forms of Governance Structure: The Case of the Telecommunication Equipment Industry', *Research Policy*, 23: 395–412.

Gersick, C. J. G. (1991), 'Revolutionary Change Theories: A Multilevel Exploration of the Punctuated Equilibrium Paradigm', *Academy of Management Review*, 16: 10–36.

Gibbons, M., Limoges, C., Nowotny, H., Schwartzman, S., Scott, P., and Trow, M. (1994), *The New Production of Knowledge: The Dynamics of Science and Research in Contemporary Societies* (London, Sage).

Giola, D. A., and Chittipeddi, K. (1991), 'Sensemaking and Sensegiving in Strategic Change Initiation', *Strategic Management Journal*, 12: 433–48.

Glatter, R., and Woods, P. (1994), 'Competitive Arenas in Education: Studying the Impact of Enhanced Competition and Choice on Parents and Schools', in W. Bartlett *et al.* (1994), 56–77.

Glendon, I. (1992), 'Radical Change within a British University', in D-M. Hosking, and N. Anderson (eds.), *Organisational Change and Innovation: Psychological Perspectives and Practices in Europe* (London, Routledge).

Glennerster, H. (1991), 'Quasi Markets for Education', *Economic Journal*, 101 (Sept.), 1268–1276.

——Power, A., and Travers, T. (1991), 'A New Era in Social Policy: A New Enlightenment or a New Leviathan?', *Journal of Social Policy*, 20/3: 389–414.

——Matsaganis, M., Owens, P., and Hancock, S. (1994), *GP Fund Holding: Wild Card or Winning Hand*, in R. Robinson and J. Le Grand (eds.), *Evaluating the NHS Reforms* (London: King Fund's Institute), 74–107.

Glover, D. (1994), 'Is Marketing Making You Aggressive?', *Management in Education*, 8/ 2: 22–3.

Goldsmith, M., and Willetts, D. (1988), *Managed Health Care: New System for a Better Health Service* (London: Centre for Policy Studies).

Golembiewski, R. T. (1972), *Renewing Organisations: The Laboratory Approach to Planned Change* (Brooklyn, NY: Itasca Peacock).

——Billingsley, K., and Yeager, S. (1975), 'Measuring Change and Persistence in Human Affairs: Types of Change Generated by O.D. Designs', *Journal of Applied Behavioural Science*, 12/2: 133–57.

Goodsir, J. (1993), 'Footing the Bill: Professionalisation and the Police Service', paper to the Professions and Management Conference, Stirling University.

Grace, G. (1993), 'On the Study of School Leadership: Beyond Education Management', *British Journal of Educational Studies*, 41/4 (Dec.), 353–65.

Granovetter, M. (1985), 'Economic Action and Social Structure: The Problem of Embeddedness', *American Journal of Sociology*, 91/3: 481–510.

——(1992), 'Economic Institutions as Social Constructions: A Framework for Analysis', *Acta Sociologica*, 35: 3–11.

——and Swedberg, R. (1992), *The Sociology of Economic Life* (Oxford: Westview Press).

Grant, R. M. (1991), 'The Resource Based Theory of Competitive Advantage: Implications for Strategy Formulation', *California Management Review*, 33/3: 114–22.

Gray, A., and Jenkins, B. (1995), 'Implementing the Next Steps: A Choreography of Management Change', in O'Toole and Jordan (1995), 37–54.

Green, D. G., Flew, A., Le Grand, J., Seldon, M., Robinson, D., and Carr-Hill, R. (1991), (eds.), *Empowering the Parents: How to Break the Schools Monopoly*, (Choice in Welfare, 9) (London: Institute of Economic Affairs, Health and Welfare Unit).

Greenley, G. E. (1989), *Strategic Management* (Herts: Prentice Hall).

Greenwood, R., Hinings, C., and Brown, J. (1990), 'Strategic Management in Professional Partnerships' *Academy of Management Journal*, 33/4: 725–55.

——————(1993), 'Understanding Strategic Change: The Contribution of Archetypes', *Academy of Management Journal*, 36/5: 1052–81.

Greiner, L. (1977), 'Patterns of Organisational Change', *Harvard Business Review*, 45/3: 119–30.

——and Barnes, L. (1970), 'Organisation Change and Development', in G. Dalton, P. Lawrence, and L. Greiner (eds.), *Organisational Change and Development* (Homewood, Ill.: Irwin Dorsey).

Griffiths Report (1983), *NHS Management Enquiry* (London: HMSO).

Griffiths, R. (1988), 'Does the Public Service Serve?' *Public Administration*, 66 (Summer), 195–204.

Grinyer, P. H., and Norburn, D. (1974), 'Strategic Planning in 21 UK Companies', *Long Range Planning*, 7/4: 60–88.

——Mayes, D., and McKiernan, P. (1988), *Sharpbenders: The Secrets of Unleashing Corporate Potential* (Oxford: Basil Blackwell).

Gunn, L. (1989), 'Public Management: A Third Approach', *Public Money and Management*, 8: 21–5.

Gyford, J., Leach, S., and Game, C. (1989), *The Changing Politics of Local Government* (London: Unwin Hyman).

Hafferty, F. (1988), 'Theories at the Crossroads: A Discussion of Evolving Views on Medicine as a Profession', *Millbank Quarterly*, 66/2: 202–25.

Hage, J., and Dewar, R. (1973), 'Elite Values Versus Organisational Structure in Predicting Innovation', *Administrative Science Quarterly*, 18: 279–90.

Hales, C. (1986), 'What Do Managers Do? A Critical Review of the Evidence', *Journal of Management Studies*, 23/1: 88–113.

Halpin, D., Power, S., and Fitz, J. (1991), 'Grant Maintained Schools: Making a Difference Without Being Really Different', *British Journal of Educational Studies*, 39/4: 409–24.

Ham, C. (1989), 'Managing for Cosumers: The New Role of the Health Service Authorities', NAHA Conference Speech.

——and Towell, D. (1985), 'Policy Theory and Policy Practice: An Encounter in the Field of Health Service Management Development', *Policy and Politics*, 13/4: 431–45.

——and Matthews, T. (1991), *Purchasing With Authority: The New Role of DHAs* (King's Fund College Papers, 1; London: King's Fund).

——and Spurgeon, P. (1992), *Effective Purchasing* (Health Services Management Centre Discussion Paper, 28; University of Birmingham).

Hambleton, R. (1988), 'Consumerism, Decentralisation and Local Democracy', *Public Administration*, 66 (Summer), 125–47.

Hamel, G. (1991), 'Competition for Competence and Interpartner Learning within International Alliances', *Strategic Management Journal*, 12: 83–103.

Handy, C. (1990), *The Age of Unreason* (Boston: Harvard University Press).

Hannan, M. T., and Freeman, J. (1988), *Organizational Ecology* (Cambridge, Mass: Harvard University Press).

Hardy, C. (1985), *Managing Organisational Closure* (Aldershot: Gower).

Hargreaves, A. (1994), *Changing Teachers, Changing Times: Teachers' Work and Culture in the Post Modern Age* (London: Cassell).

Harrison, J., and Nutley, S. (1993), 'Professions and Management in the Public Sector: The Experience of Local Government and the NHS in Britain', Paper to the Professions and Management in Britain Conference, University of Stirling.

Harrison, S., Hunter, D., Marnoch, G., and Pollitt, C. (1992), *Just Managing: Power and Culture in the NHS* (Basingstoke: Macmillan).

——and Pollitt C. (1994), *Controlling Health Professionals: The Future of Work and Organisation in the NHS* (Buckingham: Open University Press).

Harrow, J., and Willcocks, L. (1990), 'Public Services Management: Activities, Initiatives and Limits to Learning', *Journal of Management Studies*, 27/3: 281–304.

Hart, S., and Banbury, C. (1994), 'How Strategic Making Processes Can Make a Difference', *Strategic Management Journal*, 2: 263–9.

Hartley, J. (1983), 'Ideology and Organisational Behaviour', *International Studies of Management and Organisation*, 13/3.

Harwood, A., and Boufford, I. J. (1993), 'Managing Clinical Services: A Consensus Statement of Principles for Effective Clinical Management', British Association of Managers in Medicine; BMA; Institute of Health Services Management; RCN.

Haug, M. (1973), 'De-Professionalisation: An Alternative Hypothesis for the Future', *Sociological Review Monograph*, 20: 195–211.

——(1975), 'The Deprofessionalisation of Everyone?', *Sociological Focus*, 3: 197–213.

——(1988), 'A Reexamination of the Hypothesis of Physician Deprofessionalisation', *Millbank Quarterly*, 66: 48–56.

——and Lavin, B. (1983), *Consumerism in Medicine: Challenging Professional Authority* (Beverley Hills: Sage).

Haywood, S., and Hunter, D. (1982), 'Consultative Processes in Health Policy in the UK: A View from the Centre', *Public Administration*, 69/2: 143–62.

Hedlund, G. (1994), 'A Model of Knowledge Management in the N Form Corporation', *Strategic Management Journal* (Summer Special Issue), 15: 73–90.

Heginbotham, C., and Ham. C., (with Cochrane, M., and Richards, J.) (1992), *Purchasing Dilemmas* (London: King's Fund College and Southampton and South West Hampshire Health Authority).

Helps, R. (1994), 'The Allocation of Non-Contract Time to Deputy Headteachers in Primary Schools', School Oraganization, 14/3: 243–6.

Hemmings, S., Deem, R., and Brehony, K. (1990), 'Governors Working with Schools: Towards a New Partnership?' paper to the British Educational Research Association Annual Conference, Roehampton Institute.

Hendrych, D. (1993), 'Transforming Czechoslovakian Public Administration: Traditions and New Challenges', *Public Administration*, 71 (Spring/Summer), 41–54.

Herbst, P. G. (1974), *Sociotechnical Design: Strategies in Multi-disciplinary Research* (London: Tavistock).

Herman, E. S (1981), *Corporate Control, Corporate Power* (New York: Cambridge University Press).

Hinings, C., and Greenwood, R. (1988), *The Dynamics of Strategic Change* (Oxford: Basil Blackwell).

——Brown, J., and Greenwood, R. (1991), 'Change in Autonomous Professional Organisations', *Journal of Management Studies*, 28/4: 375–93.

——Thibault, L., Slack, T., and Kikulis, L. M. (forthcoming), 'Values and Organisational Structure', *Human Relations*.

HM Inspectorate (1992), 'The Implementation of Local Management of Schools, 1989–1992', A Report of HM Inspectorate, London, Dept. of Education.

Hocking, J. (1991), 'Managing in the Marketplace: Universities and Institutional Change in the late 1980s and the Early 1990s' (MBA Diss., University of Warwick)

Hodge, M. (1991), *Quality, Equality and Democracy: Improving Public Services* (Fabian Pamphlet, 549; London: Fabian Society).

——and Thompson, W. (1994), *Beyond The Town Hall: Reinventing Local Government* (Fabian Pamphlet, 561; London: Fabian Society).

Hodgson, R. C., Levinson, D. J., and Zaleznik, A. (1965), *The Executive Role Constellation* (Boston: Harvard University Press).

Hoggett, P. (1991), 'A New Management in The Public Sector?', *Policy and Politics*, 19/4: 243–56.

Hogwood, B. W. (1993), 'Restructuring Central Government: The "Next Steps" Initiative in Britain, in Eliassen and Kooiman (1993).

——and Gunn, L. A. (1986), *Policy Analysis for the Real World* (Oxford: Oxford University Press).

Holton, V., and Rabbetts, J. (1989), 'Powder in the Boardroom: Report of a Survey of Women on the Boards of Top UK Industrial Companies (Berkhamsted: Ashridge Management Research Group).

Hood, C. (1991), 'A Public Management for all Seasons?', *Public Administration*, 69 (Spring), 3–19.

Hospital and Health Services Yearbook (1994), (London: Institute of Health Service Managers).

Howe, E., and McRae, S. (1991), *Women on the Board* (London: Policy Studies Institute).

Hoyes, L., and Means, R. (1993), *Quasi Markets and the Reform of Community Care*, in J. Le Grand, and W. Bartlett, (eds.), *Quasi Markets and Social Policy (London: Macmillan), 93–124*.

Hughes, D., and Dingwall, R. (1990), 'Sir Henry Maine, Joseph Stalin and the Reorganisation of the NHS', *Journal of Social Welfare Law*, 5: 296–309.

Hunter, D. (1980), *Coping With Uncertainty: Policy and Politics in the NHS* (Letchworth: Wiley).

The Independent (1993), (28 Mar.).

———(1995), (2 Mar.).

Institutional Shareholders Committee (1991), *The Roles and Duties of Directors: A Statement of Best Practice* (London: Institutional Shareholders Committee).

Isabella, L. A. (1990), 'Evolving Interpretations as Change Unfolds: How Managers Construe Key Organisational Events', *Academy of Management Journal*, 33/1: 7–41.

Jarratt Report (1985), *Report of the Steering Committee for Efficiency Studies in Universities* (London: Committee of Vice Chancellors and Principals).

Jensen, M. C., and Meckling, W. H. (1976), 'Theory of the Firm: Managerial Behaviour, Agency Costs and Ownership Structure', *Journal of Financial Economics*, 3: 305–60.

Johnes, G., and Cave, M. (1994), 'The Development of Competition Among Higher Education Institutions', in W. Bartlett *et al.* (1994), 95–122.

Johnson, G. (1987), *Strategic Change and the Management Process* (Oxford: Basil Blackwell).

Jones, A., and Hendry, C. (1992), *The Learning Organisation: A Review of Literature and Practice* (London: Human Resource Development Partnership).

Jones, A. M. (1994) 'Creating a Learning Organisation', PhD Thesis, University of Warwick: Centre for Corporate Strategy and Change.

Jowell, R., and Witherspoon, S. (1985) *British Social Attitudes: The 1985 Report* (London: Gower).

Kanter, R.M. (1983), *The Change Masters: Corporate Entrepreneurs at Work* (New York: Counterpoint).

———(1989), *When Giants Learn to Dance* (New York: Irwin).

———Stein, B., and Jick, T. (1992), *The Challenge of Organisational Change* (New York: The Free Press).

Kearns, A. (1990), *Voluntarism Management and Accountability* (Glasgow: Centre for Housing Research, Glasgow University).

Keat, R., and Abercrombie, N. (1991), *Enterprise Culture* (London: Routledge).

Keep, E. (1992), 'Schools in the Marketplace? Some Problems with Private Sector Models', in G. Wallace (ed.), *Local Management of Schools Research and Experience (BERA Dialogues, 6; Clevedon: Multilingual Matters Ltd.)*.

Keman, H. (1993), *Proliferation of the Welfare State*, in Eliassen and Kooiman (1993: 13–33).

Kimberly, J. R. (1989), 'Change in the NHS: A View from America', Presentation to Centre for Corporate Strategy and Change Open Seminar 'Managing Change in Health Care Systems: Slogan or Reality?' University of Warwick, Sept.

———de Pourvourville, G., and associates (1993), *The Migration of Managerial Innovation: DRGs and Health Care Administration in Western Europe* (San Francisco: Jossey Bass).

King, E. (1994), 'Campaigning Against Opting Out', *Forum*, 36/2: 57–8.

King's Equal Opportunity Task Force (1990), *Ethnic Minority Health Authority Membership: A Survey* (Paper, 5; London: King Edward's Hospital Fund).

Klein, R. (1984), 'The Politics of Ideology (vs) the Realities of Politics: the Case of Britain's NHS in the 1980s', *Millbank Memorial Fund Quarterly, Health and Society*, 62/1: 82–109.

———(1994), 'Lessons from the Financial Scandals in Wessex and the West Midlands', *British Medical Journal*, 308: 215–16.

———and Lewis, J. (1976), *The Politics of Consumer Representation* (London: Centre for Studies in Social Policy).

Knapp, M., Wistow, G., Forder, J., and Hardy, B. (1994), 'Markets for Social Care—Opportunities, Barriers and Implications', in W. Bartlett *et al. (1994), 123–57*.

Korman, N., and Glennerster, H. (1990), *Hospital Closure* (Milton Keynes: Open University Press).

Korn Ferry (1989), *International Boards of Directors Study, UK (London: Korn/Ferry)*.

Kosnik, R. D. (1987), 'Greenmail: A Study of Board Performance in Corporate Governance', *Administrative Science Quarterly*, 32: 163–85.

Kotter, J. P. (1982), *The General Manager* (New York: Free Press).

Kovner, A. R. (1974), 'Hospital Board Members as Policy Makers: Role, Priorities and Qualifications', *Medical Care*, 12/12: 971–82.

Lachman, R. (1985), 'Public and Private Sector Differences: CEOs' Perceptions of their Role Environment', *Academy of Management Journal*, 28/3.

Larkin, G. V. (1988), 'Medical Dominance in Britain: Image and Reality', *Millbank Quarterly*, 66/2: 117–32.

Laughlin, R. (1991), 'Can the Information Systems for the NHS Internal Market Work?', *Public Money and Management*, 11: 37–41.

———(1992), *Accounting Control and Controlling Accounting: The Battle for the Public Sector* (Discussion Paper, 92.29; Sheffield University Management School).

———Broadbent, J., Shearn, D. (1992), 'Recent Financial and Accountability Changes in General Practice: An Unhealthy Intrusion into Medical Autonomy?', *Financial Accountability and Management*, 8/2: 129–48.

Lawson, R. (1993), 'The New Technology of Management in the Personal Social Services', in P. Taylor-Gooby and R. Lawson (eds.), *Markets and Managers: New Issues in the Delivery of Welfare* (Buckingham: Open University Press), 69–84.

Leach, S. (1990), 'Accountability in the Post Abolition Metropolitan Government System', *Local Government Studies* (May/June), 13–31.

Leask, M. (1992), 'School Development Plans: Their History and their Potential', in G. Wallace (ed.), *Local Management of Schools* (Clevedon, BERA).

Lee, K., and Mills, A. (1982), *Policy Making and Planning in the Health Sector* (London: Croom Helm).

Lee, T. (1992), 'Finding Simple answers to Complex Questions: Funding Special Needs under LMS', in G. Wallace, (ed.), *Local Management of Schools, Research and Experience* (BERA Dialogues, 6; Clevedon: Multilingual Matters Ltd).

Le Grand, J. (1991), 'Quasi Markets and Social Policy', *Economic Journal*, 101 (Sept.), 1256–67.

———(1994), 'Evaluating the NHS Reforms', in R. Robinson and J. Le Grand (eds.), *Evaluating the NHS Reforms (London: King's Fund Institute), 243–60*.

Levacic, R. (1992), 'The LEA and its Schools: The Decentralised Organisation and the Internal Market', in G. Wallace (ed.), *Local Management of Schools: Research and Experience* (BERA Dialogues, 6; Clevedon: Multilingual Matters Ltd.).

———(1994), 'Evaluating The Performance of Quasi Markets in Education', in W.

Bartlett, C. Propper, D. Wilson, and J. Le Grand (eds.), *Quasi Markets in the Welfare State* (Bristol: School of Advanced Urban Studies), 35–55.

Levy, A. (1986), 'Second Order Planned Change: Definition and Conceptualisation', *Organisational Dynamics* (Summer), 5–20.

Lewin (1948) *Resolving Social Conflicts* (New York: Harper & Row).

Lewis, D., and Wallace, H. (1984), *Policies into Practice: National and International Case Studies in Implementation* (London: Heinemann Education Books).

Lewis, J. (1987), 'From Public Health to Community Medicine: The Wider Context', in L. Willcocks and J. Harrow (eds.), *Rediscovering Public Service Management* (London, McGraw Hill).

——— (1993), 'Developing the Mixed Economy of Care: Emerging Issues for Voluntary Organisations', *Journal of Social Policy*, 22/2: 173–92.

Lippitt, R., Watson, J., and Westley, B. (1958), *Dynamics of Planned Change* (Harcourt Brace & Co.).

Local Government Training Board (1987) *Management in the Public Domain* (Luton: Local Government Training Board).

Lorsch, J., and MacIver, J. (1989) *Pawns or Potentates: The Reality of America's Corporate Boards* (Boston, Mass: Harvard Business School Press).

Lovelady, L. (1984a), 'The Process of Organisational Development: A Reformulated Model of the Change Process', *Personnel Review*, 13/2: 2–11.

——— (1984b) 'Change Strategies and the Use of OD Consultants to Facilitate Change: Part 1 — Alternative Change Strategies Reviewed', *Leadership and OD Journal*, 5/2: 3–10.

Lundberg, C. C. (1984), 'Strategies for Organisational Transitioning', in J. R. Kimberly and R. E. Quinn *Managing Organisational Transitions* (Homewood, Ill.: Irwin), 60–82.

Mace, M. L. (1971), *Directors: Myth and Reality* (Cambridge, Mass.: Harvard University Press).

McGovern, R. (1992), 'A View from the Front', in G. Wallace (ed.), *Local Management of Schools* (Clevedon: BERA).

McHugh, M., and McMullen, L. (1995), 'Headteacher or Manager? Implications for Training and Development', *School Organisation*, 14/1: 23–9.

McKee, L. (1988), 'Conflicts and Context in Managing the Closure of a Large Psychiatric Hospital', *Bulletin of the Royal College of Psychiatrists*, 12/8 (Aug), 310–20.

McKinlay, B. (1988), 'Introduction: The Changing Character of the Medical Profession', *Millbank Quarterly*, 66/2: 1–9.

——— and Stoeckle, J. (1988), 'Corporatization and the Social Transformation of Doctoring', *International Journal of Health Services*, 18: 191–205.

Mackintosh, M., Jarvis, R., and Heery, E. (1994), 'On Managing Hybrids: Some Dilemmas in Higher Education Management', *Financial Accountability and Management*, 10/4: 339–53.

MacNeil, I. (1974), 'The Many Futures of Contracts', *Southern California Law Review*, 47: 691–816.

——— (1978), 'Contracts: Adjustments of Long Term Economic Relations Under Conditions of Classical, Neo Classical and Relational Contract Law', *Northwestern University Law Review*, 72: 854–906.

——— (1983), 'Values in Contract: Internal and External', *Northwestern University Law Review*, 77: 340–418.

McNulty, T., Whittington, R., Whipp, R., and Kitchener, M. (1994), 'Implementing Marketing in NHS Hospitals', *Public Money and Management*, 14/4 (July/Sept.), 51–9.

March, J. G., and Olsen, J. P. (1989), *Rediscovering Institutions: The Organisational Basis of Politics* (New York: Free Press).

——————(1983), 'Organising Political Life: What Administrative Reorganisation Tells Us about Government', *American Political Science Review*, 77: 281–96.

Marren, E., and Levacic, R. (1994), 'School Management, Classroom Teacher and Governor Responses to Local Management of Schools', *Educational Management and Administration*, 2/1: 23–9.

Marsh, I. (1994), 'The Changing Ethos of Public Service: Guest Editor's Introduction', *Australian Journal of Public Administration*, 53/3: 277–86.

Massey, A. (1993), *Managing the Public Sector: A Comparative Analysis of the UK and the US* (Cambridge: Edward Elgar).

Maynard, A. (1991), 'Developing the Health Care Market', *Economic Journal*, 101: 1277–86.

——————(1993), '*Creating Competition in the NHS: Is It Possible? Will It Work?*', in I. Tilley, (ed.), *Managing The Internal Market* (London: Paul Chapman).

Meek, V. L (1988), 'Organisation Culture: Origins and Weaknesses', *Organization Studies*, 9/4: 453–73.

Merton, R. K (1936), 'The Unanticipated Consequences of Purposive Social Action', *American Sociological Review*, 1: 894–904.

Metcalfe, L. (1993), 'Evolving Public Management Cultures', in Eliasson and Kooiman (1993), 106–24.

——————and Richards, S. (1984) 'The Impact of the Efficiency Strategy: Political Clout or Cultural Change?', *Public Administration*, 62/4: 439–54.

——————(1990), *Improving Public Management* (London: Sage).

Meyer, J. W. and Rowan, B. (1977), 'Institutionalised Structures: Formal Structure as Myth and Ceremony', *American Journal of Sociology*, 83/2: 340–63.

Meyerson, D., and Martin, J. (1987), 'Cultural Change: An Integration of Three Different Views', *Journal of Management Studies*, 24/6 (Nov.), 623–47.

Miles, R. E., and Snow, C. C. (1978), *Organisation Strategy, Structure and Process* (New York: McGraw-Hill).

Miller, D., and Friesen, P. H (1984), *Organisations: A Quantum View* (Englewood Cliffs, NJ: Prentice-Hall Inc.).

Milliband, D. (1991), 'Markets, Politics and Education beyond the Education Reform Act' (Education and Training, 3; London: Institute for Public Policy Research).

Mintzberg, H. (1973), *The Nature of Managerial Work* (New York: Harper Row).

——————(1979), *The Structuring of Organisations* (Englewood Cliffs, NJ: Prentice Hall).

——————(1983), *Structure in Fives: Designing Effective Organisations* (Englewood Cliffs, NJ: Prentice Hall).

——————(1987), 'Crafting Strategy', *Harvard Business Review*, 87/4: 66–75.

——————(1989), *Mintzberg on Management* (New York: Free Press).

——————(1990), 'The Design School: Reconsidering the Basic Premises of Strategic Management', *Strategic Management Journal*, 11: 171–95.

——————and Waters, J. A (1985), 'Of Strategies: Deliberate and Emergent', *Management Science*, 24/9: 257–72.

Mizruchi, M. S. (1992), *The Structure of Corporate Political Action* (London: Harvard University Press).

Molz, R. (1985), 'The Role of the Board of Directors: Typologies of Interaction', *Journal of Business Strategy*, 5/4: 86–93.

Monck, E., and Kelly, A. (1992), *Managing Effective Schools, Local Management and its Reform* (London: Institute for Public Policy Research).

Morgan, G., Frost, J., and Pondy, L. (1983), 'Organisational Symbolism', in L. Pondy, J. Frost, G. Morgan, and T. Dandridge (eds.) *Organisational Symbolism* (Greenwich, Conn.: JAI Press).

Morgan, R. (1992), 'Prisons: Managing for Change', *Public Money and Management*, 12/1: 17–22.

Mumford, E. (1972), '*Job Satisfaction: a Study of Computer Specialists*', (London: Longman).

———(1981), '*Values, Technology and Work*', (Groningen: Martinus Nyhoff BV).

Munn, P. (1991), 'School Boards, Accountability and Control', *British Journal of Educational Studies*, 39/2 (May), 173–89.

Murphy, C. (1993), 'The Conditions for Locality Purchasing', MBA diss., University of Warwick.

Murray, T., Dingwall, R. and Eekelaar, J. (1983) 'Professionals in Bureaucracies', in R. Dingwall, and P. Lewis, (eds.) *The Sociology of the Professions: Lawyers, Doctors and Others* (London: Macmillan).

Nadler, D. (1987), 'Managing Organisational Change: An Integrative Perspective', *Journal of Applied Behavioural Science*, 17/2: 191–211.

Nelson, R. (1988), *Partners with Power*, (Berkeley & Los Angeles: University of California Press).

———and Winter, S. (1982), *An Evolutionary Theory of Economic Change* (London: Belnap Press).

NHS Management Executive (1992a), *Local Voices* (London: NHS Management Executive).

———(1992b), *Alliances for Health* (London: NHS Management Executive).

Niskanen, W. A. (1971), *Bureaucracy and Representative Government* (Chicago: Aldine-Atherton).

———(1993), *Health Systems* (Health Policy Studies, 3; Paris: OECD).

OECD (1994), *Economic Outlook*, 56(Dec.) (Paris).

Office of Population Census and Surveys (1983), *General Household Survey* (London: HMSO).

Olmosk, K. (1972), '*Seven Pure Strategies of Change*', Annual Handbook for Group Facilitators (San Diego, Calif.: Pfeiffer & Co.).

Oppenheimer, M. (1973), 'The Proletarianisation of the Professional', *Sociological Review Monograph*, 20: 213–37.

Osborne, D., and Gaebler, T. (1992) *Reinventing Government: How the Entrepreneurial Spirit is Transforming the Public Sector* (Reading Mass.: Addison-Wesley).

O'Toole, B. J., and Jordan, G. (1995), *Next Steps: Improving Management in Government?* (Aldershot: Dartmouth).

Ottaway, R. (1976), 'A Change Strategy to Implement New Norms, New Styles and New Environment in the Work Organisation', *Personnel Review*, 5/1: 13–18.

Ovreteit, J. (1985), 'Medical Dominance and the Development of Professional Autonomy in Physiotherapy', *Sociology of Health and Illness*, 7: 76–93.

PAC, House of Commons (1993a), *West Midlands Regional Health Authority: Regionally Managed Services Organisation*, Session 1992/93, 57th Report, HCP 485 (London: HMSO).

—— (1993*b*) *Wessex Regional Health Authority: Regional Information Systems Plan* Session 1992/3, 63rd Report, HCP 658 (London: HMSO).

—— (1994), *The Proper Conduct of Public Business*, Session 1993/4, 8th Report, HCP 154 (London: HMSO).

Packwood, T. (1991), 'The Three Faces of Medical Audit', *Health Services Journal* (26 Sept.), 24–6.

Parffrey, V. (1994), 'Exclusion: Failed Children or System Failure?', *School Organisation*, 14/2: 107–20 .

Parkin, F. (1979), *Marxism and Class Theory* (New York: Columbia University Press).

Parsons, T. (1951), *The Social System* (London: Tavistock).

Parston, G., Liddell, A., and Adams, S. (1991), 'Over the Road to Health Gain', *Health Services Journal* (11 July), 20–1.

Partin, J. J. (1973)(ed.) *Current Perspectives in Organisation Development* (Reading, Mass.: Addison Wesley).

Payer, L. (1988), *Medicine and Culture, Varieties of Treatment in the U.S.A., England, West Germany and France* (New York: Henry Holt).

Pearce, J. A., and Zahra, S. A. (1991), 'The Relative Power of CEOs and Boards of Directors: Associations with Corporate Performance', *Strategic Management Journal*, 12: 135–53.

Pedler, M., Burgoyne, J., and Boydell, T. (1991), *The Learning Company* (London: McGraw Hill Book Company).

Penney, D., and Evans J. (1995), 'Changing Structures; Changing Rules; the Development of the Internal Market', *School Organisation*, 15/1: 13–22.

Perrow, C. (1981), *Markets, Hierarchies and Hegemony*, in A. Van de Ven, and W. Joyce (eds.) *Perspectives on Organisational Design and Behaviour* (Chichester: John Wiley).

Peters, T. (1992), *Liberation Management* (Basingstoke: Macmillan).

—— and Waterman, R. H. (1982), *In Search of Excellence* (London: Harper & Row).

Pettigrew, A. M (1973), *The Politics of Organisational Decision Making* (London: Tavistock).

—— (1985), *The Awakening Giant* (Oxford: Basil Blackwell).

—— (1987), 'Context and Action in the Transformation of the Firm', *Journal of Management Studies*, 24/6: 649–70.

—— (1990), 'Is Corporate Culture Manageable?' in D. Wilson, and R. Rosenfeld, *Managing Organisations* (London: McGraw Hill).

—— (1992), 'On Studying Managerial Elites', *Strategic Management Journal*, 13 (Winter special ed.), 163–82.

—— and Whipp, R. (1991), *Managing Change for Competitive Success* (Oxford: Blackwell).

—— McKee, L., and Ferlie, E. B. (1988), 'Understanding Change in the NHS', *Public Administration*, 66/3 (Autumn), 297–318.

—— Ferlie, E., and McKee, L. (1992), *Shaping Strategic Change-Making Change in Large Organisations: The Case of the NHS* (London: Sage).

—— and McNulty, T. (1995), 'Power and Influence around the Boardroom', *Human Relations*, 48/8 (Summer), 845–73.

Pfeffer, J. (1972), 'Size, Competition and Function of Hospital Boards of Directors: a Study of Organisational–Environmental Linkage', *Administrative Science Quarterly*, 18: 349–64.

Pfeffer, N., and Pollock, A. (1993), 'Public Opinion and the NHS', *British Medical Journal*, 307 (25 Sept.), 750–1.

Player, E., and Jenkins, M. (1994), *Prisons after Woolf: Reform through Riot* (London: Routledge).

Podolny, J. (1992), 'The Matthew Effect and the Constraints of Status: A Sociological Perspective on Markets', unpublished manuscript from Stanford University Graduate School of Business.

Polanyi, K. (1957), *The Economy as Instituted Process*, in K. Polanyi, C. Arensberg, and C. M. Pearson (eds.), *Trade Market in the Early Empires*, (New York: Free Press), 483–98.

Pollitt, C. (1985), 'Measuring Performance: A New System for the NHS', *Policy and Politics*, 12/1: 1–15.

——(1986), 'Beyond the Managerial Model: The Case for Broadening Performance Assessment in Government and the Public Services', *Financial Accountability and Management*, 2/3 (Autumn), 155–70.

——(1988), 'Editorial: Consumerism and Beyond', *Public Administration*, 66 (Summer), 121–4.

——(1990), *The New Managerialism and The Public Services: The Anglo American Experience* (Oxford: Basil Blackwell).

——Harrison, S., Hunter, D., and Marnoch, G. (1991), 'General Management in the NHS: The Initial Impact 1983–1988', *Public Administration*, 69: 61–83.

Porter, M. E. (1980), *Competitive Strategy: Techniques for Analysing Industries and Competitors* (New York: Free Press).

——(1985), *Competitive Advantage: Creating and Sustaining Superior Performance* (New York: Free Press).

——(1991), 'Towards a Dynamic Theory of Strategy', *Strategic Management Journal*, 12: 95–117.

Powell, W. W. (1991), 'Neither Market nor Hierarchy: Network Forms of Organisation', in G. Thompson, J. Frances, R. Levacic, and J. Mitchell, *Markets, Hierarchies and Networks* (London: Sage), 265–76.

——and Di Maggio, P. J. (1991), *The New Institutionalism in Organisational Analysis* (London: University of Chicago Press).

Power, M. (1994), *The Audit Explosion* (Demos Paper, 7, London: Demos).

Prahalad, C. K., and Hamel, G. (1990), 'The Core Competencies of the Corporation', *Harvard Business Review* (May–June), 79–91.

Pressman, J., and Wildavsky, A. (1973), *Implementation* (Berkeley & Los Angeles: University of California Press).

Prior, D., Stewart, J., and Walsh, K. (1993), *Is the Citizen's Charter a Charter for Citizens?* (London: Local Government Management Board, The Belgrave Papers, No. 7).

Pro–Ned (1987), *Code of Recommended Practice on Non-Executive Directors* (London: Pro–ned).

Quinn, J. P. (1980), *Strategies for Change: Logical Incrementalism* (Homewood, Ill.: Irwin).

Raelin, J. A. (1985), 'The Basis for Professionals Resistance to Managerial Control', *Human Resource Management*, 24/2 (Summer), 147–75.

Ranade, W. (1985), 'Motives and Behaviours in DHAs', *Public Administration*, 63/2 (Summer), 183–200.

Ranson, S. (1993), 'Markets or Democracy for Education', *British Journal of Educational Studies*, 41/4: 333–52.

——and Stewart, J. (1989), 'Citizenship and Government: The Challenge for Management in the Public Domain', *Political Studies*, 37: 5–24.

————(1994), *Management for the Public Domain: Enabling the Learning Society* (London: Macmillan).

Rees, T. (1990), *Selecting HA Members: Lessons from the Wessex Experience* (Institute for Health Policy Studies, Occasional Paper, Feb., University of Southampton).

Rhodes, R. A. W. (1994), 'Reinventing Excellence: Or How Best Sellers Thwart the Search for Lessons to Transform the Public Sector', *Public Administration*, 72 (Summer), 281–9.

Rice, A. K. (1963), *The Enterprise and Its Environment* (London: Tavistock).

Richards, S. (1993), 'Management of Change in the Civil Service, Pity the Poor Bloody Infantry', *Public Money and Management* (Apr./June), 3.

Robertson, D. (1993), 'Establishing Strategic Direction in Higher Education Institutions', *Public Money and Management* (July–Sept), 45–51.

Robinson, R., and Le Grand, J. (1994), *Evaluating the NHS Reforms* (London: King's Fund Institute).

Romanelli, E. (1991), 'The Evolution of New Organisational Forms', *Annual Review of Sociology*, 17: 79–103.

——and Tushman, M. L. (1994), 'Organisational Transformation as Punctuated Equilibrium: An Empirical Test', *Academy of Management Journal*, 37/5: 1141–66.

Rorty, R. (1991), *Objectivity, Relationism and Truth* (Cambridge: Cambridge University Press).

Rumelt, R. P., Schendel, D., and Teece, D. J. (1991), 'Strategic Management and Economics', *Strategic Management Journal*, 12 (Winter special issue), 5–29.

Russell, J., Petersson, G., Davies, J., Posner, T., and Philo, J. (1994), *'Londoners' views on the future of Healthcare'* (London: King's Fund Institute/King's Fund Commission on the Future of Acute Services in London).

Sales, A. L., and Mirvis, P. H. (1984), 'When Cultures Collide: Issues in Acquisition', in J. R. Kimberley, and R. E. Quinn, *Managing Organisational Transitions* (Homewood, Ill.: Irwin).

Salter, B. (1993), 'The Politics of Purchasing in the NHS', *Policy and Politics*, 21/3: 171–84.

Scarborough, H. (1995), 'Introduction', in H. Scarborough (ed.) *The Management of Expertise*, (London, Macmillan).

Schein, E. (1983), 'The Role of the Founder in Creating Organisational Culture', *Organisational Dynamics* (Summer), 13–28.

——(1985), *Organisational Culture and Leadership: A Dynamic View* (San Fransico, Jossey Bass).

Schofield, J. (1994), 'The Case of the Purchasing Plan: Differing Perspectives and Persuasions amongst Health and Social Care Managers', paper presented at the Implementing Health Care Reforms Conference, Templeton College, Oxford, 11–12 Apr.

Schultz, R., and Harrison, S. (1986), 'Physician Autonomy in the Federal Republic of Germany, Great Britain and the United States', *International Journal of Health Planning and Management*, 2: 335–55.

Scott, W. R. (1985), 'Conflicting Levels of Rationality: Regulators, Managers and Professionals in the Medical Sector', *Journal of Health Administration Education*, 3/2(2): 113–31.

Senge, P. (1990), *The Fifth Discipline* (New York: Random Books).

Shearn, D., Broadbent, J., Laughlin, R., and Willig-Atherton, H. (1995), 'The Changing Face of School Governor Responsibilities: a Mismatch Between Government Intention and Actuality?', *School Organisation*, 15/2: 175–88.

Shortell, S. M., Morrison, E., and Friedman, B. (1990), *Strategic Choices for America's Hospitals: Managing Change in Turbulent Times* (San Fransisco: Jossey Bass).

Simkins, T. (1994), 'Efficiency, Effectiveness, and the Local Management of Schools', *Journal of Education Policy*, 9/1: 15–33.

Skelcher, C. (1993), 'Involvement and Empowerment in Local Public Services', *Public Money and Management* (Summer), 13–19.

———and Stewart, J. (1993), *The Appointed Government of London* (Birmingham: Inlogov, University of Birmingham.

———and Davis, H. (1995), *Opening the Boardroom Door: The Membership of Local Appointed Bodies* (York: Joseph Rowntree Foundation).

Slack, T., and Hinings, B. (1994), 'Institutional Pressures and Isomorphic Change: An Empirical Test', *Organization Studies*, 15/6: 803–27.

Sloan, A. P. (1963), *My Years with General Motors* (London: Sedgewick & Jackson).

Smircich, L. (1983), 'Organisations as Shared Meanings', in L. Pondy, P. Frost, G. Morgan, and T. Dandridge (eds.) *Organisational Symbolism* (Greenwich, Conn.: JAI Press).

Sorensen, R. J. (1993), 'The Efficiency of Public Service Provision', in Eliassen and Kooiman (1993), 224–43.

Starks, M. (1993), *Public Services and Market Forces: The BBC Experience* (London: Office for Public Management).

Sternberg, E. (1993), 'Preparing for the Hybrid Economy: The New World of Public–Private Partnerships', *Business Horizons*, 36/6: 11–15.

Stewart, J. D. (1986), *The New Management of Local Government* (London: Allen & Unwin).

———and Clarke, M. (1987), 'The Public Service Orientation: Issues and Dilemmas', *Public Administration*, 65/2 (Summer), 161–78.

———and Ranson, S. (1988), 'Management in the Public Domain', *Public Money and Management* (Spring/Summer), 13–18.

———(1992), 'The Rebuilding of Public Accountability' in J. Stewart, N. Lewis, and D. Longley, *Accountability to the Public* (London: European Policy Forum).

———(1993), 'The Limitations of Government by Contract', *Public Money and Management* (July/Sept.), 7–12.

———(1994), 'Accountability and Democracy in the Emerging System', in M. Clarke (ed.), *The New Local Governance* (London: European Policy Forum).

———and Walsh, (1992), 'Change in the Management of Public Services', *Public Administration*, 70: 499–518.

———Greer, A. and Hoggett, P. (1995), 'The Quango State: An Alternative Approach' (Commission for Local Democracy Research Report, 10; London: Commission for Local Democracy).

Stewart, R. (n.d.), *Involving Doctors in General Management* (Templeton Series, 5; Bristol, NHS Training Authority).

———(1975), *Contrasts in Management* (London: McGraw Hill).

———(1991), 'Chairmen and Chief Executives: An Exploration of their Relationship', *Journal of Management Studies*, 28/5: 511–27.

——— Gabbay, J., Dopson, J., Smith, P., and Williams, D. (1987),*DGMs and the DHA: Working with Members'* (Templeton Series, 3; Bristol: NHS Training Authority).

Sunday Times (1995), (4 June).

Taylor, M., and Hoggett, P. (1994), 'Quasi Markets and the Transformation of the Independent Sector', in W. Bartlett, C. Propper, D. Wilson, and J. Le Grand, (eds.) *Quasi Markets in the Welfare State* (Bristol: School of Advanced Urban Studies).

Thomas, H. (1988), 'Local Management in Schools', Unpublished paper, Centre for Education Management and Policy Studies, University of Birmingham.

Thompson, J. L. (1990), *Strategic Management* (London: Chapman & Hall).

Tichy, N. (1983), *Managing Strategic Change: Technical, Political and Cultural Dynamics* (Chichester: J. Wiley).

Times Educational Supplement (1993), (22 Jan).

Tolbert, P., and Zucker, L. (1983), 'Institutional Sources of Change in the Formal Structure of Organisation: The Diffusion of Civil Service Reform, 1880–1935', *Administrative Science Quarterly*, 28: 22–39.

Tomlinson Report (1992), *Report of the Enquiry into London's Health Service, Medical Education and Research* (Chairman Sir Bernard Tomlinson) (London: HMSO).

Tooley, J. (1995), 'Markets or Democracy for Education? A Reply to Stewart Ranson', *British Journal of Educational Studies*, 43/1: 21–34.

Torrington, D., and Weightman, J. (1989), 'The Management of Secondary Schools', *Journal of Management Studies*, 26/5 (Sept.), 519–30.

Tricker, R. I. (1984), *Corporate Governance: Practices, Procedures and Powers in British Companies and their Boards of Directors* (Aldershot: Gower).

Trist, E., Higgins, G. W., Murray, L., and Pollack, A. R. (1963), *Organisational Choice*, (London, Tavistock).

Trow, M. (1992), 'Thoughts on the White Paper of 1992', *Higher Education Quarterly*, 46/3: 213–26.

Tsoukas, H. (1995), 'The Ubiquity of Organizational Diversity: A Social Constructivist Perspective' (University of Warwick, Warwick Business School).

Tushman, M., and Romanelli, E. (1985), 'Organisational Evolution: A Metamorphosis Model of Convergence and Reorientation', *Research on Organisational Behaviour*, 7: 171–222.

——Newman, W., and Romanelli, E. (1988), 'Convergence and Upheaval: Managing the Unsteady Pace of Organisational Evolution', in K. S. Cameron, R. I. Sutton, and D. A. Whetten, *Readings in Organisational Decline* (Cambridge, Mass.: Ballinger).

Useem, M (1984) *The Inner Circle* (New York: Oxford University Press).

——(1993) *Executive Defense: Shareholder Power and Corporate Reorganisation* (Cambridge, Mass.: Harvard University Press).

Van de Ven, A., Angle, H. L. and Poole, M. (1989), *Research on the Management of Innovation: The Minnesota Studies* (New York: Harper & Row).

Walby, S. and Greenwell, J. (1994), 'Managing the National Health Service', in J. Clarke, A. Cochrane, and E. McLaughlin, (eds.), *Managing Social Policy* (London: Sage).

Warmington, A., Lupton, T., and Gribbin, C. (1977), *Organisation Behaviour and Performance, An Open Systems Approach to Change* (London: Macmillan).

Weber, M. (1946), 'Bureaucracy', in H. H. Gerth, and C. W. Mills (eds.) *From Max Weber: Essays in Sociology* (New York: Oxford University Press), 196–245.

——(1947), *The Theory of Social and Economic Organisation*, trans. and ed. by A. M. Henderson and T. Parsons (New York: Free Press), 328–40.

Weick, K. (1979), *The Social Psychology of Organising*, (Reading, Mass.: Addison Wesley).

Weir, S., and Hall, W. (1994), *Ego Trip* (Democratic Audit, 2; University of Essex: Human Rights Centre).

West, A., David, M., Hailes, J., and Ribbens, J. (1995), 'Parents and the Process of Choosing Secondary Schools: Implications for Schools', *Educational Management and Administration*, 23/1: 28–38.

White, H. (1981), Where do Markets Come From?, *American Journal of Sociology*, 87/3: 517–47.

Whitley, R. (1989), 'On the Nature of Managerial Tasks: Their Distinguishing Characteristics and Organisation', *Journal of Management Studies*, 26/3 (May), 209–40.

Whittington, R. (1993), *What Is Strategy—and Does It Matter?* (London: Routledge).

———McNulty, T., and Whipp, R. (1994), 'Market Driven Change in Professional Services: Problems and Processes', *Journal of Management Studies*, 31/6: 829–46.

Whyte, W. H. (1956), *The Organisation Man* (New York: Simon & Schuster).

Widdicombe Report (1986), *The Local Government Councillor Research*, xi. Committee of Enquiry into the conduct of Local Authority Business. Cmnd. 9799 (London: HMSO).

Willcocks, L., and Harrow, J. (1992) (eds.) *Rediscovering Public Services Management* (London: McGraw-Hill).

Williamson, C. (1992), *Whose Standards? Consumer and Professional Standards in Health Care* (Buckingham: Open University Press).

Williamson, O. E. (1975), *Markets and Hierarchies: Analysis and Anti Trust Implications* (New York: Macmillan).

———(1985), *The Economic Institutions of Capitalism* (New York: Free Press).

———(1991), 'Comparative Economic Organisation: The Analysis of Discrete Structural Alternatives', *Administrative Science Quarterly*, 36: 269–96.

Wilson, D. (1992), *A Strategy of Change* (London: Routledge).

———and Butler, R. (1990), *Managing Voluntary and Non Profit Organisations: Strategy and Structure* (London: Routledge).

Winch, G., and Schneider, E. (1992), 'Managing the Knowledge-Based Organisation: The Case of Architectural Practice', paper given to the Knowledge Workers in Contemporary Organisations conference, University of Lancaster, Sept.

Wistow, G., Knapp, M., Hardy, B., and Allen, C. (1992), From Providing To Enabling: Local Authorities and The Mixed Economy of Social Care, *Public Administration*, 70 (Spring), 25–42.

———and Barnes, M. (1993), 'User Involvement in Community Care: Origins, Purposes and Applications', *Public Administration*, 71: 279–99.

———, Knapp, M., Hardy, B., and Allen. C. (1994), *Social Care in a Mixed Economy* (Buckingham: Open University Press).

Wistrich, E. (1992), 'Restructuring Government New Zealand Style', *Public Administration*, 70 (Spring), 119–35.

Wommack, W. W. (1982), 'The Board's Most Important Function in Boards of Directors, pt 2', *Harvard Business Review*, 1977–1981 (Boston: Harvard University Press).

Wright Mills, C. (1956), *The Power Elite* (New York: Oxford University Press).

Yorke, D. A. (1990), 'Developing an Interactive Approach to the Marketing of Professional Services', in D. Ford, (ed.) *Understanding Business Markets* (London: Academic Press), 347–58.

Zahra, S. A. (1990), 'Increasing the Board's Involvement in Strategy', *Long Range Planning*, 23/6: 109–17.

Zajac, E. (1993), *From Interlocking Directorates to the Study of Boards of Directors* (Evanston, Ill.: Kellogg School of Management, Northwestern University).

Zald, M. (1969), 'The Power and Functions of Boards of Directors: A Theoretical Synthesis', *American Journal of Sociology*, 75: 97–111.

Zifcak, S. (1994), *New Managerialism: Administrative Reform in Whitehall and Canberra* (Buckingham: Open University Press).

Zucker, L. G. (1988), *Institutional Patterns and Organisations: Culture and Environment* (Cambridge, Mass.: Ballinger).

INDEX